D0722798

Installing and Upgrading

Identify system upgrade potential and compatibility of installable components.

Chapters 1 through 5, 11

Identify commonly used drivers and their functions and configuration.

Chapters 4 through 12

Identify methods related to upgrading Windows and DOS.

Chapters 1, 3, 4, and 9 through 12

Diagnosis

Identify common questions that should be asked when determining a customer's hardware and software problems.

Chapters 11 and 12

Identify common hardware and software failures.

Chapters 11 and 12

Identify and understand system boot sequences.

Chapters 5 through 7, 11, and 12

Repair

Understand methods for replacing hardware components (FRUs).

Chapters 11 and 12

Understand methods for solving software problems.

Chapters 11 and 12

A+: Windows/DOS Study Guide

A+: Windows®/DOS® Study Guide

David Groth

SYBEX®

San Francisco • Paris • Düsseldorf • Soest

Associate Publisher: Guy Hart-Davis
Acquisitions Manager: Kristine Plachy
Acquisitions & Developmental Editor: Neil Edde
Editor: Doug Robert
Technical Editor: Jay Tarbox
Book Designer: Catalin Dulfu
Electronic Publishing Specialist: Robin Kibby
Production Coordinator: Eryn L. Osterhaus
Indexer: Ted Laux
Cover Design: Design Site
Cover Illustration: Design Site
Chapter and Part Art: Chris Gillespie

Library of Congress Card Number: 98-84005
ISBN: 0-7821-2182-9

Manufactured in the United States of America

10 9 8 7 6 5 4 3 2

Dedicated to my wife Linda
and to the geek in all of us

ACKNOWLEDGMENTS

I've never known how a movie star feels when accepting an Academy Award, until now. I'm not saying this book is an award-winning book, but who knows? There are so many people to thank, and so little space. I'll begin by thanking my wife. She tirelessly edited the glossary, listened to my rants about the books, and gave me a "swift kick" when and where I needed it.

Then there's my Dad, who always told me that "You've gotta do what you've gotta do." Thanks, Dad. And Mom, for encouraging me to do whatever I wanted to, as long as I did the "have to's" first.

To my contributing writers: Your tireless work and patience made my life easier. Yes, I asked a lot, but I think you'll be proud to have your names here, in print. Who says you should never go into business with your friends?

Dan Newland, MCT, MCSE: Dan is a coworker who wrote the chapters "A Brief History of Operating Systems," "Prerequisites for Installation [DOS]," and "Windows Interface Overview." I look forward to collaborating with him on many projects in the future.

Michael Jones: A technical writer and PC specialist, Michael was a last-minute (but valuable) addition to my author team. He wrote the chapters "DOS Startup and Configuration" and "Basic DOS Commands." I applaud his ability to finish the chapters under extreme time pressure.

Neil Edde and Doug Robert, my editors, have turned my chicken scratchings into a professional study guide. I can't thank these gentlemen enough, for without them, I would not be writing this acknowledgment. Many thanks also to Jay Tarbox for double-checking the technical accuracy and relevance of the materials, and to Robin Kibby and Eryn Osterhaus for taking all the pieces and turning them into a good looking book.

Finally, I would like to thank you, the reader, for purchasing this book. I firmly believe that the A+ Study Guides are the best study guides available today for the A+ certification exams. I hope that you get as much out of this one as I put into it.

CONTENTS AT A GLANCE

TABLE OF CONTENTS

INTRODUCTION: THE A+ CERTIFICATION PROCESS

There are a lot of people in the world today who consider themselves to be computer "experts," but they all started out knowing nothing about computers. It starts with the question "How do I...?" People get frustrated when they recognize that they paid a couple of thousand dollars for a computer and they don't know anything about it. Then they ask the question "How do I ...?" They may find the answer in a book or a magazine, or from a friend who knows the answer. Little by little, they find out more about their computer until they feel comfortable enough to add new hardware to their computer.

Their first attempt may not be successful. To be sure, it probably was a disaster. They probably had to pay to have it fixed. But they learn from it. They realize where they went wrong, and the next time they try, they may succeed. They have more successes and more failures until they come to the point where they have developed critical thinking skills. This is how computer service technicians are born. One of the most valuable skills a service technician has is the ability to troubleshoot problems. To do this, he or she needs to be able to think critically. When there is a problem, service technicians must rely on their critical thinking abilities and their background knowledge to fix the problem.

What Is A+ Certification?

A+ is a certification program designed to quantify the level of critical thinking skills and general industry knowledge demanded of computer service technicians. It was developed by the Computer Technology Industry Association (CompTIA) to provide an industry-wide recognition of those service technicians who have attained this level of knowledge. For example, Novell has developed their Certified Novell Engineer (CNE) program to provide the same recognition for network professionals that deal with their NetWare products. Also, Microsoft has their Microsoft Certified Service Engineer (MCSE) program. The theory behind these certifications is that if you need to have service performed on any of their products, a technician who has been certified in one of their certification programs should be the one you call, because they know the product.

The A+ certification program was created to be a wide-ranging certification involving products from many vendors. In any situation, if computer service is needed, an A+ certified technician should be able to solve the problem.

Benefits of A+ Certification

Why should you get A+ certified? There are several good reasons. The CompTIA "Candidate's Information" packet lists five major benefits: It demonstrates proof of professional achievement, it increases your marketability, it provides greater opportunity for advancement in your field, it is increasingly found as a requirement for some kinds of advanced training, and it raises customer confidence in your and your company's services.

It's Proof of Professional Achievement

The A+ certification is quickly becoming a status symbol in the computer service industry. Organizations that contain members of the computer service industry are recognizing the benefits of A+ certification and are pushing for their members to become certified. And more people every day are putting the emblem of the "A+ Certified Technician" on their business cards.

It Increases Your Marketability

A+ certification makes an individual more marketable to a potential employer. Also, that individual may be able to receive a higher base salary, because the employer won't have to spend as much money on vendor-specific training.

What Is an AASC?

More service companies are becoming A+ Authorized Service Centers (AASCs). This means that over 50% of the technicians employed by that service center are A+ certified. At the time of the writing of this book, there are over 1,400 A+ Authorized Service Centers in the world. Customers and vendors alike recognize that AASCs employ the most qualified service technicians. Because of this, an AASC will get more business than a non-authorized service center. Also, because more service centers want to reach the AASC level, they will give preference in hiring to a candidate who is A+ certified over one who is not.

It Provides Opportunity for Advancement

Most raises and advancement are based on performance. A+ certified employees work faster and more efficiently, thus making them more productive. The more productive an employee is, the more money they will make for their company. And of course, the more money they make for the company, the more valuable they will be to the company, so if an employee is A+ certified, their chances of getting promoted will be greater.

It Fulfills Training Requirements

A+ certification is recognized by most major computer hardware vendors, including (but not limited to) IBM, Hewlett-Packard, Apple, and Compaq. Some of these vendors will apply A+ certification toward prerequisites in their own respective certification programs. For example, an A+ certified technician is automatically given credit towards HP laser printer certification without having to take prerequisite classes and tests. This has the side benefit of reducing training costs for employers.

It Raises Customer Confidence

As the A+ moniker becomes more well-known among computer owners, more of them will realize that the A+ technician is more qualified to work on their computer equipment than a non-certified technician is.

How to Get A+ Certified

A+ Certification is available to anyone who wishes to pay the registration fees. You don't have to work for any particular company. It's not a secret society. It is, however, an elite group. In order to become A+ certified you must do two things:

- Pass the A+ certification *Core* exam (which is the focus of the *A+: Core Module Study Guide*, also published by Sybex).

- Pass one of the A+ certification *Operating System Specialty* exams (the focus of this book is the DOS/Windows module; if you wish, you can take the Macintosh module in addition to or instead of the DOS/Windows module).

You don't have to take both exams at the same time; you have ninety days from the time you pass one test to pass the second.

The exams are administered by Sylvan Prometric and can be taken at any Sylvan Prometric Testing Center, with locations throughout the US. Arrangements can also be made for testing in Canada, the UK, and Australia. If you pass both exams, you will get a certificate in the mail from the CompTIA saying that you have passed, as well as a lapel pin and business card.

To register for the tests, call Sylvan at (800) 77-MICRO (776-4276). You'll be asked for your name, Social Security number (an optional number may be assigned if you don't wish to provide your SSN), mailing address, phone number, employer, when and where (i.e., which Sylvan testing center) you want to take the test, and your credit card number (arrangement for payment must be made at the time of registration).

NOTE
Note that although you can save money by arranging to take more than one test at the same seating, there are no other discounts—for example, if you have to take a test more than once in order to get a passing grade, you have to pay both times.

It is possible to pass these tests without any reference materials, but only if you already have the knowledge and experience that come from reading about and working with personal computers. Even experienced service people, however, tend to have what you might call a 20/80 situation with their computer knowledge—they may use 20 percent of their knowledge and skills 80 percent of the time, and have to rely on manuals or guesswork or phone calls for the rest. By covering all the topics that are tested by the exam, this book can help you to refresh your memory concerning topics that until now you might have only seldom used. (It can also serve to fill in gaps that, let's admit, you may have tried to cover up for quite some time.) Further, by treating all the issues that the exam covers, i.e., problems you may run into in the arenas of PC service and support, this book can serve as a general field guide, one that you may want to keep with you as you go about your work.

NOTE   In addition to reading the book, you might consider practicing these objectives through an internship program. (After all, all theory and no practice make for a poor technician.) Companies that offer training programs are listed in Appendix C.

DOS/Windows Module Objectives

The following are the areas in which you must be proficient in order to pass the A+ DOS/Windows Module exam:

Configuring

- Identify hardware components of the system and necessary set-up procedures.

- Determine the appropriate commands and parameters to initialize media and to back up data.

- Identify software configuration tools and commands in Windows and DOS.

- Identify major system files of Windows and DOS and how they are used.

- Identify methods of system optimization.

Installing and Upgrading

- Identify system upgrade potential and compatibility of installable components.

- Identify commonly used drivers and their functions and configuration.

- Identify methods related to upgrading Windows and DOS.

Diagnosis

- Identify common questions that should be asked when determining a customer's hardware and software problems.

- Identify common hardware and software failures.

- Identify and understand system boot sequences.

Repair

- Understand methods for replacing hardware components (FRUs).

- Understand methods for solving software problems.

How to Use This Book

This book has been written to provide you with the knowledge you need to pass the A+ certification exams. It has been written at a medium technical level. You should already be familiar with the concept of what a PC is and its basic function. The material in this book will hopefully "fill in the gaps" in your knowledge. I would recommend reading the review questions at the end of the chapter to gauge your level of knowledge of the subject. If you pass (greater than 80%), move on to the next chapter. If not, read the chapter, then re-take the review questions. Hopefully your score will increase.

Good Luck!

For the latest pricing on the exams and updates to the registration procedures, call (800) 77-MICRO (776-4276). If you have further questions about the scope of the exams or about related CompTIA programs, refer to the CompTIA website at *http://www.comptia.org/*.

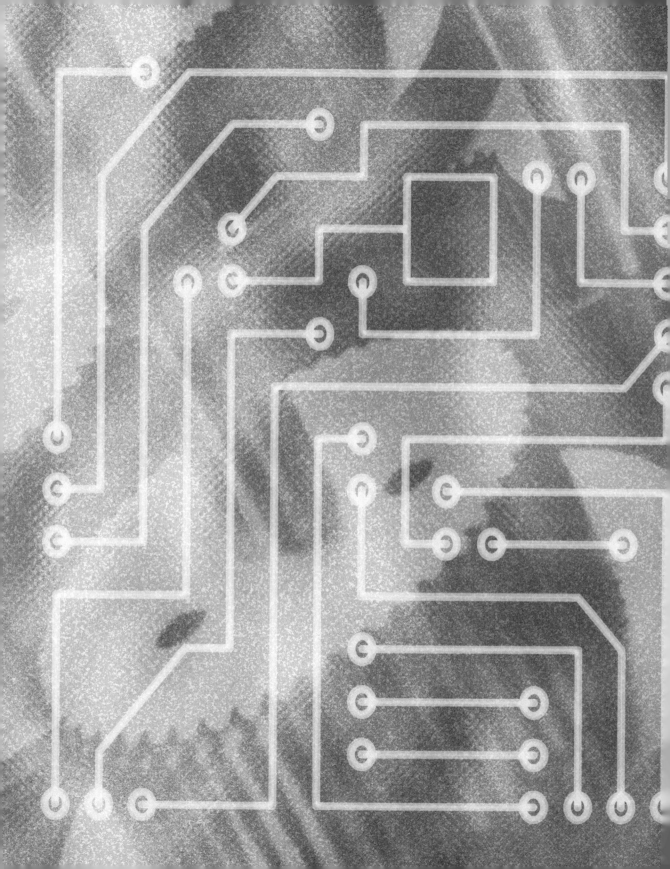

CHAPTER

ONE

1

A Brief History of Computer Operating Systems

- CP/M

- MS-DOS and PC-DOS

- Windows Interfaces to DOS

- Windows 95/98 and NT

- OS/2

- High-End Operating Systems

The role of the computer has changed drastically over the course of history. It has gone from table-making to the complex demands of the world today, including data entry and Internet access. This chapter takes a step back in time to map the directions the personal computer has taken, in terms of its main software component: the operating system. In this chapter, we will cover the following important developments in Intel platform PC operating systems:

- CP/M

- MS-DOS and PC-DOS

- Windows Interfaces to DOS

- Windows 95/98 and NT

- OS/2

- High-End Operating Systems

An Overview of Operating Systems

In the past twenty years, the emergence of computer hardware, which is continually becoming smaller and more powerful, has necessitated the development of new software to access and optimize this hardware. The foundation of computer software is the *operating system* (abbreviated *OS*). Operating system software gives the user an interface by means of which they can enter commands to the computer. The interface communicates with the computer's hardware to execute those commands. It offers commands for controlling disk and file management, device management, and memory management. By doing this, operating systems also provide a consistent environment for other software such as word processors and spreadsheets to execute. Rather than having to access devices and memory themselves, the programs simply request that the OS does it for them. This saves substantially on software overhead, as much of the executable code is "shared"—meaning it is used by multiple programs. These software add-ons are called *applications*, and they generally run only on the OS for which they were written.

In order to understand the emergence of modern graphical operating systems, you should have an idea of the technologies that led to our present systems. You should also understand the critical relationship between hardware and software. Graphics, speed, GUI interfaces and multiple programs running concurrently are all made possible by software designers taking full advantage of the hardware they are designing their software for.

This chapter will introduce a few of the major operating systems of the past twenty years, and will briefly describe how they work. These are not the only operating systems out there, but rather are simply the ones that were accepted by a large enough segment of the PC market to become de-facto standards. As you read about these different software products, try to think about the ways they differ from one another, and the reasons they were designed in the fashion they were. By knowing the options available on the Intel platform, you can better decide which operating system will work best in a particular situation, and therefore be better prepared to recommend a particular OS to your customers. We will be discussing these operating systems in roughly chronological order.

CP/M

The first operating system we will discuss is one you may never have heard of—CP/M. The reason for this is that it is no longer in widespread use on modern PCs. The *Control Program for Microcomputer* OS, written in 1973 by Gary Kildall using Kildall's PL/M programming language, initially ran on the Intel 8008. It was later ported to the 8080 chip, and was in many ways very similar in function to DOS. As a matter of fact, it looks quite similar to DOS, as you can see in Figure 1.1.

FIGURE 1.1:

A typical CP/M
command line

```
Z80 C>SUBMIT AUTOEXEC.Z80
Z80 C>set_bdos min
Z80 C>set_cpmecho off
Z80 C>set_cpmlist lpt1
Z80 C>set_cpmpun com1
Z80 C>set_cpmrdr com1
Z80 C>set_cpu z80
Z80 C>set_fake off
Z80 C>set_illop fault
Z80 C>set_iobase 400
Z80 C>set_mask on
Z80 C>set_source z80
Z80 C>set_term h19
Z80 C>set_vars on
Z80 C>coldboot
Z80 C>
Z80 C>
```

The similarities between CP/M and DOS are underscored by the following bit of computer folklore, which, despite questionable authenticity, has become well known in the industry. In 1981, IBM decided to begin marketing machines to the home user and small offices. They decided that for reasons of time and efficiency they would rather simply license an operating system, rather than develop and support one of their own. To that end, they scheduled a meeting with Gary Kildall. The IBM representative arrived for the meeting at Kildall's house, but Gary wasn't there. He was out flying his plane, and after an unsuccessful meeting with Kildall's wife and lawyer, the IBM rep left without an OS. Not long after, IBM found a different system, entering into a contract with Bill Gates (Microsoft) and licensing DOS. Kildall says that this is not accurate, and in fact claims that Bill Gates was the first to tell the apocryphal story. One way or the other, the fact remains that Kildall lost a huge opportunity. At the time that IBM came calling, CP/M was in fact the de facto industry standard for low-cost computers on the Intel platform. Within a few years of losing the IBM contract, it was nothing but a memory.

NOTE For more information on CP/M, check out the Caldera CP/M website for fans of CP/M at *http://www.caldera.com/dos/html/legacyindex.html*. This page includes information about CP/M, sources for software, and links to several other CP/M sites.

MS-DOS and PC-DOS

When dealing with most PCs made from the early 1980s to the early 1990s, you will find that the operating system that shipped with the machine was some version of the *Disk Operating System* (*DOS*) created by Microsoft—MS-DOS. There are a number of manufacturers of DOS, but most of them produce relatively similar versions—they differ only in syntax and a few utilities. The important differences between DOSes are to be found from one chronological version to the next.

NOTE A version is a particular revision of a piece of software, normally described by a number, which tells you how new the product is in relation to other versions of the product. MS-DOS, for instance, is currently in its sixth major version. Major revisions are distinguished from smaller ones in this manner: DOS 5.0 to 6.0 was a major revision, while 6.0 to 6.2 was a minor revision. This way of marking changes is now relatively standard in marking changes in other OS and application software as well.

In next section, we will look at the origins of DOS, and the way it has evolved, version by version, over time. In the following chapters, we'll examine the commands and syntax of the DOS OS, as you will need a very strong knowledge of this operating system before taking the A+ exam.

The Origins of DOS

As noted, the story behind MS-DOS is one of the most often told of all computer fables. But the intrigue goes far further than the mystery of why Gary Kildall missed his meeting with IBM. As noted, Microsoft contracted with IBM to write the operating system for their new Intel-based microcomputer project. Although Bill Gates and his partner Paul Allen were both experienced programmers, they had gained their success through the creation of programming languages, not operating systems.

Gates and Allen had created the BASIC language in 1976, and had also released versions of COBOL and FORTRAN for Intel-based machines. However, they had never created an operating system from scratch. Yet this is exactly what they promised to IBM. Microsoft also took an active role as consultants on the type of hardware that should be used, and Gates was instrumental in IBM's decision to go with the 8086 chip, rather than the cheaper (and less powerful) 8080 processor IBM had originally planned. Microsoft also argued that the machine should have 64KB of memory, rather than the 16KB that IBM initially had thought would be sufficient.

In an interesting twist, just as Seattle-based Microsoft was finishing up a very secretive deal with IBM, Tim Patterson of Seattle Computer Products began writing an operating system specifically for use with the 8086-based computer. Patterson was dissatisfied with how long it was taking for an x86 version of CP/M to be released, so he named his operating system *Quick-and-Dirty Disk Operating System (QDOS)*, and showed it to Microsoft even as they were in the middle of talks with IBM. Paul Allen soon contracted with Seattle Computer Products to purchase QDOS, for sale to an unnamed client (IBM, of course). The purchase price of around $100,000 bought Microsoft an operating system, and a few months later Patterson followed his operating system: he quit SCP and took a job with Gates and Allen. Microsoft acquired all rights to QDOS and renamed it to MS-DOS.

From there, QDOS was modified for use with the new IBM minicomputer, and in the fall of 1981, IBM announced the IBM 5150 PC Personal Computer. The 5150 had a 4.77MHz Intel 8088 CPU, 64KB RAM, 40KB ROM, one 5.25-inch floppy drive, and an OS called *PC-DOS 1.0*. PC-DOS, of course, was simply IBM's moniker for the MS-DOS they were licensing from Microsoft. Color graphics capability was also available.

NOTE   Before the PC, most computers were sold as kits. This meant that the customer had to assemble the machine, install the OS, et cetera. IBM debuted the PC as a machine that anyone could use, because it was "ready to go" right out of the box.

There is only one more element to the story that we are going to discuss, but it is, in fact, a crucial detail. As noted above, IBM PCs shipped with a version of MS-DOS called PC-DOS. But Gates and Allen had contracted to allow IBM to use their operating system, rather than IBM buying it outright. Moreover, IBM had not been granted any type of exclusivity over DOS, hence Microsoft was able to also license versions of DOS to other companies, effectively allowing the creation of what were originally called "IBM clone" machines. These machines ran on the same Intel chip as the IBM PC, and used a similar version of the operating system. Because this allowed for any number of companies to make hardware that was roughly compatible with that of other vendors, software companies could begin to create and market programs for a wider and wider market. These programs were not dependent upon proprietary technology other than the Intel chipset and the Microsoft operating system which formed the nucleus of these computers. From 1981 on, the future of the personal computer was to be largely determined by the increasingly powerful processors created by the Intel Corp., and the increasingly sophisticated operating systems Microsoft wrote to take advantage of Intel's enhancements.

The remainder of this chapter will deal with the evolution of the MS-DOS operating system, and will examine the major changes in microcomputer architecture and standards which are reflected in each revision. Smaller revisions—1.0 to 1.1, 6.0 to 6.1—are not enumerated, but their changes are included in the overall enhancements made to the overall version.

You will notice as you read about and use DOS that most of the versions of this operating system are very similar, as the OS proved to be very stable in its original design. Although various enhancements or features may or may not be available to you depending on the version you are using, in a general sense you can trust that if you learn one version, you can probably use any of them.

MS-DOS 1.0

The original version of DOS was, to put it mildly, a "no-frills" operating system. It had no provisions for networking, did not include any sort of graphical shell program, and had limited ability to manage system resources. The good news was that most of these features would have been too complex for the hardware that version 1.0 was designed for anyway, so no one really noticed.

NOTE
PC-DOS and MS-DOS were very similar, differing mainly in the fact that PC-DOS was specific to IBM machines, while MS-DOS was sold on clone microcomputers. They generally share version numbers, and version x.1 of PC-DOS should have most of the same enhancements as version x.1 of MS-DOS. There are, of course, some technical differences, which will be enumerated in the following chapter, "An Overview of DOS."

Approximately a year after the release of DOS, a revision—DOS 1.1—added support for double-sided 320KB floppy drives. Double-sided disks were important, as they effectively doubled the machine's storage and retrieval capacity. It is difficult to grasp this concept today, when a one- or two-gigabyte hard drive is standard on most new desktop machines, but in 1981 internal hard drives were neither easily available nor supported by DOS. Users generally had only a single 5.25" drive, so the OS, any programs the users wanted to run, *and* any data they wanted to retrieve all had to be accessed through the 5.25" floppies, which stored a maximum of either 320 KB and 640 KB depending on whether it was single-sided or double. For comparison, consider that you would need more than 1,600 double-sided 640KB floppies to store a single gigabyte of information.

DOS 1.25 followed soon after 1.1, and was designed to be sold with "clone," non-IBM, hardware. Any machine that could run DOS 1.25 could lay claim to at least some level of "IBM compatability."

MS-DOS 2.0

In early 1983, IBM introduced the IBM PC XT. The XT featured a 10MB hard drive, a serial interface, and three additional expansion slots. It also had 128 KB of RAM and a 360KB floppy drive (40 KB more capacity than that of single-sided floppies on the previous PC). Users of this new PC needed an operating system which would allow them to take advantage of this new hardware, and Microsoft did not disappoint them.

The XT shipped with MS-DOS 2.0, a revision of the DOS operating system which had to be redone almost from the ground up. It closely fit the machine it was built for, and supported 10 MB hard drives and the new 360 KB floppy disks. It also introduced the hierarchical "tree" structure to the DOS file system. The PC Jr., which was one of IBM's first real microcomputer failures, used PC-DOS 2.1.

MS-DOS 3.0

With DOS 3.0, released in summer 1984, Microsoft continued to include additional DOS features, and to support more powerful hardware. DOS 3.0 supported hard drives larger than 10MB, as well as enhanced graphics formats. Three revisions—3.1, 3.2, and 3.3—provided additional innovations. The IBM PC AT was the first machine shipped with DOS 3.0. It had 256 KB of RAM, an Intel 80286 processor (6 MHz!), and a 1.2MB 5.25" floppy drive. A 20MB hard drive and color video card were also available.

DOS 3 was revised three times—3.1, 3.2 and 3.3. Version 3.1 was notable because it featured the first DOS support for networking. The IBM PC Network was a simple Local Area Network structure that was similar to today's workgroup networks.

> **NOTE** A network is any group of computers that have a physical communication link between them. Networks allow computers to share information and other resources quickly and securely.

DOS 3.2 introduced the XCOPY command, enabling the user to identify more than one file at a time to be copied, and it made important modifications to other DOS commands. It was also the first version to support IBM's Token Ring network topology, and the first to allow for 720KB 3.5" floppies. Version 3.3, introduced in 1987, offered additional enhancements to numerous existing commands, and introduced support for 1.44MB floppy disks. Logical partition sizes could be up to 32 MB, and a single machine could support both a primary and a secondary partition on each disk.

NOTE Partitions and other disk concepts will be covered in more depth in Chapter 4.

It was around the same time that DOS 3.3 was introduced that Microsoft and IBM announced the creation of a second PC operating system, OS/2. We will discuss OS/2 later in this chapter.

MS-DOS 4.0

By 1988 it was apparent that the wave of the future was the graphical interface, and DOS 4.0 provided users with the DOS Shell, a utility much like the Windows File Manager. Actually, DOS Shell was simply a scaled-down version of Windows (which we will look at in a minute) that allowed users to manage files, run programs, and do routine maintenance all from a single screen. The DOS Shell even supported a mouse! (That's right, there was no ability to use a mouse within DOS before this version.) For all versions of DOS after version 4.0, you will find that most of the improvements were relatively small, and involved tinkering with and refining existing utilities and commands.

NOTE
A *shell* is a program that runs "on top of" the operating system and allows the user to issue commands through a set of menus or some other graphical interface. Shells make using an operating system easier to use by changing the user interface. The two shells we will be looking at most closely are Microsoft's DOS Shell (a menuing system) and Windows (a fully graphical user interface).

MS-DOS 5.0

There were several important features introduced in the 1991 release of DOS 5.0. First of all, the ability to load drivers into reserved (upper) memory was a relief to those people who were constantly running out of conventional memory. This feature allowed more complex DOS programs (that took up more conventional memory) to be developed.

In addition to this feature, several software utilities made their debut. The most commonly used utility introduced at this time was EDIT.COM. This ASCII text editor has since become one of the most popular text editors for simple text files (and a welcome relief from the single-line view of EDLIN.COM—previously the only choice for a text editor). In DOS 5 (and 6), MS-DOS included the program QBASIC.EXE, which EDIT required in order to run. QBASIC also allowed BASIC programs to be written and run.

Another DOS 5 utility that has become a favorite among technicians is DOSKEY.COM. When loaded, this utility allowed DOS *macros* to be programmed and executed. Additionally, this utility will store, in memory, the last few commands typed at the DOS prompt. You can then press the up-arrow key to cycle through the last few commands instead of retyping them. It makes issuing repetitive commands much simpler.

Finally, with DOS 5 came the release of the "uns"—UNFORMAT
.EXE and UNDELETE.EXE. The UNFORMAT utility can recover
from an accidental disk format, as long as the format had been performed with the /U (unconditional) switch. The UNDELETE utility
can recover accidentally deleted files.

WARNING When performing file or disk maintenance on a machine set
up for DOS 5.0, never interrupt a format or deletion. If you let
it finish, you improve the chance that you can then use the
UNDELETE or UNFORMAT commands to undo it.

MS-DOS 6.0

Released in 1993 to excellent sales (and a lawsuit for patent infringe-
ment) DOS 6.0 offered a number of new commands and configurable
options. It included new antivirus and backup software, a defragmentation utility, drive compression (the lawsuit was over this),
and the ability to pool EMS and XMS memory using EMM386.EXE.
Please note that DOS 6.0 has subsequently been revised a number
of times, including once (DOS 6.2 to 6.21) because of a court order!
Microsoft was found to have violated Star Electronics' patent rights
in the creation of the DoubleSpace utility for 6.0, and the only real
difference between 6.2 and 6.21 is that DoubleSpace is removed.
Never to be denied, though, Microsoft later released DOS 6.22. Its
new feature? A disk compression program called DriveSpace! As of
this writing, DOS 6.22 is the most current version available as an
operating system. (Although Microsoft has made modifications to
certain DOS commands for use within Windows 95, Microsoft does
not consider DOS a separate operating system under Windows 95,
and so does not sell it separately as a new version, or even identify
it as such.)

Microsoft Windows

Any real understanding of the success of DOS after 1987 requires a knowledge of Windows. In the early years of its existence Microsoft's DOS gained great acceptance and became a de facto standard as a PC operating system. Even so, as computers became more powerful and programs more complex, the limitations of the DOS command-line interface were becoming apparent (as well as the aforementioned conventional memory limitation).

The solution to the problem was to make the operating system easier to navigate, more uniform, and generally more "friendly" to the user. IBM had understood that the average user did not want to receive their computer in pieces, but preferred to have it ready-to-go out of the box. Oddly, they did not understand that the same user who wanted their *hardware* to be ready-to-go did not want to edit batch files or hunt through directories using CD or DIR commands either. Because of this, when Microsoft came to IBM with a graphical user interface (GUI) based on groundbreaking work done by Xerox PARC labs, IBM was not interested, preferring to go onward with the development of OS/2, a project it had already started with Microsoft.

NOTE
The Xerox corporation maintained a think tank of computer designers in Palo Alto, California called the Palo Alto Research Center (PARC). One of the results of their work was the Alto workstation, which is generally thought to be the forerunner of all modern graphical operating systems. The Alto had a mouse and a GUI interface, and communicated with other stations via ethernet. Oh, and it was finished in 1974! Both Microsoft and Apple viewed the Alto, and incorporated its technology in their own systems.

Regardless of IBM's interest, Microsoft continued on its own with its development of the GUI—which it named *Windows* after its rectangular work areas—and released the first version to the market in 1985. Apple filed a lawsuit soon after, claiming that the Microsoft GUI had been built using Apple technology, but the suit was dismissed. Apple's Macintosh and Microsoft's DOS-with-Windows combo have both continued to evolve, but until a recent deal between Apple and Microsoft, tensions have always been high. Mac and PC *users*, of course, still remain adamantly chauvinist about their respective platforms.

The Windows interface to MS-DOS is really just a shell program that allows users to issue DOS commands through a graphical interface. The introduction of a mouse—a legacy of the Xerox Alto computer on which both the Macintosh and Windows GUIs are based—further freed the user from DOS in that it allowed them to escape the use of the keyboard for issuing commands. Word processors, spreadsheets, and especially games were revolutionized as software manufacturers happily took advantage of the ease of use and flexibility that Windows added to DOS.

You will find that after the development of Windows, many of the enhancements made to subsequent versions of DOS were designed to help free up and reallocate resources to better run Windows and Windows-based applications. Similarly, PC hardware continued to evolve far past the limits of DOS's ability to effectively use the power available to it, and later versions of Windows would be designed to hide and overcome the limitations of the operating system.

Windows 1.0

Version 1.0 of Windows already featured the tiling windows, mouse support, and menu systems which still drive next-generation operating systems such as Windows 95, Windows 98, and Windows NT. It also offered "cooperative multitasking"—meaning more than one Windows application could run concurrently. This was something that MS-DOS up to this point could not do.

There were several things Windows 1.0 could not do, however. For one thing, it didn't use icons. Windows 1.0 was basically a fuller-featured graphical version of the DOS SHELL.EXE program.

Windows 2.0

Version 2.0, released in 1987, added icons and allowed application windows to overlap each other as well as tile. Support was also added for PIFs (program information files), which allowed the user to configure Windows to run their DOS applications more efficiently. Later in 1987 Microsoft also released another version of Windows, designed for the Intel 386 processor, which came to be known as Windows/386. (Because of this, version 2.0 is often referred to as Windows/286.) Windows/386 allowed for multiple DOS sessions in extended memory, but in most other ways was the same as Windows 2.0. Although they were an improvement over version 1.0, it would not be until the 1990 release of Windows 3.0 that the Windows interface would be widely used.

Windows 3.0

Windows 3.0 featured a far more flexible memory model, allowing it to access more memory than the 640KB limit normally imposed by DOS. It also featured the addition of the File Manager and Program Manager, allowed for network support, and could operate in "386 Enhanced mode." 386 Enhanced mode used parts of the hard drive as "virtual memory," and was therefore able to use disk memory to supplement the RAM in the machine. Windows today in fact is still quite similar to the Windows of version 3.0.

Windows 3.x

In 1992, a final revision of Windows 3.0, known as Windows 3.1, provided for better graphical display capability and multimedia support. It also improved the Windows error-protection system, and let applications work together more easily through the use of object linking and embedding (OLE).

Windows after the introduction of version 3.1 took a marked turn for the better, in that Microsoft started making a serious effort to make the change to a full 32-bit application environment. With version 3.11, also known as Windows for Workgroups, Windows could now offer support for both 16-bit and 32-bit applications (Windows 3.1 could only support 16-bit applications). Significant progress on that front was not to be made, however, until very late in 1995, when Microsoft introduced Windows 95.

NOTE   With the introduction of Windows for Workgroups (Windows 3.11), people who knew that there were two "flavors" of Windows 3.1 started referring both to version 3.1 and to version 3.11 as *Windows 3.x.*

OS/2

Even as Windows 3.1 was in development, Microsoft was also participating in a joint effort with IBM to create a next-generation operating system for use with 286 and higher processors. This operating system was the second generation OS, or OS/2. The creation of the initial version caused a number of disagreements, though, and the partnership soon broke up. IBM continued the development of OS/2, while Microsoft took part of the technology and began to develop LAN Manager, which would eventually lead to the development of Windows NT.

With OS/2 version 2.0, IBM made OS/2 a 32-bit system which required at least a 386 processor to run. Although this made it vastly more stable and powerful than Windows 3.1, both it and Microsoft's NT product had a problem finding a market. The main reason for this was probably that most users simply did not have powerful enough computers (or couldn't afford them) to properly use the system.

With version 3.0 (OS/2 Warp), IBM created a multitasking, 32-bit OS which required a 386 but preferred a 486. Warp also required a staggering 4 MB of RAM just to load. With a graphical interface and the ability to do a great deal of self-configuration, the Warp OS was a peculiar cross between DOS and a Macintosh. Warp featured true preemptive multitasking, did not suffer from the memory limitations of DOS, and had a desktop similar to the Macintosh.

For all of its tremendous features, OS/2 Warp had a funny name, and it was, unfortunately, badly marketed. It never really established a wide user base. Nonetheless, until Windows NT 3.51 was released in 1995, OS/2 was the operating system of choice for high-end workstations, and the OS retains a small but faithful following.

Windows 95

Although it dominated the market with its DOS operating system and its add-on Windows interface, Microsoft found that the constraints of DOS were rapidly making it difficult to take full advantage of rapidly improving hardware and software developments. The future of computing was clearly a 32-bit, preemptively multitasked system such as IBM's OS/2, but many current users had DOS-based software or older hardware—generally referred to as "legacy" devices—which were specifically designed for DOS and would not operate outside of its Windows 3.1, cooperatively multitasked environment.

Multitasking—or How to Do More Than One Thing at a Time!

Preemptive and cooperative multitasking are two ways that computers are able to manage the way that the processor is controlled. Cooperative multitasking depends on the application itself to be responsible for using and then freeing access to the processor. This is the way that Windows 3.1 manages multiple applications. Because of this, if any application locks up while using the processor, it will be unable to properly free the processor to do other tasks, and the entire system locks, usually forcing a reboot.

Cooperative multitasking is different, in that the operating system allots each application a certain amount of processor time, and then forcibly takes back control and gives another application or task access to the processor. This means that if an application crashes, the operating system takes control of the processor away from the locked application, and passes it on to the next app, which should be unaffected. Although unstable programs still lock, only the locked application will be stalled, not the entire system.

NOTE Legacy devices are generally defined as devices (sound cards, modems, etc.) that do not support the Plug-and-Play standard used by Windows 95, or are simply too old to properly interface with more modern computers. Legacy devices are either not able to dynamically interact with the Windows 95 system, or not able to function at all. They therefore require manual configuration (which is not generally necessary on newer devices), or must be replaced by newer devices.

Because of this problem, in the fall of 1995 Microsoft released a major upgrade to the DOS/Windows environment. Named Windows 95, the new product integrated the operating system and the shell. Whereas previous versions of Windows had simply provided a graphic interface to the existing DOS OS, in Windows 95 the graphical interface *is* the OS! Moreover, Windows 95 was designed to be a hybrid of the features of previous DOS versions and newer 32-bit systems. To this end, it is a preemptively multi-tasked system which is able to emulate and support cooperative multitasking for programs which require it. It also supports both 32-bit drivers and DOS drivers, although the 32-bit drivers are strongly recommended over the DOS ones, as they are far more stable and faster.

WARNING Currently the A+ test does not test your knowledge of the Windows 95 operating system. Regardless of this, you will find that the Win95 OS is rapidly taking over the desktops of both corporate and home users, and soon Win98 will probably continue the takeover at an even faster rate. Taking time to study Windows 95/98 should be a crucial part of your preparation for a job as a service technician. An unfortunate fact of the computer industry is that about the time you master a product, it is obsolete. The only defense against this is constant re-education and studying. To this end, I'm providing an appendix at the end of this book, covering the basics of the Windows 95/98 OS.

Windows NT

The DOS+Windows 3.x combo and Windows 95 are currently the most important PC operating systems on the market. Still, for users who need more power, other options are available. One of these is the Windows NT operating system. NT (which unofficially stands for New Technology) is an OS that was designed to be far more powerful than any previous Windows version. It uses an architecture based entirely on 32-bit code, and is capable of accessing up to 4 gigabytes (4,000 megabytes) of RAM. Windows NT can support huge drive sizes and more than one processor, and has numerous other advantages over Windows 95 and DOS. NT is often used as a workstation for users who use large files or complex programs. CAD (computer-aided design) programs are a good example of the sort of applications which run better under NT than under other versions of Windows. Windows NT also allows for better security than previous versions of Windows, and is more stable. Naturally, each version of NT that has come out has also been more expensive than the current version of Windows 3.x or 95, and needed a significantly more powerful machine to run well. NT 3.1 was released as both a workstation and a server product in 1993, and has subsequently been upgraded to 3.5, 3.51 and 4.0. Versions 3.1 through 3.51 look much like Windows 3.1, while 4.0 uses the Windows 95 GUI.

High-End Operating Systems

High-end operating systems are those that are used by "power users" (a user who does several high-end task concurrently—for example, people involved in the process of software development must perform several types of tasks simultaneously as they write, compile, debug, and test their programs). Generally speaking, these operating systems have higher hardware requirements than the personal computer systems used by typical business workers. Some of these operating systems may require the use of more than one processor.

UNIX

One option for high-end users is UNIX, which is an operating system that has been in use for more than two decades in some form. UNIX is compatible with DOS or Windows applications through the use of additional software, and there are versions of UNIX that run on Intel-based PC hardware (like Linux, FreeBSD, Solaris X86, and SCO for Intel). UNIX is an extremely powerful and extremely complex system. It features many of the advantages of Windows NT, and because of its design UNIX machines can be made to perform many different tasks. The most popular use of UNIX today is as the foundation of the Internet. All of the protocols and programs used on the Internet have their basis in UNIX in some form or another. For example, World Wide Web server software was only available on the UNIX OS before the Internet really took off.

The most important disadvantage of UNIX is that it is not totally compatible with PC software. Additionally, UNIX is not what most people would describe as a "user-friendly" operating system (although I have some friends who would debate that statement).

NeXTSTEP

In addition to these operating systems, other companies have been developing their own "next generation" operating systems. One company that had its own operating system was NeXT Computer. Founded by ousted Apple Computer executive Steve Jobs, NeXT Computer started by developing hardware (basically a souped-up Macintosh) that ran their special operating system called NeXTSTEP. Their operating system was unique in that it represented every entity in the operating system with logical "objects". Hence the term *object-oriented OS*.

Eventually Jobs realized that the OS was where the money was to be made, and NeXT abandoned its hardware ventures. The NeXTSTEP OS was primarily used by programmers and system administrators.

Recently, Apple acquired NeXT and the rights to use its operating system technologies and incorporate them into Apple's next operating system release, code-named Rhapsody. Rhapsody has been in development for some time now. The main benefit to this operating system is supposed to be that it will be hardware independent. It is intended to run on both Intel and Motorola-based computers.

> **NOTE**   It is important that we know where we have been and how we have gotten to where we are. Although the information in this chapter is not literally included on the A+ exam, knowing this background is an essential part of being an informed and effective computer support person or service technician, and certainly accords with the overall goals of certification. Customers and clients will be more confident of your abilities when you can show that you have a solid understanding of your industry.

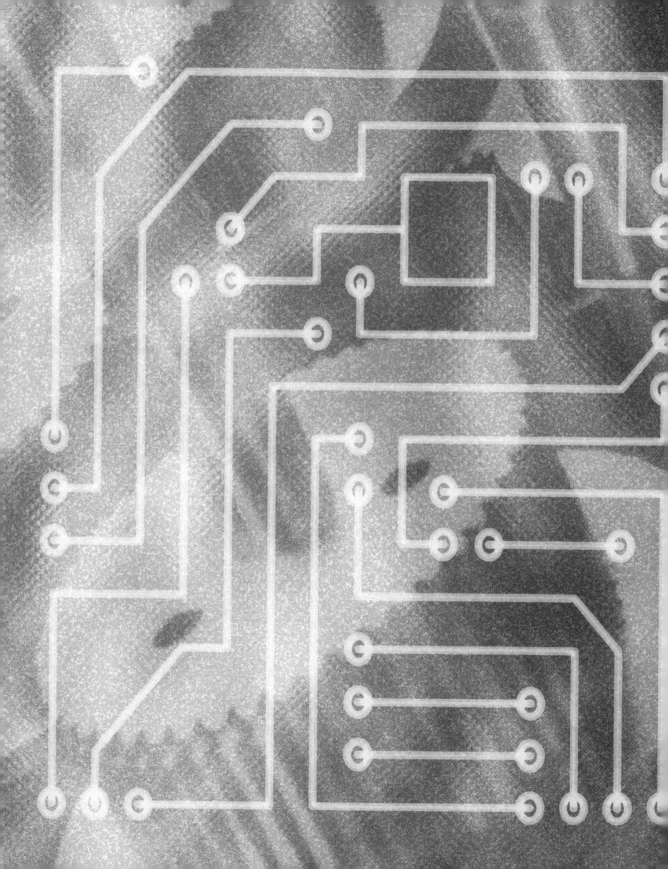

CHAPTER

TWO

2

An Overview of the DOS Operating System

- Varieties of DOS

- The Primary Functions Provided by DOS

- The Major Elements of DOS

Now that we have taken a brief look at the different operating systems that are available today, it is time to focus on the OS that has dominated the PC market for the better part of the last two decades. Microsoft's Disk Operating System—DOS for short—is a simple yet very powerful OS that has proved to be both flexible and configurable. Even as newer operating systems have come onto the market that are better suited to the strains of running state-of-the-art applications on new machines, DOS continues to be a viable desktop operating system in many environments. It is also a necessity for technicians because of its usefulness as a configuration and diagnostic tool.

This chapter, then, will give you an overview of the capabilities of the DOS operating system, and will familiarize you with many of the concepts and terms you will be studying in later chapters, including the following:

- Varieties of DOS

- The Primary Functions Provided by DOS

- The Major Elements of DOS

NOTE   Use this chapter as a brief introduction to the later chapters. If something particularly interests you, feel free to skip to that chapter and find out more. Remember, though, that knowledge builds throughout the book and some information assumed in later chapters may not be familiar to you if you do not follow through the book in order.

Varieties of DOS

Throughout this book, when I mention DOS, I am referring to Microsoft MS-DOS by default. When I need to specify another DOS, for example, IBM's PC-DOS, I will specify it, as appropriate. As you might expect, there are even more DOSes out there. Let's examine a few of these briefly.

Microsoft DOS (MS-DOS)

Of all the versions of DOS, the most popular by far is Microsoft DOS, which is usually abbreviated as MS-DOS, or just "DOS" to people who may be unaware that there are other makers. As we discussed in the previous chapter, MS-DOS was developed by Microsoft for IBM's bold computer venture of the early eighties, the IBM PC.

As enumerated in the previous chapter, the MS-DOS operating system has occasionally been updated, and a new "version" of the OS would be released to the public. This version would then become the standard DOS version on new machines, or could be purchased as an "upgrade" by owners of previous DOS versions.

TIP   An upgrade can be a comparatively inexpensive way to purchase a new version of any software product. Most companies will offer a discounted price to customers who are upgrading from a previous purchase of the same product. They do this both to reward loyal customers and to help them keep track of which sales are to new consumers and which are to returning customers. If a customer already has a piece of software and you know they may be thinking of buying a newer version of the same program, advise them to see if the software manufacturer offers a discounted upgrade price.

Keeping track of versions is not the only source of confusion that PC technicians have to deal with. This is because besides occasionally issuing upgrades, which would introduce new commands and possibly change (or phase out) existing utilities, Microsoft also licensed DOS to a number of other companies, who then began making their own DOS operating systems. Although these were generally very close to Microsoft's product, they were not usually identical. For the most part, the other manufacturers took their lead from Microsoft by bringing out similar versions around the same time as Microsoft, but often with slightly different names or functionality on certain utilities. You may run into slight differences in your work with customers or clients, so you should try to become familiar with a few other kinds of DOS. However, as a general rule, if you know MS-DOS, you know DOS. Any other varieties will work in basically the same way, and will have almost all of the same features.

IBM PC-DOS

PC-DOS is IBM's own DOS variety. It was developed by IBM after a disagreement they had with Microsoft over the new operating system they were co-developing (which was called OS/2). Both companies went their separate ways, but that left IBM without a new version of DOS when Microsoft revised MS-DOS for the ever growing population of non-IBM users, and OS/2 wasn't quite ready for shipment. Hence PC-DOS.

In general, PC-DOS is extremely similar to Microsoft's MS-DOS, but has a few changes in particular commands or utilities. For example, you use EDIT.COM in MS-DOS to edit an ASCII text (DOS text) file. But in PC-DOS, you will use E.EXE. People that normally use a version of MS-DOS and are used to its commands can get confused when they start using a machine that has PC-DOS installed. They may type **EDIT FILE.TXT** and get a "Bad Command or File Name" message because EDIT.COM doesn't exist on that machine. Instead, they will need to type **E FILE.TXT** to be able to edit the file.

TIP

When dealing with a non-Microsoft DOS variety, you may need to confirm that the "command syntax" (the proper order and spelling of commands and command options) for the commands you normally use in MS-DOS is supported in the variety you are using. A good way to do this is to access help on the command in question. Typing the command followed directly by /? on the same line will bring up the DOS help screen for that command. This works in nearly any variety or version of DOS. The help screen displays the syntax of the command.

Other Varieties

Generally speaking, MS-DOS and PC-DOS are the two most popular varieties of DOS. There have been a couple of key players in the DOS world that aren't associated with either of these two (except for the fact that their operating systems share similar names). Let's look a couple of the other key players.

DR-DOS 6

About the same time that MS-DOS was having operating system disputes with IBM, a company by the name of Digital Research came out with an alternative to MS-DOS. They called their operating system Digital Research DOS or DR-DOS for short. Just like the other versions of DOS, basic functionality was still the same. DIR, COPY, and DEL worked the same as their "older brother" counterparts (MS-DOS & PC-DOS).

But here's where the story gets interesting. Novell, a networking software company based out of Provo, Utah, wanted to leverage its investment in networks and break into the desktop OS market. In short, they wanted to buy a product that would directly compete with Microsoft's MS-DOS 5. They found DR-DOS to be a perfect solution. So, they bought *DR-DOS 6* (and all the source code) from Digital Research and recommended that all customers load DR-DOS on their workstations at the same time they loaded NetWare on their servers.

Novell DOS 7

As time passed people generally ignored DR-DOS 6 because they could get the same features cheaper through MS-DOS (it was pre-loaded on most new computers, so people were getting it for free). That's when Novell countered with *Novell DOS 7*. Novell's idea was that people weren't buying their DOS because it didn't offer any new features. So they decided to completely revamp DR-DOS 6 and add several major new features.

The first new feature to be added was the ability to run several programs at once (called *multitasking*). This was something that MS-DOS (or any other variety, including DR-DOS) had never been able to accomplish. If a user was in a word processor and wanted to switch to a spreadsheet program to look up a set of numbers, they would have to exit the word processor and run the spreadsheet. With Novell DOS 7's multitasking feature, users could run multiple programs and switch between them with a keystroke.

At the time, Novell NetWare held almost 90% of the network operating system market share (meaning that 9 out of 10 servers in use at that time had NetWare installed on them). Novell decided to put their networking savvy to use in their version of DOS. So, they came up with a product (introduced at the same time as Novell DOS 7) called Personal NetWare. Personal NetWare is a peer-to-peer *network operating system* (*NOS*). It allows computers to function as both servers and workstations on small networks. If a computer had Personal NetWare installed on it (as well as Novell DOS 7), it could share files out to other computers at the same time they were running their word processing program. With a feature like that, how could they miss?

Well, believe it or not, they could. Two factors contributed to the demise of Novell DOS 7 and Personal NetWare. First of all, a computer that would be running both products would be running neither of them very well. The memory and disk space requirements were bulky, and Personal NetWare would sometimes crash, either locking up the computer or requiring a reboot. Second, Novell did most of its marketing through their dealer channel. They let the product sell itself on its own merits. Unfortunately, just because a product is technically superior doesn't mean the public will buy it. (The "build a better mousetrap..." adage just doesn't work in the technology market.)

Novell DOS 7 is still around, but it was sold to Caldera in 1995 and became *OpenDOS*. It is basically the same OS as DOS 7, just with a different name.

The Primary Functions Provided by DOS

In order to be useful, an operating system must provide services, both to the user and to the computer. MS-DOS does this in numerous ways, but the basic types of services can be placed into four general categories.

- Executing code (programs)
- Managing files
- Managing disks
- System management

We will talk about each of these briefly here, and each will be covered in greater depth in a later chapter. Remember that these services are not in any way unique to DOS. They are, in fact, the same standard tasks that every machine from a Commodore 64 to a Cray supercomputer needs to address. It is the way that DOS addresses these needs that interests us, and which sets it apart—in good ways and bad—from other operating systems.

Executing Programs

The primary reason for having a computer is to use it for particular tasks. Be they word processors, spreadsheets, or games, all tasks that need to be completed on a computer must be implemented in the form of some sort of *program*.

NOTE Even the command-line DOS utilities we will be looking at later are technically just programs provided with DOS, but in general when a person is talking about a program they're referring to a piece of software that is purchased separately from DOS. Examples of this would be WordPerfect 5.1, Paradox 4.0 for DOS, and even—of course—Windows 3.1!

Programs consist of at least one file that is accessed by DOS, and which then issues instructions. These instructions are interpreted by DOS, and then passed on to the processor, which executes the code. This will then produce a result, which the operating system will either pass on to the monitor, the printer, or another device.

Installing and Running a Program

In early versions of DOS, most PCs had little or no hard drive storage space, and programs were normally written with the idea that they would be run directly off a single diskette, and that the user would have to insert another diskette if work needed to be saved for later use. This worked, but was incredibly tedious, and keeping track of disks and finding files was a user management headache.

As PC hardware evolved, and greater amounts of storage became available, programs began to get larger and more feature-laden. This made running programs from the floppy drive difficult if not impossible, and software needed to be transferred to the hard drive—that is, *installed*—before it could be used. This process works well, and most vendors supply an installation program with their software products to make the process as painless as possible. This program, usually named either INSTALL.EXE or SETUP.EXE, has a dual purpose: to transfer the program files for the desired program to the hard drive and to configure DOS to use that product. Some DOS programs do not need any particular configuration, and will run as long as the files they need are available to them. Others need additional changes to be made to DOS. These changes, and how they can be made, will be discussed in Chapter 6.

NOTE The setup process for two different software packages—MS-DOS and Windows 3.1—are described in depth later in this book. Chapter 5 deals with installing DOS, while Chapter 9 is dedicated to the Windows 3.1 setup. Remember that as Windows 3.1 is actually just a program that runs on top of DOS (like WordPerfect 5.1 or other software), it needs DOS to already be installed before it can be put on the system.

You will find that the newer a piece of software is, the more resources it is likely to consume. These programs also are more likely to make system modifications, and it is partly because of this that you can't just copy files from the installation disk to the hard drive—you have to run the installation program.

You must be certain before you spend your money on a new program that the software you want to use does not require a different operating system than the one you have. If you do not have Windows, make certain that the program is not designed to run under Windows. Even DOS programs often require more overhead than your old machine might be able to offer. For example, a new DOS program may require any or all of the following:

- greater amounts of free drive space to install the software
- a newer version of DOS in order to run properly
- more memory (RAM)
- a faster system (updated CPU, etc.)
- a CD-ROM drive as the preferred installation drive

Windows applications, such as Microsoft's Word for Windows, simply do not function without Windows installed and running.

Once a DOS program has been installed, the process of running that program is relatively straightforward. Each program will have either an executable file or a batch file that must be run to begin the execution of the program. Until this file has been executed, the computer acts as though the program does not exist, and will not contain in its memory any information on how to complete that program's tasks. As a matter of terminology, the program is only active while the executable file is *open*. Exiting the program usually unloads its code from memory and stops execution of any tasks that are underway. In this way, DOS allows another program to be started, and to make use of the resources previously used by another program.

TIP

The executable file or batch file for a program is usually specified in the setup instructions for the program, but these files are also recognizable by their filename *extensions*. Extensions are the characters that appear after the dot in a DOS filename (the extension is one, two, or three characters long; most files use all three). The extension defines the file's type and function. Executables, for instance, have a .EXE or .COM extension, and batch files, which have a different function, have a .BAT extension.

Managing Files

Another important task of the operating system is file management. File management is accomplished through the use of a number of "external" commands. I will cover those commands later (in Chapter 7), but the basic idea is that for a program to run it must be able to read information off of the disk, and write information back. In order to be able to organize and access information—especially in larger new systems which may have thousands of files—it is necessary to have a structure and an ordering process.

DOS provides this process by allowing you to create directories in which to organize files, and it also regulates the way that files are named and what the properties of the file are. Each file created in DOS has to follow certain rules, and any program that accesses files through DOS must comply with these rules. Files created on a DOS system will have the following:

- a filename of 1 to 8 characters, with no spaces or punctuation

- an optional extension of 1 to 3 characters

The TREE command allows you to examine your file structure by letting you "see" the relationships of the directories and subdirectories you have created. See Figure 2.1 for a simple DOS file system tree.

FIGURE 2.1:

A DOS tree

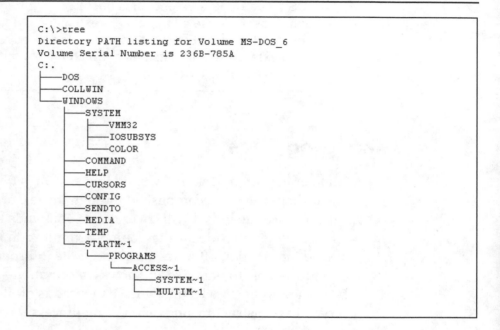

```
C:\>tree
Directory PATH listing for Volume MS-DOS_6
Volume Serial Number is 236B-785A
C:.
├───DOS
├───COLLWIN
└───WINDOWS
    ├───SYSTEM
    │   ├───VMM32
    │   ├───IOSUBSYS
    │   └───COLOR
    ├───COMMAND
    ├───HELP
    ├───CURSORS
    ├───CONFIG
    ├───SENDTO
    ├───MEDIA
    ├───TEMP
    └───STARTM~1
        └───PROGRAMS
            └───ACCESS~1
                ├───SYSTEM~1
                └───MULTIM~1
```

DOS also protects against duplicate filenames, as no two files on the system can have exactly the same name and *path*. A path indicates the location of the file on the disk; it is composed of the logical drive letter the file is on, and if the file is located in a directory or subdirectory, the names of the directories. For instance, an important DOS file named COMMAND.COM is located in the "root" of the C: drive—that means it is not within a directory, and so the path to the file is simply C:\COMMAND.COM. Another important DOS file, the file FDISK, is located in the DOS directory off of the root of C:, so the path to FDISK is therefore C:\DOS\FDISK.EXE.

WARNING Saving a new file named WORK.TXT into a directory that already has a file of that name will overwrite the old file and replace it with the new one. To avoid this, either name the new file something different—for instance, WORK2.TXT—or put the file into a different directory. Both C:\WORK.TXT and C:\FILES\WORK.TXT can exist on the same system, because although the files have the same name, they have different paths. Also, DOS is not case sensitive. To the DOS OS, WORK.TXT and work.txt are the same file.

Additionally, DOS provides four attributes that can be set for files to modify their interaction with the system. These attributes are:

- **Read-Only**: Prevents a file from being modified, deleted, or overwritten.

- **Archive**: Used by backup programs to determine whether the file has changed since the last backup and needs to be backed up.

- **System**: Used to tell the OS that this file is needed by the system, and should not be deleted.

- **Hidden**: Used to keep files from being seen in a normal directory search. This is useful to prevent system files and other important files from being accidentally moved or deleted.

Attributes are set for files using an external DOS command called ATTRIB, which I'll present along with a number of other commands in Chapter 7.

Managing Disks

Besides governing the way in which files are named and organized, DOS also has utilities that allow it to manage physical disks—both hard drive and floppy disks—so that they are usable. DOS provides a number of disk-related services, including:

- Creating and deleting partitions on hard drives

- Formatting partitions and floppy drives

- Copying and backing up disks

- Compressing files to increase the number of files stored on a drive

---

NOTE   I'll be explaining these concepts in numerous places throughout the next few chapters. Chapter 4 focuses on the preparation and formatting of a disk, and the COPY, XCOPY, and BACKUP utilities are examined in Chapter 7.

System Management

Not all functions of DOS are directly related to running applications, yet are still important to the health of your system. One example of this is the ability of DOS to adjust a PC's internal clock. The hour, minute, and second can be set with the TIME command, and the date can be changed with the DATE command (see Figure 2.2). This can be crucial to some programs, as different applications may access the computer's internal clock to time-stamp or date-stamp a document.

FIGURE 2.2:

Date and Time commands

```
C:\>date
Current date is Sat 12-13-1997
Enter new date (mm-dd-yy):

C:\>time
Current time is  7:18:19.53p
Enter new time:
```

DOS gives you utilities to help configure the system as well, and in Chapter 7 ("Basic DOS Commands") you will see how the EDIT program included with DOS can be used to modify key DOS startup files. Lastly, DOS has utilities built into it that allow you to examine the system's configuration and resource usage. Two such programs are MEM, which allows you to examine the total memory and used memory on the system, and MSD, which stands for Microsoft Diagnostics. MSD is a program that gives you the ability to examine many different aspects of a system's hardware and software setup. A screen shot of the main MSD menu, showing the various category "buttons" you can activate to show more information, is shown in Figure 2.3.

FIGURE 2.3:

The main
MSD (Microsoft
Diagnostics) menu

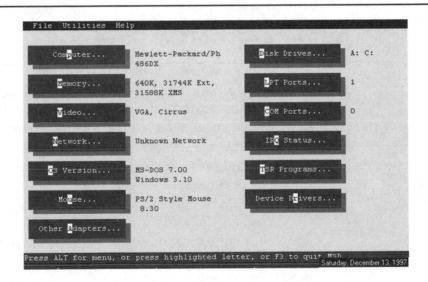

These, then, are the main tasks that the DOS OS accomplishes. We will now turn our attention to the main components that make up this operating system and allow it to do its work.

The Major Elements of DOS

In the first chapter of this book you learned what an operating system is, and also looked at how PC operating systems have evolved over the past twenty years. You have also seen some of the major responsibilities of an OS. Now we will look at the major components of the DOS operating system, and how these components allow DOS to accomplish the tasks it needs to accomplish. The major elements we'll consider fall into two major categories:

- User interaction with DOS

- DOS interaction with hardware

User Interaction with DOS

The file COMMAND.COM, which is located in the root of the C: drive on a DOS-based computer, is the primary vehicle for allowing you to communicate with your computer, and vice-versa. Also known as the command interpreter, or the command processor, COMMAND.COM is very much like a person who is interpreting for two people who speak different languages. When dealing with the user, the command interpreter presents a *command-line prompt* (which usually looks like C:\> or something similar) and waits for the user to type in a command next to the prompt. Both the prompt and the commands that DOS is waiting to receive are in words and letters that are more or less recognizable as English, so you should be able to understand and remember them once you become familiar with them.

On the other side of the command interpreter are the actual DOS system files, which are written in such a way that we cannot communicate with them directly. These files are the ones that provide most of the real functionality of DOS. They are also the files that communicate with the hardware and the BIOS.

NOTE   I'll present the DOS system files in detail in Chapter 6.

Just as an interpreter is simply supposed to translate one person's words into a language that another person can understand, COM-MAND.COM takes commands issued by the user through their text strings and translates them into calls that can be understood by lower layers of DOS. Although its prompt is the user's primary contact with the OS, COMMAND.COM has little ability to do anything on its own, and can execute only very common tasks by itself without needing to pass the command on to a different place. The beauty of this, though, is that this single interface to DOS allows users to do their work completely unaware of what part of the operating system is performing the tasks they are requesting. The use of this front-line command interpreter allows for a single, consistent interface for all tasks.

DOS Interaction with Hardware

The command interpreter, as we have seen, takes requests from user input and translates them into calls that can be understood by the DOS system. The DOS system files then communicate with the special memory of the computer. The special computer memory is called *ROM* (*Read-Only Memory*), and it contains information that was written into it at the factory. Unlike RAM, ROM does not dynamically load and unload information based on which programs are running.

There are several ROM chips inside any computer. The most inportant of these is the ROM BIOS. BIOS stands for *Basic Input/ Output System*, which pretty much describes the function of this part of the computer. All requests to access hardware and all responses from hardware go through the BIOS.

Just as the command interpreter took our text commands, translated them into a form the DOS system could understand, and passed them to the system, the system does further translation before passing the request on to the ROM BIOS, and the ROM BIOS does a final translation itself before passing the request to the hardware. Of course, once the request has been executed, the response from the hardware must be returned to the system or the user, and in such a case the entire translation process must be reversed for the response to pass up through these layers and eventually be displayed as a message or an action.

As you go through the next chapters, and see all of the functions that can be accomplished with DOS, remember that every one of these must follow this complex path up and down the system, probably thousands of times, to accomplish even the smallest task.

Review Questions for Chapter 2, An Overview of the DOS Operating System

Answers to the review questions may be found in Appendix A.

1. Which of the following is *not* true of an upgrade?

    A. usually cheaper than a new purchase

    B. requires the buyer to own an earlier version of the software

    C. available only for applications, not operating systems

    D. created to add new features to an existing piece of software

2. Which of the following is *not* a standard feature of DOS?

    A. network support

    B. running programs

    C. managing files

    D. managing disks

3. Which of these is used to add and configure new software?

    A. SETUP.EXE

    B. ADDPROG.EXE

    C. INSTALL.EXE

    D. both A and C

4. Which of the following is a program?

    A. Windows 3.1

    B. WordPerfect 5.1

    C. FORMAT.EXE

    D. all of the above

5. Which of the following are typical requirements of newer applications? (Circle all that apply.)

   A. need greater amounts of free drive space to install the software

   B. need newer versions of DOS to run properly

   C. more likely to run off of a floppy drive instead of the hard disk

   D. need more memory (RAM) and a faster system (updated CPU, etc.)

6. Which of the following filenames are invalid in DOS?

   A. myfile.txt

   B. my file.txt

   C. myfile

   D. myfile.

   E. MYFILE.TXT

7. Which is a disk-related service provided by DOS?

   A. creating and deleting partitions on hard drives

   B. compressing files to increase the number of files stored on a drive

   C. copying and backing up disks

   D. all of the above

8. Which utility allows you to view memory usage?

   A. MEM

   B. MEMORY

   C. TIME

   D. FORMAT

9. Which utility allows you to view the system's processor type?

    A. MEM

    B. MSD

    C. FDISK

    D. PROC

10. Which of the following actually talks to a computer's hardware?

    A. the ROM BIOS

    B. the DOS System Files

    C. COMMAND.COM

    D. the processor

11. What is the Basic Input/Output System also known as?

    A. RAM

    B. ROM

    C. COMMAND.COM

    D. BIOS

12. Which is *not* a function of COMMAND.COM?

    A. provide a consistent user interface to all DOS system files

    B. present the results of a command to the user

    C. receive input from the user

    D. format requests so they can be sent directly to the processor

13. Which DOS attribute is used by backup programs?

    A. Read-only

    B. Archive

    C. Hidden

    D. System

14. Which command allows you to see the syntax of the DATE command?

    A. DATE /?

    B. DATE ?

    C. HELP /DATE

    D. HELP /DATE /SYNTAX

15. What do you have to do to run a Windows-based program in DOS without the Windows interface?

    A. Use the DOS Shell to run the program.

    B. Configure DOS to support a mouse.

    C. Run the Windows program as the only program on the machine.

    D. Dream on. Windows programs do not run under DOS alone.

16. Which DOS command displays your current directory structure, including any subdirectories?

    A. SUBDIR

    B. DIRSTRUCT

    C. TREE

    D. DIR

17. It is possible to have two files, one having the name file.txt and another having the name FILE.TXT in the same directory. True or false?

    A. True

    B. False

18. The exact location of a file in the DOS directory structure is known as the file's _____.

    A. absolute reference

    B. path

    C. reference

    D. location

19. If the COMMAND.COM file was missing from the boot disk of a computer, which of the following would you not be able to do?

    A. interact with DOS

    B. boot the computer

    C. run programs

    D. none of the above

20. Which function of DOS deals with file compression?

    A. managing hardware

    B. managing disks

    C. managing files

    D. executing programs

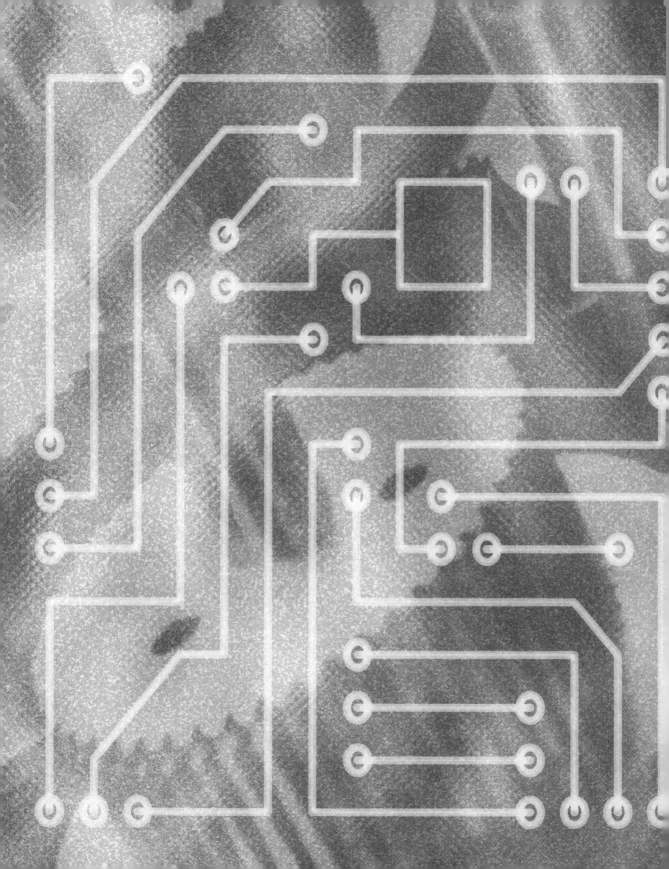

CHAPTER

THREE

3

Prerequisites for Installation

- Verifying the Type of Computer

- Checking to See If Disk Space Is Available

- Backing Up Existing Data

- Preparing the Disk for Installation

Although DOS is a fairly simple operating system, it does require a little bit of preparation before installation. If these prerequisites aren't completed, then DOS either won't install properly or can't be installed at all. In this chapter we will discuss the most important of the prerequisites. Pre-installation procedures for DOS include the following:

- Verifying the Type of Computer
- Checking to See If Disk Space Is Available
- Backing Up Existing Data
- Preparing the Disk for Installation

This chapter assumes that the drive or drives to be configured have already been properly installed, and that they can be accessed by the computer. The initial installation of the DOS operating system can only be completed on a disk that has been properly prepared.

NOTE The information necessary to accomplish these tasks was covered in the first book in the A+ Certification Study Guide series, *A+: Core Module Study Guide*.

Similarly, later additions to the physical disk configuration—for instance, the addition of a second IDE hard drive as a slave drive—must be configured for use by DOS. The hard drive configuration process takes a number of steps, and should be undertaken with care, especially on systems that have existing data.

Verifying the Type of Computer

In order for DOS to function on a computer, that computer must be an IBM-compatible computer. This means that the computer must have a processor that is compatible with the original IBM PC 8088.

Motherboards that contain Intel, AMD, and Cyrix CPUs fall into this class. Macintoshes don't. DOS cannot be installed on Macintosh computers or their compatibles. They use their own proprietary operating system called the Macintosh OS. There are special expansion cards that can be installed in Macs that will allow DOS to run on a Mac, but these cards simply include their own processor and are really "PCs on a card." There are special *DOS emulators* that allow a special version of DOS to be used on a Mac. Basically, DOS doesn't run on the Mac without special help.

Most personal computers today use either a 486, Pentium, Pentium Pro, or Pentium-II processor, or something compatible to one of these processors. All of these processors are backwards-compatible to the original IBM PC's Intel 8088 processor; that is why DOS will run on these machines.

Checking to See If Disk Space Is Available

Assuming you have a computer that can run the DOS operating system, the next prerequisite is that the disk drive have enough space available to accept it. The core components of the MS-DOS operating system—COMMAND.COM, MS-DOS.SYS, and IO.SYS—take only a few kilobytes. However, with all the utilities and options, DOS can take up to seven megabytes of disk space!

There are several methods you can use to check the available disk space. The first is rather obvious. If you install a brand new disk into a computer, that computer will be blank and the entire disk will be available to store information. Alternatively, if you are upgrading from a previous version of DOS, you can use its DIR command to show the available disk space (Figure 3.1). As you can see, the available space is listed, in bytes, at the bottom of the directory listing.

FIGURE 3.1:

Using the DOS DIR command to show available disk space

```
C:\tmp>dir

 Volume in drive C has no label
 Volume Serial Number is 4017-1CEB
 Directory of C:\tmp

 .                <DIR>           08-22-97  3:16p .
 ..               <DIR>           08-22-97  3:16p ..
RESOURCE 1         9,086,574      10-01-96  1:52p resource.1
INSTALL  BAT             311      09-26-96  1:39p install.bat
DEICE    EXE          36,064      09-26-96  1:32p deice.exe
RESOURCE DAT             196      10-01-96  2:30p resource.dat
INSTALL  PIF             967      11-01-97  8:23a install.PIF
         5 file(s)        9,124,112 bytes
         2 dir(s)     2,616,696,832 bytes free
```

This line reports the amount of space still available on the drive.

TIP

Since DIR is an internal DOS command (that is, one that is internal to COMMAND.COM), it is also available on bootable DOS diskettes.

Another DOS program (included with DOS starting with version 5.0) that can show disk space is the CHKDSK.EXE program. Again, this is only available for use if DOS is already installed and you're just planning on ugrading. CHKDSK can provide information about the size of the disk as well as how much space is left on the disk (in bytes). Figure 3.2 shows a sample display of the output of CHKDSK.

FIGURE 3.2:

The output of the CHKDSK.EXE program, showing available disk space

```
Volume Serial Number is 4017-1CEB

4,215,435,264 bytes total disk space
2,605,768,704 bytes available on disk

      4,096 bytes in each allocation unit
  1,029,159 total allocation units on disk
    636,174 available allocation units on disk

    655,360 total bytes memory
    627,392 bytes free
```

This line reports the amount of space still available on the drive.

Finally, during the installation of DOS, the SETUP.EXE program will *check* the amount of disk space that is available on the destination disk (the disk you are trying to install DOS to) and display a warning if there is not enough space.

Backing Up Existing Data

This prerequisite applies only if you are using a disk that has DOS already installed on it and you are upgrading to a newer version. If that is the case, you should *back up* (that is, make a copy of) your existing data before continuing with the upgrade. Installing DOS is normally a non-destructive process, but accidents do happen, and those accidents have a very small chance of causing data loss. If your files are unimportant to you, you can skip this step.

There are several programs available commercially for backing up your data easily. These programs can back data up to floppy disks, magnetic tape, and optical disks as well as other types of backup media. Since there are so many different companies that make backup software, we won't discuss all of them here, but we'll touch on the basic principles of the operation by presenting a competent backup program that comes with DOS (version 5.0 and later).

The DOS program BACKUP.EXE is useful for backing up a relatively small amount of data to floppies. (For some people, it is the only backup program they have ever used.) On the plus side, it contains a menu interface and is pretty friendly to the user (meaning, it works predictably). It does have its limitations, however. BACKUP can only back up to floppy disk, so you need to have a whole stack of floppy disks within arm's reach if you want to back up an entire hard disk. It also doesn't do compression "on the fly." That means that BACKUP will use more floppy disks than a commercial program would, since any commercial program that sells for more than a dollar should by all rights incorporate compression.

Preparing the Disk for Installation

Once you have determined that there is enough space available on the disk, you can begin the final step: preparing the disk to accept the DOS operating system. If the disk has had DOS installed on it before, this final step is unnecessary. There are two main steps to this process:

- Partitioning the disk with FDISK.EXE
- Formatting the disk

Partitioning involves "carving out" a space on the disk that DOS can use and then formatting the partition so that DOS can save files on the disk. Formatting involves creating the DOS File Allocation Table (FAT) so that DOS can find the files once it has saved them on the disk. The disk you install DOS on must have been formatted with the /S switch so that the disk is bootable. If you have partitioned the disk and rebooted, the disk will automatically be formatted for you.

If you want to do things simply, you can use the DOS SETUP program to perform both of these operations in one step, as outlined in the following section.

Configuring a Drive with DOS Setup

If you have just installed and configured a new hard drive in a personal computer, your next objective will be to prepare the drive for use by an operating system. All operating systems require that a drive be partitioned and formatted before use. The process of partitioning is a relatively standard one, and involves little more than allocating the space on the drive into specific physical spaces—partitions. In most cases all the space on the drive can simply be partitioned into just one large physical partition, but there are times when you might want to subdivide this space into smaller fragments. Once you've created at least one usable partition on the disk, you must then format that partition to meet the needs of the operating system that will be running off of it. Some operating systems, such as Microsoft's Windows NT, can use more than one type of format. DOS can only use one, the FAT file system.

NOTE　The File Allocation Table (FAT) is simply an index of the locations and lengths of all the files on the hard drive. When the OS wants to find a file, it references the FAT. The FAT file system is the native system of DOS. It uses a linked-list structure to allow it to store information on the drive. The information is written in 64KB blocks (storage locations), and at the end of each block is one of two commands. If the block is the final one in a file, a "stop" command is written, which tells the OS that it has all of the information it needs. If it is not, the last information is where to go to get the next block.

To begin preparing a new disk for use, make certain that you have the computer put back together properly, and that the keyboard, monitor, etc. are all attached. Once you have this completed, plug in the power cord (always the last cord to be attached!).

Let's take a detailed look at how to let SETUP configure the drive.

Booting the Computer and Executing SETUP.EXE

Insert the first DOS setup disk into the floppy drive. For the examples in this section, we will be using MS-DOS 6.22, but most versions of DOS are very similar in the way they perform the tasks in this chapter. The first disk has a file named SETUP.EXE on it, and is configured to run Setup automatically when the computer is booted to this disk. The computer will boot from this floppy disk. During this time, the following words will appear in the upper left-hand corner of your screen:

Starting MS-DOS...

Within a few seconds (the actual time varies by machine) you should see a blue setup screen appear, which says:

```
Microsoft MS-DOS 6.22 Setup
```

This screen welcomes you to the setup program, and presents you with three options.

- To set up MS-DOS now, press Enter.
- To learn more about Setup before continuing, press F1.
- To exit Setup without installing MS-DOS, press F3.

Setup also warns you about backing up any files on the hard drive before continuing. If you've only now remembered that there is some valuable data on this drive and you might be up a creek if that data got trashed, doing a backup before installing is a *very* good idea, so you might have to press F3 to exit Setup for the time being until you've used the BACKUP.EXE program (or another backup program). If you think you're ready to proceed with the setup operation, but you're interested in reading Microsoft's version of what Setup is going to do, and how to navigate through the process, press the F1 key.

Configuring the Disk Space

Hit Enter (to "set up MS-DOS now") in order to continue using Setup. The program should detect that the drive contains no usable space (remember, in this example we're assuming that we're installing to a new hard drive), and will present a screen that says:

```
Setup needs to configure the unallocated space on your hard disk for
use with MS-DOS. None of your existing files will be affected.
To have Setup configure the space for you, choose the recommended
option.
```

The recommended option ("Have SETUP configure the space for you") should already be selected. If it is, hit Enter. If it is not, use the up or down arrow keys on your keyboard to select it, and then hit Enter. DOS Setup will then present you with a screen asking you to press Enter to restart the computer. Make certain the first Setup disk is still in the floppy drive, and hit Enter.

NOTE The numerous restarts in this process each represent a specific phase of the disk preparation process, and after each phase (like the creation of the partition in the first phase) the machine must be reconfigured to recognize that changes have occurred. This is accomplished through a restart, which resets and reinitializes the hardware and software on the machine.

Finishing Setup

The computer restarts, and DOS Setup reappears. This time, however, the Setup program presents a different screen, and shows you that it is formatting your hard drive for use by MS-DOS. This may take a while, depending on the size of the drive and the speed of the computer, so do not shut off the machine as long as the "% of drive formatted" reading keeps increasing. Restarting now would require you to start the format over from the start! Once the format process is complete, the computer will reboot again, and Setup will reappear a third time. At this time, your drive will be ready to accept the DOS operating system, and the actual installation of MS-DOS 6.22 can begin.

This is by far the easiest way to prepare a drive for use. Setup creates a single partition out of all of the free space on the drive, and then formats that space with the FAT file system. There are times, though, when you may not want all of the space on the drive to be used for a single partition, or when you need to modify the partition structure of an existing system. In this case, you must use other utilities that give you more control, but which are more complex to use. An example is given in the following section.

Configuring a Drive with FDISK.EXE

If you have already installed the disk drives, and now need to configure unused space on your drive for use, you will need to use the FDISK command. FDISK.EXE is a DOS program that allows you to access and modify information about your fixed disks (hence the name). It is used for four major tasks:

- Viewing the current partition configuration

- Creating DOS partitions or logical DOS drives

- Setting active partitions

- Deleting partitions or logical DOS drives

These functions can be used on any of the physical disks in your machine, as long as those disks are considered to be permanent, that is, *fixed*, drives. Hard drives, whether they are SCSI or IDE or EIDE, are all fixed. Once installed, they are expected to be permanently attached to the system, and if one is removed, extensive reconfiguration may need to be done on the system. Floppy drives and CD-ROM drives are designed to support removable, interchangeable media, and as such are not configurable under FDISK.

To run the FDISK utility, type **C:\DOS\FDISK.EXE** at a command prompt.

TIP

If you have a PATH statement that points to the DOS directory, you may be able to simply type **FDISK.EXE** from any directory and the FDISK program will be found and started. Also, the .EXE extension is not technically necessary, so just typing **FDISK** should start the program. If this does not work, check your PATH statement, and also make certain that your DOS directory has the FDISK.EXE file.

At this point, the Fixed Disk Setup Program main screen should appear (see Figure 3.3). You will either have four or five options. The fifth option (not shown here, but it says "Change current fixed disk drive") allows you to select a different disk to administrate, appears only if the program detects at least two fixed disks on the system.

FIGURE 3.3:

The FDISK main menu

```
                            FDISK Options

Current fixed disk drive: 1

Choose one of the following:

1. Create DOS partition or Logical DOS Drive
2. Set active partition
3. Delete partition or Logical DOS Drive
4. Display partition information


Enter choice: [1]




Press Esc to exit FDISK
```

Viewing Partition Information with FDISK

Before you make any major changes to your disk configuration, it is a good idea to check the current configuration. The first step in this process is to boot the computer to DOS. Once DOS has loaded, type **FDISK**. The FDISK utility loads, and you are given a menu. Select the fourth option:

4. Display partition information

and hit Enter. This will display the partition information for the drive (Figure 3.4). You will see that currently the drive has only one partition. The partition has been given the logical drive letter C:. It is identified as a "PRI DOS" (primary DOS partition) of "500 Mbytes" (500 MB). The drive is used completely by this partition, as you can see with the 100% under Usage. These terms and concepts will be explained in the following section.

```
                     Display Partition Information
Current fixed disk drive: 1

Partition  Status   Type    Volume Label  Mbytes   System   Usage
  C: 1        A     PRI DOS                 500      FAT     100%




Total disk space is   500 Mbytes (1 Mbyte = 1048576 bytes)




Press Esc to continue
```

Hit the Escape key (Esc) as instructed on the screen, and you will be returned to the main FDISK menu. Once you have observed the current partition information and total drive size, you then need to decide whether you actually want to delete the existing partition and reconfigure the drive.

Deleting and Creating Partitions Using FDISK

The first option in the FDISK utility is "Create DOS partition or Logical DOS Drive." This option allows you to take an area of free space on your disk and configure that space for use by the system. To create a partition, you must have a disk that has no existing partitions, or you must delete the existing partition to free up space. Because of this, the option "Delete DOS partition or Logical DOS Drive" is closely linked to the Create option, and we will therefore examine them together. Often, these options are used to delete an existing DOS partition or other operating system and then recreate it with a new drive configuration.

NOTE Currently, DOS 6.22 supports a maximum partition size of 2 GB. This is usually not a problem with standard IDE disks (their maximum size is 540 MB), but older versions of DOS (namely DOS 3.3) could only support partition sizes of up to 32 MB. If you were to install DOS 3.3 on a 100MB hard disk, you would have to make 2-32 MB partitions (A primary and an extended) and waste 36 MB!

Partition Concepts The partitioning process is relatively simple, but does involve a number of important concepts you should remember. Selecting "1" on the initial screen ("Create DOS partition or Logical DOS Drive") brings up a second selection menu, giving you three choices:

1. Create Primary DOS Partition

2. Create Extended DOS Partition

3. Create Logical DOS Drive(s) in the Extended DOS Partition

If, instead of selecting "1" at the initial screen you chose "3" ("Delete partition or Logical DOS Drive"), you would get these options:

1. Delete Primary DOS Partition

2. Delete Extended DOS Partition

3. Delete Logical DOS Drive(s) in the Extended DOS Partition

4. Delete Non-DOS Partition

WARNING Be EXTREMELY careful when using any of the Delete choices! Do not create or delete any partitions on a system containing valuable data unless you are very sure of how your actions will impact the system. Remember that deleting a partition will permanently and irrevocably delete all data on it. Recreating a new partition in the same space will only give you new usable blank space!

Each physical disk (e.g., hard drive, fixed disk) can have only one primary partition and one extended partition. Because of this, the current disk configuration will always determine which option you will choose in the Create menu, as you will have only one choice. If the disk is new or unpartitioned, a primary partition must be created first. This has to exist before DOS will allow you to create an extended partition. Then, if free space remains on the drive, you can create an extended partition.

If your disk does not have free space, things become more difficult. Once created, partitions cannot be resized! Rather, you must delete the large existing partition. This returns the space occupied by the partition to free space, and you can then create new partitions from that free space. If your 500MB disk has a single primary partition that takes up the entire volume of the disk, and you want two 250MB partitions instead, you must back up the data on the existing partition to a tape drive or another hard drive. You can then delete the original partition and create a 250MB primary partition and a 250MB extended partition from the newly created free space.

Once you have created a primary partition, it will be assigned the logical drive letter C: by the FDISK program. A logical drive letter is an alphabetic character assigned to a physical space on your system. This letter represents the physical space, and gives users of the DOS operating system an easy way to reference these spaces.

NOTE The letter C: is always assigned to the active primary partition on the DOS-based computer. This is the drive that is used to boot the system, and is the drive on which you will find your DOS directory and other crucial system files.

Once the primary partition has been created and assigned a drive letter, the extended partition can be created. Unlike the primary, though, the extended partition can be subdivided into a number of smaller parts. Because of this, even though you can have only two *physical* spaces (partitions) on a single drive, you could in theory have twenty-four logical spaces (logical drives represented by letters) through the use of the divisible properties of the extended partition. The number of logical drives is limited only by the number of letters—26—that can be assigned to them. As A: and B: are usually reserved for floppies and C: references the primary partition, D: through Z: are available for use in the extended partition as logical drive letters.

A possible extension of our earlier scenario would be that after creating our 250MB primary partition (logical drive C:), we would create the 250MB extended partition, and then divide it into two logical drives.

Deleting Partitions   The following is a step-by-step guide to doing exactly the operation dEscribed above. This exercise is intended for use on a machine already running DOS—but take note: the existing partition (and the DOS installation) will be completely destroyed by this exercise. Therefore, DO NOT perform this exercise on a machine that contains necessary data.

NOTE It is not necessary for you to actually perform these steps, but read them carefully and if possible use this as a hands-on exercise.

This example assumes that, before you begin, DOS has been installed on a workstation through a standard setup; i.e., the entire drive is one partition. No extended partition or free space exists. The drive in the example is 500 MB, but this is largely irrelevant. Any drive under 2 GB will yield the same results.

As we do want a second partition on the drive, our next step is to select option #3:

```
3. Delete Partition or Logical DOS Drive
```

Press Enter, and the Delete options appear, as shown in Figure 3.5.

FIGURE 3.5:

FDISK's "Delete Partition" menu

```
                Delete DOS Partition or Logical DOS Drive
Current fixed disk drive: 1

Choose one of the following:

1.  Delete Primary DOS Partition
2.  Delete Extended DOS Partition
3.  Delete Logical DOS Drive(s) in the Extended DOS Partition
4.  Delete Non-DOS Partition



Enter choice: [ ]



Press Esc to return to FDISK Options
```

As you saw in the partition display screen, currently our only partition is a primary DOS partition. Therefore, we must choose the following:

```
1. Delete Primary DOS Partition
```

The process of deleting multiple partitions, like the process of creating them, has a particular order. Primary partitions must be created first, followed by extended partitions, and finally logical drives. They are deleted in exactly the opposite order. All logical drives must be deleted before an extended partition can be deleted, and the extended partition must be gone before the primary can be deleted. Thus, if we had an additional partition, we would have to go through both options 3 and 2 before 1. For now, though, select 1 and hit Enter.

The DELETE Primary DOS Partition screen appears, and DOS asks you which primary partition you wish to delete. It may seem strange that FDISK needs to ask this, because, as you may recall, DOS can only create and use one primary per drive. The option is necessary, though, because other operating systems, such as Windows NT and UNIX, can create multiple primary partitions, and for DOS to use that space these additional primaries must be deleted and replaced by an extended partition.

WARNING The WARNING message flashing in the bottom left corner of this screen is extremely important. It reminds you that deleting a partition irrevocably destroys all information on that partition. DO NOT delete a partition until you are certain it is safe to do so! Undelete and other utilities are useless in recovering data from deleted partitions. If you need to delete a partition that has valuable data, back up the data beforehand so that it will not be lost.

We have only one primary, so type **1** and press Enter. You will be prompted to enter the Volume Label (which in this case is **MS-DOS_6**) and then press Enter again. At this point, you receive a final confirmation. Note that the default value is N, and also that you can abort this process at any time by hitting Esc. Type **Y**, and press Enter a last time. FDISK returns a message:

```
Primary DOS Partition deleted
```

Hit Esc, and you will be taken back to the main options screen.

WARNING   Once you have deleted the primary partition, the DOS directory and the FDISK.EXE program are both gone—they have been permanently deleted along with everything else on the C: drive. FDISK continues to run, but only because it is loaded into the dynamic memory (RAM) of the computer. If you shut off the power or hit Esc before recreating a primary partition, you will need to run FDISK off of a floppy disk to finish this procedure. This is not disastrous, but it is unnecessary extra work. All of these steps should be done in a single, uninterrupted FDISK session.

Creating a Primary Partition   At this point, the disk is once again nothing but blank space. We will now create two separate physical spaces on the disk, each of them 250 MB. The first step in this part of the process is to select option #1:

```
1. Create DOS partition or Logical DOS drive
```

When you highlight this option and hit Enter, the "Create options" menu appears. Initially we will be choosing option #1 again:

```
1. Create Primary DOS Partition
```

Remember that this must be the first partition on a new disk. Select "1" and hit Enter. FDISK will then ask if you wish to use the maximum available size (all the free space on the disk) for this partition, as shown in Figure 3.6. The default answer is Y, but that would give us another single 500 MB partition. Instead, type **N**, and then hit the Enter key.

FIGURE 3.6:

FDISK's "Create Partition" menu

```
                          Create Primary DOS Partition


Current Fixed disk drive: 2

Do you wish to use the maximum available size for a Primary DOS Partition
[Y/N]..................................................................?[Y]








Press   Esc   to return to FDISK Options
```

You are then presented with the total disk space, and the maximum amount that is available for the new partition. The partition size default is the maximum amount available, or in this case 500 MB. Change this value to 250, and then hit Enter. You should now see a screen that states:

Primary DOS Partition created

Hit Esc, and you will be taken back to the main FDISK menu. Select the Create option again, and you will once again be at a menu with three choices. Select option #1:

1. Create Primary DOS Partition

You will get the following message:

```
Primary DOS Partition already exists
```

This message tells us that we already have a primary partition. Hit Esc to return to the main menu.

Creating an Extended DOS Partition and Assigning Logical Drive Letters   Now that we have a primary partition, we can create an extended DOS partition. From the main menu, select the Create option. This time, select option #2:

```
2. Create Extended DOS Partition
```

and press Enter. The existing primary partition will be displayed, along with the total and available disk space. You will again be asked to specify the size of the new partition, with the default option being all available space—in this case 250 MB. Hit Enter to continue, and the new partition will be displayed on the screen along with a message stating that the partition has been created.

TIP   In most cases, you will want to use the default value, which uses all available drive space when creating the extended partition. The reason is that DOS can only recognize two physical partitions, so leaving any space left over after the primary and extended partitions are created is a waste (unless you also install another operating system that can access additional partitions).

Hit Esc, and FDISK will then prompt you to create logical drives to fill the newly created extended partition, as shown in Figure 3.7. (If you don't create logical drives, the space in the extended partition is unusable.)

FIGURE 3.7:

FDISK's "Create Logical Drive" screen

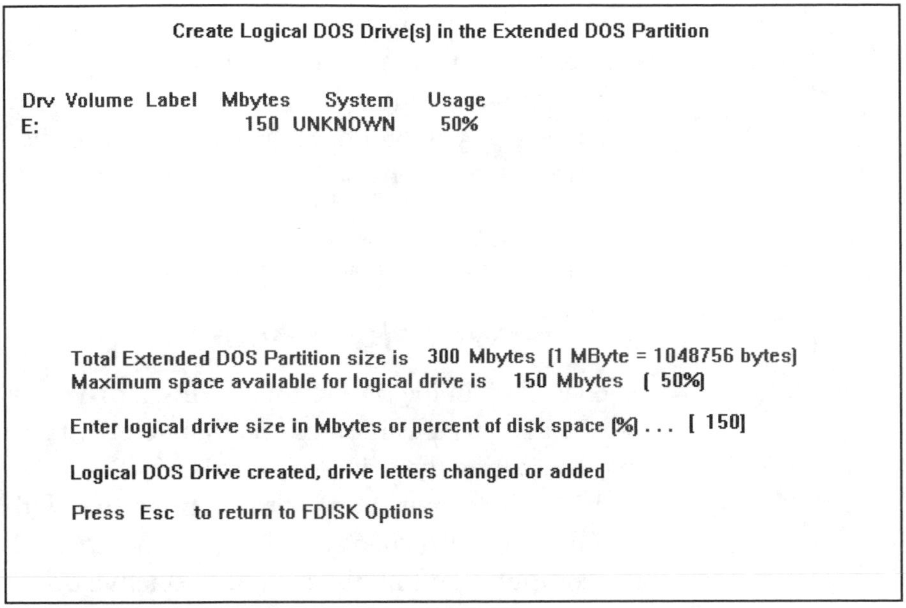

```
              Create Logical DOS Drive(s) in the Extended DOS Partition


Drv  Volume Label   Mbytes   System    Usage
E:                    150   UNKNOWN     50%








     Total Extended DOS Partition size is  300 Mbytes  (1 MByte = 1048756 bytes)
     Maximum space available for logical drive is   150 Mbytes  ( 50%)

     Enter logical drive size in Mbytes or percent of disk space (%) . . .  [ 150]

     Logical DOS Drive created, drive letters changed or added

     Press  Esc   to return to FDISK Options
```

As we want to create two logical drives, we cannot use the entire 250 MB partition for the first drive. Type in **150** as the desired size of the first new logical drive, and hit Enter. You should get the following message:

```
Logical DOS Drive created, drive letters changed or added
```

At this point, you can either leave the remaining space unused or create another logical drive. Hitting Esc would return us to the main menu, and would leave the space unusable. We do want to use the remaining 100 MB, though, and as all the remaining free space should go to the new drive, you can simply hit Enter and the default value of 100 will be used. The system displays both new logical drives, and displays the following message:

```
All available space in the Extended DOS Partition is assigned to
logical drives.
```

At this point, you can hit Esc and return to the main menu. Two partitions have now been created in the space where previously only one existed, and a total of three drives—one for the primary and two in the extended—have been created. At this point, only one task remains, and you will have successfully reconfigured the drive. The bottom of the screen should have a message that reads as follows:

```
WARNING! No partitions are set active - - disk 1 is not startable
unless a partition is set active.
```

Making a Partition Active

The last step in the process of making a drive usable by DOS is to set the primary partition on the disk to be "startable." This is done by designating the primary partition as the *active partition* for the system. The active partition is the partition that will be read at startup, and thus will be expected to have the necessary system files to boot the computer. Setting the primary as active does not create these files, but it does tell the computer where to look for them.

> **NOTE**
> The process of installing the necessary boot files on the active partition is known as "SYSing the drive," because the active partition is also known as the System partition. The DOS SYS.COM program can be used to perform this operation.

To set the new primary partition as active, select option #2 from the main FDISK menu:

```
2. Set Active Partition
```

and hit Enter. The disk utility then asks you to choose which partition to make active. If you choose 2—the extended partition—you will get an error, because only primaries can be active. Type **1** and press Enter. The screen confirms the action by displaying the following message:

```
Partition 1 made active
```

Press Esc to return to the main menu. The FDISK process is now finished, and the fixed disk is available for use. If you have multiple drives in the machine, this process must be repeated with each drive. The exception to this, of course, is that only one of the primary partitions you create can be set as active at any time, so the final part of this process—setting the active partition—is done only once.

It is always a good idea to take a final look at the system configuration (option #4) to make sure your configuration of the disk worked the way you planned. If anything is incorrect, repeat the Delete and Create processes until it is right, and then exit the FDISK utility by hitting Esc one final time. At this point, the screen will display the following:

```
System will now restart
Insert DOS system diskette in drive A:
Press any key when ready . . .
```

Insert Disk 1 of the DOS Setup set (or any other DOS system diskette) into the floppy drive, and press a key. The computer will reboot, and you will be able to prepare for the install of the DOS operating system on this newly reconfigured drive. The first step involved in reinstalling DOS is the use of the FORMAT command, which is covered in the next section, and which prepares the partition to accept an OS.

Formatting a Disk for DOS

Besides creating at least one partition to provide space in which files, programs, and data files can be stored, you must also prepare this partition to be readable by the operating system. To do this, you need to use the FORMAT.COM program.

The FORMAT command is an external command, just like FDISK, in that it consists of a DOS-executable program stored in a specific file, FORMAT.COM. This program prepares the partition to store information using the FAT (File Allocation Table) system that is required by DOS. Unlike FDISK, the FORMAT utility does not have a menu system, but rather is a command-line program controlled through a series of "switches" added to the end of the command.

NOTE
External programs are very common in DOS, and we've already mentioned a number of them, including XCOPY and EDIT. Command-line DOS programs are utilities that work only with DOS, but that are not part of the basic functionality of the DOS operating system. Simply put, they need DOS but DOS doesn't need them. To use an external program, the file or files necessary for that program to run must be available to the operating system.

Formatting Using the DOS Setup Program

If a drive contains a partition or partitions that have just been created, the DOS Setup program will automatically allow you to *format* that partition before it goes about setting up DOS. To use this method of formatting the primary partition, insert DOS Setup disk 1 into the floppy drive of the machine and turn it on. The Setup program will load, and you will be presented with setup options. Hit Enter to continue to the second screen, and Setup will inform you of the present drive status:

```
Hard disk drive C is not formatted. MS-DOS 6.22 cannot use
unformatted drives.
```

Setup then gives you the option of having the drive formatted for you, or of exiting the Setup program and formatting it yourself. Simply hit Enter to accept the default value ("Format this drive") and Setup will begin the format. The percent of the format completed will eventually reach 100%, at which point you will be prompted to format any additional partitions available to DOS. Note that unlike our previous setup example, the Setup program does not create a single partition of the drive. This is because if a usable partition exists—that is, a primary partition of 10 MB or larger—DOS Setup will use the existing partition structure. Once all logical drives have been formatted, the disk is prepared to accept DOS, and the installation can continue.

Using the FORMAT.COM Command

In many cases, you will want to format a partition without using the DOS Setup process. This will require that you have DOS already installed on the system, or that you have a DOS-bootable disk with the FORMAT.COM program copied onto it.

Once you have booted to DOS, you will have access to the FORMAT command, and will be able to use it on any logical drive on the system.

WARNING   Although it's not as destructive as deleting a partition, formatting a logical drive is not something you should do without first giving it careful thought. Formatting a drive destroys all information on the drive, in many cases irreversibly. Formatting should be reserved for use on new installations or for thoroughly cleaning a drive that is to be used for a different role than it is currently performing. It is not used for routine maintenance or on a drive that has data you still need.

To format a logical drive, simply type in the FORMAT command, and then add the letter of the drive to be formatted. To format the first drive in the extended partition, for instance, type **FORMAT D:** and hit Enter. This will cause the system to return a warning to you, and you will be asked to confirm your wish to delete all information on the drive and reformat. Note that the default is "No," which reminds you that FORMAT is generally used only with great care. If you are at all uncertain about whether the drive in question holds useful information, hit Enter to end the format. If you are sure everything on the drive is useless, and you want to reformat, select Yes and then hit Enter.

NOTE

If you reformat the C: drive—the logical drive on the primary partition—you will lose your DOS installation in the process, and will have to reinstall DOS from diskette after the format is complete. This is generally not advisable unless the operating system is horribly corrupted, is infected with an uncleanable virus, or is otherwise unusable. If none of these pertains, and you simply want to free up some space for data or programs, use more conventional methods for deleting unneeded files—notably the DELETE command for individual files, and DELTREE command for entire directories. These methods leave the machine still operational, and are less work for you.

When formatting a floppy disk, you type the following at a DOS prompt: **FORMAT A:.** DOS will then return the following prompt:

```
Insert new diskette for drive A:
and press ENTER when ready...
```

When you are ready to start the format, insert the disk in drive A: and press the Enter key. This will start the format, and DOS will return a message telling you that it's formatting the disk. It will also indicate how far along it is, like so:

```
Checking existing disk format.
Formatting 1.44M
2 percent completed.
```

When the format is complete, FORMAT will indicate "Format Complete" and ask for a volume label (a name that identifies the disk). You can type one in (11 characters or fewer) and press Enter to continue. Or, if you don't want to enter a volume label (it's not required), you can just press Enter. If the diskette you just formatted was a high-density floppy disk, DOS will display something similar to the following:

```
1,457,664 bytes total disk space
1,457,664 bytes available on disk
 512 bytes in each allocation unit.
2,847 allocation units available on disk.

Volume Serial Number is 2A27-1ECD

Format another (Y/N)?
```

You can answer with **Y** for Yes and press Enter if you want to format another disk. If not, type **N** and press Enter. FORMAT will return control back to the DOS command prompt.

As you can see, the basic process of formatting a logical drive is not at all complicated. FORMAT is a relatively complex utility, though, and through the use of switches we can modify the way it works, and what optional tasks it can be made to carry out.

Using FORMAT with Switches

As with most standard DOS commands, you can find out the options available to you with the FORMAT command by simply typing the command name followed by /? on the same line. In this case, when you type **FORMAT /?** at a command prompt (and hit Enter), the DOS help system returns the information shown in Table 3.1. Note that the FORMAT command, unlike FDISK, also works with floppy disks, each of which has to be individually formatted before being used. Because of this, some switches are specifically intended only for use with floppies.

TABLE 3.1: Switches Used with the Format Command

Switch	Used To
/?	Show all the possible switches that can be used with the FORMAT command. (Also called the "Help" switch.) When the FOMAT command is used with this switch, all other switches are disabled (i.e., the disk will not start formatting, just the help screen will appear).
/v	Specify the volume label. This switch allows you to create a name for the new volume, such as "DANS DRIVE" "MY C DRIVE". A label can be up to 11 characters, and can include spaces, as well as any letters or numbers. It can also include any of the following symbols: ~ ! @ # $ % ^ & ( ) - _ { }. It cannot include the following: + = : ; " ' ? / \	. < >.
/q	Perform a quick format. This option allows you to rapidly perform the reformatting of a drive that has already been formatted with the FAT system. Quick formatting is not a usable option on the initial format of a logical drive.
/u	Perform an unconditional format. Versions of DOS that are 5.0 or higher include the UNFORMAT utility. When you reformat a drive using FORMAT in these versions of DOS, the program clears the data from the boot record, the root directory, and the File Allocation Table, but it does not delete this data. Rather, it stores this data in the MIRROR image file. This is done so that if the drive is accidentally formatted (even after all of the precautions we have been through!) the UNFORMAT command can be used to access the MIRROR file and restore the boot record, the root directory, and the FAT. From these, all the rest of the data can be recovered as well. An unconditional format purposefully overwrites all data on the drive, and does not make a backup of the boot record, root, or FAT. This is usually done to assure that sensitive data is permanently erased from a disk, or to save the overhead of storing the unformat information when it is known that the drive will not need to be restored.
/f:size	Specify the size of the floppy disk to format (the options are 160, 180, 320, 360, 720, 1.2, 1.44, 2.88). This switch is only usable on floppy drives, and is generally not something you need to worry about if you are using 1.44MB floppies.
/b	Allocate space on the formatted disk for system files. This switch applies only to DOS 4.01 and earlier, and allows disks to be made bootable by these earlier versions of DOS.
/s	Copy system files to the formatted disk. This switch is very important in the creation of a bootable DOS disk, in that it copies needed system files and the COMMAND.COM file to the newly formatted disk. This switch and its use will be discussed more fully in the next topic, "Creating a Bootable DOS Disk."

TABLE 3.1 CONTINUED: Switches Used with the Format Command

Switch	Used To
/t:*tracks*	Specify the number of tracks per disk side. This switch is largely unused in newer DOS versions, with its functionality being replaced by the /f switch.
/n:*sectors*	Specify the number of sectors per track. Used in conjunction with /t. This switch too has been replaced by /f in newer versions of DOS.
/1	Format a single side of a floppy disk. Usually used with the /8 switch to format a disk usable by very early versions of DOS.
/4	Format a 5.25-inch 360KB floppy disk in a high-density drive. As with /t and /n, this switch has been replaced in newer DOS versions with /f.

The particular syntax, or order, of these statements is defined by the four lines above the switches. As noted in the table, some switches depend on others. Multiple switches can be used with FORMAT in a single command. The syntax of FORMAT therefore will follow one of the following sequences:

```
Syntax:
format drive: [/v[:label]] [/q] [/u] [/f:size] [/b | /s]
Example:
FORMAT C: /v:[NEW C DRIVE] /Q /U /S


Syntax:
format drive: [/v[:label]] [/q] [/u] [/t:tracks] [/n:sectors] [/b |
/s]
Example:
FORMAT C: /v:[NEW C DRIVE] /Q /U /T:99 /N:99 /S


Syntax:
format drive: [/v[:label]] [/q] [/u] [/1] [/4] [/b | /s]
Example:
FORMAT C: /v:[NEW C DRIVE] /Q /U /1 /4 /S
```

```
Syntax:
format drive: [/q] [/u] [/1] [/4] [/8] [/b | /s]
Example:
FORMAT C: /Q /U /1 /4 /8 /B
```

In most cases, you will use only the /s and the /u or /q commands on newer DOS systems, but the others can be useful in special circumstances. Now that we have seen these switches, let's look at how switches can be used to perform a particular sort of format on a floppy disk.

Making a Bootable DOS System Disk

One of the most useful tools that a PC repair technician can have is a trusty old DOS boot disk. A boot disk is simply a diskette that allows the technician to load a limited version of DOS and then perform troubleshooting and configuration tasks on the PC. A boot disk is characterized by three characteristics:

- It's formatted using another DOS machine.

- It has system files installed.

- It has a number of useful DOS external programs, such as EDIT.COM, FORMAT, and FDISK on it.

NOTE   Creating a basic DOS boot disk is a simple process, but you will find that as you improve your skills with DOS your boot disk will become increasingly complex and powerful. You may even design multiple disks for use in particular situations. CD-ROM drivers, other device drivers, and numerous other useful utilities can be added to the boot disk over time. You will know you have been using DOS too long when you start bragging about how perfect your boot disk is to other technicians.

The process of creating a boot disk requires a working DOS install, and two DOS utilities (FORMAT.COM and SYS.COM).

Formatting the Disk   To format the disk, do the following:

1. Insert a new floppy into the floppy drive, and type **Format A:**. You will be prompted to insert a diskette into the drive. Verify that the disk is there, and hit Enter. This will prepare the disk to accept the DOS system files, and allow you to store and retrieve information from the disk using DOS.

2. Once the format is complete, you will be asked to supply a volume label for the new disk. Type a label if you want, or simply hit Enter to leave the label blank.

3. You will be prompted to format another. Type **N** and hit Enter. At this point, the format is complete. Now you can type **a:** and hit Enter. A directory listing of the floppy can then be displayed by typing **dir**. The listing will show that although the disk is usable (i.e., DOS can access and browse it) there is no information on it.

Transferring System Files   Our next task is to transfer the crucial system files that allow DOS to boot a PC. Here's how:

1. Return to the c: drive by typing **c:** and pressing Enter. You have to do this, because a disk cannot have the system files transferred to it if it is the current drive.

2. Type **sys a:** and hit Enter. Within a few seconds, the screen will display the following message:

    ```
    System transferred.
    ```

3. Now repeat the process of doing a directory listing on a:, and you should find a single file, COMMAND.COM. Do a second directory listing, but this time search for hidden files. To do

this, type **dir a:*.* /ah** and hit Enter. You will see that three other hidden files have also been added to the disk—IO.SYS, MSDOS.SYS, and DBLSPACE.BIN. These are the basic files that are added to a disk when it is first "SYSed."

TIP

Instead of typing both FORMAT and SYS separately, you can call the SYS command from FORMAT using the /s switch as shown earlier. Typing **format a: /s** will both format the floppy and make it bootable.

Adding Functionality to the DOS Boot Disk   Once the DOS boot disk has been created, your next task is to copy important files from the C:\DOS directory onto the disk to give it additional functionality. EDIT.COM, QBASIC.EXE, FORMAT.COM, SYS.COM, and FDISK.EXE are some of the most important ones for a general troubleshooting disk.

NOTE

QBASIC.EXE has no function in and of itself, but it is a file necessary for the use of EDIT.COM, and must be present for the EDIT program to function.

Once these files have been copied to the DOS boot disk, the disk will allow you to troubleshoot, configure, partition, and format systems that can boot to a floppy. This can be very useful for new installations as well. If the default DOS Setup options are not what you want, you can use the boot disk to configure the partitions and format the drives, and then run Setup afterward.

Review Questions for Chapter 3, Prerequisites for Installation

Answers to the Review Questions may be found in Appendix A.

1. Format is what type of DOS command?

    A. core

    B. internal

    C. external

    D. extended

2. FDISK allows all of the following except:

    A. creating a partition

    B. deleting a partition

    C. moving a partition

    D. marking a partition as active

3. Logical drives exist for which of the following?

    A. primary partition

    B. extended partition

    C. floppy drives

    D. all of the above

4. Formatting a partition will delete the files on that partition in which of the following circumstances?

    A. only if the partition is a primary partition

    B. only if the partition is an extended partition

    C. Never. (Formatting never deletes existing data.)

    D. Always. (Formatting always deletes existing data.)

5. Which switch tells FORMAT to transfer the system to a newly formatted partition?

   A. /s

   B. \s

   C. -s

   D. -t

6. Which file system type is used by DOS?

   A. NTFS

   B. HPFS

   C. FAT

   D. CP/M

7. Which partition type can have more than one logical drive?

   A. extended partition

   B. primary partition

   C. both A and B

   D. neither A nor B

8. Which utility can *sometimes* recover a partition that has been reformatted with DOS 6?

   A. FORMAT with the /u switch

   B. UNDELETE

   C. UNFORMAT

   D. No utility can do this. The information is gone.

9. What is the maximum partition size with DOS 3.3?

   A. 12 MB

   B. 23 MB

   C. 32 MB

   D. 42 MB

10. On a new drive, in which order must the following commands be executed in order to install DOS? (Assume that at least two logical drives are needed on the drive.)

    A. FORMAT

    B. SYS

    C. FDISK

    D. DOS SETUP

11. Which utility allows you to view the current disk configuration of a system?

    A. FDISK.EXE

    B. SYS.COM

    C. FORMAT.COM

    D. COMMAND.COM

12. When can the /q switch be used with FORMAT?

    A. on a new partition only

    B. on any partition

    C. only on partitions with an existing FAT file system

    D. only on an extended partition

13. Which of the following utilities allows you to recover a partition deleted through FDISK?

    A. UNDELETE

    B. UNFORMAT

    C. none, because partitions cannot be deleted through FDISK

    D. none, because partitions deleted through FDISK cannot be recovered

14. Which of the following commands work on floppy disks?

    A. FDISK

    B. FORMAT

    C. SYS

    D. both B and C

    E. A, B, and C

15. SYS can be performed on which of the following partition types?

    A. primary

    B. extended

    C. both A and B

    D. neither A nor B

16. In a normal DOS install, where are FORMAT and FDISK located on the hard drive?

    A. Nowhere. They are only available if you have a boot disk.

    B. the root of the C: drive

    C. C:\DOS

    D. C:\DOSUTILS

17. A boot disk can have which of the following?

    A. DOS system files

    B. DOS external commands

    C. specific device drivers

    D. all of the above

18. Which of these cannot be part of a DOS volume label?

    A. a blank space

    B. \

    C. !

    D. %

    E. all of the above

19. What is the maximum length of a volume label?

    A. 8 characters

    B. 11 characters

    C. 16 characters

    D. 24 characters

20. If you need only one partition on a new 500 MB drive, and want to use all the space on the drive for that partition, *and* you want to format the partition and install DOS, what is the most efficient way to do this?

    A. Use a boot disk to configure the partition and format it, then run DOS Setup.

    B. Run DOS Setup.

    C. Run SYS, then DOS SETUP.

    D. You cannot create just one partition on a drive.

21. How many primary partitions can be created on a DOS disk using FDISK?

     A. 1

     B. 2

     C. 3

     D. several

22. How many Extended partitions can be created on a DOS disk using FDISK?

     A. 1

     B. 2

     C. 3

     D. several

23. You cannot adjust the size of partition, once it has been created, using the FDISK program. True or false?

     A. True

     B. False

24. Which drive letter is assigned to the first, active, primary partition in DOS?

     A. A:

     B. B:

     C. C:

     D. D:

25. Which DOS command(s) can be used to make a disk bootable?

    A. SYS

    B. FDISK

    C. FORMAT

    D. BOOT

26. Which FORMAT switch(es) can be used to format a 360KB low-density floppy disk in a high-density drive?

    A. /1

    B. /f

    C. /4

    D. /8

27. Which utilities can be used to format a hard disk?

    A. FORMAT.COM

    B. FORMAT.EXE

    C. the DOS SETUP.EXE program

    D. INSTALL.EXE

28. Suppose your hard disk contains two partitions, a primary and an extended partition. There are three logical drive letters in the extended partition (D:, E:, & F:). You want to delete the primary partition and recreate it. What do you do?

    A. Using FDISK, delete the primary partition and recreate it.

    B. Using FDISK, delete the extended DOS partition, then the primary partition.

    C. Using FDISK, delete the drive letters in the order D:, E:, F:, then the extended partition, then the primary partition.

    D. Using FDISK, delete the drive letters in the order F:, E: ,D:, then the extended partition, then the primary partition.

29. What must be created before you can create the logical drive letter D: on the first disk?

   A. the primary partition

   B. the secondary partition

   C. the extended partition

   D. the logical drive pointer C:

   D. none of the above

   E. all of the above

30. Before you can boot to a hard disk, what three things must you do to it?

   _____

   _____

   _____

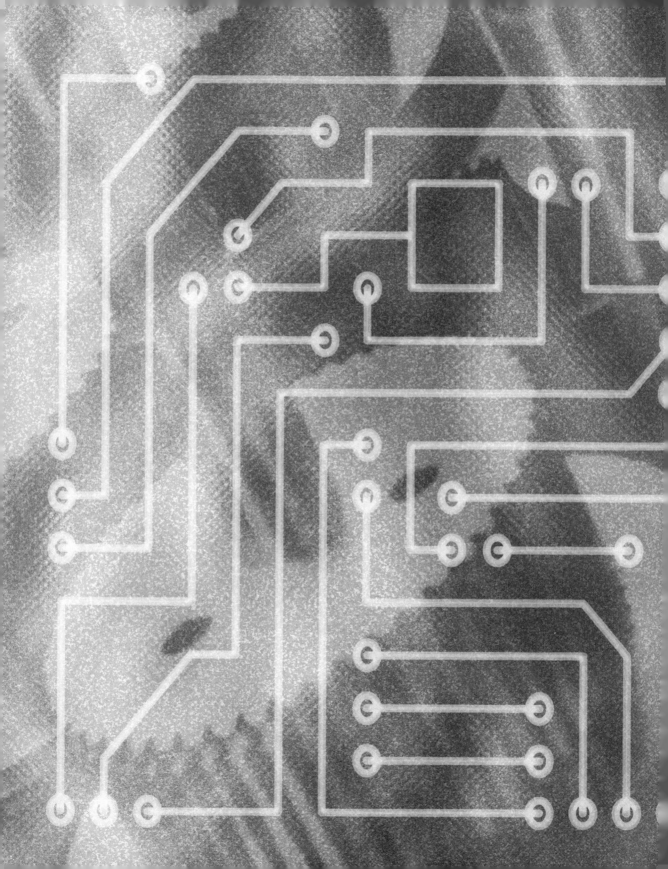

CHAPTER
FOUR

4

Installing DOS

- Installing on a Fresh Drive

- Upgrading an Existing Version of DOS

At this point, you should have the computer prepared to accept the operating system files (as covered in Chapter 3). The next step is to install the operating system. In this chapter we will cover the steps that need to be followed in order to install MS-DOS. The steps to install PC-DOS or some other flavor of DOS are very similar and can be considered to be identical. (The installation steps for PC-DOS aren't covered on the A+ exams anyway.) We will also assume MS-DOS version 6.22 (the most current version) for all discussions, unless otherwise noted.

The chapter is split into two topics:

- Installing on a Fresh Drive
- Upgrading an Existing Version of DOS

Installing DOS

Installing DOS is a relatively simple task. There are menus at every step to guide you through the process. As mentioned above, the following sections detail the installation steps of MS-DOS. For these sections we will make a few assumptions. First, we'll assume that you are installing MS-DOS version 6.22, the most current version available for installing on a PC. IBM's PC-DOS installation is very similar. Second, we'll assume that the disk has already been partitioned and formatted (with the /S switch to make it a bootable hard disk), as described in Chapter 3. Finally, we'll assume that you are installing DOS to a hard disk. We will make special notations for installing to a floppy disk, where appropriate.

Starting SETUP.EXE

There are three disks used to install MS-DOS. They are labeled Disk 1, Disk 2, and Disk 3, surprisingly enough. Disk 1 is the disk that is bootable and contains the SETUP.EXE program that is used to install

DOS. In order to install DOS, you need to insert the Disk 1 disk in the A: drive and turn the computer on.

If you have more than one floppy drive, you can boot to a floppy in drive A: and place Disk 1 in drive B:. In order to get SETUP.EXE to execute in this case, you will need to manually type the following at a command prompt:

```
A:\> B:
B:\> SETUP
```

The setup program will then start and you can begin the installation process.

Since this disk is bootable, the computer will boot and automatically start the SETUP.EXE program. You will know that this process has completed successfully when you see a blue screen with the following message:

```
Please Wait.
Setup is determining your system configuration.
```

At this point, you know that SETUP.EXE is functioning normally. After a small delay (a few seconds), a welcome screen will be shown that indicates that you are ready to install DOS. Pressing F1 at this point will display a help screen detailing information about the installation process.

TIP   You can press F3 twice to escape to the DOS command prompt at this point (or at any time during the installation). Also, you can press F5 at any time to change the screen colors that SETUP uses to display information. This may be useful to those people who are color blind and can't see certain contrasting colors. Additionally, if you are installing to a floppy disk, you need to press F7 and Enter to choose this option.

TIP	When you are ready to continue with the installation, press Enter.

Entering MS-DOS Machine Settings

At this point, SETUP has determined what type of machine you are installing DOS on and will present you with the system settings information it has found. Figure 4.1 shows a screen similar to what you might find.

FIGURE 4.1:

The MS-DOS system settings information setup screen

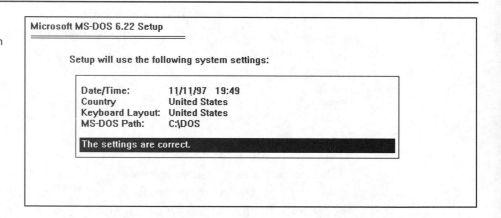

In this menu, SETUP will display both the configuration it detected for your system and the default installation parameters to use for this installation. The settings it normally shows are those for Date & Time, Country, and Keyboard Layout. Notice that the default for the selection bar is "These settings are correct." MS-DOS SETUP is rather arrogant in its assumption that it did everything right the first time and that you want to put everything where it tells you to. However, it can afford to be arrogant because it's usually right.

On the off chance that SETUP made an error, you do have the ability to change the settings. To change a setting:

1. Use the arrow keys on your keyboard to move the selection bar so that the value you want to change is highlighted.

2. Press Enter.

3. You will be prompted to either enter a new value (Date/Time) or be presented with a list of possible settings (Country and Keyboard Layout). Enter the new value for the setting and press Enter to accept the new value.

4. Repeat steps 1 through 3 for any other settings that need to be changed.

When you've finished changing the installation parameters, highlight "These settings are correct" and press Enter. This indicates to SETUP that all configuration information is correct and installation can proceed normally.

Setting the DOS Installation Directory

The next screen that is presented asks where you would like to install the DOS files (Figure 4.2). The default directory is C:\DOS. This is normally the directory in which you'd want to place these files. To change the path where SETUP puts the DOS files, simply hit Backspace to delete all of the current installation directory and enter your own. If the directory doesn't exist, SETUP will create it for you. When you have entered the correct directory (or you are accepting the default directory), press Enter and the SETUP program will continue.

NOTE At this point, as soon as you press Enter, SETUP will begin copying files and making changes to your system. If you press F3 to exit, no changes will have been made to your system (except any FDISKing or FORMATing you may have done).

FIGURE 4.2:

Selecting the location
for the MS-DOS files

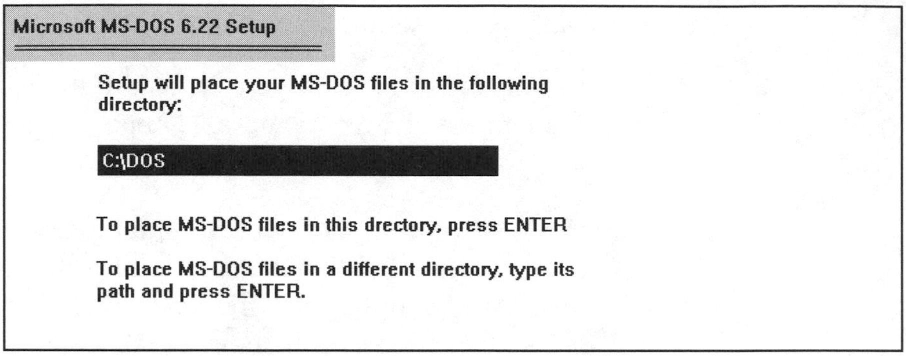

> **Microsoft MS-DOS 6.22 Setup**
>
> Setup will place your MS-DOS files in the following
> directory:
>
> C:\DOS
>
> To place MS-DOS files in this drectory, press ENTER
>
> To place MS-DOS files in a different directory, type its
> path and press ENTER.

Copying MS-DOS Files

At this point, SETUP starts copying files. An installation progress
bar at the bottom of the screen will indicate to you how far SETUP
is into the installation with a yellow bar that increases in size as the
installation progresses. SETUP also indicates progress with a "%
Complete" figure above the progress bar. This setup screen will
also tell you that now is a good time to fill out your registration
card (Figure 4.3). That is, in fact, a good idea because it lets Microsoft know who you are and that you have legally purchased their
software.

> **TIP**
>
> Watch the lower right-hand corner of the SETUP screen dur-
> ing installation. SETUP will display what files it is reading
> from the setup disk, and then what files it is writing to the
> hard disk (or floppy disk). If you encounter a problem read-
> ing or writing a file, you will know which file is causing the
> problem by paying attention to this corner of the screen.

FIGURE 4.3:

MS-DOS Setup shows the progress by means of a "% Complete" barometer.

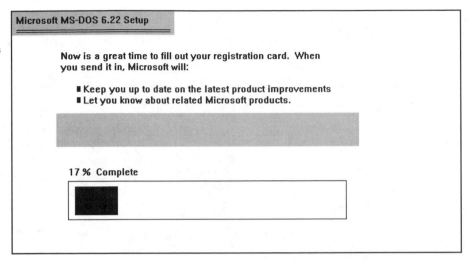

When the SETUP progress bar reaches "25% complete," a screen will appear that tells you to insert the next MS-DOS setup disk into your A: drive (Figure 4.4). Insert the MS-DOS Setup disk that is labeled "Disk 2" (remember, there are three MS-DOS setup disks). Eject the first disk by pushing the eject button on your floppy drive and remove the first disk. Insert the second disk, as instructed, and press Enter to continue.

FIGURE 4.4:

SETUP asking you to insert Disk #2

> Please insert the following disk in drive A:
>
> Setup Disk #2
>
> When you are ready to continue, press ENTER.

At this point, SETUP goes into what I like to call "the long copy," during which it will copy several files to your hard disk. During this time, SETUP will flash several screens of information about some of the new features of MS-DOS 6.22, including MemMaker, Disk Compression, and MS-DOS Anti-Virus.

When the progress indicator reaches 58%, it will present another screen that asks for MS-DOS Setup Disk 3 (Figure 4.5). Remove Disk 2 and insert Disk 3. Press Enter to continue and start the final file copy.

FIGURE 4.5:

SETUP asking you to insert Disk #3

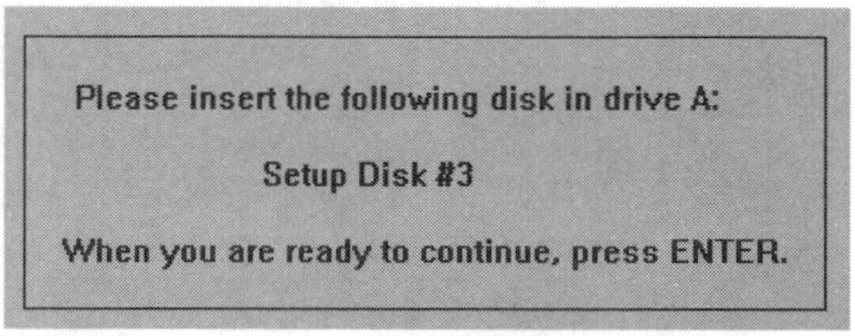

> Please insert the following disk in drive A:
>
> Setup Disk #3
>
> When you are ready to continue, press ENTER.

The final file copy will take slightly less time than the second. When the indicator reaches 100% Complete, the disk activity stops and the screen in Figure 4.6 appears, telling you to remove the MS-DOS setup disk from the floppy drive in preparation for a restart. At this point, all files have been copied and the computer has DOS installed. Remove all disks from all floppy drives and press Enter.

FIGURE 4.6:

At the end of the install process, SETUP asks you to remove the floppy disks.

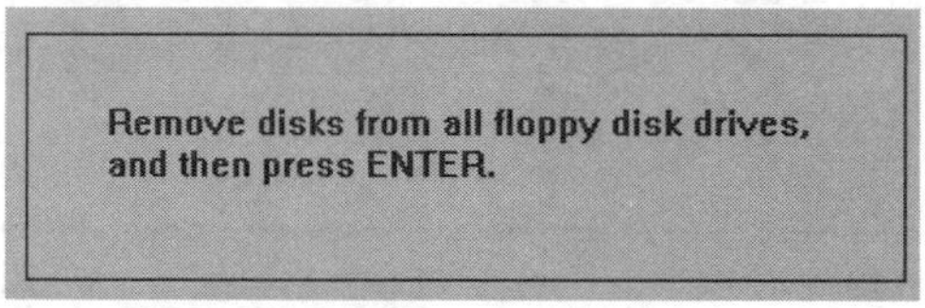

> Remove disks from all floppy disk drives, and then press ENTER.

Finalizing Setup

When you press Enter at the previous screen, the screen shown in Figure 4.7 is displayed. This screen instructs you what to do next. If you want to reboot the computer and start MS-DOS 6.22, go ahead and press Enter.

FIGURE 4.7:

The MS-DOS final
setup screen

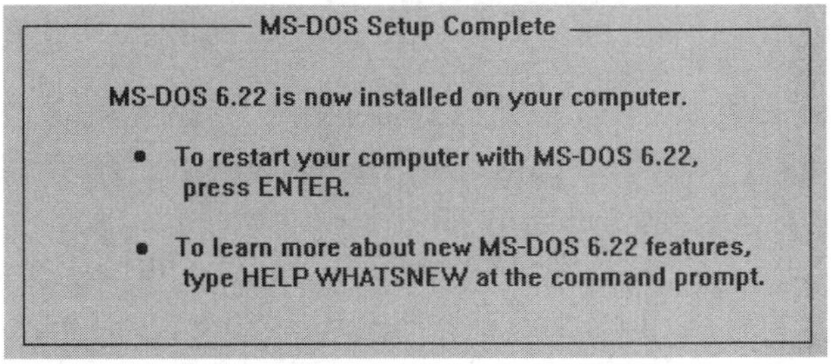

```
┌──────────── MS-DOS Setup Complete ────────────┐
│                                               │
│   MS-DOS 6.22 is now installed on your computer. │
│                                               │
│   •  To restart your computer with MS-DOS 6.22, │
│      press ENTER.                             │
│                                               │
│   •  To learn more about new MS-DOS 6.22 features, │
│      type HELP WHATSNEW at the command prompt. │
│                                               │
└───────────────────────────────────────────────┘
```

Note that if you want to learn about the new features, you still have to press Enter to reboot first. However, after you've rebooted, you can type the following to get information about the new commands:

HELP WHATSNEW

This will bring up a DOS help file that explains what's new about MS-DOS since the previous version.

After you've pressed Enter, the machine will reboot and the default AUTOEXEC.BAT and CONFIG.SYS will be executed. You can make changes to them if you wish. You can also install new hardware and install the drivers for them at this point, now that the AUTOEXEC.BAT and CONFIG.SYS have been created.

Pat yourself on the back. You have just successfully installed MS-DOS.

Upgrading DOS

Occasionally, you will be asked to upgrade a version of MS-DOS. The machine that already has DOS installed will present only a few, minor issues for a technician. We have already discussed the prerequisites for installing MS-DOS. Of those prerequisites, the two most important for performing upgrades are checking available disk space and backing up existing data.

You want to back up anything that may change during the installation process. For example, it would be a good idea to have backups of your configuration files (AUTOEXEC.BAT, CONFIG.SYS, and any Windows .INI files, if present). All of these configuration files should easily fit on a blank, high-density (1.44MB) floppy disk. It also wouldn't hurt to have a backup of your entire system, in case something goes drastically wrong (like the floppy disk drive going bad in the middle of an install).

These next sections will cover the steps necessary to upgrade MS-DOS to version 6.22. We will compare an upgrade to a normal DOS install, where appropriate. Again, there are a few assumptions. First, we assume the computer already has an older version of DOS installed on the hard disk. Second, there is a version of Windows installed (let's say it's version 3.1).

Starting SETUP.EXE

To start the upgrade of DOS, turn off the computer and insert the "MS-DOS Setup Disk 1" disk into the A: drive and boot the computer. Your computer will start SETUP.EXE automatically. You will receive the same "Please wait. SETUP is checking your system configuration information" as before.

TIP
If you are upgrading from MS-DOS version 6.0 or above, you don't have to use the three setup diskettes. Instead, you can boot to the STEPUP disk (a special disk included when you purchase the *MS-DOS 6.22 Upgrade* software package. This disk contains a special SETUP.EXE program which installs only the changes between the two versions of DOS and modifies any existing files to include those changes. This is a much faster way of upgrading DOS on your machine if the version of DOS isn't that old.

The next screen that appears is the screen that welcomes you to MS-DOS Setup and details the various options you have for running SETUP. These options are the same as they were in the normal install. Press Enter to start the upgrade.

Starting the Upgrade

The first difference between an install and an upgrade SETUP is the next screen (Figure 4.8). This screen indicates that, because this is an upgrade, you may have some problems. To help preempt some of these, SETUP will make duplicates of your current configuration and some of your old DOS information to one or more *uninstall* diskettes. You will need to have a couple of high-density (1.44MB) blank diskettes available during the installation process to store this information.

FIGURE 4.8:

Directions for creating the Uninstall diskettes

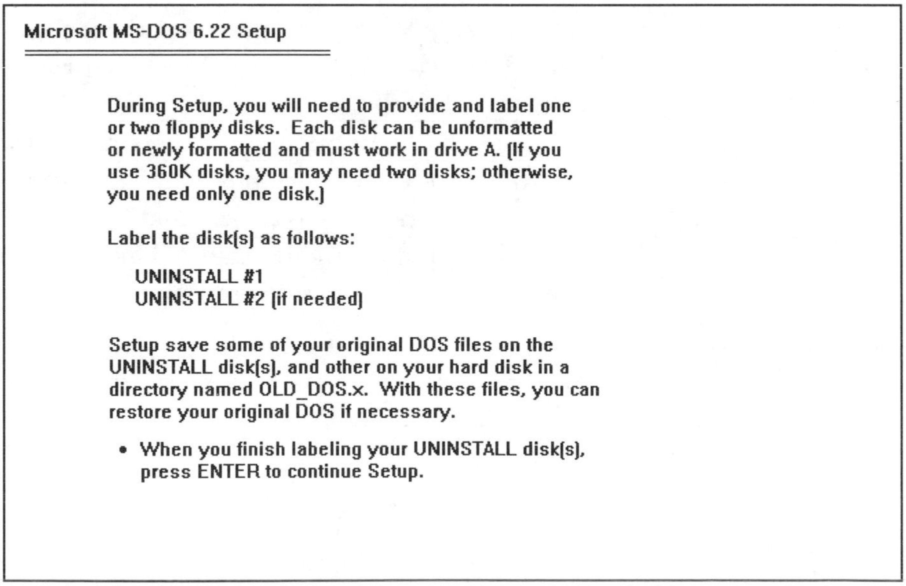

Microsoft MS-DOS 6.22 Setup

During Setup, you will need to provide and label one
or two floppy disks. Each disk can be unformatted
or newly formatted and must work in drive A. (If you
use 360K disks, you may need two disks; otherwise,
you need only one disk.)

Label the disk(s) as follows:

UNINSTALL #1
UNINSTALL #2 (if needed)

Setup save some of your original DOS files on the
UNINSTALL disk(s), and other on your hard disk in a
directory named OLD_DOS.x. With these files, you can
restore your original DOS if necessary.

• When you finish labeling your UNINSTALL disk(s),
  press ENTER to continue Setup.

NOTE During the upgrade, SETUP saves some of your old DOS files to a directory called C:\OLD_DOS.*x* (where x is the version of DOS you are upgrading *from*). If your upgrade fails, you can use the uninstall diskettes you made at this stage to boot the computer. Another program will then run and assist you in restoring your computer to "pre-upgrade" status. This will remove all traces of the new version of DOS and restore your old version.

Pressing Enter will create the uninstall diskette(s). SETUP will prompt you for each disk as they are needed. When you have finished creating your uninstall diskettes, press Enter to resume the upgrade.

Entering MS-DOS Upgrade Settings

The next screen presented in the upgrade process is a combination of two of the screens in the normal SETUP process. The screen in Figure 4.9 asks for all the upgrade settings (location information and MS-DOS installation path) in one screen, rather than getting the information from two separate screens. Changing the information on this screen is done in the same manner as in the regular SETUP process. When you have made any necessary changes, highlight "The settings are correct" and press Enter to continue with the upgrade.

FIGURE 4.9:

The MS-DOS upgrade settings screen

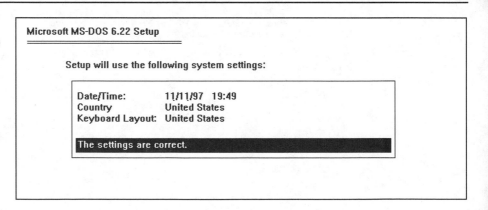

```
Microsoft MS-DOS 6.22 Setup
═══════════════════════════════

    Setup will use the following system settings:


    ┌─────────────────────────────────────────────────┐
    │ Date/Time:        11/11/97   19:49               │
    │ Country           United States                  │
    │ Keyboard Layout:  United States                  │
    ├─────────────────────────────────────────────────┤
    │ The settings are correct.                        │
    └─────────────────────────────────────────────────┘
```

Adding MS-DOS Windows Components

If you have Windows installed on the computer you are upgrading, you will be presented with a screen like the one in Figure 4.10. This screen indicates that the Windows versions of the programs listed will be the only ones listed (as opposed to the DOS versions of the same programs). If you press Enter with "Install the listed programs" highlighted, *only* the Windows versions of those programs will be installed (this is the default setting). To install both Windows and MS-DOS versions, on the one hand, or, on the other hand, the MS-DOS versions only, or neither version, you must change the default. Do this by using the arrow keys to select the program option you want to change, and press Enter. You will then be presented with a list similar to the one in Figure 4.11. Select the appropriate option with the arrow keys and press Enter to select it.

FIGURE 4.10:

Installing Windows and DOS versions of MS-DOS utilities

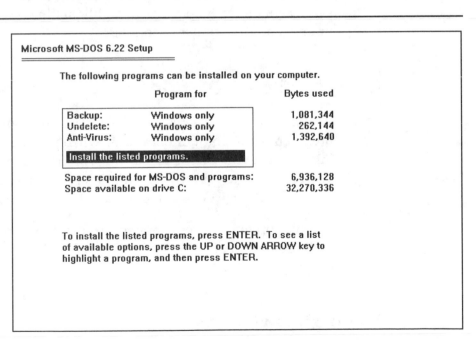

FIGURE 4.11:

Selecting which ver-
sion of an MS-DOS
utility to install

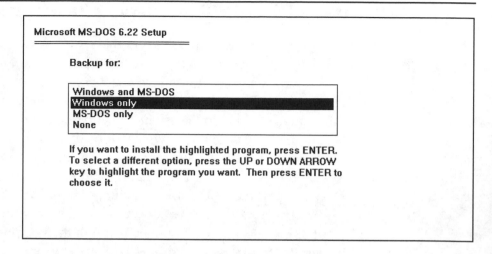

Once you have finished changing any of these options (if necessary), and are ready to proceed, highlight "Install the listed programs" and press Enter to continue.

Copying MS-DOS Files

At this point, no changes have been made to your system yet. The
next step is the point of no return. When you have finished entering settings, you will be presented with the screen in Figure 4.12. If
you are ready to perform the upgrade, press the Y key. SETUP will
create the OLD_DOS.X directory and begin the upgrade.

The file copying process happens exactly the same as with a normal installation of DOS. You will be asked for disks as SETUP
needs them.

Finalizing the Upgrade

After all the MS-DOS files are copied, SETUP will display the message shown in Figure 4.13. This message says that the original

AUTOEXEC.BAT and CONFIG.SYS were renamed to AUTOEXEC
.DAT and CONFIG.DAT, then saved to the uninstall disk(s). This
message is basically saying "Hey, we're finished!" To finish the
upgrade, remove all disks from any floppy drives and press Enter
to reboot the computer.

FIGURE 4.12:

The "Point of No
Return" screen

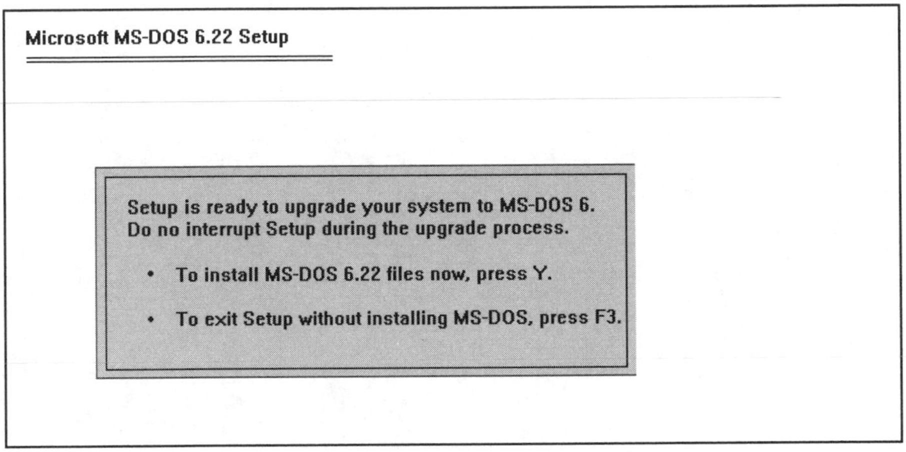

Microsoft MS-DOS 6.22 Setup

Setup is ready to upgrade your system to MS-DOS 6.
Do no interrupt Setup during the upgrade process.

- To install MS-DOS 6.22 files now, press Y.

- To exit Setup without installing MS-DOS, press F3.

FIGURE 4.13:

At the end of the
upgrade process,
you're instructed to
reboot the computer
by pressing Enter. Be
sure to remove any
floppies first.

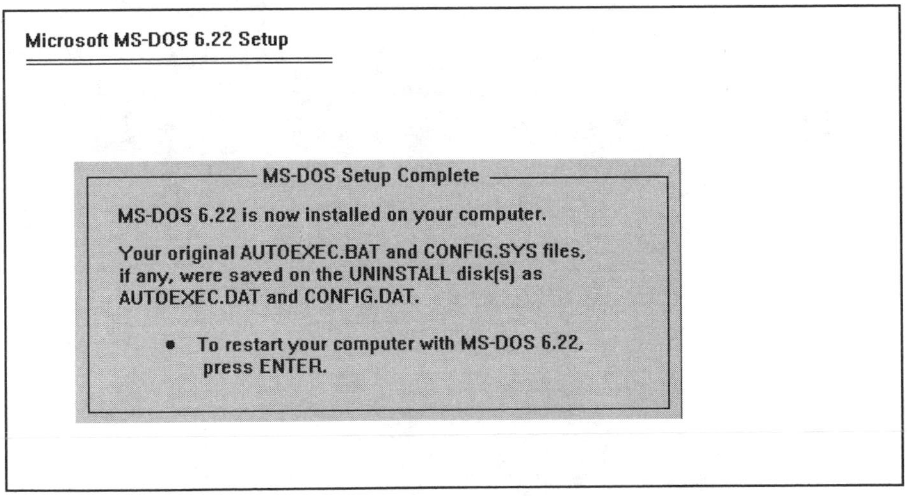

Microsoft MS-DOS 6.22 Setup

——————— MS-DOS Setup Complete ———————

MS-DOS 6.22 is now installed on your computer.

Your original AUTOEXEC.BAT and CONFIG.SYS files,
if any, were saved on the UNINSTALL disk(s) as
AUTOEXEC.DAT and CONFIG.DAT.

- To restart your computer with MS-DOS 6.22,
  press ENTER.

If you experienced problems anywhere along the process, simply reboot the computer with the first uninstall diskette in the A: drive and follow the prompts. The UNINSTALL program will restore your system configuration back to its original state.

Review Questions for Chapter 4, Installing DOS

Answers to the Review Questions may be found in Appendix A.

1. Which program is used to install DOS?

    A. INSTALL.EXE

    B. INSTALL.BAT

    C. SETUP.EXE

    D. STEPUP.EXE

2. Which utility (or utilities) can be used to determine the amount of disk space on a machine that already has a version of DOS installed? (Circle all that apply.)

    A. DIR

    B. CHKDSK

    C. SPACE /DISK

    D. DISK /SPACE

3. When upgrading DOS, SETUP renames the AUTOEXEC.BAT to what?

    A. AUTOEXEC.BAK

    B. AUTOEXEC.001

    C. AUTOEXEC.OLD

    D. AUTOEXED.DAT

4. DOS can be installed on IBM-compatible computers. True or false?

    A. True

    B. False

5. How many disks are required to do a regular DOS installation?

   A. 1

   B. 2

   C. 3

   D. 4

6. If you are upgrading from MS-DOS 6.20 to 6.22, how many disks (not counting uninstall diskettes) will you use to do the upgrade?

   A. 1

   B. 2

   C. 3

   D. 4

7. It is necessary to back up the entire hard disk before doing a DOS upgrade. True or false?

   A. True

   B. False

8. Which of the following prerequisites is *not* required to upgrade DOS?

   A. Back up the configuration files.

   B. Verify that the computer is IBM-compatible.

   C. Ensure that the computer has more than 10 MB of available disk space.

   D. Format the hard disk.

9. When installing DOS for the first time, you must do which of the following?

    A. FDISK and FORMAT the disk.

    B. Delete any unnecessary files.

    C. Back up the entire disk.

    D. Turn off the computer, then turn it back on.

10. If you are installing DOS onto the A: floppy drive, you must:

    A. Boot to the C: drive. Insert the DOS Setup Disk 1 in the A: drive and run SETUP from the A: drive manually.

    B. Boot to the C: drive. Insert the DOS Setup Disk 1 in the B: drive and run SETUP from the B: drive manually.

    C. Boot to Drive B:. Insert DOS Setup Disk 1 in the A: drive and run SETUP from the A: drive manually.

    D. Boot to Drive A:. Insert DOS Setup Disk 1 in the B: drive and run SETUP from the B: drive manually.

11. Which function key, when pressed, will halt SETUP and leave you at a DOS command prompt?

    A. F1

    B. F3

    C. F5

    D. F7

12. Which program is used to upgrade DOS from version 6.20 to 6.22?

    A. SETUP.COM

    B. SETUP.EXE

    C. STEPUP.EXE

    D. STEPUP.COM

13. Which function key will display help in the SETUP program?

    A. F1

    B. F3

    C. F5

    D. F7

14. Which of the following is a DOS installation step unique to a DOS upgrade?

    A. booting to the A: drive

    B. adding Windows components of DOS utilities

    C. running SETUP.EXE

    D. pressing F3 to exit

15. A computer with an AMD K5 processor (an Intel-compatible CPU) can run MS-DOS. True or false?

    A. True

    B. False

16. You can install DOS 6.22 on Macintosh computers without any special hardware or software. True or false?

    A. True

    B. False

17. Which key could you press to give you information about the SETUP process while running it?

    A. F1

    B. F3

    C. F5

    D. F7

18. Suppose you have just performed an upgrade from MS-DOS 6.0 to MS-DOS 6.22. You are wondering what the new features of this new version of DOS are. What command can you type at the C:\> prompt to detail these commands and features?

    A. HELP

    B. INFO

    C. HELP WHATSNEW

    D. WHATSNEW INFO

19. What executable is used to upgrade DOS to a new version?

    A. INSTALL.EXE

    B. SETUP.EXE

    C. UPGRADE.EXE

    D. INSTALL.BAT

20. How many disks are used to install DOS?

    A. 1

    B. 3

    C. 5

    D. 4

21. How many disks are used to upgrade DOS? (Assume the current version of DOS is 6.0 and you are upgrading to 6.22.)

    A. 1

    B. 2

    C. 3

    D. as many as 4

22. Assume that you don't have an operating system installed on the hard disk of your computer. You insert the disk labeled "Disk 1 – SETUP" into the A: drive and turn the computer on. What do you have to do next?

    A. Use a different disk. "Disk 1" isn't bootable.

    B. Type **SETUP** from the C:\> prompt, when it appears.

    C. Type **INSTALL** at the C:\> prompt, when it appears.

    D. Nothing, the installation program will start automatically.

23. During a DOS upgrade, you happen to drop something on your keyboard and it hits the F5 key. What happens?

    A. Nothing.

    B. Your screen changes color.

    C. The installation quits.

    D. Your computer reboots, forcing you to delete the DOS directory and start over.

24. Which system settings can you change during a fresh DOS install? (Circle all that apply.)

    A. time zone

    B. date

    C. hardware configuration

    D. time

    E. keyboard layout

    F. DOS components to install

25. The DOS installation installs some Windows programs. True or false?

    A. True

    B. False

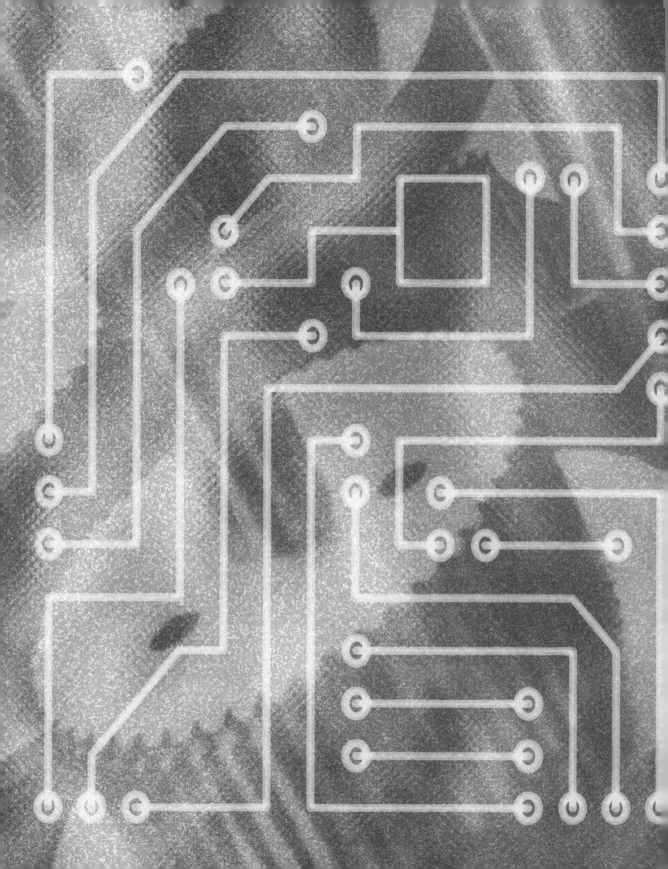

DOS Startup and Configuration

- The Boot Process

- MS-DOS Boot Files

- PC-DOS Boot Files

- DOS Configuration Files (CONFIG.SYS and AUTOEXEC.BAT)

- Using PROMPT, PATH, and SMARTDRV in AUTOEXEC.BAT

An understanding of the DOS boot process and the essential files of the DOS operating system provide a foundation for understanding the rest of the operating system. This chapter details this information in reference to MS-DOS and PC-DOS, and also describes system configuration options available through the CONFIG.SYS and AUTOEXEC.BAT files.

DOS is a highly configurable system. The topics of this chapter include:

- An explanation of the boot process

- Definitions of the essential DOS files and their roles in the boot process

- An analysis of how DOS may be configured through alterations made to the CONFIG.SYS file, including memory management commands, Multiconfig, and the disk-compression program DoubleSpace

- A discussion of how you can configure DOS by including programs and commands in the AUTOEXEC.BAT file

Startup and the Startup Files

Startup of a computer is generally referred to as *booting* or *bootstrapping*. This term is derived from an expression that was more meaningful in an older age of lesser technology—to pull oneself up by the bootstraps.

This section of the chapter describes what happens when you flip the power switch on a DOS-based computer, and devotes special attention to the software involved in that process. An understanding of what *should* be taking place during bootup will aid you greatly in any effort to diagnose a malfunctioning system.

MS-DOS = IO.SYS + MSDOS.SYS + COMMAND.COM

While the equation given in this section's heading does not contain the profound mathematical truths of Einstein's theory of relativity, it does describe a truth that is fundamental to the world of DOS. The three files—IO.SYS, MSDOS.SYS, and COMMAND.COM—constitute the essential parts of the DOS operating system. These three files are the only ones that are absolutely necessary to your computer for it to properly boot up into DOS.

- **IO.SYS** is a hidden, read-only, system file that manages the input/output routines of your computer. The .SYS extension defines it as a file that should not be deleted, because it is part of the operating system. IO.SYS deals with the nuts and bolts issues of data communication between the various hardware devices attached to your computer, such as the hard disk, printers, floppy disk drive, etc.

- **MSDOS.SYS** is also a hidden, read-only, system file. Its job is to handle program management and file management, and in doing so it provides a platform for COMMAND.COM to do its work.

- **COMMAND.COM** is the vital command interpreter for your computer. It is the most personable of these three files in that, unlike IO.SYS and MSDOS.SYS, it interacts with the user directly, via the keyboard and screen. COMMAND.COM exhibits the DOS prompt on screen, and when the user types in a command this file will interpret the command on behalf of DOS so that DOS can take action. COMMAND.COM itself contains some of many basic DOS commands like DIR and DEL. (These commands are called *internal* DOS commands because they are part of COMMAND.COM.)

Understanding the Boot Process

When you turn the power switch on your computer, your computer goes through a series of test routines that are part of the BIOS software. The test routines constitute the *Power On Self Test* (*POST*), which takes inventory of the system and tests memory, ROMs, video, keyboard, and other components of your computer. The BIOS software then gathers hardware configuration information from the computer's CMOS chip before moving on to the next phase of the boot process, loading the operating system. Up to this point, any messages displayed on screen, such as the memory test output, a copyright notice, or initialization messages, will be authored by the main BIOS or by additional BIOSes contained in ROMs on circuit boards.

The loading of the operating system takes place in several steps, as follows:

1. The BIOS first looks for a bootable disk first in drive A:.

    *   If there is a bootable disk in drive A:, the BIOS looks on the first sector of the disk for the *DOS Boot Record* (*DBR*), and passes control to it. The rest of the boot process is described below, beginning with step 3 (in other words, when the system is booting from a floppy, it skips step 2).

    *   If there is a non-bootable disk is in drive A:, it will display the following message: "Non-System disk or disk error. Replace and strike any key when ready." You can put a bootable floppy in the drive and press any key to have the BIOS read that floppy's DOS Boot Record (as mentioned in the previous bulleted paragraph), *or* you can simply eject the floppy disk and press Enter to continue the booting process.

2. If there is no bootable floppy in place, BIOS looks for and loads the *Master Boot Record* (*MBR*). The BIOS now passes control to the MBR. The MBR contains information on how the hard disk is divided into partitions, and it will run its Partition Table program, which is designed to locate a bootable partition. Once found, it will load the first sector of the partition into memory, and pass control to whatever program is residing there—the DOS Boot Record, in this case.

The MBR consists of 512 bytes located on the first sector of the hard disk. If there is a problem with the MBR, most likely the system will freeze and will not display any error messages. If the MBR is functioning properly but cannot locate a bootable partition, it will display this message:

```
Missing Operating System
```

3. The DOS Boot Record (DBR) then looks for the two hidden system files, IO.SYS and MSDOS.SYS. (If it can't find them in the root directory, it will again display the message, "Non-System disk or disk error. Replace and strike any key when ready.") When it finds them, the DBR passes control to IO.SYS.

4. IO.SYS first tests itself to confirm that it has properly loaded into memory, then it checks MSDOS.SYS with the same purpose in mind. IO.SYS contains a pointer to the CONFIG.SYS file. If all is well, IO.SYS begins processing the commands in CONFIG.SYS, in the order in which they are listed in the file.

5. IO.SYS also contains a pointer to COMMAND.COM, which must reside in the root directory. The usual exception to this is when a SHELL statement in CONFIG.SYS points IO.SYS to an alternate directory. Different versions of DOS also include different versions of COMMAND.COM, IO.SYS, and MSDOS.SYS. The version of COMMAND.COM must match the version of the two hidden DOS files, or an error will be displayed.

6. At this point COMMAND.COM runs the AUTOEXEC.BAT file.

This completes the boot process. Your interactive options during this time are discussed later in this chapter and involve bypassing all or part of the CONFIG.SYS file and/or the AUTOEXEC.BAT file by using the F5 or F8 keys during startup.

MS-DOS Boot Files and Root Directory

The root directory of your computer must contain the command interpreter COMMAND.COM in addition to IO.SYS and MSDOS.SYS. When you boot your computer it will default to the root directory, which is usually represented by the C:\> for the hard drive or the A:\> for the floppy drive.

If one of these files is missing from the root directory or corrupted, your computer will not boot. As a safety precaution it is wise to be prepared for this by first formatting a floppy with the following command:

FORMAT A: /S

This /S (system) switch will result in the format of a bootable floppy disk with IO.SYS, MSDOS.SYS, and COMMAND.COM copied onto it. When the format is complete, DOS will display how much space has been used up and how much is left to store additional files.

TIP

If you're using a simple DIR command to view the contents of the floppy, IO.SYS and MSDOS.SYS will not appear in the list, because they are hidden files. To include the hidden files in your list of files, you must append to the DIR command the switch that tells it to list hidden files—**DIR /A:H.**

Cold Boots and Warm Boots

A "cold boot" is what you get when you first turn on the computer's power switch. When a computer is already on, you can force the computer to perform what is referred to as a *warm boot* by pressing Ctrl+Alt+Del. A warm boot does not perform all of the hardware and memory checks that a cold boot initiates. Pressing Ctrl+Alt+Del can be helpful in the event your system freezes, but there is a chance that any files you have open could be destroyed. Fortunately, Windows and various other programs may intercept the Ctrl+Alt+Del combination and present an alternative to a warm boot such as shutting down your current program or task. The reason for this is that Windows is more susceptible than DOS to problems stemming from an improper shutdown of the system.

Internal versus External DOS Commands

The user interface of DOS is COMMAND.COM. It is called the *command interpreter*, which means that it takes what you type at the keyboard and attempts to interpret it for DOS. COMMAND.COM also displays on screen the C:\> prompt in addition to your typed commands. Let's take a closer look at COMMAND.COM and how it operates.

Internal DOS Commands

COMMAND.COM contains a large number of *internal* commands. These commands are typically the more essential and smaller DOS commands. The advantage of this is that it can execute these programs faster than it can execute external commands, because they are already present in memory. Each internal command constitutes a small program residing within COMMAND.COM. Here is a list of the internal commands:

BREAK	ERASE	REM
CALL	EXIT	REN
CD	FOR	RENAME
CHCP	GOTO	RMDIR
CHDIR	IF	SET
CLS	LH	SHIFT
COPY	LOADHIGH	TIME
CTTY	MD	TYPE
DATE	MKDIR	VER
DEL	PATH	VERIFY
DIR	PAUSE	VOL
ECHO	PROMPT	

External DOS Commands

The DOS commands that are not contained within COMMAND.COM are referred to as *external* commands. They are represented by a .COM or .EXE extension.

When you type in text at the command line and press Enter, COMMAND.COM assumes you've typed a command and parses the text into sections. The main sections of a command are as follows:

- The *name* of the command, such as DIR

- The *parameters* for the command, which determine basically *where* this command will be executed. The parameters are separated by spaces. Depending on the command and its context, parameters are not always required.

- The optional *switches* for the command. Switches determine which of the options are used and, sometimes, how they are used, and are usually preceded by the forward slash.

An example of this would be the FORMAT A: /S command. When reading this, COMMAND.COM uses the spaces—which are therefore crucial to its correct interpretation of the command—to determine that it will parse this command into three sections, FORMAT, A:, and /S. "FORMAT" is the command; "A:" is the parameter for the command, which in this case means that the A: drive is where the command will be carried out; and "/S" is an optional switch, which in this case tells DOS to format the disk as a bootable floppy (in other words, S stands for "system"—it tells DOS to include the necessary system files).

Names are assigned by COMMAND.COM to the parsed sections of the command. The first section becomes %0, the second section becomes %1, the third section %2, and so on up to %9. In our FORMAT A: /S example, /S would be named %2. This issue becomes significant to users when writing batch files, because they can use the %*n* to represent a changing parameter (more on that in Chapter 7).

Except for its own internal commands, COMMAND.COM does not know what the parsed portions of the command mean. In other words, when it's processing FORMAT A: /S, it loads the FORMAT command, and lets FORMAT figure out what to do with the A: and the /S.

The process by which COMMAND.COM searches for the command that it reads from the first parsed portion of the command line is an ordered and exact process. First, COMMAND.COM performs a self-check to see if the command in question is an internal command. If it is, it will execute the command. If the command is not internal, it will search until it has found a file with the correct name and a .COM extension. If unsuccessful, it will search for a file with the correct name and a .EXE extension, and if that doesn't work, it will start looking for a .BAT extension if necessary. An example of this follows:

1. You enter **EDIT DOC3** at the command line, and COMMAND .COM investigates whether it carries EDIT as in internal

command. If it finds the command it will execute it. If it does not find the command, it will proceed to step 2.

2. COMMAND.COM will look for EDIT.COM in the default directory. If it finds it, it will order DOS to execute it. If it does not find the file, it will move to step 3.

3. COMMAND.COM will look for EDIT.EXE in the same manner, and execute it if it finds it; otherwise it proceeds to step 4.

4. COMMAND.COM will look for EDIT.BAT and execute it, or proceed to step 5 if it does not find it.

5. COMMAND.COM will start its search for the command all over again, but this time it will look in the directories that are listed in the PATH environment variable. If COMMAND.COM can't find any of these files in any of the directories of the path, then it will display the following message:

```
Bad command or file name
```

The PC-DOS Startup Files

PC-DOS is the version of DOS owned by IBM. The three essential files of the PC-DOS operating system are:

- IBMBIO.COM
- IBMDOS.COM
- COMMAND.COM

IBMBIO.COM and IBMDOS.COM are the PC-DOS equivalents of IO.SYS and MSDOS.SYS, respectively (refer to the preceding discussions of the MS-DOS boot process). During the bootup phase, the DOS Boot Record locates and loads IBMBIO.COM and IBMDOS. COM. IBMBIO.COM then takes over from the DBR and runs CON-FIG.SYS and COMMAND.COM. As in MS-DOS, COMMAND.COM finalizes the boot process by running the AUTOEXEC.BAT file.

Customizing DOS with CONFIG.SYS

We have already looked at the elements of DOS that are unalterably programmed into your computer. Unless you're a DOS programmer, undertaking to change these elements would be tantamount to proposing to wreak havoc on the operating system.

Unlike the files discussed previously, however, CONFIG.SYS is a system file that is *made* to be changed, much like a new car is made to be individually adjusted according to the taste of its owner. When buying a new car, a prospective buyer selects from a list of possible options and pays to have those options included in the vehicle. The CONFIG.SYS file can be compared to the dashboard of your car. A standard-model automobile's dashboard contains, in addition to the standard dials and buttons, various unused "plugs" which are waiting to be utilized should the buyer decide to purchase additional special features. The dashboard's dials and plugs correspond to the commands located within the CONFIG.SYS file—they are device drivers and commands that are placed in the CONFIG.SYS file. The unused plugs in this hypothetical dashboard correspond to the full range of available commands that may be used in the CONFIG.SYS file, many of which are described in detail later in this chapter.

This file can be used for vital tasks such as memory management, which has to do with arranging the memory addresses used by DOS programs. Many users include the DOUBLESPACE program in their CONFIG.SYS, allowing the doubling of disk space through disk compression. There are also multi-configuration options available, which allow you to change your configuration at bootup depending on your occasional needs. Other options include things like the VSAFE command, which allows for automatic virus-protection for your system.

In the bootup process, CONFIG.SYS loads into memory prior to COMMAND.COM. To view its contents, you must first be in the root directory of your hard drive, which will be indicated by the C:\> prompt. Alongside this prompt, type the following:

```
EDIT CONFIG.SYS
```

In all likelihood you will see a file that looks something like this:

```
DEVICE=C:\WINDOWS\HIMEM.SYS
DEVICE=C:\WINDOWS\EMM386.EXE NOEMS
BUFFERS=23,0
FILES=30
DOS=UMB
LASTDRIVE=E
FCBS=4,0
```

(Or you may see something longer and somewhat more intimidating.) The rest of this chapter will explain much of what you're likely to see.

Before editing the CONFIG.SYS file it is a good idea to make a copy of it so you can restore its previous settings. This may be necessary because it is possible to render your system nonfunctional through incorrect changes to the file. To make a copy, type the following command:

```
COPY CONFIG.SYS CONFIG.BAK
```

If you later need to restore the previous settings you can then use the following commands, in the following order:

```
RENAME CONFIG.SYS CONFIG.OLD
RENAME CONFIG.BAK CONFIG.SYS
```

These commands will replace the existing CONFIG.SYS with one that is known to work.

Main Parameters of CONFIG.SYS

The following sections describe the most commonly used parameters for CONFIG.SYS and how they are used. The commands must follow a proper format, as shown in the command's syntax.

FILES

The FILES command describes how many *file handles* DOS can keep track of simultaneously. A file handle is simply another name for an open file. If DOS discovers that a program exceeds this limit as it tries to open a file, DOS responds by saying that there are too many files open. In light of that, it seems logical to make FILES the highest number the system will allow (which is 255), except that the memory available to the system is reduced slightly whenever this number is increased. Setting the FILES to 30 would be typical. Documentation that comes with programs will often specify the minimum FILES setting for their program.

The syntax for the FILES commands is:

```
FILES=n
```

Here is an example of the FILES command:

```
FILES=30
```

BUFFERS

Not unlike the FILES command, the BUFFERS command determines the number of buffers DOS creates, so that it can store disk information in RAM rather than on disk. This will lessen the need for constantly accessing the hard drive, reducing the number of reads and writes, and speeding up overall operation of the computer. As with the FILES command, the higher this number is set to the more memory it will use. Setting BUFFERS to 50 would be typical on a hard drive of 120 MB or more.

The BUFFERS command should be reduced on systems running a disk caching program such as SMARTDRV. In this case BUFFERS should be set to a lower number, such as 15. Windows automatically installs SMARTDRV in the AUTOEXEC.BAT file, so a Windows computer should have the BUFFERS command set low.

The syntax for the BUFFERS command is:

BUFFERS=n

An example of this command in use is:

BUFFERS=50

DEVICE

Every device that is connected to a computer, such as a hard drive, CD-ROM, or printer, relies on a piece of software called a *device driver* in order to communicate with the operating system. These drivers are sometimes included with DOS. Drivers for those devices that are not included with DOS (a CD-ROM is a typical example) must have a pointer in the CONFIG.SYS file that directs DOS to the correct address for the driver. This pointer is the DEVICE command. Typically, the driver for a piece of hardware will come on a disk included with the hardware. In the hardware's documentation there will be instructions explaining how to load the driver on your hard drive and how to modify your CONFIG.SYS file so that DOS can find the driver when it boots up.

When the DEVICE command is executed at bootup, DOS will find the driver and load it into memory.

The syntax for the DEVICE command is:

DEVICE=[d:path]filename

Here is an example of the DEVICE command in use:

```
DEVICE=C:\SB16\SB16.SYS
```

Many kinds of *software* also require the use of a device driver. DOS includes many examples of such software, such as its own memory management software. The memory management drivers are HIMEM.SYS and EMM386.EXE. Other drivers include DOUBLE-SPACE.SYS, which is the device driver for DOS's DoubleSpace disk compression program. We will look at the memory management programs in detail later in this chapter.

Memory Management Parameters of CONFIG.SYS

Memory management involves loading portions of DOS or complete DOS programs into areas of memory that are not normally accessible. This is an essential aspect of optimizing DOS for high performance, as it makes more memory available to other programs, including Windows. Some DOS programs require contiguous blocks of memory to run, and using memory management may allow them to fit into memory, even in cases where they may have been squeezed out and rendered nonfunctional before.

DOS is capable of working with 1,024 KB of memory addresses under most circumstances. The reason for this is that DOS was originally designed to work with the Intel 8088 CPU that IBM picked out for the original PC back around 1980. The 8088 could address 1,024 KB of memory, which at the time was a colossal amount of memory.

These early programmers also had to decide how those 1,024 KB of memory addresses would be used. They decided that the first 640 KB would be used for programs, data, and the operating system itself. This first 640 KB is referred to as *conventional memory*. Most programs written for DOS are designed to work within this first 640 KB, which is sometimes referred to as the *640K barrier*. The area from 640 KB to 768 KB is reserved for video memory. The upper area from 768 KB to 1,024 KB is referred to as the *reserved memory area* (this area is also sometimes called the *upper memory area*). This reserved memory area contains the BIOS ROM and is reserved for ROMs on circuit boards such as LAN cards or hard disk controller cards. Figure 5.1 illustrates these memory areas.

FIGURE 5.1:

DOS's main memory areas

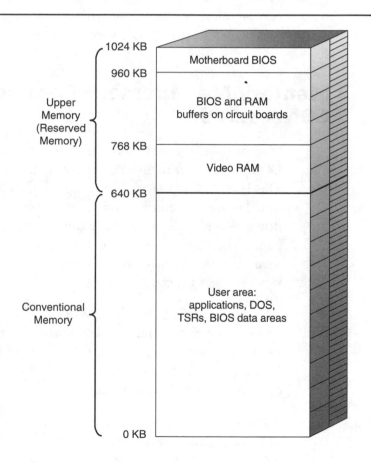

Originally, the programmers for DOS envisioned that this 640 KB would be enough memory space to run any software built for DOS. Programs grew quickly, however, and it became necessary to utilize the upper areas of memory for more and more purposes. The device drivers and commands described in this section provide ways to do that.

Memory above 1,024 KB is called extended memory, and is used by Windows and Windows-based programs. Extended memory cannot be accessed unless the HIMEM.SYS memory manager is used. The lowest 64 KB of extended memory, from 1,024 KB to 1,088 KB, is called the High Memory Area (HMA). Portions of DOS can be loaded into this area using a memory manager.

NOTE For more detailed information about the DOS memory map and other PC memory topics, refer to the first book in the A+ Study Guide series, the *A+ Core Module Study Guide*.

HIMEM.SYS

HIMEM.SYS is the DOS memory manager that enables extended memory above 1,024 KB on your system, including the High Memory Area from 1,024 KB to 1,088 KB. Windows cannot load at all without HIMEM.SYS, and for this reason it automatically invokes it whether it is present in the CONFIG.SYS file or not.

The syntax for HIMEM.SYS is as follows:

```
DEVICE=[d:\path]HIMEM.SYS [switches]
```

Here is an example of HIMEM.SYS being used:

```
DEVICE=c:\dos\HIMEM.SYS /int15=1024
```

Table 5.1 describes the switches that can be used with HIMEM.SYS.

TABLE 5.1: Switches Used with the HIMEM.SYS Command

Switch	Purpose
/a20control:on|off	Determines status of the HMA A20 line.
/cpuclock:on|off	Determines whether HIMEM.SYS will modify system clock speed. The default is off.
/eisa	Allocates maximum amount of extended memory. Required for EISA systems with 16 MB of memory or more.
/hmamin=*nnn*	Specifies minimum memory space a program must request in order for DOS to load it into the HMA. The number *nnn* will be in kilobytes. Only one program can load into HMA. The default size is 0 KB.
int15=*nnn*	Reserves *nnn* kilobytes for handling of Int 15, which is used by certain older programs. The default size is 0 KB.
/machine:*name*	Defines the specific computer type using a predefined code. (Required by some systems that HIMEM.SYS cannot detect.)
/numhandles=*nn*	Maximum memory block handles for extended memory. The default is 32.
/shadowram:on|off	Sets the status of shadow RAM.
/verbose	Calls for status messages by HIMEM.SYS when it starts up.

DOS=HIGH and DOS=UMB

The DOS=HIGH command is used to load part of DOS into the High Memory Area between 1,024 KB and 1,088 KB. The DOS=UMB command enables DOS to manage *upper memory blocks* (*UMBs*). Upper memory blocks are the blocks of free memory in the upper memory area between 640 KB and 1,024 KB. Using DOS=UMB will mean that DOS is empowered to load programs and device drivers into UMBs.

DOS=HIGH and DOS=UMB can be left as separate commands or combined into one statement as shown here:

```
DOS=HIGH,UMB
```

The syntax for this command is as follows:

```
DOS=HIGH|LOW[,UMB|,NOUMB]
```

TIP

The "|" symbol that appears twice in the preceding syntax line above indicates that you can use one or the other, but not both, of the items that are separated by the symbol.

The DOS=HIGH command will not work unless the HIMEM.SYS device driver is installed. The DOS=UMB command requires that the EMM386.EXE driver be loaded.

EMM386.EXE

The EMM386.EXE reserved memory manager provides DOS with the ability to utilize upper memory blocks (UMBs) to store programs and device drivers. UMBs reside in the 640 KB to 1,024 KB region of memory. The EMM386.EXE is also used to simulate expanded memory for DOS applications that utilize 386 Enhanced mode.

The syntax for the command is:

```
DEVICE=[d:\path]EMM386.EXE [switches]
```

An example of the EMM386.EXE invocation is:

```
DEVICE=C:\DOS\EMM386.EXE NOEMS I=B000-B7FF
```

EMM386.EXE comes with numerous optional switches, which are summarized in Table 5.2.

TABLE 5.2: Switches Used with EMM386.EXE

Switch	Purpose
nnnn	Quantity of extended memory allocated for expanded memory emulation, represented in kilobytes.
on | off | auto	Set or change operational status of EMM386.EXE.
/p*nnnn*	Specifies page frame address.
/pn=*address*	Specifies address for segment *n*.
a=*altregs*	Assigns alternate register sets used for multitasking. The default is 7.
altboot	Enables an alternate process for warm boots initiated by Ctrl+Alt+Del; for use when warm boots malfunction.
b=*address*	Specifies the starting address for EMS memory swapping; the default is hex address 4000h.
d=*nnn*	Retains DMA buffering equal to nnn KB.
frame=*address*	Specifies the 64KB page frame's starting address.
h=*handles*	Number of file handles that EMM386.EXE can utilize.
i=*range*	Include this memory range as available memory addresses.
l=*nnnn*	Directs EMM386.EXE to leave available a specified quantity of extended memory after loading itself.
min=*nnnn*	Describes minimum amount of expanded memory provided by EMM386.EXE. The default EMS memory is 256 KB.
m*n*	Specifies a page-frame address; will be a number from 1 to 14, representing a pre-defined base address.
noems	Prevents LIM3.2 expanded memory.
novcpi	Disallows VCPI.
nohi	Directs EMM386.EXE to load itself into memory below 640 KB.
highscan	Restricts upper memory scanning.
quiet	Suppresses display of EMM386.EXE loading messages.

TABLE 5.2 CONTINUED: Switches Used with EMM386.EXE

Switch	Purpose
ram=*range*	Specifies segment addresses for UMBs; also enables UMBs and expanded memory.
rom=*range*	Allocates memory addresses for shadow RAM.
verbose	Calls for status messages by EMM386.EXE when it starts up.
win=*range*	Specifies an address range to be used by Windows rather than EMM386.EXE.
x=*range*	Excludes this memory range from available memory addresses.

NOTE   All the *range* addresses specified in Table 5.2 are in hexadecimal.

NOEMS is a commonly used option for disabling expanded memory. The *I=range* and *X=range* switches are commonly used both by the MemMaker program and by anyone performing manual memory mapping of the system.

The EMM386.EXE driver is often used in conjunction with the DEVICEHIGH and LOADHIGH commands. The LOADHIGH command is covered in detail later in this chapter, in the section pertaining to the AUTOEXEC.BAT file. LOADHIGH or LH is used to load an application program into an upper memory block.

DEVICEHIGH

This command functions precisely as the device command, but with the following exception: It will load the device drivers into upper memory blocks, thereby freeing up space in conventional memory. If there is insufficient space in the UMBs, DOS will load the device driver into conventional memory. This command requires the

EMM386.EXE invocation to be in place in CONFIG.SYS. It is possible that you may encounter some older drivers that will not execute properly if they are loaded into UMBs. If you know you're using some older drivers, you may want to load one driver at a time into upper memory. After rebooting you should then verify that the system is working correctly.

The syntax for the command is:

```
DEVICE=[d:path]filename
```

An example of the DEVICEHIGH command is:

```
DEVICE=C:\lsrjt\lsr.sys
```

Using MEM to Verify Memory Usage

Once the preceding commands are in place, you can view the results of memory management by rebooting to initiate the changes, and then typing MEM at the command prompt. The MEM command displays statistics as shown in Figure 5.2.

FIGURE 5.2:

Output from the MEM command in DOS 6.22

```
C:\WINDOWS>mem

Memory Type          Total        Used        Free
----------------     --------     --------    --------
Conventional          640K          44K         596K
Upper                   0K           0K           0K
Reserved              384K         384K           0K
Extended (XMS)      15,360K       2,240K      13,120K
----------------     --------     --------    --------
Total memory        16,384K       2,668K      13,716K

Total under 1 MB      640K          44K         596K

Total Expanded (EMS)                20M (20,463,616 bytes)
Free Expanded (EMS)                 13M (13,434,880 bytes)

Largest executable program size    596K (609,968 bytes)
Largest free upper memory block      0K       (0 bytes)
MS-DOS is resident in the high memory area.
```

The row displaying Upper Memory is most significant for memory optimization. In Figure 5.2 notice that the Upper Memory row shows that there is no upper memory available (and none being used).

Typing **MEM /C** at the command prompt displays a very useful and important table. This table describes where each specific program loads, whether into conventional or upper memory. After setting up memory optimization on your system and rebooting, use the MEM /C command. Read the name of those drivers or programs that you attempted to load into UMBs, then check the Upper Memory column to see which of them *did* in fact load into the upper memory area. If a program loaded into conventional memory instead, there may not be sufficient contiguous memory space available for it in a UMB.

NOTE Contiguous memory is memory that occurs in a single continuous block. Programs usually won't function when loaded into different areas of memory; for this reason DOS requires that there be a single memory block available that is large enough to contain an entire program before it will load the given program.

The task of working out which programs can fit into upper memory becomes a time-consuming task, and for that reason it is often simpler to run the MemMaker program included with DOS to optimize memory.

NOTE MemMaker and DOS memory management are covered in detail in Chapter 11.

Using Multiconfig to Customize PC Startup

One of the most powerful and attractive features that came along with version 6.2 of DOS is *Multiconfig*. Before Multiconfig, it was necessary to maintain different CONFIG.SYS files if you wanted to utilize different system configurations at different times. The real problem with this approach was that you either had to rename or move your CONFIG.SYS files after booting up, and then boot the system again in order to use the altered configuration. Users who required programs that used a lot of memory, or users who liked to run scads of memory-gripping TSRs, were often forced into this tedious repetition.

DOS 6.2 included special commands that allowed different configurations to be maintained within a single CONFIG.SYS file. These different configurations are made available to choose from at bootup, when a menu appears offering a choice of bootup configurations. The menu can also be set to default to a certain configuration for occasions when no user is present to make a menu selection. This is helpful for those who hate to sit idly by while their computer boots; they can still go off and grab a coffee during the moments it takes for the computer to boot.

The following analysis will provide step-by-step explanations for a multiple configuration. Suppose you had two simple CONFIG.SYS files that you wanted to merge into one Multiconfig. The first file describes a very basic setup:

```
FILES=30
BUFFERS=30
DEVICE=C:\DOS\ANSI.SYS
DEVICE=C:\WINDOWS\SETVER.EXE
```

The second CONFIG.SYS file is set up to use upper memory in order to effectively run a hypothetical memory-hogging DOS game called BigRAMhog.

```
DEVICE=C:\DOS\HIMEM.SYS
DEVICE=C:\DOS\EMM386.EXE NOEMS
DOS=HIGH,UMB
FILES=30
BUFFERS=30
DEVICEHIGH=C:\DOS\ANSI.SYS
DEVICE=C:\BIG\BIGRA.SYS
```

Once you combine the two files into one CONFIG.SYS file, you need to add titles in square brackets. A bracketed title must precede each section that was formerly a complete CONFIG.SYS file. These sections are called *blocks*. The result of joining the two files would be this:

```
[basicsetup]
FILES=30
BUFFERS=30
DEVICE=C:\DOS\ANSI.SYS
DEVICE=C:\WINDOWS\SETVER.EXE
[bigramsetup]
DEVICE=C:\DOS\HIMEM.SYS
DEVICE=C:\DOS\EMM386.EXE NOEMS
DOS=HIGH,UMB
FILES=30
BUFFERS=30
DEVICEHIGH=C:\DOS\ANSI.SYS
DEVICE=C:\BIG\BIGRA.SYS
```

Now, a *menu block* must be factored into the picture. This block of commands goes at the top of the Multiconfig file. Again, this is also created with a bracketed title, and this block will contain specific *menuitem* commands. The syntax of the menuitem command is this:

```
MENUITEM BlockName,[menutext]
```

Blockname refers to the bracketed name preceding the two configurations. *Menutext* is what will actually appear on the menu that is seen during bootup. After adding in these commands under the [menu] block title, here is what the CONFIG.SYS file looks like:

```
[menu]
menuitem basicsetup,Basic setup
menuitem bigramsetup,Bigramhog setup
[basicsetup]
FILES=30
BUFFERS=30
DEVICE=C:\DOS\ANSI.SYS
DEVICE=C:\WINDOWS\SETVER.EXE
[bigramsetup]
DEVICE=C:\DOS\HIMEM.SYS
DEVICE=C:\DOS\EMM386.EXE NOEMS
DOS=HIGH,UMB
FILES=30
BUFFERS=30
DEVICEHIGH=C:\DOS\ANSI.SYS
DEVICE=C:\BIG\BIGRA.SYS
```

NOTE
It is also important to create a common block at the end of the Multiconfig file (by adding the word *common* in brackets at the end of the CONFIG.SYS file, like this: **[common]**). This is important because installation programs will sometimes update your CONFIG.SYS file automatically, by tacking a command at the end of the file. Commands in the common block are automatically executed by all configurations. If the common block is missing, automatic updates to CONFIG.SYS will land at the end of last configuration block, and thus will take effect only if the last configuration block is selected. This is generally undesirable. Some software will edit existing lines in CONFIG.SYS when installed, and will do this with no awareness of Multiconfig. After automatic installations, it is wise to check to see if this has occurred. If it has, the changes will need to be manually made to any blocks that were not updated.

The next step is to assign a default configuration and a timeout specifying how long the system will wait until it boots into the default configuration. This can be accomplished with the *menudefault* command:

```
menudefault BlockName,[timeoutvalue]
```

The *timeoutvalue* specifies in seconds how long Multiconfig will wait for you to select one of the configurations. The menudefault command should be placed into the menu block in CONFIG.SYS. Suppose your primary interest in the computer is to play video games. To this end, you would want the default configuration to be *bigramsetup*. Type this in the menu block:

```
menudefault bigramsetup,5
```

CONFIG.SYS now appears like this:

```
[menu]
menuitem basicsetup,Basic setup
menuitem bigramsetup,Bigramhog setup
menudefault bigramsetup,5
[basicsetup]
FILES=30
BUFFERS=30
DEVICE=C:\DOS\ANSI.SYS
DEVICE=C:\WINDOWS\SETVER.EXE
[bigramsetup]
DEVICE=C:\DOS\HIMEM.SYS
DEVICE=C:\DOS\EMM386.EXE NOEMS
DOS=HIGH,UMB
FILES=30
BUFFERS=30
DEVICEHIGH=C:\DOS\ANSI.SYS
DEVICE=C:\BIG\BIGRA.SYS
[common]
```

Reboot the computer at this point and DOS will display the following:

```
MS-DOS 6 Startup Menu
=====================
1. Basic setup
2. Bigramhog setup
Enter a choice: 2      Time remaining: 5
```

The "Enter a choice" line contains a 2 because the menudefault command in CONFIG.SYS specifies that bigramsetup will be the default configuration. Pressing Enter at this point will automatically select the default configuration, and the processing of the Bigram-setup block in CONFIG.SYS will begin immediately. Hitting 1 and then Enter will select the Basic setup.

Meanwhile, the time remaining will count down to zero, and if nothing is pressed prior to this, the computer will begin processing the Bigramsetup block. If any number is pressed, DOS stops its countdown while waiting for the Enter key.

Another valuable command in Multiconfig is *Include*. Here's the syntax for it:

```
Include [blockname]
```

Include is especially useful in CONFIG.SYS files that contain numerous commands that are common to more than one configuration block. To use it, the common commands must be placed in a separate block, and the block must be given a name. The Include command is then invoked from within the other blocks.

In the example configuration, the following lines are common to both blocks:

```
FILES=30
BUFFERS=30
```

Revising the configuration with the Include command would produce the following results:

```
[menu]
menuitem basicsetup,Basic setup
menuitem bigramsetup,Bigramhog setup
menudefault bigramsetup,5
[all]
FILES=30
BUFFERS=30
DEVICEHIGH=C:\DOS\ANSI.SYS
[basicsetup]
INCLUDE all
DEVICE=C:\WINDOWS\SETVER.EXE
[bigramsetup]
INCLUDE all
DEVICE=C:\DOS\HIMEM.SYS
DEVICE=C:\DOS\EMM386.EXE NOEMS
DOS=HIGH,UMB
DEVICE=C:\BIG\BIGRA.SYS
[common]
```

Note here that the DEVICEHIGH command will load ANSI.SYS into conventional memory (below 640 KB) rather than upper memory if the basic setup is selected. This is because the basic setup does not contain the HIMEM.SYS and the EMM386.EXE drivers that it needs in order to utilize upper memory.

Bypassing CONFIG.SYS

Certain occasions of troubleshooting hardware or software malfunctions may necessitate using the *clean boot* feature of DOS. The way to perform a clean boot is to press the F5 key while your machine is booting up. Please note that the keystroke must occur *after* the message comes up that says:

```
Starting MS-DOS...
```

When you press F5 during the appropriate interval, a message informs you that DOS is booting without the CONFIG.SYS and AUTOEXEC.BAT files. The system will then use built-in default values in its revised minimal configuration. Memory management, for example, will not take place, and any customized PROMPT or PATH settings will be eliminated. A similar result may be obtained by pressing and holding down the Shift key instead of F5; if the Shift key is used, it must be held down until the bootup process is completed.

TIP   DoubleSpace, DOS's disk compression program, will load regardless of whether you bypass the configuration files by means of the F5 key. If you really want to bypass Double-Space, use Ctrl+F5 instead.

The typical scenario for problems that necessitate your using a clean boot is that some new hardware or software has just been installed and your computer fails to boot (or otherwise malfunctions) in the aftermath. The device driver for the new equipment may prove incompatible with your system or with another installed program or driver. If the computer successfully boots with the F5 option, this indicates the problem lies with a particular line in CONFIG.SYS or AUTOEXEC.BAT.

Another option during bootup is the F8 key, which will engage the interactive boot feature of DOS when pressed, like F5, as DOS is starting up. The F8 option is useful when you have already determined that a problem lies in CONFIG.SYS or AUTOEXEC.BAT but you must narrow it down to a particular line of text. In the earlier years of DOS, a troubleshooting technique used in this situation consisted of putting the REM command at the beginning of suspect lines in CONFIG.SYS or AUTOEXEC.BAT. The REM would classify that line as a "remark," thus rendering it non-executable. This method was time-consuming, however, as every reboot required further editing of CONFIG.SYS or AUTOEXEC.BAT. The interactive boot offered by the F8 option is far more efficient. When F8 is pressed during the interval between the "Starting MS-DOS" message and what would have been the next message, each command in the CONFIG.SYS file will be displayed one at a time during bootup, followed by a [Y, N]? query, as in the following example:

```
DEVICE=C:\HIMEM.SYS [Y,N]?
```

Here, DOS is requesting that you tell it whether you want this particular command to be processed or ignored. After you respond, it will bring up the next command in your CONFIG.SYS file. When you have answered Y or N to each query, another question will appear:

```
Process Autoexec.bat [Y,N]?
```

If you answer Y to this question, DOS will step you through the AUTOEXEC.BAT file in a similar manner. If you answer N, AUTOEXEC.BAT will not run at all.

Customizing DOS with the AUTOEXEC.BAT

A *batch file* is a file with a .BAT extension that contains other DOS commands. The power of a batch file is that by simply typing the name of the batch file and pressing Enter, DOS will process all of the batch file commands without need for any additional user input. Once created, a good batch file will save you time every time you use it. The batch file will also save you from lost time due to typos, and from having to look up commands for which you can't remember the correct syntax or the optional switches. Batch files are the subject of Chapter 7. In this section we will describe one batch file, the AUTOEXEC.BAT file, because of its special role in the startup and configuration of DOS-based system.

The power of the AUTOEXEC.BAT file is simply this; it runs every time you boot your computer. It is the last stage of the bootup process, and is automatically executed by COMMAND .COM before your C:> prompt appears.

There are certain programs and commands that are pertinent to your system configuration, and these are often most effective when placed in the AUTOEXEC.BAT file. A few of these programs and commands will be examined in the next several sections.

An example of an AUTOEXEC.BAT file is as follows:

```
@ECHO OFF
PATH C:\DOS\;C\WINDOWS;C:\UTILITY
PROMPT $P$g
cls
C:\DOS\SMARTDRV
MOUSE
```

The first line, @ECHO OFF, issues a command reversing a DOS default setting. By default, DOS will display, or "echo" on screen, every command that it processes. Normally, this happens when you type in the command. However, DOS will also display the commands as they run from a batch file, just as if you'd typed them in, which may amount to unwanted screen output. Turning off this echo with the ECHO OFF command will prevent DOS from doing this. The @ symbol acts as an ECHO OFF command, but affects only its own command line. Without the @ symbol, AUTOEXEC.BAT will actually display the command "ECHO OFF" before executing the command.

The CLS command in the fourth line is a directive to clear the screen of all text except the command prompt. The MOUSE command invokes the mouse driver. The other elements require a more detailed explanation, and will be discussed below.

Customizing the DOS Prompt Using the PROMPT Command

The PROMPT command is used to modify the appearance of the command line prompt, which usually appears as the C:\> for the hard drive or A:\> prompt for the floppy disk drive. In this case, the C: or A: refers to the current drive; the backslash refers the current directory, and both are followed by the > symbol. The command used to produce this prompt is PROMPT pg. In this command, the "p" directs DOS to include the current drive and path in the DOS prompt, and the "g" directs DOS to include the greater-than sign.

The syntax for the command is:

PROMPT $symbolcode$symbolcode

The symbol codes that can be used with the PROMPT command are given in Table 5.3. They can be used to display features like date and time within the DOS prompt, or to invoke more complex video alterations (like making the prompt flash on and off, or appear in a different color) by calling on the ANSI.SYS driver. The $ sign followed by a character is used to delineate a special code, summarized in Table 5.3.

Additionally, the PROMPT command can be used to place text onscreen instead of (or in addition to) using one PROMPT's special symbols. Type this line at the DOS prompt:

PROMPT Yeah?

Enter it, and your command line will henceforth display a little more personality:

Yeah?_

TABLE 5.3: Symbols for Use after "$" in the PROMPT Command

Symbol	Output in the Prompt
a	The & symbol
c	The (symbol
f	The) symbol
e	The Esc key, used to invoke ANSI.SYS
s	Blank space
p	Designates the current drive and path
g	The > symbol
n	Designates the current drive
d	Date
t	Time
v	The DOS version in use
l	The < symbol
b	The | symbol
q	The = sign
h	Backspace (deletes character left of cursor)
_	Underscore (moves cursor to next line)

Understanding the PATH Command

As mentioned earlier in the chapter, COMMAND.COM is the lucky agent who gets to do the dirty work when DOS is looking for a program. If COMMAND.COM does not locate the program in the current directory as a .COM, .EXE. or .BAT file, it will search along the current *path*. The current path on your system refers to the order in which COMMAND.COM searches specified subdirectories for programs typed in and entered at the command prompt. The current path can be ascertained by typing PATH without any parameters at the command line:

```
PATH
```

The current path, which is the output from the preceding command, may appear like this:

```
PATH C:\DOS;D:\
```

The path statement indicates to DOS that if COMMAND.COM is unable to find a requested program in the current directory, it will search the C:\DOS subdirectory and then the D:\ root directory in search of it. When failing to find a particular program along the path, it will display the message

```
Bad command or file name
```

The PATH command is used to view or modify the current path. The syntax for the command is as follows:

```
PATH d1:\path1;d2:\path2...
```

If your path statement is poorly configured, or if you have added programs that reside in their own separate subdirectories or disk partitions, or if you'd like to rename directories or move critical files to different locations, your path statement becomes very important. Understanding how it functions is dependent upon an understanding of how the DOS directory system works.

As an example, suppose your job entails frequent travel, and the necessity to download compressed files from your headquarters on a regular basis. You need to run your DOS decompression program, PKZIPW, which your company purchased for you and loaded into a

PKWARE subdirectory. When you boot up each morning, the computer displays the familiar C:\ prompt. One morning, a little sleepy, you forget to change to the PKWARE directory before you type PKZIPW. You are abruptly informed:

```
Bad command or file name
```

This occurs, of course, because DOS cannot process this command until you have switched to the PKWARE subdirectory:

```
CD\pkware
```

Instead of issuing this CD command before each downloading session, you could add the PKWARE subdirectory to your path statement, as follows:

```
PATH C:\dos;C:\pkware
```

From that point on, you can type PKZIPW and run the program without having to switch directories. Typically, the external commands for DOS will be found in the DOS subdirectory. It is logical, therefore, to make sure that the DOS subdirectory is included on the path.

The path can be eliminated completely by typing this:

```
PATH ;
```

In this case, DOS will produce the following message when the current path is next requested:

```
No Path
```

While you can use the PATH command to rewrite the entire current path, the APPEND command is the best way to simply modify the path. The syntax for APPEND is:

```
APPEND d1:\path1;d2:\path2... /x
```

The subdirectories included with the APPEND command will also be examined when DOS is looking for a program. The /x switch must be used for this command to work.

Using SMARTDRV.EXE to Cache Disk Reads and Writes

SMARTDRV.EXE is a disk-caching program that will almost always improve performance on a DOS-based system. A disk-caching program's job is to intercept data that is being read from disk. The program will store this data in RAM, in a place referred to as the *cache*. Often, the operating system or an application will make multiple calls for the same piece of data. Frequently, this data can be retrieved from the cache, suspending the need to access the hard drive, and thus taking advantage of the vastly superior speed of RAM memory.

Writes to disk can also be cached by most disk-caching programs. This works the same way, but in reverse. When a program calls for data to be written to disk, it is intercepted and stored in the cache for a specific interval of time, at the conclusion of which it will be written to disk.

The syntax for invoking the SMARTDRV command is:

```
[d:path]SMARTDRV.EXE [switches]
```

Software cache programs must be configured when the system is started. For this reason Smartdrive should be placed in the AUTOEXEC.BAT file. Alternatively, it can be placed in CONFIG.SYS with the following command:

```
DEVICE=[d:path]SMARTDRV.EXE [switches]
```

Options for SMARTDRV.EXE consist of the switches shown in Table 5.4.

TABLE 5.4: Switches for Use with SMARTDRV

Switch	Purpose
Device [+|-]	Enables or disables read/write caching.
InitCacheSize *WinCacheSize*	Defines cache size.
/C	Forces data in the write cache to be written to disk.
/F	Empties cache before returning to command prompt.
/L	Forces SMARTDRV to load itself in memory below 640 KB.
/N	Displays a command prompt without forcing cached data to disk.
/Q	Tells SMARTDRV to forego the display of status messages when loading.
/R	Restarts SMARTDRV after clearing cache.
/S	Displays status information on SMARTDRV's efficiency.
/U	Prevents CD-ROM caching portion of SMARTDRV from loading.
/V	Tells SMARTDRV to display status messages when loading.
/X	This default setting disables write-caching for all drives, and is countered by the d:+ parameter.
/E:*elementsize*	Minimum number of bytes SMARTDRV will process at once.
/B:*buffersize*	Number of bytes in read-ahead buffer.

The Device [+ I -] option overrides the SMARTDRV default setting, which is to cache read and write requests for hard disks, read requests fro151m floppy disks, and to overlook network drives completely. Multiple drives can be indicated here if they are separated by spaces. The plus sign tacked onto a drive will enable both read and write requests for that drive, while the minus sign will negate them. Adding the drive letter without the plus or minus sign will result in the caching of reads but disable write caching.

The *Initial Cache Size* (or *InitCacheSize* as it's listed in the table) is the amount of cache memory SMARTDRV reserves at the outset when running DOS. It is also the maximum size of the cache. *Windows Cache Size* (or *WinCacheSize*) describes the smallest cache that Windows must preserve for SMARTDRV if it chooses to allocate additional memory to its operations. This additional memory can actually be taken temporarily out of the cache reserved under InitCacheSize. This tends to make the cache fluctuate during operations. Upon exit from Windows, the cache is restored to its InitCacheSize value.

The default cache sizes, which are usually adequate, are shown in Table 5.5.

TABLE 5.5: DOS 6.22 Default Cache Sizes

Extended Memory		InitCacheSize	WinCacheSize
Up to 1 MB	All extended	Zero (no caching)	
Up to 2 MB	1 MB	256 KB	
Up to 4 MB	1 MB	512 KB	
Up to 6 MB	2 MB	1 MB	
6 MB or greater	2 MB	2 MB	

The size of the cache can be changed easily in the AUTOEXEC.BAT file. An example of this that will create a 1MB InitCacheSize and a 1MB WinCacheSize would be the one created by the following command:

```
C:\DOS\SMARTDRV 1024 1024
```

The /E:*elementsize* option determines the minimum number of bytes SMARTDRV will process at once. Although 8 KB is the default, smaller values may be entered.

/B:*buffersize* refers to the SMARTDRV buffer. The buffersize value, a multiple of the elementsize, is the number of bytes that will be placed into memory cache during disk reads. The default is 16 KB.

The /L option is irrelevant unless upper memory is enabled with EMM386.EXE. SMARTDRIVE loads into upper memory by default unless forced into low memory with the /L option.

The /S option is a useful tool that can be used to analyze the performance of SMARTDRV. Output from invoking SMARTDRV /S will look like Figure 5.3. This screen informs us that the cache size is 256 KB and remains 256 KB while running Windows. This indicates Windows is not requiring the use of cache for running applications. A *cache miss* indicates that the system did not find required data in the cache, which necessitated a disk read. A *cache hit* indicates a successful read from the cache. Figure 5.3 shows about a 75% rate of cache hits. This percentage could be increased by increasing the WinCacheSize, which at 256 KB is set below its default and may be too low for optimum performance on this system.

FIGURE 5.3:

Output from the SMARTDRV /S command in DOS 6.22

```
Room for    32 elements of   8,192 bytes each
There have been   1,643 cache hits
     and    498 cache misses

Cache size:   262,144 bytes
Cache size while running Windows:   262,144 bytes


              Disk Caching Status
drive   read cache   write cache   buffering
-------------------------------------------
  A:       yes          no           no
  B:       yes          no           no
  C:       yes          yes          no
  D:       yes          yes          no
Write behind data will be committed before command prompt returns.
```

TIP

If the drives displayed by SMARTDRV /S all read "No" under the "Buffering" column, be sure your CONFIG.SYS file does not contain the /DOUBLEBUFFER option following a SMART-DRV invocation. The double buffering may be necessary on some older equipment, but if so, the SMARTDRV /S option will reveal that by displaying a least one yes in the buffering column.

Review Questions for Chapter 5, DOS Startup and Configuration

Answers to the Review Questions may be found in Appendix A.

1. Place the following MS-DOS files in order by placing a number next to them to indicate their loading order (i.e., 1=first, 2=second, and so on).

   _____ MSDOS.SYS

   _____ CONFIG.SYS

   _____ IO.SYS

   _____ AUTOEXEC.BAT

   _____ COMMAND.COM

2. If SMARTDRV.EXE is used, which CONFIG.SYS parameter's value should be reduced?

   A. FILES=20

   B. CACHE=10

   C. BUFFERS=50

   D. SMARTDRV=10

3. The PATH environment variable specifies what kind of directories?

   A. directories that DOS uses

   B. directories that COMMAND.COM searches to find programs to run

   C. directories that COMMAND.COM searches to find files

   D. directories that DOS searches to find files

4. Which memory driver controls access to the High Memory Area (HMA)?

   A. HIMEM.SYS

   B. EMM386.EXE

   C. SMARTDRV.EXE

   D. MEM.EXE

5. Which DOS components can be used for caching?

   A. BUFFERS=

   B. CACHE=

   C. SMARTDRIVE

   D. SMARTDRV

6. Name the three files that MS-DOS requires in order to boot.

   _____

   _____

   _____

7. Name the three files that PC-DOS requires in order to boot.

   _____

   _____

   _____

8. Which command replaces the "DEVICE=" command in the CONFIG.SYS, but performs the same function and adds the ability to load drivers into free UMBs?

   A. LOADUMB=

   B. DEVICEUMB=

   C. LOADHIGH=

   D. DEVICEHIGH=

9. Which MS-DOS file must be loaded in order for the AUTOEXEC
   .BAT to execute?

   A. MSDOS.SYS

   B. COMMAND.COM

   C. IO.SYS

   D. IBMBIO.COM

10. Which MS-DOS command controls the appearance of the
    MS-DOS command prompt?

    A. CSET

    B. DOSPROMPT

    C. PROMPT

    D. CONFIG.SYS

11. Which CONFIG.SYS area (in a multiconfig setup) contains
    commands that execute regardless of the menu option chosen?

    A. :ALL

    B. [ALL]

    C. :COMMON

    D. [COMMON]

12. Which CONFIG.SYS loads device drivers into memory?

    A. DEVICE=

    B. LOAD=

    C. START=

    D. DOS=

13. Which type of DOS command is contained within COMMAND
.COM?

    A. .EXE

    B. Internal

    C. External

    D. .COM

14. What DOS utility is used for disk compression?

    A. DRVSPACE

    B. DISKSPACE

    C. DUBDRIVE

    D. DoubleSpace

15. Which of the following is *not* an internal DOS command?

    A. CLS

    B. COPY

    C. MORE

    D. PAUSE

16. Which DOS system file(s) must be loaded in order for the
CONFIG.SYS to be executed?

    A. IO.SYS

    B. MSDOS.SYS

    C. COMMAND.COM

    D. MSDOS.COM

17. You are troubleshooting a computer that is having CD-ROM read problems. You look on the CD-ROM manufacturers web site and discover that the driver has an incompatibility with SMARTDRV. The customer requires SMARTDRV for use with their proprietary program. What do you do?

   A. Inform the customer they will need to buy a new CD-ROM, one that is compatible with SMARTDRV.

   B. Disable CD-ROM caching at the SMARTDRV command line with the /U switch.

   C. Disable CD-ROM caching at the SMARTDRV command line with the /CD switch.

   D. Disable CD-ROM caching at the SMARTDRV command line with the /Q switch.

18. You want to change the DOS prompt to look like

   `C:\=`

   What prompt command do you place in the AUTOEXEC.BAT?

   A. PROMPT=PE

   B. PROMPT=PV

   C. PROMPT=PQ

   D. PROMPT=PS

19. Which key(s) can be pressed at the appearance of the message "Starting MS-DOS…," and will bypass the CONFIG.SYS and AUTOEXEC.BAT, preventing them from being executed?

   A. F5

   B. Ctrl

   C. Esc

   D. Shift

20. Suppose you have a Token Ring network adapter card installed in a computer. The computer keeps locking up on boot-up. It usually does this right after the phrase "HIMEM.SYS is testing Extended Memory." Since your computer uses Expanded memory, you conclude that the problem is that there were no memory range exclusions on the EMM386.EXE command line for the Token Ring card's ROMs. How would you modify the DEVICE=EMM386.EXE line in the CONFIG.SYS?

   A. Add the line I=<*Memory Range*> after EMM386.EXE on the same line.

   B. Add the line X=<*Memory Range*> after EMM386.EXE on the same line.

   C. Add the line NOEMS after EMM386.EXE on the same line.

   D. Add the line ROM=<*Memory Range*> after EMM386.EXE on the same line.

21. Which MS-DOS Startup Menu command determines which menu option will be chosen automatically after a timeout period?

   A. Menutimeout

   B. Menuoption

   C. Menudefault

   D. Menuchoice

22. Which key(s) can be pressed at the appearance of the message "Starting MS-DOS...," and will allow you to "step through" the CONFIG.SYS and AUTOEXEC.BAT, allowing commands or preventing them at each step at your discretion?

   A. F2

   B. F3

   C. F5

   D. F8

23. Which is the proper way to indicate CONFIG.SYS sections for use with the MS-DOS Startup Menu?

   A. :*<Section Name>*:

   B. [*<Section Name>*]

   C. :*<Section Name>*

   D. [*<Section Name>*

24. Which DOS system file is responsible for processing the CONFIG.SYS?

   A. IO.SYS

   B. MSDOS.SYS

   C. COMMAND.COM

   D. AUTOEXEC.BAT

25. Which kind of DOS command is TIME in MS-DOS?

   A. Internal

   B. External

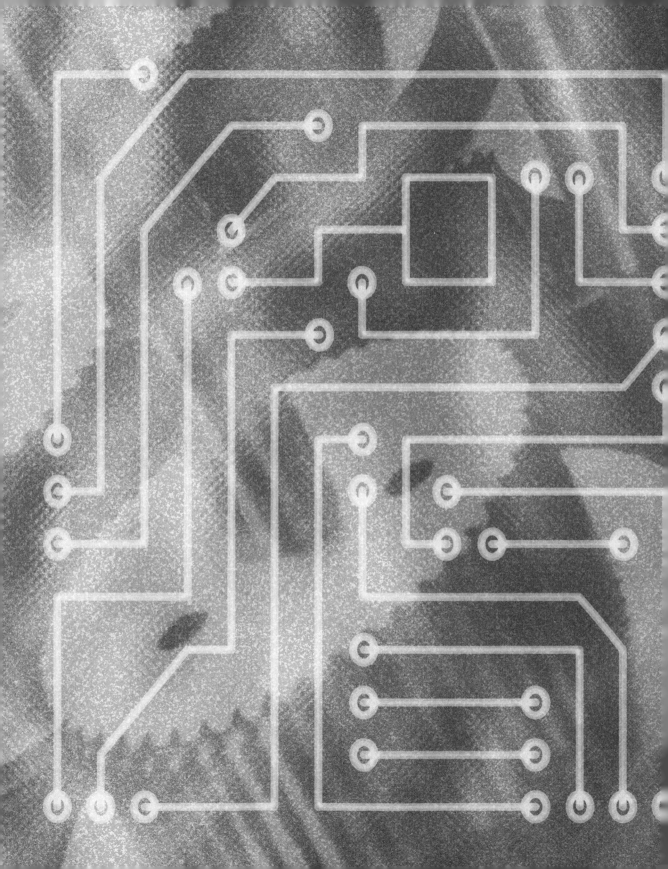

CHAPTER
SIX

Basic DOS Commands

- Ten Essential Commands for MS-DOS 6.22

- MS-DOS Commands vs. PC-DOS Commands

The successful navigation of MS-DOS or PC-DOS requires a basic level of familiarity with their most common commands. It is the purpose of this chapter to teach you those commands. Learning how to use the commands described here will provide you with a measure of control that is necessary to fully utilize the DOS information you have already read about in the preceding chapters.

- Ten Essential Commands for MS-DOS 6.22
- MS-DOS Commands vs. PC-DOS Commands

Ten Essential Commands for MS-DOS 6.22

Commands are either internal or external. *Internal* commands are contained within COMMAND.COM. *External* commands will have a corresponding .EXE or .COM file usually located in the C:\DOS or C:\WINDOWS directory. Typing the command and then pressing Enter will run the file and thus invoke the command. An external command will not execute unless one of the following conditions if true:

- You are issuing the command from within the directory where the command resides.
- *Or,* your system's PATH statement includes the directory where the command resides.

The more versatile commands described in this section will include table listings containing the optional switches for a command. The switches must be used according to a fixed command structure. In previous chapters you have seen examples of the syntax for DOS commands, such as this:

```
DEVICE=[d:\path]filename [switches]
```

There are three parts to the preceding command: the *command*, its *parameters*, and its *switches*:

1. The command itself is DEVICE=.

2. The parameters for the command are [*d:\path*] *filename*. A command's parameters usually specify where the command will take place.

3. The fairly extensive list of switches, usually represented by */n*, are simply summarized as [*switches*]. Switches resolve the question of how a command will be executed or what special features will be invoked.

Bracketed sections of a command's syntax indicate that it is a non-essential feature of the command and can be left out in many circumstances. The DEVICE= command above, for example, does not need the drive and path if the filename is contained along the current system path. The current system path can be ascertained by typing **PATH** at the DOS prompt. It is important to note that the switches are bracketed, which means they are optional. Except in cases where switches contradict each other, they can be used in combination.

DIR and Wildcards

DIR, which stands for *directory*, is an internal command contained within COMMAND.COM. The DIR command is the principal means by which you can list the contents of your computer's storage media, be it hard disk, floppy disk, or CD ROM. You will use DIR to find the names and relative locations of files or subdirectories you need to access. Additionally, you can use it to gather information such as how much space each file occupies and how much space is available on a specified drive.

To examine the contents of your current directory, simply type **DIR** at a command line. This will produce a list of files and directories for whatever directory the command prompt belongs to. The output is preceded by a header such as the following:

```
Volume in drive C is C_DRIVE
Volume Serial Number is 2280-0DE1
Directory of C:\MSOFFICE
```

TIP

The last line of the DIR header tells us we are in the MSOFFICE directory. If someone has modified the command prompt so that it no longer displays the current directory (this can be done via the PROMPT command), then this element of DIR output can be quite useful.

The syntax for the DIR command is as follows:

```
DIR [d:path][filename] [switches]
```

A sample of file and directory output following the DIR header information is shown in Figure 6.1.

Standard DIR output contains the following information in a six-column display:

1. Column 1 shows the name of the file or subdirectory. The filename will include its three digit extension.

2. Column 2 indicates whether the name stands for a subdirectory. (If it does, it displays the indicator <DIR>.)

3. Column 3 shows the size of a file in bytes.

4. Column 4 shows the date the file was last modified.

5. Column 5 shows the time of day the file was last modified.

6. Column 6 shows the name of the file or directory again, but this time it shows the *full* filename for any file that uses the "long filenames" convention. (To compare, Column 1 shows only the conventional "eight-dot-three" version of the filename.)

FIGURE 6.1:

Sample output of
a DOS 6.22 DIR
command

```
Volume in drive C has no label
Volume Serial Number is 228D-0DE1
Directory of C:\MSOFFICE

.               <DIR>         04-13-97   2:44a .
..              <DIR>         04-13-97   2:44a ..
ACCESS          <DIR>         04-13-97   2:44a ACCESS
CLIPART         <DIR>         04-13-97   2:52a CLIPART
EXCEL           <DIR>         04-13-97   2:44a EXCEL
MS-BTTNS        <DIR>         04-13-97   2:44a MS-BTTNS
MSOFFCUE HLP        139,136   04-05-94  12:00a MSOFFCUE.HLP
MSOFFICE EXE        193,600   04-05-94  12:00a MSOFFICE.EXE
MSOFFICE HLP        237,533   04-05-94  12:00a MSOFFICE.HLP
MSOFFWEL HLP         10,890   04-05-94  12:00a MSOFFWEL.HLP
OFREADME HLP         16,944   04-05-94  12:00a OFREADME.HLP
OHELP    DLL          7,664   04-05-94  12:00a OHELP.DLL
POWERPNT        <DIR>         04-13-97   2:44a POWERPNT
PSSINFO  HLP         22,509   04-05-94  12:00a PSSINFO.HLP
SETUP           <DIR>         04-13-97   2:44a SETUP
WINWORD         <DIR>         04-13-97   2:45a WINWORD
           7 file(s)       628,276 bytes
           9 dir(s)     18,202,624 bytes free
```

The footer at the bottom of Figure 6.1 shows the total amount of space used by the files in this directory.

DIR can also be used to locate specific files. When you're at a prompt for the root directory, type the following:

```
DIR AUTOEXEC.BAT
```

The resulting directory listing will contain only the AUTOEXEC.BAT file. This feature becomes still more useful when *wildcard characters*— either a single asterisk (*) or several questionmarks (?)—are used in place of letters or words. For example, you can type an asterisk to signify that you are looking for any number of characters between that point in the filename and the period (or, to techies, the "dot" or "dot separator"). Suppose you want to know what .EXE programs are contained in a directory. You can elicit this information from DOS by typing

```
DIR *.EXE
```

Press Enter and all files with a .EXE extension in the current directory will be listed. Searching for files in this manner can be useful when you need to launch an application program but can't remember how to spell the command that launches it. This command will be the name of a file with a .COM, .EXE, or—not as commonly—a .BAT extension. Therefore, searching for a file in a directory by typing DIR *.COM or DIR *.EXE is a fast means of locating the command you need to type in to start the program.

You can be more precise about which filenames you'd like to have DIR list for you through the use of the command's switches (listed in Table 6.1). You can also use one or more questionmark (?) wildcards with the DIR command if you can identify exactly which position in the filename you'll allow the search to operate on. The questionmark and asterisk wildcards are explained further in the sidebar on the next page.

TABLE 6.1: Using Switches with the DIR Command

Switch	Purpose
/P	*Pauses* the screen display so that a large directory can be viewed before it scrolls off the page.
/W	Displays a directory in *wide* format, five columns wide, and excludes detailed information such as file size and date last modified.
/A:*attrib*	Displays files according to their *attributes.* Using /A with no attribute will display all files, including hidden files. Attributes that can be used are *a, d, h, r,* and *s.*
	a is used to display files that have been altered since the last time the directory was backed up. (You may also hear this described as setting the archive bit to on.) *d* displays subdirectories. *h* displays hidden files. *r* displays read-only files. *s* displays system files.
	Preceding an attribute with a hyphen or a minus sign will suppress the display of files with the chosen attribute.

TABLE 6.1 CONTINUED: Using Switches with the DIR Command

Switch	Purpose
/O:*sort*	Sorts the files in specified *order* upon display. Sort options include the following: *c* sorts by compression ratio. *d* sorts by date and time. *e* sorts alphabetically by extension. *g* prioritizes (groups) directories before files. *n* sorts alphabetically by filename. Sort order can be reversed if the sort option letter is preceded by a hyphen or a minus sign.
/S	Searches *subdirectories* in addition to current directory.
/B	Incorporates file extension into displayed filename. (Also referred to as *bare* format, because no date, size, etc. are displayed.)
/L	Uses *lowercase* letters for directory display.
/C	Can be used only if DoubleSpace is running. This switch sorts by *compression* ratio, lowest to highest. (Will sort from highest to lowest if preceded by a hyphen or a minus sign.)

The Way Wildcards Work

Wildcards work very well when you want to do a particular operation with several files at once. They can be used to greatly reduce the amount of typing. However, there is one special case with the "*" wildcard that deserves particular attention.

When you want to show a listing of all the filenames of text files that end in "OCT" for example, you would think that you could type something like this:

```
DIR *OCT.TXT
```

continued on next page

In fact, what you get with this command is a listing of every text file, not just the ones that end in "OCT." This is because of the way the "*" wildcard is treated by most commands. This command is interpreted as "anything from this point on to the period." When the DIR command sees the "*OCT," it *ignores the characters following the asterisk,* because they are part of the "anything from this point to the period."

The opposite does work, however. If you wanted to find all the files that begin with "OCT," you could do that by typing:

```
DIR OCT*.TXT
```

and you would get a listing of all the files that start with "OCT."

To work around this, use questionmarks to replace anything to the left of "OCT," like so:

```
DIR ?????OCT.TXT
```

You must use the same number of question marks as there are letters in the filename. For example, the above command wouldn't find "NOCT.TXT" because the first part of the name doesn't contain eight characters. You would have to do this command once for each number of characters in a potential filename, like so:

```
DIR ?OCT.TXT
DIR ??OCT.TXT
DIR ???OCT.TXT
DIR ????OCT.TXT
DIR ?????OCT.TXT
```

Two of the switches in Table 6.1 warrant special attention because they are so frequently used. They are the /P and /W switches. By default, the DIR command produces directory listings with a great deal of information, which is not always needed. To obtain a succinct listing of the filenames without any extra information, type this:

```
DIR /W
```

Figure 6.2 shows output from this command.

FIGURE 6.2:

DOS 6.22 output of DIR /W

```
[ACCESS]        [ACROREAD]    [ADS]         [AOL30]        [AOL30A]
[AOL30B]        [ARCADE]      [AUDRACK]     AUTOEXEC.DOS   AUTOEXEC.BAT
[A_MATE~1]      [BAD]         [BIN]         [COLLWIN]      COMMAND.DOS
COMMAND.COM     [COMPRESS]    CONFIG.DOS    CONFIG.ALL     CONFIG.OLD
CONFIG.ALT      CONFIG.WIN    CONFIG.SYS    [CRIDE]        [DIAGS]
[DOS]           DOSEDIT.COM   EXPERI~1      [FILES]        [GAMES]
[GRAPHICS]      [GWSWIN]      [LIB]         LOGFILE.TXT    MCD.BAT
[MK'SDOCS]      [MOUSE]       [MSOFFICE]    [NC4]          NETLOG.TXT
[NEWSUB]        [PKWARE]      [PROGRA~1]    SCANDISK.LOG   SHORTC~1.PIF
[STEREO]        [TEMP]        TEST.BAT      [TMP]          [USER0000]
[UTILITY]       [VLPROD]      [WEP]         [WINDOWS]      [WINPROJ]
```

Notice there is no information pertaining to the size of specific files or the date or time that files were last modified; notice also that the files and directories are displayed side by side in several columns. (Subdirectories are now indicated by brackets.) DIR /W is an extremely useful command when displaying extensive directories, because it shows a much larger number of files on one screen.

An extensive directory listing is practically impossible to read because it scrolls so quickly off the screen after the DIR command is issued. If you want to take a little longer to read the listing than your computer allows, you can use the /P switch, which will cause the display to *pause* when the screen is filled up. A message at the bottom of the display says,

```
Press any key to continue...
```

When you press a key, the screen will be filled with another screen's worth of the listing (followed by the same prompt for a keystroke if there are still more files to appear). The /W and /P switches can also be used effectively in combination.

TIP

It is easy to change the *default* DIR command display by setting what is known as an *environmental variable* (DIRCMD in this case). To do this place the following line in your AUTOEXEC.BAT file: **SET DIRCMD= /o:n /p**. Notice that these switches are standard DIR switches. The original default sorting order for the DIR command is by modification date; the new default DIR command that this DIRCMD environmental variable will implement will use the /on switch to sort files by filename instead. In addition to this change to the sorting order, the /p switch will pause the display before any lengthy directory listing scrolls off the screen.

CD

The CD or CHDIR internal command is used to change the current or default directory. The default directory is the answer DOS would give to the question, "Where am I?" if you were to ask it that question. Since DOS generally applies typed-in commands to the default directory unless you tell it otherwise, you'll have to make sure you're at the correct directory before you issue your DOS commands. The CD command is the primary means for getting there, as it enables you to move around in the hierarchy of directories that DOS maintains.

DOS reminds you what directory you're in by displaying the default directory in the DOS prompt. For example, the prompt you will generally see when you're in the *root directory* is simply

    C:\>

(or something very similar). The drive letter is generally separated from the rest of the prompt by a colon; next to the colon is the name of the directory you're in (in this case, it's the root directory, represented by the backslash); and the angle bracket is the actual prompt.

If you were in a *subdirectory* of the root directory, that subdirectory will appear between the root directory's backslash and the angle bracket:

C:\WINDOWS>

Terminology: Roots and Subdirectories

The main DOS directory, or root directory, ultimately contains all other subdirectories and is represented by the drive letter and a backslash (for example, C:\). The term "root directory" is somewhat misleading, because a hierarchical system usually depicts its foremost or all-encompassing member at the top of the hierarchy, and *root* would imply it resides at the bottom.

In regard to all directories apart from the root directory, the terms "directory" and "subdirectory" are interchangeable. It is, however, more meaningful to refer to a directory as a subdirectory when it is described in relationship to other directories.

NOTE   The DOS prompt can be customized to show more than just the name of the current directory. For instance, the prompt may include the time and date. (On the other hand, it can also be customized to *leave off* the name of the current directory.) For this reason, it's possible that the DOS prompt you see on your machine will display something slightly different than the examples you're seeing here. (The command for changing the appearance of the DOS prompt is the PROMPT command. It is not generally necessary to what most people will be doing with DOS, so we won't be discussing it in this chapter.)

The syntax for CD is:

```
CD [[d:]path]
```

The *path* is the list of directories and subdirectories between the current directory and the one you want to change to. Thus, to move to a subdirectory of your current directory, all you have to type is **CD** followed by the name of the subdirectory. To move to a subdirectory of a directory you're *not* currently in, however, you have to tell DOS where to start from. (In many cases, you'll have to type in the path starting from the root directory; in those cases, therefore, don't forget to begin your path with a backslash.)

TIP   To move to a directory via a path that starts from the root directory of any drive, you have to remember to type the backslash that signifies the root directory. To move to a subdirectory of a directory you're already in, you have to leave off the backslash that signifies the root directory.

For example, to find the Templates subdirectory residing in the Word subdirectory in the Windows subdirectory, you would need to issue the following CD command:

```
CD \WINDOWS\WORD\TEMPLATES
```

If you were already in the Windows directory, however, you would only have to issue the following version:

```
CD WORD\TEMPLATES
```

After pressing Enter, the DOS prompt again reflects your altered default directory:

```
C:\WINDOWS\WORD\TEMPLATES>
```

Sometimes, all you want to do is move upward one level in the directory structure. To avoid the task of typing the path to that directory starting from the root, you can take advantage of DOS's "two-dot shortcut," as shown here:

```
CD ..
```

For example, if you entered that simple command from the Windows\Word\Templates directory mentioned above, you would end up at the Windows\Word directory. If you wanted instead to move to a "sister" directory of your parent directory, you could enter that subdirectory after the parent dots. For example, you could move to the Windows\Word\Help directory from the Windows\Word\Templates directory with the following command:

```
CD ..\HELP
```

DOS will remember what directory is current on your other drives, so if you simply issue **CD A:** or **CD D:**, then DOS will know to go to whatever directory you last used on those drives. Actually, most people only ever use the root drive on a floppy, so this doesn't save very many keystrokes, but for other media (like a CD-ROM drive or a tape drive), DOS's memory of current directories can be quite useful.

NOTE The CD command can be dropped when switching drives. For example, you can simply type **A:** (instead of **CD A:**) at a command prompt to make the A drive current. Similarly, typing **C:** when you're at another drive's DOS prompt will make the C drive current.

MD

The MD or MKDIR command stands for *make directory*; this is the DOS command used to create new directories. MD is an internal command contained within COMMAND.COM. This command, though easily mastered, is important to grasp. It is a basic DOS file and directory management tool.

The syntax for the MD command is:

```
MD [d:\path] directoryname
```

If the drive and path are not included, the directory will be created in the current directory. For example, if you are in the C:\Utilities directory, and you type:

```
MD SCRNSV
```

then a directory named Scrnsv will appear within the Utilities directory.

If you wish to create a directory on a drive or directory other than the current directory, then you must include the path in the command. For example, to create a Files directory in the Windows\Word subdirectory, type this:

```
MD C:\WINDOWS\WORD\FILES
```

Creating a Files directory in the root directory of a floppy disk is equally simple:

```
MD A:\FILES
```

NOTE The RD or RMDIR command stands for *remove directory*. RD is used in exactly the same way as MD, except it produces the opposite effect and will delete a directory from disk. RD cannot be used to delete *files*, however, which means that the directory must be empty before RD can remove it. Files within a directory must be erased using the ERASE (or DEL) command before the RD command can be used to delete the directory. (If you want to delete all the files and subdirectories in a directory all at once, use the DELTREE external command.)

ATTRIB

The ATTRIB command is used to alter a file's *attributes*. Attributes determine whether a file is an archive, hidden, read-only, or system file. ATTRIB is an external command. The symbols for the four attributes are as follows:

A = Archive

H = Hidden

R = Read-only

S = System

The archive bit is used to mark files that have been modified since they were last backed up. This is significant when performing incremental backups.

Hidden files will not appear in directory listings and cannot be deleted.

Read-only files can be viewed but not modified. (Nor can they be deleted without first changing the read-only attribute).

The system attribute marks a file as part of the operating system. It will also prevent the file from deletion. If the system attribute is set, the other attributes cannot be cleared out—that is, until the system bit is also cleared. For example, if you wish to edit MSDOS.SYS by first clearing its read-only attribute, you must also clear its system attribute, or nothing will happen and a message will come up:

```
Not resetting system file filename
```

The syntax for ATTRIB is:

```
ATTRIB [+attribute|-attribute][[d:\path]filename][/S]
```

The +*attribute* or -*attribute* is ATTRIB's method of assigning or clearing an attribute. To make a file named DOC1 a read-only file, type this:

```
ATTRIB +r doc1
```

To simply check whether an attribute has been assigned to a file, enter the command without any attributes:

```
ATTRIB doc1
```

DOS will then display the attribute settings for the DOC1 file. Typing ATTRIB without parameters *and* without a filename will display the attribute status for all the files in the current directory. This will even display hidden files, and as such, is a little faster than using DIR /a:h. The command DIR /a:h, however, restricts its output to hidden files only, which may be more useful for you, since its relative brevity may make it less difficult to read. A sample of output from typing ATTRIB is shown in Figure 6.3.

FIGURE 6.3:

Output from ATTRIB
without parameters

```
      SHR     IO.DOS          C:\IO.DOS
      SHR     MSDOS.DOS       C:\MSDOS.DOS
       R      COMMAND.DOS     C:\COMMAND.DOS
  A           COMMAND.COM     C:\COMMAND.COM
  A           CONFIG.OLD      C:\CONFIG.OLD
  A           AUTOEXEC.OLD    C:\AUTOEXEC.OLD
  A           CONFIG.DOS      C:\CONFIG.DOS
  A           AUTOEXEC.SYD    C:\AUTOEXEC.SYD
  A    H      BOOTLOG.PRV     C:\BOOTLOG.PRV
  A           AUTOEXEC.DOS    C:\AUTOEXEC.DOS
  A           SCANDISK.LOG    C:\SCANDISK.LOG
  A    H      BOOTLOG.TXT     C:\BOOTLOG.TXT
  A           AUTOEXEC.BAT    C:\AUTOEXEC.BAT
  A           CONFIG.SYS      C:\CONFIG.SYS
       H      MSDOS.---       C:\MSDOS.---
  A    H      SETUPLOG.TXT    C:\SETUPLOG.TXT
      HR      SUHDLOG.DAT     C:\SUHDLOG.DAT
      SHR     MSDOS.SYS       C:\MSDOS.SYS
  A   SH      DETLOG.TXT      C:\DETLOG.TXT
  A           NETLOG.TXT      C:\NETLOG.TXT
      HR      W95UNDO.DAT     C:\W95UNDO.DAT
      HR      W95UNDO.INI     C:\W95UNDO.INI
      SH      DETLOG.OLD      C:\DETLOG.OLD
      SHR     SYSTEM.1ST      C:\SYSTEM.1ST
      SHR     IO.SYS          C:\IO.SYS
  A           F0603.TXT       C:\f0603.txt
```

Multiple attributes can be set or cleared simultaneously on the same command line. For example:

```
ATTRIB -r -h doc1
```

Wildcard characters can also be used in filenames. For example, to remove the hidden file status from every file in the C:\Word\Files directory, type this:

```
ATTRIB -h C:\WORD\FILES\*.*
```

TIP   The /S switch can be used with ATTRIB to include subdirectory files in the processing of the command.

COPY

The COPY command is an internal DOS command which is used to copy files. This command is able to copy multiple files, rename files, copy files onto other drives or directories, merge files, and even send copies to the console (CON) or printer. The syntax for COPY is:

```
COPY [d:\path]SOURCE FILENAME [d:\path][DESTINATION
FILENAME][switches]
```

If the source file is located in the current directory there is no need to include the source file's path in the command. To copy the Janbudg file to the C:\Word\Budgets directory, type:

```
COPY janbudg C:\WORD\BUDGETS
```

DOS will inform you that the file has been successfully copied:

```
1 file(s) copied
```

To change the name of the Janbudg file to Janbu96 while copying it, enter this command:

```
COPY janbudg C:\WORD\BUDGETS\janbu96
```

Copying the file DOC1 from your floppy disk to the Files directory on your hard drive is accomplished like this:

```
COPY A:\DOC1 C:\WORD\FILES
```

Wildcard characters may be used to specify groups of files to be copied, such as using *.txt in place of the source filename.

The screen or a printer can also be used in place of a destination filename. To copy a file to the screen use CON (for console) as the destination; use PRN to copy a file to the printer. CON can also actually be used in place of the source filename. This will initiate the transmission of text that you're typing at your keyboard directly to a destination file. The transmission will not end until Ctrl+Z is pressed.

Table 6.2 shows the switches that may be employed in conjunction with the COPY command.

TABLE 6.2 Using COPY with Switches

Switch	Purpose
/A	Used to mark the file as an *ASCII* file. Does not copy end-of-file notation; but it does place an end-of-file notation at the end of the destination file.
/B	Used to mark the file as a *binary* file. Copies end-of-file notations into destination file.
/V	*Verifies* that the copied file is identical to its source file.
/Y	Instructs COPY to overwrite existing files bearing the same name without requesting confirmation.
/-Y	Suspends the environmental variable SET COPYCMD=/Y.

You can merge a pair of ASCII text files by using the following format with the /A switch:

```
COPY fileA + fileB /A fileC
```

By default COPY displays the following message before it overwrites identically named files in the destination directory:

Overwrite *d:\path\DESTINATION FILENAME* (Yes/No/All?)

Answering Y, N, or A will produce the desired result. The /Y switch, which reverses the default COPY setting, instructs COPY to overwrite files without displaying this warning. The /Y switch can be made permanent by using the SET COPYCMD=/Y command.

XCOPY

XCOPY is similar to the copy command but is used to copy entire subdirectories or the entire contents of disk. This latter function is especially useful for copying floppy disks. XCOPY is an external DOS command.

The syntax for XCOPY is:

XCOPY *source* [*destination*] [/A|/M] [/D:*date*] [/P] [/E] [/V] [/W]

For example, to copy the C:\Documents directory from the hard disk to a floppy disk in drive A, type:

XCOPY C:\DOCUMENTS A:

Use the following command to copy the contents of a disk in drive A to the C:\Word\Templates directory on drive C:

XCOPY a: c:\WORD\TEMPLATES

NOTE   Before XCOPY overwrites identically named files, it will display a prompt requesting confirmation.

Table 6.3 shows the switches that can be used in combination with the XCOPY command.

TABLE 6.3: Using XCOPY with Switches

Switches	Purpose
/A	Copies only files whose *archive* attribute is on.
/E	Used in combination with /S switch. Copies directories even if the directory is *empty* (i.e., contains no files).
/M	Copies only files whose archive attribute is on (indicating that the file has been *modified* since the last backup); turns off the archive attribute while copying.
/D:*date*	Copies files created or modified after the specified *date*.
/P	*Prompts* you to confirm the creation of each destination file.
/S	Includes copying of all *subdirectories*.
/V	*Verifies* that each copied file is identical to its source file.
/W	*Waits* for you to respond to a prompt that requests confirmation before copying.
/Y	Instructs XCOPY to overwrite existing files bearing the same name, without requesting confirmation.
/-Y	Suspends the environmental variable SET COPYCMD=/Y.

The SET COPYCMD environmental variable affects the use of XCOPY. Any of the switches from Table 6.3 can be used according to this format:

```
SET COPYCMD= [switches]
```

Placing the preceding line in your AUTOEXEC.BAT file will ensure that any of the switches you've specified there will be in effect as the new default settings for your use of XCOPY.

RENAME

The RENAME or REN command is an internal command used to change the name of a file. RENAME is similar in form to the COPY command. Its syntax is as follows:

`RENAME [d:\path]oldfilename newfilename`

Notice that the drive and path are not included in the syntax for the new filename. This is indicative of the fact that RENAME cannot be used to move a file to another directory. The renamed file will be in the same directory as the original file.

If the new filename is identical to another file in the same directory an error message will be displayed after typing the command and pressing Enter.

Changing a file in the Files directory from Novskej to Decskej would be accomplished in this manner:

`REN C:\WORD\FILES\NOVSKEJ DECSKEJ`

Wildcard characters may be used with REN to rename multiple files. This feature works best when used to change the three-digit filename extensions, as when a program prefers its files to have special extensions. Word, for example, likes its files to have .DOC extensions. The following example will rename all .TXT files with .P65 extensions:

`REN *.TXT *.P65`

DEL

DEL is an internal command contained within COMMAND.COM. (ERASE can be used in its place to accomplish the same purpose.) DEL is used to delete files from a disk. The syntax for DEL is as follows:

`DEL [d:path]filename [/P]`

or

```
DEL d:path | directoryname
```

If the path is not specified, DEL will delete the file only if it resides in the current directory. For example, to delete DOC1 from the current directory, type this:

```
DEL DOC1
```

Enter the following command to delete the Janbud file from the Files directory on the floppy disk:

```
DEL A:\FILES\JANBUD
```

To quickly delete all files within the Word directory, use this command:

```
DEL C:\WINDOWS\WORD
```

Before deleting all the files in the Word directory, DOS will prompt you, giving you a last chance to change your mind:

```
All files in directory will be deleted!
Are you sure? (Yes/No?)
```

TIP If you accidentally delete files, you may be able to use the UNDELETE command to try to recover them. This works best if you haven't written to the disk between the time the file was deleted and the moment you try the UNDELETE command. The more disk writes that have been performed in this period, the lower the chance that you will be able to recover the deleted file (because each disk write runs the risk of writing over part of the file you want to recover). The syntax of this command is UNDELETE [*d:path*] *filename*.

Wildcard characters can also be used to delete files. For example, the following command will delete all .DOC files in the Word directory:

```
DEL C:\WINDOWS\WORD\*.DOC
```

Files that have their system, hidden, or read-only attribute set are protected from deletion. Before you can delete such files, you must first use the ATTRIB command to remove these attributes.

EDIT

The EDIT command in MS-DOS invokes the MS-DOS Editor, which is used to create new text files or modify existing text files. The syntax for the EDIT command is:

```
EDIT [d:path \filename][/switches]
```

If the filename you type following the EDIT command does not exist in the specified directory, a new text file is created. If the filename does exist, EDIT will open the file so that you can read it and/or make any desired alterations.

Table 6.4 shows the switches for use with EDIT.

TABLE 6.4 Using Switches with the EDIT Command

Switch	Purpose
/B	Changes display to black-and-white.
/G	Increases update speed of a CGA monitor.
/H	Orders maximum resolution for the Editor's video display.
/NOHI	Reduces Editor to 8 colors rather than 16.

NOTE   In earlier versions of DOS, EDLIN was a secondary command used to engage DOS line-editing features for text files. EDLIN was limited to single line modifications, however. EDIT, on the other hand, brings up a full-screen editor.

When you open the DOS Editor you will see a typical set of word-processing menus. Each menu is easily manipulated with a mouse. Alternatively, you can press the Alt key along with the first letter of the menu name to pull down the menu. Table 6.5 shows the DOS Editor menus and describes the commands available within each menu.

TABLE 6.5: DOS Editor Pull-Down Menu Options

Menu	Option	Description
File		
	New	Creates an unnamed text document.
	Open	Opens an existing file.
	Save	Saves the file.
	Save As	Saves the current file as a new file; new directory location for the file can be specified.
	Exit	Exits DOS Editor and returns to command prompt.
Edit		
	Cut	Cuts highlighted text, saves it in the clipboard (a temporary holding area) so that it can be copied elsewhere with the Paste command.
	Copy	Makes a copy of highlighted text, saves it in the clipboard to be copied elsewhere with the Paste command.
	Paste	Copies text in the clipboard to current cursor location.
	Clear	Deletes highlighted text.

TABLE 6.5 CONTINUED: DOS Editor Pull-Down Menu Options

Menu	Option	Description
Search		
	Find	Searches for a specified word or set of characters contained in the current open file.
	Repeat Last Find	Continues search for previously specified words or characters.
	Change	Overwrites specified words or characters while performing a search; replaces them with alternate words or characters.
Options		
	Display	Manages video display and screen colors.
	Help Path	Points Editor to the Editor's Help file.
Help		
	Getting Started	Opens Editor's control screens.
	Keyboard	Opens keyboard help screens.
	About	Gives information on your version of the Editor.

The Edit menu's commands take effect on highlighted text. The simplest method of highlighting text is to drag and click with a mouse. The Shift+arrow key approach is the alternative keyboard command used to highlight text.

The Search menu commands take effect on text that *follows* the cursor, so the cursor should be placed at the before the region of text that you are searching.

MSBACKUP

MSBACKUP allows you to make "backup copies" of all your programs and data that are stored on the hard disk. You can even copy your entire directory structure along with your files, and use the backup disks to restore the programs and/or the data as needed. MSBACKUP is an external DOS command. MSBACKUP is menu-driven, and allows you to set up options that you can use each time you back up your hard drive. MSBACKUP can copy to floppy disks, or to other DOS-compatible devices. However, MSBACKUP will not work with tape backup units.

The utility offers three types of backups that you can select to suit your needs:

- **Full Backup** copies all the files you select.

- **Incremental Backup** copies all the files that have changed since your last backup, either full or incremental.

- **Differential Backup** copies files that have changed since your last full backup.

TIP

Every hard drive *will* fail, eventually. It is important that you schedule a regular time to back up your hard disk. There is no other way to prevent or minimize the loss of your work. The more frequently you back up, the less data you will lose when your hard drive fails, and therefore the less data you'll have to recreate.

The MSBACKUP program has a shell, so that you can use on-screen dialog boxes. You have the option of using either keyboard or mouse to make your choices.

To start MSBackup, type the program's name at the command line:

```
MSBackup
```

and press Enter. Follow the on-screen directions. You can access help at any time by pressing F1. MSBACKUP will bring you first to the initial MSBACKUP dialog box. Here, the following options are presented:

- Backup
- Compare
- Restore
- Configure

The first time you use MSBACKUP, have two blank floppies available, and select Configure. This option runs a compatibility test to be certain that the program operates properly with your system. Simply follow the on-screen instructions. You only need to run the test once, unless you change hardware. If you change hardware it is important to reconfigure MSBACKUP to your new system by repeating the compatibility test. If you skip the test, you might not get reliable copies.

Subsequent use of MSBACKUP will bring you back to the initial program screen, from which you should select Backup. This will bring you to the main MSBACKUP screen, where you can specify various parameters for the backup to be performed:

- **Backup To** determines the destination drive for the backup.
- **Backup From** determines the source drive to be backed up.
- **Select Files** permits specific files to be selected for (or excluded from) backup.
- **Setup File** allows you to use a saved configuration (called a *setup file*) for your backup.
- **File** (pull-down menu at the upper left) allows a Save As option to save your selected options as a new setup file.

- **Options** allows options such as verifying backups, compressing backups, requiring confirmation before overwriting files, error correction, etc.

- **Start Backup** initiates the backup.

When you want to back up only certain files, choose the Select Files button in the main MSBACKUP screen. Highlight the files you want, and select them with the right mouse button or the spacebar. If you change your mind about a particular file, highlight the file and press the right mouse button or the spacebar again.

The display button at the bottom of the Select Files screen lets you view and specify files by name, either to back them up or to exclude them. If you have run the compatibility test and configured MSBACKUP to your system, the most likely source of problems is incorrect configuration of the destination disk drive.

MSBACKUP allows you to save your settings in a setup file, so you can use the same settings for your next backup. You can save up to 50 different setup files! Simply choose Save Setup As from the File pull-down menu in the main MSBACKUP screen, and enter an eight-character filename. Use the description box to further identify your setup file for future use. To use a setup file you have saved, select the Setup File box from the main MSBACKUP dialog box. A list of saved files appears for you to select from.

MSBACKUP creates a *backup set catalog* file and stores it to your hard disk and to the last disk of your most recent backup. You can use this file to compare files and select files to restore. You can select Compare from the initial MSBACKUP screen to verify that the backup files are identical to the original files.

MSBACKUP is capable of restoring backed up files to a hard disk or to another computer. Follow the on-screen dialog boxes to restore the files.

NOTE   To restore backup files created by a DOS version earlier than DOS 6.2, you must use the RESTORE command. Specify the source and destination drives; include the /S switch if you want to restore subdirectories.

MS-DOS Commands versus PC-DOS Commands

The evolution of MS-DOS and PC-DOS began moving along divergent lines in the later years of their development. The early differences between the two operating systems were not significant to a casual user, and may not have been noticed at all except for a few hints gathered by a close examination of the hidden files in the root directory of a PC-DOS computer, where IBMBIO.COM and IBMDOS. COM quietly resided.

As powerful add-on DOS utilities increased in popularity, many of these utilities were incorporated into the off-the-shelf versions of the operating system. With the notable exception of the two versions of the DOS Editor, most of the differences between MS-DOS and PC-DOS lay in the add-on utilities. Some of these differences are described here.

- **Disk compression programs:** Doublespace and SuperStor are the disk compression programs for MS-DOS and PC-DOS respectively. Doublespace includes a full-screen user interface and is included with DOS 6.22. As of PC-DOS 6.3, SuperStor remains an add-on which must be purchased separately.

- **Backup programs:** MSBACKUP is the MS-DOS backup program and is based on Norton Backup. The PC-DOS version is Central Point Backup (CPBACKUP). CPBACKUP has several advantages over MSBACKUP, including especially the option to perform unattended backups using the Scheduler program. CPBACKUP also supports different user-experience levels.

- **Data recovery programs:** Both versions of DOS use recovery programs based on Central Point Undelete. UNDELETE in MS-DOS, however, is a simplified version of the program. It does not include a full-screen user interface option as does the PC-DOS UNDELETE. The PC-DOS version of UNDELETE has a greater range of effectiveness in recovering data in destroyed files and deleted directories.

- **Antivirus programs:** Like UNDELETE, both versions of DOS use an anti-virus utility based on a program by Central Point called CP ANTIVIRUS. As with Undelete, MS-DOS uses a more simplified version called MSAV. The PC-DOS version is named IBMAVD and is capable of detecting twice the number of viruses as MSAV. IBMAVD also makes use of the Scheduler program to arrange for automatic virus scanning, if desired.

- **Text editors:** The MS-DOS Edit program is a full-screen editor, like the PC-DOS E program. The MS-DOS editor is easier to use, but the PC-DOS editor does provide for certain extended functions.

The text editor and the backup program will be the subject of this portion of the chapter. Of the ten basic commands in MS-DOS described previously in this chapter, eight of them are essentially identical in PC-DOS. The two remaining commands, E and CPBACKUP, are quite different and will be detailed in this section. The E editor is the text editor program, and CPBACKUP is the PC-DOS backup program.

Using E

The E command starts the PC-DOS editor, which is used to create and edit ASCII text files. From the E editor it is also possible to print text files. Its counterpart in MS-DOS is the EDIT command.

The syntax for the E command is:

`E [=][d:path\filename.ext][/Q]`

The E editor has a number of features that differ from the MS-DOS editor, including the ability to open multiple files and a word wrap feature. The E editor, however, responds only to keystrokes. (The MS-DOS editor, though less versatile, does offer the convenience of a mouse and pull-down menus.)

The = sign directs DOS to use the previously specified path. It can be used to instruct the E editor to open multiple files, as in this example:

`E \programs\doc1 =doc4`

The preceding example would open Doc1 and Doc4 in the Programs subdirectory. As with the MS-DOS editor, if Doc1 or Doc4 did not exist, the editor creates a new file or files with these respective names. Using a wildcard command to open multiple files is also permitted:

`E *.txt`

This command would open all the files in the current directory that have a .TXT extension.

Another command that is often used with E is the /Q switch. The /Q switch turns off the "Loading..." message that is displayed upon opening the E editor. This will decrease the time it takes to load the editor when loading lots of files to edit.

When you open the E editor you will see a screen with command options and a command line listed at the bottom of the page. The text you are editing is placed between a "Top of file" header and a "Bottom of file" footer which expands downward as you type.

One of the extended features of the E editor is the ability to set margins and use the word wrap feature (Very useful when adding a large amount of text to a file). To set margins and utilize the word wrap feature, take the following steps:

1. Move your cursor to the command line at the bottom of the page by pressing ESC.

2. Type the MARGINS command according to this format:

```
MARGINS [left margin[right margin[new paragraph margin]]]
```

An example of this is:

```
MARGINS 1 60 4
```

3. Hit Enter.

4. Hit ESC to put your cursor back in the text area.

The word wrap feature is automatically engaged as you type, which will cause text to wrap around to the next line when it passes the right margin. This occurs without your having to hit the Enter key. It is preferable to set margins when you begin a text document, because the MARGINS command will not reformat previously existing text.

Using Central Point Backup

Central Point Backup is the PC-DOS equivalent of MSBACKUP. CPBACKUP is the external command that runs the program. CP-BACKUP allows you to back up the data from your hard disk to other types of storage devices, including tape drives. Without backups, there is a greater risk of losing most or all of your work when the inevitable hardware, software, or power supply problems occurs (or, more often, as a result of making simple or stupid mistakes that erase data). With backup copies you can restore data in the event of problems.

Central Point Backup will perform four types of backups:

- **Full Backup** backs up all selected files. This is the default setting, and you must tell the system if there are files you do not wish to back up.

- **Incremental Backup** backs up every file that has changed since the last full or incremental backup.

- **Differential Backup** backs up files that have been changed since the last full backup.

- **Unattended Backup** backs up files to the destination you specify at a time you specify.

Additional features allow you to compare and verify accuracy of your copied data, and restore lost data. Central Point Backup is designed for use in a network, and will allow backup of files to various network connections.

Installation of Central Point Backup can be installed during initial installation of DOS, but can be installed at any later time by using DOS Setup. Use this procedure:

1. Place your Central Point Backup diskette into drive A:.

2. From the DOS prompt, type the following:

   ```
   a:setup /e
   ```

NOTE　　The /e switch allows you to use the optional tools selection menu for DOS, an option not normally found on the PC-DOS installation.

---

3. Follow the directions in the on-screen boxes to install Central Point Backup.

The first time you use Central Point Backup, or after making system changes, you must configure CPBACKUP by running the confidence test and configure the program to your system. Follow the on-screen instructions. Your choices will be saved in a file called CPBACKUP.CFG. Help is available by pressing the F1 key.

The program can operate at various speeds, but your computer may not be compatible with the higher speeds. The program starts your test with high speed, and re-runs at the next lower speed until satisfactory results are obtained. In this way backups will take place at the highest possible speed.

After you have configured Central Point Backup, you will work from the main Backup window, which displays three options:

- Backup
- Restore
- Compare

Selecting Backup will bring you to the CPBACKUP Express window, where you will decide on parameters for the current backup. The Express window offers most of the same options that appear in the main program screen for MSBACKUP. Unlike MSBACKUP, CPBACKUP offers three user levels: Advanced, Intermediate, and Beginner. The higher levels offer additional command options that can be confusing for inexperienced users, but offer increased convenience for more advanced users. The default setting is Advanced, but you can select a lower level if you desire.

NOTE   The scheduling option in the Express window offers one tremendous advantage over MSBACKUP. With this option you can configure CPBACKUP to run unattended using the PC-DOS Scheduler program.

Central Point Backup includes some preconfigured setup files that allow you to back up easily on a regular basis, or restrict the areas you want to back up. To use it, select from the Setup Files list in the Express window. You may modify the file, but you need to save your new setup if you wish to use it again.

When selecting files, the Automatic file selection option can be a helpful tool; this allows you to specify several filters that restrict the files that will be backed up. Most useful is the "Include/exclude files" command. There are more than 100 specifications available to the user. This method works with all the available backup methods.

WARNING   If you check the Save File Selections option in the Save Setup window, your selections in the include/exclude list are ignored.

The Date Range Selection option allows you to select files for backup that are only within the range of dates you specify. The date range is typed by using double digits:

`mm/dd,yy or mm/dd/yyyy`

In addition, CPBACKUP allows up to 30 characters for descriptive names for your backups to help you find the correct copies later.

TIP   Central Point Backup utilizes on-screen menus that allow the user to easily explore additional options. Remember also that the F1 key will always provide on-screen help.

Review Questions for Chapter 6, Basic DOS Commands

Answers to the Review Questions may be found in Appendix A.

1. Which DOS command(s) allow you to delete files?

    A. ERASE

    B. BEGONE

    C. DEL

    D. PURGE

2. Which DOS command(s) allow you to create directories?

    A. CREATE

    B. MD

    C. DIR

    D. CD

3. Which external DOS command is a text editor for PC-DOS?

    A. E

    B. EDIT

    C. TEXT

    D. ASCII

4. Which switch for the DIR command displays the output one page at a time?

    A. /W

    B. /O

    C. /S

    D. /P

5. The command **COPY CON FILE.TXT** will create a file called FILE.TXT on the hard drive from keyboard input, once the input has finished and the author has pressed Ctrl+Z. True or false?

    A. True

    B. False

6. If you have used the ATTRIB command to set the Hidden attribute on a file, can you delete the file?

    A. Yes

    B. No

    C. Maybe, if the file isn't a text file

    D. Maybe, if the file isn't an application (.COM or .EXE) file

7. Which files will be listed via the command **DIR *.TXT** if the command is issued at the root of the C: drive?

    A. all files

    B. all text files

    C. all files with the .TXT extension

    D. all word processing files

8. Which switch for the DIR command displays the output in "Wide" format, with no other information except for the filenames?

    A. /W

    B. /O

    C. /S

    D. /P

9. Which of these COPY commands will work?

    A. COPY A*?.DOC

    B. COPY $A.DOC

    C. COPY *A*.DOC

    D. COPY A*.DOC

10. Which program is used to backup PC-DOS disks?

    A. MSBACKUP

    B. BACKUP

    C. CPBACKUP

    D. PCBACKUP

11. Which DOS command can copy directories, subdirectories, and files all at once to a new location, preserving their structure?

    A. COPY

    B. XCOPY

    C. COPYTREE

    D. COPYFILE

12. Which syntax for the ATTRIB command is correct for setting the Read Only attribute on the file TEXT.DOC?

    A. ATTRIB +R TEXT.DOC

    B. ATTRIB –R TEXT.DOC

    C. ATTRIB +O TEXT.DOC

    D. ATTRIB –O TEXT.DOC

13. MSBACKUP will work with floppy disk and tape drive backup media. True or false?

    A. True

    B. False

14. What information will the command **XCOPY *.* /s A:** copy to the A: drive?

    A. everything in the current directory

    B. everything on the current disk

    C. everything in the current directory, including all subdirectories and files

    D. everything on the current disk, including all subdirectories and files

15. If you wanted to rename a file from JOHNS.TXT to JSMITH.TXT, how could you do it? (Choose all that apply.)

    A. REN JOHNS.TXT JSMITH.TXT

    B. REN JSMITH.TXT JOHNS.TXT

    C. COPY JOHNS.TXT JSMITH.TXT and then DELete the original

    D. COPY JSMITH.TXT JOHNS.TXT and then DELete the original

16. Which command should you use to display a directory listing in wide format, one page at a time, sorted alphabetically (backwards Z to A)?

    A. DIR /S /P /Z

    B. DIR /W /P /S:-A

    C. DIR /W /P /S:-O

    D. DIR /W /P /:-N

17. What is the name of the disk compression utility for PC-DOS?

    A. DiskComp

    B. SuperStore

    C. Disk Doubler

    D. DoubleSpace

18. Which of the following are external DOS commands?

    A. CLS

    B. FORMAT

    C. XCOPY

    D. COPY

19. Which of the following DOS utilities can be used to edit an ASCII text file?

    A. any word processor

    B. EDITOR.COM

    C. E.EXE

    D. EDIT.COM

20. Which type of backup backs up the entire hard disk at one time?

    A. Full

    B. Differential

    C. Incremental

    D. Total

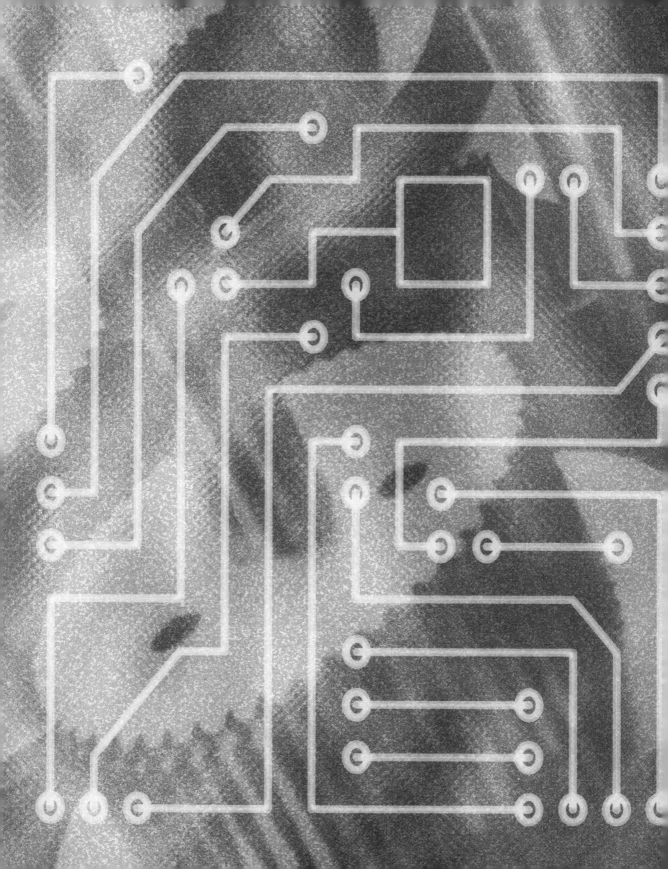

CHAPTER

SEVEN

7

Batch Files

This chapter is meant to give you a good understanding of batch files, the commands you can use in a batch file, and the most common ways of implementing batch files. As you read the following sections, remember that the AUTOEXEC.BAT file is, in fact, a batch file, and all the topics covered herein apply to the AUTOEXEC.BAT as well.

The topics we'll cover include the following:

- Creating Batch Files
- Batch File Guidelines
- Implementing Batch Files
- Executing Batch Files from AUTOEXEC.BAT
- Stopping a Batch File

What *Are* Batch Files?

Batch files are the neatest thing since sliced bread. Every technician will agree on that concept. They are used to automate long lists of commands. At least, that's the theory. Some technicians I know have elevated the science of creating batch files to an art form, as they use them to do several things that the programmers of DOS never meant for them to do. For them, it has become another programming language. For you, a simple grasp of the fundamentals should be adequate to ease your tasks with DOS.

In short, a batch file is an ASCII text file that has the DOS extension .BAT and that automates long lists of DOS commands as though they were one long command. Kind of like an operating system macro that DOS executes, batch files are primarily used as time savers. For example, if you have some files that frequently need to be copied from a particular directory to a floppy disk, you *could* go through the following every time you needed to do it:

```
C:\> CD TEMP
C:\TEMP> COPY *.* A:\
FILE1.TXT
FILE2.TXT
FILE3.TXT
   3 File(s) copied
C:\TEMP> CD\
C:\>
```

Sure, you could repeat those three commands every day (in the preceding, the commands are shown in bold, while the DOS prompts and responses are in a regular typeface); and most people would approach the task just like that. However, technicians and DOS power users are able to tap into the magic of batch files and reduce those three commands into one command. If you create a batch file called COPYTEMP.BAT (the name isn't important, other than the requirement that it contain a .BAT extension) that contains the two CD commands and the Copy command, you could reduce those three commands into a single command; like so:

```
C:\>COPYTEMP
FILE1.TXT
FILE2.TXT
FILE3.TXT
   3 File(s) copied
C:\>
```

This is especially useful if we have to do this same procedure over and over again.

Creating Batch Files

Batch files can be created very quickly. This is mainly because there only a very few major steps to creating new batch files.

1. Open a new, blank file in your text editor.

2. Enter the DOS commands into the file, one per line.

3. Save the file with the extension .BAT.

Since batch files are simple text files, we can use any text editor to edit them. The only requirement is that the program must be able to save the files as ASCII text (also referred to as *DOS text*). Examples of programs that can do this are the Windows 3.x NOTEPAD.EXE program, the MS-DOS EDIT.COM program, the PC-DOS E.EXE program, and most word processing programs.

TIP   Word processing programs normally save their documents with a proprietary file format that includes hidden formatting codes. These codes can cause a batch file to not function properly. In order to save a file as ASCII text, you usually need to choose "Save As..." and pick "ASCII (DOS) text" from the "Save As Type" drop-down list.

The first step in creating a batch file entails running the text editor and selecting New from the File menu (or whichever "Create New File" option your text editing program has). If you are using a program like EDIT.COM (MS-DOS) or E.EXE (PC-DOS) you can tell the program what you'd like to name the batch file before you even start the editor. Like so:

```
C:\> EDIT FURBLE.BAT
```

or

```
C:\> E FURBLE.BAT
```

Once you have a blank file you can start entering commands. Let's talk about how an average batch file is put together. The next section will explore the syntax that is unique to batch files and some of the commands that you can implement in them.

And Now for the Real World...

If you don't have an ASCII text editor available, you can use the COPY command to make any type of text file. To do this, type:

```
COPY CON [filename.TXT]
```

This will drop you to a blank line. You can then type the batch file one line at a time, pressing Enter after each line. When finished, press Ctrl and Z, then press Enter again (pressing F6 and then Enter will work the same). DOS will return the following message:

```
1 File(s) Copied
```

...and the file will be created. While you can't *edit* a file this way, it's a great way to create a simple, small text file. (Especially if your typing is perfect.) If you make a mistake, press Ctrl+C and the copy will be aborted.

Batch File Guidelines

No question about it, batch files can be both useful and complex—so complex, there are specific guidelines for putting them together. There are three items to consider when editing batch files: proper use of syntax, batch file commands, and variables. Let's discuss each of them in order.

Batch File Syntax

As already mentioned, batch files are lists of commands. When you create a batch file, you must enter the commands one per line. If you enter more than one command per line, DOS will interpret only the first command and interpret subsequent commands as parameters for the first. This will usually generate an error and cause the batch file to work incorrectly; or not at all. Figure 7.1 shows the right and wrong way to write commands in a batch file.

FIGURE 7.1:

Correct syntax for batch files

```
@ECHO OFF DIR                    @ECHO OFF
COPY *.* A: CD\ ECHO Hello!      DIR
                                 COPY *.* A:
                                 CD\
                                 ECHO Hello!


    Incorrect Syntax             Correct Syntax
```

Batch File Commands

As a general rule, any DOS command can be placed in a batch file. As long as it's a .COM or .EXE file, it can be executed from a batch file. You just have to place the DOS command (including the path to the executable file) in the batch file. When the command is finished executing, control will return to the batch file, which will proceed to the next command and execute it.

Some of the commands that are most often found in batch files aren't normally used by DOS. Let's take a look at the most frequently used non-DOS commands.

The ECHO Command

Batch files are like small programs. Thus, the people who write them can be considered programmers. Every programmer sitting in their Programming 101 class has written the "Hello World" program. The "Hello World" program simply writes the words "Hello World" to the screen (once or several times). This program's only purpose is to familiarize the programmer with the idea of writing a "program." It also familiarizes the programmer with the most popular command, the command that writes information to the screen. The command in batch files that does this is the ECHO command.

The ECHO command "echoes" text to the screen (very similar to the PRINT command in BASIC). When placed into a batch file, ECHO will display to the screen any text that is located after the ECHO command. For instance, this command in a batch file:

```
ECHO This is a test batch file
```

will produce the following output:

```
This is a test batch file
```

Most batch files have the statement @ECHO OFF at the top of the batch file. The ECHO OFF part of the command prevents subsequent lines from being echoed to the screen, and the @ sign prevents the ECHO OFF command itself from appearing.

Let's say you have a batch file call CP.BAT. This batch file will copy a bunch of text files from the current directory to the A: drive. The batch file looks like this:

```
ECHO This will copy files from here to A:
COPY *.txt A:
ECHO This is the end
```

To execute this batch file, you type CP at the command prompt and the following will appear at the prompt:

```
C:\>CP
C:\>ECHO This will copy files from here to A:
```

```
This will copy files from here to A:
C:\>COPY *.txt A:
FILE1.txt
FILE2.TXT
FILE3.TXT
   3 File(s) Copied
C:\>ECHO This is the end
This is the end
```

As you can see, this is not exactly the "cleanest" way to execute a file. Imagine if every program displayed its inner workings every time you ran it. To prevent this situation, you can insert the @ECHO OFF command. The @ prevents the current line from displaying, and ECHO OFF turns off the ECHOing of all subsequent commands to the screen. If you add the @ECHO OFF command to our previous example, like so:

```
@ECHO OFF
ECHO This will copy files from here to A:
COPY *.txt A:
ECHO This is the end
```

then the output will look like so:

```
C:\>CP
This will copy files from here to A:
FILE1.TXT
FILE2.TXT
FILE3.TXT
   3 File(s) Copied
This is the end
C:\>
```

A little more elegant execution, don't you think?

NOTE Most people use the ECHO command to display text to the screen, but what if you want to display a blank line (for spacing purposes)? This is accomplished with the **ECHO.** command (that is, ECHO with a period immediately following—no space). When executed, this version of the ECHO command will print a blank line instead of the period.

The CALL Command

As we have already discussed, you can execute a .COM or .EXE program from within a batch file. There is a special situation that exists when we try to execute a batch file from within another batch file. If we put the name of a second batch file into a batch file, the first batch file will start the second batch file normally, but when the second batch file is finished, it does not return control of DOS back to the first batch file. In fact, it stops batch file execution altogether and returns control of DOS back to DOS. Figure 7.2 illustrates this problem.

FIGURE 7.2:

One batch file executing another

```
FIRST.BAT                              SECOND.BAT

@ECHO OFF                              @ECHO OFF
DIR *.* /w /o                          CD\
ECHO This is the current directory     A:
C:\DOS\SECOND.BAT                      dir *.* /w /o
ECHO Hello                             ECHO This is the floppy disk directory


FIRST.BAT will do a directory of the current directory, display
"This is the current directory" and execute SECOND.BAT.  SECOND.BAT
will change to the root directory, change to the A: drive, do a directory,
then display "This is the floppy disk directory".  At this point, SECOND.BAT
batch file execution stops and the DOS command prompt is displayed.
"Hello" will never be displayed to the screen.
```

To solve this problem, you must use the CALL command. CALL executes the commands in another batch file and returns control back to the batch file that "CALLed" it. The syntax for using the call command is as follows:

CALL [*batch file name*]

This concept is illustrated in Figure 7.3.

FIGURE 7.3:

One batch file CALLing another

```
FIRST.BAT                              SECOND.BAT

@ECHO OFF                              @ECHO OFF
DIR *.* /w /o                          CD\
ECHO This is the current directory     A:
CALL C:\DOS\SECOND.BAT                 dir *.* /w /o
ECHO Hello                             ECHO This is the floppy disk directory
```

FIRST.BAT will do a directory of the current directory, display "This is the current directory" and execute SECOND.BAT. SECOND.BAT will change to the root directory, change to the A: drive, do a directory, then display "This is the floppy disk directory". At this point, control returns to FIRST.BAT. Finally, "Hello" is displayed on the screen.

The REM Command

The first rule you learn in Programming 101 is "Always Document your Code!" This makes things easier for you when you are looking over the program and need to understand what a certain line of code does (the more code you have, the harder it is to remember). Documenting batch files is done with the REM command, which you can place into a batch file before a command or set of commands to detail their use. When DOS sees REM statements, it just skips over them and continues with the next line. A sample REM statement might look like so:

REM This copies all files from C:\DATA to the A: drive (floppy)
COPY C:\DATA*.* A:\

REM statements can also be used to temporarily "turn off" a command during batch file testing. If you want to see if a particular statement is causing a batch file to not execute properly, you can edit the file and place a REM command in front of the suspect command. If you save the file and then execute it, then when DOS reaches the suspect command, it will not execute it, because there is a REM statement in front of it.

The PAUSE Command

PAUSE is a simple batch file command. It is used when several lines of text are scrolling by and you need to pause the batch file. The PAUSE command, when placed in a batch file, will halt the batch file execution until the user presses a key. When the user presses any key on the keyboard (except Shift, Alt, Ctrl, Caps Lock, PrntScrn, Scroll Lock, or Pause), batch file execution will continue.

The "Any" Key

The PAUSE command will produce a message that says "Press any key to continue." Some users (albeit the less experienced ones) may get confused by this syntax. They may get confused and look for an key labeled "Any" (hence the "Any" key). To solve this problem, some computer supply companies have come up with a sticker to place on the spacebar that says "Any". Some keyboard companies have actually considered putting another key on the keyboard that sends the same signal as the spacebar, but is labeled "Any."

The GOTO Command and Batch File Labeling

There are times when the order of lines in a program (or batch file) makes sense for programming, but not for execution. In other words, DOS may need to "jump around" within the batch file to get to the commands it needs to. You can help it do this through the use of the GOTO command and *labels*.

Labels break up the batch file into sections that can be accessed by name. Each section can be distinguished by the special label you place before each set of commands. The only requirement is that the label be a name, without spaces, preceded by a colon (:). For example, you may have commands that perform three separate functions within a batch file. It may therefore be useful to split this batch file into three sections, by using three labels, as follows:

```
:SECTION1
COMMAND
COMMAND
COMMAND

:SECTION2
COMMAND
COMMAND
COMMAND

:SECTION3
COMMAND
COMMAND
COMMAND

:END
```

The major use of batch file labels is in conjunction with the GOTO command. The GOTO command allows a batch file execution to "branch." The execution of a batch file starts at the top of the file, but if you need a batch file to be written in one order, then execute in another, you can use GOTO to specify the order of the commands. For example, if you need the above batch file commands to run in the order section1, then section3, then section2, you could modify the batch file to look like this:

```
:SECTION1
COMMAND
COMMAND
COMMAND
GOTO SECTION3
```

```
:SECTION2
COMMAND
COMMAND
COMMAND
GOTO END

:SECTION3
COMMAND
COMMAND
COMMAND
GOTO SECTION 2
:END
```

Notice the ":End" label. It is placed at the end of the file, so that you can specify the final branch (from Section 2 to the End). If you didn't specify this branch, DOS would execute the batch file in the following sequence: Section 1 first, then Section 3, then Section 2, then Section 3, then Section 2, then Section 3, … and so on. The final GOTO (in Section 2) ends the branching.

The IF… THEN… Commands

Have you ever been told by your parents, "If you eat all the food on your plate, then you can have dessert"? This type of statement is known as a *conditional statement*. There is a condition ("All the food on the plate eaten?") and a result ("Child gets dessert."). The result of any conditional statement is done if the condition can be considered "true." In our above analogy, if our condition, "all food eaten," is true, then the result is "child gets dessert." However, if that same condition comes out to be false, then the child doesn't get dessert.

These conditional statements are known as *Boolean logic* and are found throughout computer programs. This set of logical rules is how a computer makes decisions. In batch files, we use the two commands "IF" and "THEN" together to allow the computer to make a decision about how a batch file should work.

For example, if we want a batch file to display a message when a particular file exists, we use the IF ... THEN statement with the modifier EXIST, like so:

```
IF EXIST C:\DATA\MYFILE.TXT THEN ECHO File does exist!
```

This conditional statement will display the message "File does exist!" if, in fact the MYFILE.TXT file exists in the directory C:\Data. If the file does not exist, the batch file will skip this command and move on.

There are several options that are used with IF... THEN. The options are called *Boolean operators*. Table 7.1 describes the most often used Boolean operators.

TABLE 7.1: Common Boolean Operators

Operator	example	Description
AND	IF *X* **AND** *Y* THEN *Z*	If condition *X* **and** condition *Y* are BOTH true, then *Z* will be done. If one or the other are false, then *Z* will not be done.
OR	IF *X* **OR** *Y* THEN *Z*	If EITHER condition *X* **or** condition *Y* are true then *Z* will be done. Also, if both are true, then *Z* will be done. However, if neither condition is true, then *Z* will not be done.
NOT	IF *X* **NOT** *Y* THEN *Z*	If condition *X* is true and condition *Y* is **not** true then *Z* will be done. If any other condition exists, *Z* will not be done
ELSE	IF (*X* and *Y* condition is TRUE) THEN A ELSE Z	If the *X* and *Y* condition is TRUE, then do *A*, **otherwise** do *Z*
=	IF *X* = *Y* THEN *Z*	If condition *X* is **the same as** condition *Y*, then *Z* will be done. If any other condition exists, *Z* will not be done.

X and Y can be replaced by some condition. If you use our example above, X could be "Johnny eats all the food on his plate," Y could be "Johnny cleans up his room," and Z could be "Johnny can play baseball with his friends."

TABLE 7.1 CONTINUED: Common Boolean Operators

Operator	example	Description
= =	IF *X* = = *Y* THEN *Z*	If condition *X* is **not the same as** condition *Y*, *Z* will be done. If any other condition exists, *Z* will not be done.
>	IF *X* > *Y* THEN *Z*	(Where both *X* and *Y* are numbers) If *X* is **greater** than *Y* then *Z* will be done. If any other condition exists, *Z* will not be done.
<	IF *X* < *Y* THEN *Z*	(Where both *X* and *Y* are numbers) If *X* is **less** than *Y* then *Z* will be done. If any other condition exists, *Z* will not be done.
>=	IF *X* >= *Y* THEN *Z*	(Where both *X* and *Y* are numbers) If *X* is **greater** than *Y*, *Z* will be done. If *X* **equals** *Y*, *Z* will be done. If any other conditions exists, *Z* will not be done.
<=	If *X* <= *Y* THEN *Z*	(Where both *X* and *Y* are numbers) If *X* is **less** than *Y*, *Z* will be done. If *X* **equals** *Y*, *Z* will be done. If any other conditions exists, *Z* will not be done.

X and Y can be replaced by some condition. If you use our example above, X could be "Johnny eats all the food on his plate," Y could be "Johnny cleans up his room," and Z could be "Johnny can play baseball with his friends."

The CHOICE Command

Originally, batch files weren't designed to accept input. But, as I stated earlier, technicians love to make batch files do things they weren't designed to do. Early batch file programmers wanted to make menus. They didn't have a command to ask for input, so they used the DOS prompt as the input mechanism. They would create a batch file (possibly called MENU.BAT) that contains entries like the following:

```
@ECHO OFF
CLS
ECHO.
```

```
ECHO                      Dave's Menu
ECHO.
ECHO Enter the number of the program you wish to run (without
ECHO the period).
ECHO.
ECHO 1. Card Game
ECHO 2. Word Processor
ECHO 3. Spreadsheet
ECHO 4. Database
ECHO.
```

This batch file's output would look like this, when run:

```
              Dave's Menu

Enter the number of the program you wish to run (without
the period).

1. Card Game
2. Word Processor
3. Spreadsheet
4. Database

C:\>_
```

The batch file creator would have also made four additional batch files: 1.BAT, 2.BAT, 3.BAT, and 4.BAT. Each batch file would simply contain the appropriate command to run the requested program and an entry to rerun the MENU.BAT batch file. The following is an example of 1.BAT (the other three batch files would be similar; just replace the command that executes the correct program):

```
@ECHO OFF
C:\GAMES\CARDS.EXE
C:\MENU.BAT
```

This solution works, but is somewhat cumbersome. There is also a possibility that a user could accidentally delete one of the required batch files. If this happened, the user would receive a "Bad Command or Filename" message instead of seeing the program execute.

That's where the CHOICE command of MS-DOS version 6 entered the picture. This command, when placed into a batch file, will halt the batch file and allow the user to make a choice. This command is usually followed by several IF ... THEN statements (and possibly a few GOTO statements and labels) that allow the batch file to do different things depending on which choice was made.

The CHOICE command uses the following syntax:

```
CHOICE [option] text
```

For example, this command:

```
CHOICE /C:1234 Enter the number
```

will show the following result when the batch file is run:

```
Enter the number[1,2,3,4]?
```

Whichever choice is entered, CHOICE will return an "error level" to DOS that represents the choice position (error level 1 for the first choice, 2 for the second, and so on). These error levels can be placed into conditional statements with IF ERRORLEVEL=[number] THEN... statements, like so:

```
IF ERRORLEVEL=1 THEN GOTO START
IF ERRORLEVEL=2 THEN GOTO STOP
```

There are several options that can be used with the CHOICE command. Table 7.2 details some of the switches that can be used with the CHOICE command.

TABLE 7.2: CHOICE Options

Option	Use	Description
/C:[choices]	/C:ABCD	Specifies which choices the CHOICE command will accept as input. The default is YN (which will return 1 for "Y" for ERRORLEVEL).
/N	/N	When added to the command line for CHOICE, it prevents the displaying of the question mark and selection choices.
/S	/S	Treats choices as case sensitive.
/T:xx,yy	/T:1,5	Defaults to choice xx after yy seconds.

Using a combination of CHOICE, ERRORLEVEL and IF...THEN... commands, you can modify your original MENU.BAT file to be a bit more efficient. In our previous example, we had five batch files for this simple menu. You can reduce that to one by changing MENU.BAT to look as follows:

```
@ECHO OFF
:BEGIN
CLS
ECHO.
ECHO                    Dave's Menu
ECHO.
ECHO Enter the number of the program you wish to run (without
ECHO the period).
ECHO.
ECHO 1. Card Game
ECHO 2. Word Processor
ECHO 3. Spreadsheet
ECHO 4. Database
ECHO 5. Exit to DOS
ECHO.
CHOICE /C:12345 Enter Choice
IF ERRORLEVEL=1 THEN GOTO GAME
IF ERRORLEVEL=2 THEN GOTO WORDPROC
```

```
IF ERRORLEVEL=3 THEN GOTO SS
IF ERRORLEVEL=4 THEN GOTO DB
GOTO END

:GAME
C:\GAMES\CARDS.EXE
GOTO BEGIN

:WORDPROC
C:\APPS\WPR.EXE
GOTO BEGIN

:SS
C:\APPS\SS.EXE
GOTO BEGIN

:DB
C:\APPS\DB.EXE
GOTO BEGIN

:END
```

And Now for the Real World...

In this section we discussed a portion of some of the commands that can be used in a batch file. However, as I mentioned at the beginning of this chapter, some DOS users love to use batch file for everything. The inherent problem in this thinking is that batch files weren't *meant* to do everything. Batch file users found away around this problem. To solve it, they would write small .COM or .EXE programs to do what they wanted, then called them from a batch file. For example, if there is no batch file or DOS command to accept mouse input, someone will write a program to accept mouse input and pass that information to the batch file.

Batch File Parameters

In addition to commands there are also *parameters* (also called *variables*) that can be used to change how the batch files execute. Most DOS commands have switches that change the way they operate. There are two types of parameters: *DOS parameters* and *command-line execution parameters*. Each is used slightly differently in batch files.

DOS Parameters

DOS parameters are global to both DOS and batch files. These are set in AUTOEXEC.BAT and are also called *DOS environment variables*. These variables specify global things like the path that DOS searches to find executables. To set an environment variable, you use the SET command in the AUTOEXEC.BAT or CONFIG.SYS, like so:

```
SET TEMP=C:\TEMP
SET PROMPT=$P$G
SET USER=DSMITH
```

These variables can be referenced in a batch file by placing them in the batch file with a percent sign (%) on either side of the variable. When the batch file is executed, the variable will be replaced with its global value. So, if we use the examples above in a batch file, it will look like this:

```
@ECHO OFF
ECHO %TEMP%
ECHO %PROMPT%
ECHO %USER%
```

and the resultant output of this batch file will be:

```
C:\TEMP
$p$g
DSMITH
```

You could also use these variables in other commands as well. For example, if the TEMP environment variable was set to C:\ Windows\Temp in the AUTOEXEC.BAT and you wanted to copy some files there temporarily, you could write a batch file that might look like the following:

```
@ECHO OFF
COPY *.TXT %TEMP%
```

The %TEMP% would get replaced with the value of the TEMP environment variable; thus the *.TXT files would get copied to the C:\Windows\Temp directory. Additionally, if someone edited the AUTOEXEC.BAT and changed the TEMP variable to point to C:\Temp, the batch file would still work. The files would get copied to C:\Temp, instead.

Command-Line Execution Parameters

The other type of parameter that batch files can use are the *command-line execution parameters.* These parameters are passed to the batch file from the batch file's command line. They work just like the command-line parameters for regular DOS commands (i.e., the command-line switches for the DIR command, like /w, /o, etc.).

You can use up to nine command-line parameters with any batch file, then reference them within the batch file. These parameters are referenced in the batch file by their position (the first occurrence after the name of the batch file is referenced as %1 in the batch file, the second occurrence is %2, and so on up to the ninth occurrence).

NOTE   %0 is used to represent the name of the batch file itself. Use it if you need to.

Let's say you want a batch file to operate differently depending on who is using it. You might make a batch file named TEST.BAT like the following:

```
@ECHO OFF
ECHO Hello %1
cd C:\USERS\%1
COPY A:\*.* C:\USERS\%1
```

If you run this batch file with your name, like so:

```
C:\>TEST David
```

the batch file will say "Hello David," change to the directory C:\Users\David (assuming it exists), and copy all the files from the A: drive to that directory. However, if you ran the batch file like so:

```
C:\>TEST Rob
```

the batch file will the same things, except with Rob's name wherever David's was before. This type of parameter makes batch files almost infinitely flexible.

Implementing Batch Files

Once you have created a few batch files, you'll probably find they don't always work as efficiently or elegantly as you might have first envisioned. In the following sections, we'll present a few things you can do to make your batch files work better.

Executing Batch Files from the AUTOEXEC.BAT

Some batch files get run all the time. Take, as an example, the AUTOEXEC.BAT file. This batch file runs automatically at startup, executing the commands contained within it just as any other batch file would. Did you know that you can execute your own batch files automatically at startup as well? Just place a call to the appropriate batch file inside your AUTOEXEC.BAT file.

Remember to use the CALL command to execute another batch file from within the AUTOEXEC.BAT. If you are executing a menu batch file, place that command at the end of the AUTOEXEC.BAT file so that the menu executes when the rest of the AUTOEXEC.BAT is finished.

Stopping a Running Batch File

If you have an extra long batch file and want to stop its execution, there are two ways to do it. The first way is to break its action, by holding down the Ctrl key and pressing Break (this key is usually located near the Scroll Lock or PrintScreen key). At this point DOS stops and asks:

```
Terminate batch job (Y/N)?
```

If you respond with Y, the batch program will exit at its current point in the action and return control back to DOS. (If you type N instead, the batch file will continue executing.)

The second way to stop a batch file in progress is the key combination Ctrl+C.

Batch File Optimization

There are several things you can do to make batch files easier to use:

- First of all, don't forget to give each batch file a .BAT filename extension. (And remember you're limited to an eight-character filename before the extension.)

- The batch files should be named according to their *function*.

- Don't name them the same as existing DOS commands, because DOS will just execute the command of the same name; it will never look for a batch file of the same name unless the DOS command of that name is missing.

NOTE

Remember that, if given a family of commands or programs with the same filename, DOS will execute the first one it finds and then stop searching. Its search always proceeds in this order: .COM, .EXE, then .BAT.

Another thing you can do to make it easy for the user is to put all the batch files in a directory that's in the PATH environment variable. As already stated, when DOS looks for a program, it looks first in the current directory, then in the directories of the PATH variable, in order. You could make a directory called BATCH right off the root of the C: drive, and then place C:\Batch in the PATH statement in your AUTOEXEC.BAT file, like so:

```
@ECHO OFF
SET PATH=C:\DOS;C:\BATCH;C:\;C:\WINDOWS;C:\WINDOWS\SYSTEM
C:\SB16\SB16SET.EXE /I:5 /P:220
C:\DOS\MSCDEX /D:MCD0001 /B:1024
MENU.BAT
```

Finally, it's a good idea to break large batch files into several smaller batch files. For instance, break up a batch file that does several things into several batch files that do one process apiece, and call each one as necessary from the main batch file.

Review Questions for Chapter 7, Batch Files

Answers to the Review Questions may be found in Appendix A.

1. Batch files can be made with word processors. True or false?

   A. True

   B. False

2. If you name a batch file with the same name as a DOS utility or program and execute it by name only (no extension), it will run instead of the DOS utility or program. True or false?

   A. True

   B. False

3. Which batch command executes another batch file and then returns to the original?

   A. ECHO

   B. IF... THEN...

   C. CHOICE

   D. CALL

4. Which batch command displays text to the screen?

   A. ECHO

   B. IF... THEN...

   C. CHOICE

   D. CALL

5. Which of the following sample outputs would be generated by this batch file?

```
@ECHO OFF
ECHO        Menu
ECHO.
ECHO Hello, User
ECHO This is the current time
TIME
```

OUTPUT A:

```
Menu

.

Hello, User
This is the current time
11:02:56.10p
```

OUTPUT B:

```
        Menu

Hello, User
This is the current time
Current time is 11:02:56.10p
Enter new time:
```

OUTPUT C:

```
Hello, User
11:02:56.10p
```

OUTPUT D:

```
Hello, User
Current time is 11:02:56.10p
Enter new time:
```

6. Batch files can contain what commands?

    A. any DOS command

    B. ECHO, CHOICE, IF ...THEN... statements

    C. variables

    D. none of the above

    E. all of the above

7. Which key needs to be pressed to resume execution when the PAUSE command is used to halt batch file execution?

    A. Ctrl+Break

    B. Ctrl+C

    C. Any key will work.

    D. the spacebar

8. Which of the following commands would successfully interpret a variable that the user would type after the name of the batch file (when issuing the batch file at the command line) in order to specify how a batch file should executes command "*X*"?

    A. IF EXIST CMDLINE THEN *X*

    B. IF %1="Y" THEN *X*

    C. IF *Z*<=*Y* THEN *X*

    D. IF %TEMP%="C:\TEMP" THEN *X*

9. If the CHOICE command that follows is implemented, which ERRORLEVEL would be considered TRUE if the answer given is "Y"?

   CHOICE Do you want to continue?

   A. IF ERRORLEVEL=1 THEN *X*

   B. IF ERRORLEVEL=Y THEN *X*

   C. IF ERRORLEVEL=N THEN *X*

   D. IF ERRORLEVEL=0 THEN *X*

10. To use the TEMP environment variable in a batch file, which syntax must you follow?

    A. TEMP

    B. #TEMP

    C. %TEMP

    D. %TEMP%

    E. %%TEMP

11. Which programs can be used to make batch files? (Circle all that apply.)

    A. COPY

    B. EDIT.COM

    C. a word processor

    D. E.EXE

    E. none of the above

12. Batch files have to be in the DOS directory to execute. True or false?

    A. True

    B. False

13. Which of the following Boolean operators has the most conditions?

    A. AND

    B. NOT

    C. OR

    D. ELSE

14. Which command-line switch for the CHOICE command prevents the displaying of the questionmark and answer choices?

    A. /S

    B. /T

    C. /Q

    D. /N

15. Which of the following illustrates the proper syntax for the GOTO command to branch the batch file to the :END label?

    A. GOTO END

    B. GOTO :END

    C. GOTO %END

    D. GOTO %:END%

16. Which key combination(s) will halt a batch file during its execution? (Choose all that apply.)

    A. Ctrl+Break

    B. Ctrl+Del

    C. Ctrl+Alt+Del

    D. Ctrl+C

17. Which is better (that is, which is more efficient, design-wise): a large batch file, or several smaller batch files?

    A. One large batch file

    B. Several smaller batch files

18. If you create a batch file and you want it to operate differently depending on what name was placed after the name of the batch file, like so:

```
MYBATCH Name
```

then which parameter would you place in the batch file?

    A. %1

    B. %2

    C. %A

    D. %B

19. Which command(s) turn off the displaying of each batch file command?

    A. ECHO OFF

    B. ECHO

    C. DISPLAY

    D. DISPLAY OFF

20. If, within a batch file, you want to execute another batch file, then continue on in the original batch file, which command do you use?

    A. GOTO

    B. CALL

    C. RUN

    D. GOSUB

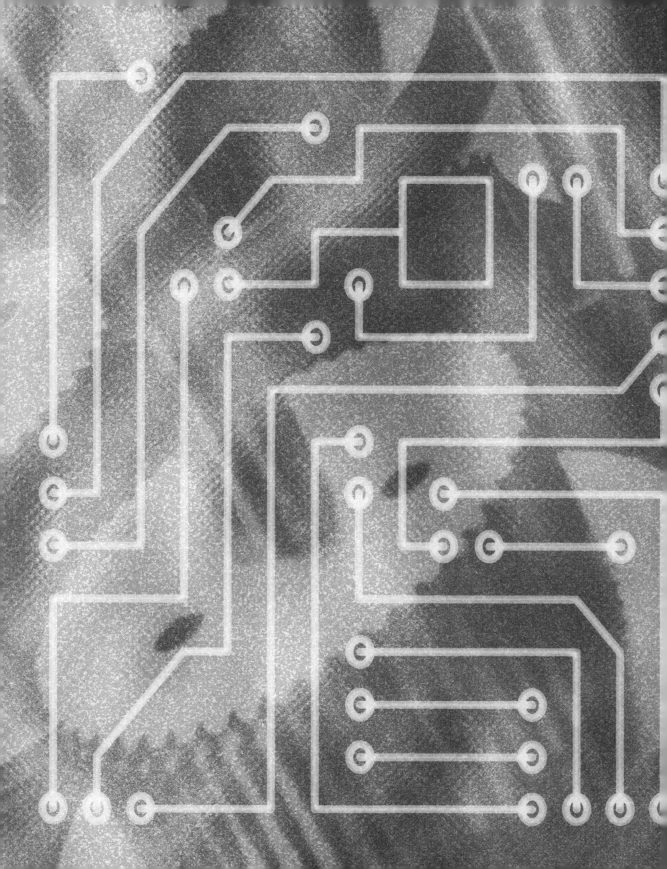

CHAPTER
EIGHT

8

Windows Interface Overview

- The Parts of the Interface

- The Desktop

- Program Manager

- File Manager

- Print Manager

- Customizing the Interface

- The Control Panel

- Windows Setup

As we have discussed in our exploration of the DOS operating system, the Windows interface to DOS has become an integral addition to most modern Desktop PCs. In this chapter, we will look a little more deeply at this interface, and at how Windows helped to add functionality and ease-of-use that would have been difficult or even impossible under DOS alone.

We will look at how the major program elements of Windows work, and give you a basic introduction to how to use the interface. We will then examine how to configure and customize systems based on the particular needs and tastes of each user.

In this chapter we'll cover the following interface topics:

- The Parts of the Interface
- The Desktop
- Program Manager
- File Manager
- Print Manager
- Customizing the Interface
- The Control Panel
- Windows Setup

As you go through, remember that this chapter is intended as an overview, so there will be times when we'll be introducing a topic without exploring that topic fully. A more comprehensive discussion of installing, configuring, optimizing, and troubleshooting Windows will follow over the next four chapters.

Interface Components

The key to the success of the Windows product has been the way in which its GUI (graphic user interface) has allowed programmers to hide the inner workings of the DOS operating system and its command-line input process from users. In order to do this, Windows provides simplified access to three major functions that users needed to use on a regular basis. These three functions are:

- Running applications

- Managing Files

- Printing

The programs that allow for this, as well as the Windows Desktop itself, will therefore be the topic of this section. Note that these features are exactly the same in both Windows for Workgroups and Windows.

WARNING The following information is best learned if Windows 3.1 or Workgroups 3.11 has been installed on a machine that you have access to as you read. This will allow you to experiment and follow along with the examples. If you do not yet have Windows installed on a machine, it would be best to install it first (the process is covered in the next chapter) and come back later to step through these exercises.

The Desktop

The Windows Desktop is best understood if you look at it as an actual, physical desktop. When you put papers on top of your desk, no matter how you organize those documents, they are still all sitting on the work surface. The Windows Desktop is a similar entity, except that it is the back *wall* of the Windows environment. As you learn to open, close and move individual program windows around on the screen, all of these windows nonetheless will have to fight for space on the Desktop, which is a flat space as large as your screen resolution.

The Desktop itself does not have any configurable options, and it does not perform any tasks. Rather, it simply contains the visible elements of Windows, and defines the limits of the graphic environment. To see the Desktop on your own Windows system, start your computer, start Windows, and click the Minimize button on the Program Manager. Assuming you have nothing else running, and the system has not been modified, you will now see a flat wall on your screen with a Program Manager icon in the lower left, as shown in Figure 8.1. If the system has been modified, you may see a pattern or a picture on the screen.

FIGURE 8.1:

The Windows Desktop

The Program Manager

When you initially start Windows, the program that starts on Windows load is called the "Shell program." By default, this shell is PROGMAN.EXE, a program that is located in the Windows directory.

PROGMAN.EXE is the file that runs the Program Manager, or the interface that allows you to organize and execute numerous commands from a single graphical window. The Program Manager shell is designed to allow users to easily access needed applications, and also allows them access to various utilities for customizing their Windows environment.

Program Manager works through the use of two major types of objects—*windows* and *icons*. The windows you use in the Windows environment are crucial to the way you use your computer. They provide the space in which a particular program or utility can function. Icons are the doors through which programs are started, and are therefore used to spawn windows. A third object—the *group*—is a special type of window found only in Program Manager.

NOTE The difference between Windows (with a capital W) and windows (with a lowercase w) may seem confusing at first, but it is important to recognize the distinction. The proper noun refers to the product, while the lowercase "window" is used when describing any particular window within the interface, or program windows in general.

Program Windows

A program window is a rectangular area created on the screen when an application is opened within Windows. This window can have a number of different forms, but most windows include at least a few basic elements. Shown below in Figure 8.2 are the Control Box, Title Bar, Minimize Button, Restore Button, and Resizable Border.

The Control Box is used to examine the state of the application, and can be used to maximize, minimize, and close the application. Clicking it once brings into view a selection menu. Double-clicking it closes the window and shuts down the application. The Minimize and Restore buttons are used to change the state of the window on the Desktop, and they will be discussed in the section on the three states of a Windows window (coming up later in this section).

FIGURE 8.2:

Basic elements of a window

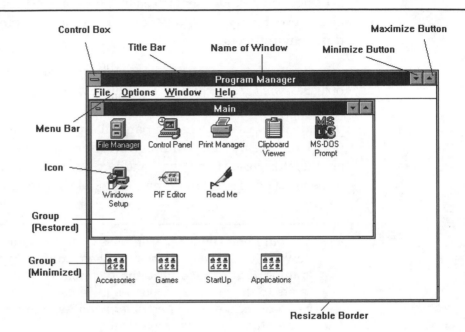

The Title Bar simply states the name of the program, and in some cases gives information as to the particular document being accessed by that program. As we learn about multitasking, the color of the Title Bar will indicate whether or not a particular window is the active window. The active window is simply the window that is currently being used, and it has two attributes. First, any keystrokes that are entered are directed there by default, and second, any other windows that overlap the active window will be pushed behind it.

The border is a thin line that surrounds the window, and allows it to be widened and shortened. This will also be explained further, later in this section.

NOTE

Double-clicking is an important mouse skill. Although we have not talked about this much, the mouse is used far more in Windows than it had been in DOS. The mouse has three main functions: the *click*, the *drag*, and the *double-click*. Clicking simply means placing the mouse pointer over an object and clicking the left button once. To drag, click and hold down the mouse button and move the object to a new location. The double-click is the toughest to get used to. Double-clicking involves rapidly clicking on an object twice without moving the mouse in the process. If you are not mouse-proficient, the double-click and the drag can be challenging skills to learn, and you should plan to give yourself some learning time.

These elements are not all found on every window, for programmers can choose to eliminate or modify them. Still, in most cases these will be constant, with the rest of the window filled with menus, toolbars, a workspace, or other application-specific elements. For instance, Microsoft Word, the word-processing program we used to write this book, adds an additional control box and minimize and maximize buttons for each document. It also has a menu bar, a number of optional toolbars, scroll bars at the right and bottom, and a status bar at the very bottom. As you might expect, then, application windows can become very cluttered.

Notepad, on the other hand, is a very simple Windows program. It has only a single menu bar and the basic elements seen in Figure 8.3. Both Word and Notepad are used to create and edit documents, but Word is far more configurable, far more powerful, and therefore has many more optional components available within its window.

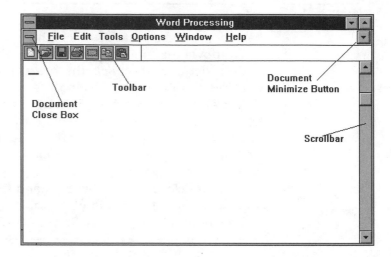

It takes more than recognizing the physical parts of a window, though, to understand what the Windows interface allows a user to do. Almost all windows are movable, stackable, and resizable, and they can be hidden behind other windows (often unintentionally!).

When an application window has been launched, it will exist in one of the three following states:

- Maximized

- Restored

- Minimized

Maximized Windows   A *maximized* window is one that takes up all the available space on the screen. When it is in front of the other programs, it is the only thing visible; even the Desktop is hidden. For an example of a maximized application, see Figure 8.4. Note that in the upper right corner the restore button displays a down-pointing triangle, and the sides of the window no longer have borders, as the window is flush with the edges of the screen. Maximizing a window provides the maximum workspace possible for that window's application, and the window can be accessed actively by the user. Still, in the process every other window is covered, making multitasking more difficult. Nonetheless, maximized mode is the preferred window size for most word processing, graphics creation, and other user applications.

Restored Windows   A *restored* window is one that, like a maximized window, can be used interactively, and is identical in function to a maximized window in just about every way except one: it does not necessarily take up the entire screen. Restored windows can be very small, or they can take up almost as much space as a maximized window. Generally, the size of the restored window is up to the user. Restored windows have a restore box with an upward pointing triangle (used to maximize the window) and they have a border going around their edge, as can be seen in Figure 8.5.

FIGURE 8.4:

A Solitaire window that has been maximized

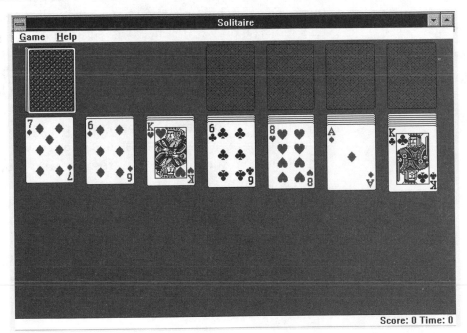

FIGURE 8.5:

A Solitaire window that has been restored

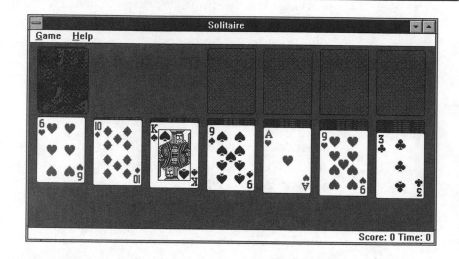

Minimized Windows   The last state of a window is that of *minimized*. Minimized program windows are represented by nothing but an icon on the Desktop (don't worry, we'll get to icons soon!) and they are not usable until they have been either ...maximized or restored! The only difference between a minimized program and a *closed* program is that a minimized program is out of the way, but is still in the same place when you return to it as when you minimized it. Let's take the Solitaire program we have been looking at in the graphics. The program is opened, and a game of Solitaire is started. If you need to open another program, though (or maybe need to stop playing because your boss has entered the room), you have two choices. You can close the program, and reopen it later. If you do this, though, your current game will be lost, and you will have to start over. Minimizing the Solitaire window, on the other hand, would leave the program open, but would remove the open window from the screen, and put nothing more than an icon in the lower left corner of the Desktop, as shown in Figure 8.6. Cover the icon with a different active window, and later you can restore the window to its previous size and finish the game in progress.

FIGURE 8.6:

A Solitaire window that has been minimized

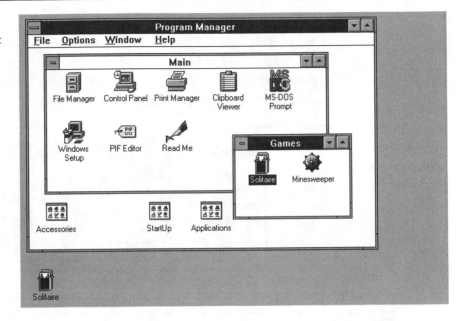

Icons

Icons are not nearly as complex as windows can be, but they are very important nonetheless. Icons are shortcuts that allow a user to open a program or a utility without knowing where that program is, or how it needs to be configured. Icons consist of four elements:

- Icon label
- Icon graphic
- Program location
- Working directory location

The label and graphic simply tell the user the name of the program, and give a visual hint as to what that program does. Solitaire, for instance, is labeled as "Solitaire" and its icon graphic is a deck of cards. By clicking on an icon once, you make that icon the *active* icon (programmers call this "setting the focus on an object"). Once an icon is active, the commands in the Program Manager menu bar will affect it only. By clicking on the word *File* on the Program Manager menu, a drop-down menu appears. One of the selections is *Properties*. Clicking this option will bring up the attributes of an icon, as shown in Figure 8.7, and is the only way to see exactly which program an icon is configured to start.

FIGURE 8.7:

The Properties window of Solitaire

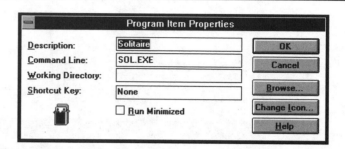

TIP   The label and graphic of an icon are, to a large extent, irrelevant to the icon's function. They are meant to give a user information on the program to be started, but only the program path actually defines that. An icon can say Microsoft Word and have a Word graphic, but someone may have set it up to have a program path leading to Microsoft Excel by mistake, or perhaps intentionally to keep unauthorized users ignorant of what the user has on their desktop.

The Working Directory line in the Program Item Properties dialog box simply apprises Windows as to where documents created through this icon are saved. Most applications provide a working directory by default when they are first installed, but a user can override it by typing a new path to the working directory of their choice.

Remember that program icons are very specialized objects, and that they occur only in the Program Manager or on the Desktop to identify a minimized window. Other types of icons do occur, as you will see when we look at the Control Panel icons later (as well as at Group icons in the section directly following).

Groups

Within Program Manager, there is actually a second type of icon besides the program icons. These are the *group icons*. Groups are created to allow icons with like purposes to be stored together. No program icon can be stored directly on the workspace of the Program Manager. All program icons must belong to a group, which then has an icon on the workspace. To use a particular icon, a user must double-click the group in which the program's icon resides. This then brings up a window containing the individual program icons, which the user double-clicks to launch the program window. In Figure 8.8, the Main and Games groups are open, and the Applications, Accessories, and StartUp groups are closed. Can you identify which one is the active window? How about the active icon?

FIGURE 8.8:

Group windows and icons

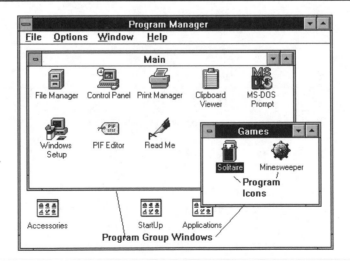

The File Manager

As we have now seen, the Program Manager is responsible for allowing a user access to applications. To manage files, though, requires the use of a different program. The Windows File Manager is a utility that allows the user to accomplish a number of important file-related tasks from a single interface. Moreover, the ability to use drag-and-drop techniques and other graphical tools to manage the file system makes the process far simpler.

The commands whose jobs are done in full or part by File Manager include:

- DIR
- MD
- CD
- MOVE
- COPY
- XCOPY
- DEL
- DELTREE
- REN
- DISKCOPY
- FORMAT

To open the File Manager, find its icon in the Main group (it looks like a yellow file cabinet) and double-click. The window will open, looking more or less like the image in Figure 8.9, and will have three major areas, plus a menu bar and a status bar.

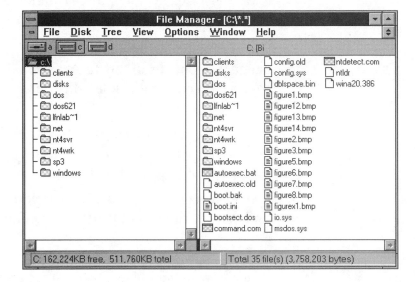

FIGURE 8.9:

Windows File Manager

Along the top of the workspace, just under the menu, is a *drive bar* where the logical drives accessible to the machine are listed. Each drive has a small icon, with a letter to the right of it. Below this are two "panes." The one to the left shows the directory structure of the current drive while the one to the right displays the contents of the currently selected directory. The machine in Figure 8.9 has two local logical drives (C: and D:) as well as a floppy drive (A:). In the root of the C: drive are 10 directories—displayed in yellow—and 26 files which have icons resembling pieces of paper. Note that the directories are listed in both panes, but the files are only on the right.

In DOS, displaying the contents of the directory C:\Aplus\Docs would require the following sequence of commands:

```
a:\> c:
c:\> CD aplus
c:\aplus> CD docs
c:\aplus\docs> dir
```

With the File Manager, all of these commands can be executed simply by using the mouse:

1. Click on the icon for the C: drive in the drive bar. This will change the contents of the directory window below to that of the C: drive, and will display the contents of the root of C: in the right window pane.

2. Double-click on the Aplus directory in the left pane. This will show the contents of the Aplus directory on the right, and will display any subdirectories of Aplus.

3. Double-click on the docs subdirectory in the left pane. This will display the contents of the directory in the right pane.

WARNING We are now going to look for a minute at how easy deleting and moving files is within Windows. This makes it even more likely than under DOS that you or one of the people you support will delete or misplace a file or a number of files that are still needed. In some cases, the UNDELETE utility can be used to recover these files, but this is risky at best, and often does not work. Educate your users on the dangers of playing in the File Manager, and take care yourself when cleaning out files.

Most of the common file commands that you have learned to execute in DOS can be accomplished through the Windows File Manager. You are simply using Windows as an interface to the DOS system, in that your mouse clicks are actually causing the Windows interface to issue the same commands to DOS that you could have typed in yourself. Copying, moving and deleting directories is now accomplished simply by selecting the files you wish to work with. To move or copy, simply click and drag to the new location. To delete, click the Del key on the keyboard after selecting the files to be purged.

Selecting objects in the File Manager usually just involves clicking on the drive, directory, or file you wish to use. At times, though, you may need to select multiple files or directories. This can only be accomplished in the right window (where subdirectories and files are displayed), and involves the use of the Ctrl or the Shift key. Holding down the Ctrl key while clicking on filenames allows you to click multiple files, and instead of changing the focus to a new file as you click it, the focus is shared between files already selected and the new file. Clicking a file and then holding down Shift and selecting another file selects not only both files but any files between them in the list. If the File Manager is new to you, try these to see how they work.

Some other utilities in the File Manager also are very useful. Finding files in a large and complex file structure can be difficult, and the Search option in the File menu can be used to scan the *names* of files and directories on a drive looking for a particular name, phrase, or pattern. The contents of the files are not searched. Standard DOS wildcards can also be used, allowing, for instance, a search for all files with text (.txt) extensions. This would be accomplished using an asterisk (*) as a stand-in for the filename. Asterisks are used to take the place of any number of letters or numbers in a search, while question marks (?) are used to take the place of a single number or letter. To try this, click on File, and then on Search. The Search window will open, and you will be prompted for the Search information. Type ***.txt** in the Search For text box, and in the Start From box enter **C:**. Make sure the checkbox allowing you to search subdirectories is selected (has an X in it), as shown in Figure 8.10, and click OK.

FIGURE 8.10:

The Search window

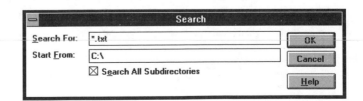

Windows will now search the C: drive, and will eventually display a Search Results window with all of the files it has found.

Besides simplifying most file management commands, the File Manager also allows you to more easily complete a number of disk management tasks. Floppy disks can be formatted and labeled, in addition to having the DOS system files installed. They can also be copied through the Copy Disk option (which uses the DOS DISKCOPY utility). These commands are all located in the Disk menu.

> **NOTE** Most formatting and management of your fixed drives will still be done with the FDISK utility in the DOS directory. The File Manager cannot modify partitions or format hard drives.

Network Options

One of the areas in which the basic Windows product and its Windows for Workgroups cousin differ is the way in which they access information on the network. While Windows depends on a third-party DOS client (such as the DOS Client for Microsoft Networks or the NetWare client software) Windows for Workgroups has networking software built into it, and the Workgroups File Manager has the additional functionality of being able to attach the user to network resources. The regular Windows File Manager cannot do this, but will display and allow access to any drive mappings that already have been mapped using a DOS client. Figure 8.11 shows such a drive, shown as I:, being accessed within Windows 3.1's File Manager.

Networking is not covered on the A+ exam, so we are not going to look at this in detail, but it is a good idea to remember that the Windows 3.11 networking capability does add functionality unavailable in Windows 3.1. Don't be caught unaware if you run into it.

FIGURE 8.11:

Accessing a network
drive

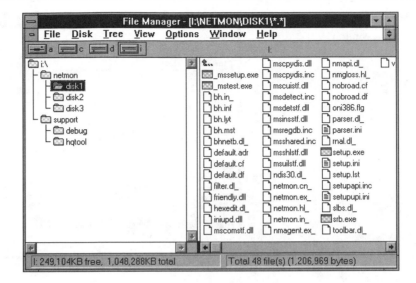

Print Manager

Like file management, the creation and use of printers has been integrated into the Windows interface. This allows you to capture printer ports, install Windows printer drivers, and even examine the print queue Windows creates for your documents. Moreover, Windows is able to help make the print process more efficient, and can save a great deal of time for your users.

The Print Manager is the program that manages all of this, and its icon (a picture of a printer with paper coming out) is in the Main group. If you have not yet installed a printer, the Print Manager window will be relatively blank when you first open it. The Pause, Resume, and Delete buttons will be unavailable (the icons will be grayed out) until a printer is installed. This graying of unavailable options is a characteristic of all well-written Windows programs. The first step toward using this utility is installing a printer, and to do this you need to click on the Options menu, and then select *Printer Setup*. You'll see the dialog box shown in Figure 8.12.

FIGURE 8.12:

The Printers window

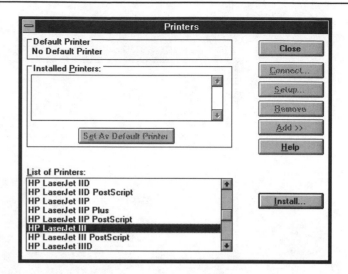

If you have a printer that is listed in the box labeled List of Printers, you should select the printer and click Install. You will then be asked to insert at least one of the Windows installation disks (probably Disk 6). If your printer is not listed, you have to acquire the Windows driver for your particular printer, perhaps from the printer manufacturer's website, and then select *Install Unlisted or Updated Printer*. You will then be asked for the location of the updated driver.

Once the printer is installed, it will appear in the Installed Printers list. You can then select the printer, and click on the Setup button to the right. This will allow you to see additional configuration information for that particular printer. In Figure 8.13 you can see that these options can include the installed fonts, the paper source, and other settings. Generally, these do not need to be configured, as the defaults work well in most situations, but if the printer is not providing you with adequate results using the defaults, check its documentation to see if any of its settings may be modified to remedy the situation.

FIGURE 8.13:

The Setup window for an HP LaserJet III printer

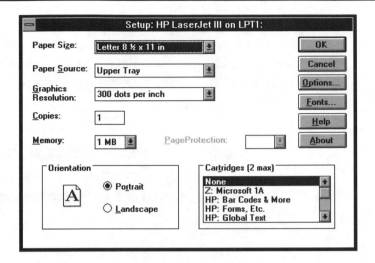

TIP

As some printers are far more complex than others are, they also have more options. Because of this, do not expect all printers to have the same setup options. For instance, a color printer will have color settings options that are not listed on printers that do not have color available. Check each new printer type you install to see what options are available for that model.

Note that the top of the screen also tells you which *local port* the printer is being redirected to. As with DOS, Windows needs to be able to send the job to a specific place. In Figure 8.13 this is LPT1:, but it could potentially have been any of a number of different ports listed in the window that comes up in response to clicking the Connect button seen back in Figure 8.12. Any printer, even one on the network, must be routed through a logical port in DOS and Windows.

Once one printer is installed, other printers may be added, or by clicking Close you can return to the main Print Manager window. The Pause and Resume buttons will now be active, and the printer will be listed below them, as in Figure 8.14. Notice that you do not have to have the printer physically installed on the port to add the print driver. (Nonetheless, if it isn't physically connected you will get errors if you try to print.) Also, since drivers are specific to each printer, if you change the printer you must install the new printer's driver for best performance.

FIGURE 8.14:

The Print Manager window

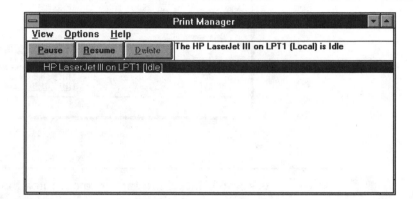

Customizing the Windows Interface

Although for the most part the Windows system is functional from the time it is first installed, Microsoft realized that if people were going to be using computers regularly, they would probably want to be able to customize their environment so that it would be better suited to their needs, or at least more fun to use. Because of this, the Windows environment has a large number of utilities that are intended to give the user control over the look and feel of the Desktop.

This was, of course, an excellent idea. It was also a bit more freedom than some less-than-cautious users seem to be capable of handling, and you will undoubtedly serve a number of customers who have called you in to restore their configuration after a botched attempt at changing one setting or another. More than likely, you will also have to reinstall Windows yourself a few times because of accidents you've created while studying or testing the system's limits. This is actually a good thing, since no competent computer technician can say that they have never had to reinstall because of an error—you can't really know how to fix Windows until you are very experienced in breaking it! It is extremely important to experiment, and to find out what can be changed in the Windows environment, what results from that change, and how to undo any unwanted results! To this end, we will be examining the two most common configuration utilities in Windows—the Control Panel and the Windows Setup utility.

The Control Panel

Located in the Main group, and represented by a computer with a clock, the Control panels are the graphical entryway to the heart of Windows' configurable settings. One of the few applications in Windows that contains icons of its own, the Control Panel utility houses a number of other options. The standard Control Panel icons are shown in Figure 8.15, but various applications and add-on products can add others. We will be taking only a brief look at the uses of these panels, but a number of them are worth exploring closely on your own. For now, though, here is an introduction that focuses on the three most commonly used panels and describes the function of the others.

The Color Panel

The Color panel, represented by three crayons, is one of the most commonly used Control panels. Its purpose is to allow a user to select a color scheme for their Windows Desktop which is easier to see or more appealing aesthetically than the default gray, white, and blue that loads when Windows is first installed.

The Control Panel

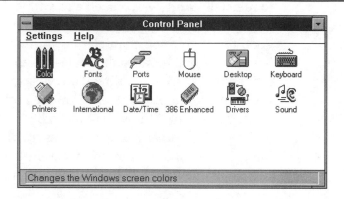

One of the more appealing aspects about the Windows interface is that it is designed to be very responsive to the user, and to give the user the ability to configure a work environment that is unique to them. To this end, the Color panel has two sections, as shown in Figure 8.16.

FIGURE 8.16:

The Color panel

The top part of the Color panel has a drop-down menu with a list of different color combinations that can be used on the system. Each of these color combinations—called "schemes"—specifies the color to be used by every element of the Windows environment, from the Desktop color to the color of the menus to the color of the buttons and their text.

NOTE Drop-down menus are a common device for allowing a user to enter input graphically. The drop-down menu is easily recognized; it's a selection box with a button on its right side that has a down arrow. You can use the mouse to drop down a list box, or clicking the up and down arrows on the keyboard to make a selection.

Experiment a bit with the different schemes available, and look to see what your options are. Trying "Hot Dog Stand" is highly recommended, just so you can see the hideous results that can be produced if you take colors to extremes. Notice that as you select a color scheme, the small window below the menu changes to show the way that the different screen elements would be colored. To test a scheme on the system as a whole, click OK. (You have to scrutinize the screen a little more carefully than usual on this one, because the OK button in the display window doesn't do anything—the real OK is in the lower left!)

To change the scheme back, or to try a different one, double-click Colors again. To modify the color patterns even further, use the "Color Palette >>" button near the bottom of the control panel, which allows you to customize the color schemes themselves. Pressing this button increases the size of the Color panel, as shown in Figure 8.17, and gives the user a color palette from which they can then assign particular colors to individual elements.

Moreover, the Define Custom Colors button in the lower right of this new, larger window allows you to further customize by actually creating colors from the spectrum brought up on the left.

FIGURE 8.17:

The Color control panel customization window

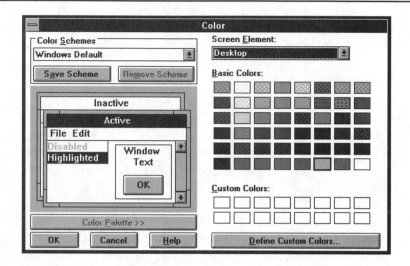

> **NOTE**
>
> If this seems a bit ridiculous to you, you are almost certainly in the majority. Still, it is Microsoft's success at giving people options and making an interface that is almost ludicrously changeable that has made Windows successful.

One of the only real dangers with the Color panel is that an unwary user can accidentally set their foreground and background colors to the same value. This effectively makes some parts of the interface invisible, and makes the system extremely annoying to use. Fortunately, you should be able to simply select a different color scheme (probably the trusty Windows Default scheme) and return the components to usable colors.

The Desktop Panel

Much like the Color control panel, the Desktop panel is used to configure the system so that it is more easily usable and more attractive to look at. The Desktop panel allows a variety of settings:

- Setting a Pattern or a Wallpaper for the Desktop
- Turning on and off the "Alt-Tab" switching feature
- Enabling and configuring a screen saver
- Configuring icon spacing, border sizing, and cursor blink rate

The Pattern and Wallpaper options both apply only to the Windows Desktop, and both affect the way that the Desktop looks, as shown in Figures 8.18 and 8.19. They are different, though, in that the Pattern option applies a texturing or pattern to the surface, while the Wallpaper option places a bitmap file of top of it. Bitmap files can be relatively large. For this reason, loading a Wallpaper consumes more system resources than the comparably small Pattern files do. For highest performance, it is best to use neither, and simply accept the flat Desktop background.

FIGURE 8.18:

The Desktop with a pattern (Weave)

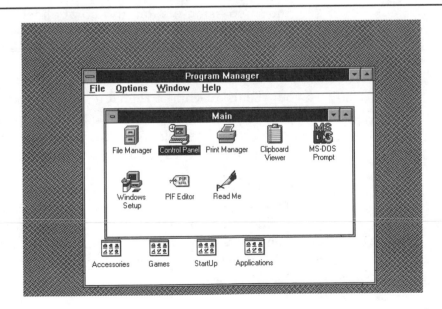

FIGURE 8.19:

The Desktop with the egypt.bmp wallpaper

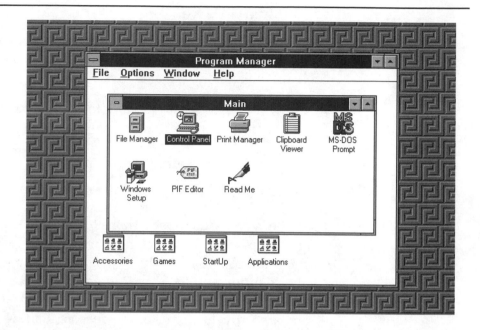

NOTE

Bitmaps are the default image type for Windows. Windows bitmaps have a .BMP extension, and are usually created and modified using the Paintbrush application which can be found in the Accessories group.

It pays to be familiar with the variety of screens you may encounter on your clients' machines. Therefore, before proceeding with your study, try this out: Go into the Desktop panel and try some of the patterns and wallpapers. (First, though, make sure your Program Manager is restored to such a size that you can see the Desktop behind it.)

The other option that you'll find your clients using often is the Screen Saver. Screen savers were initially designed to prevent "burn-in" on older monitors, which could develop permanent "shadows" of screen images that were left on for too long. Screen savers were designed to ensure that after a certain period of time the entire screen would become active, and thus the monitor would be safe from having particular portions of it being burned from overuse. Interestingly, as newer monitors came out that do not generally get damaged by being left on with a static image, the screen saver took on an entertainment function instead, and Windows comes with a number of interesting—and sometimes hypnotizing—screen saver options. To see one of these, click the down arrow in the Name box under the Screen Saver area, as shown in Figure 8.20, and select Starfield Simulation. You'll feel like you're sitting on the bridge of the Starship Enterprise.

FIGURE 8.20:

Selecting the Starfield Simulation on the Desktop panel

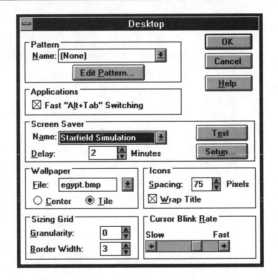

The Delay option below the Name box allows you to set the number of minutes the machine must be idle (no keyboard or mouse input) before the screen saver is loaded. In Figure 8.20, the delay has been set to 2 minutes. Next, click the Setup button to the right. This shows a new dialog box, as shown in Figure 8.21. Here, we can set the particular properties of this screen saver. We can also set a password, so that once it has loaded the screen saver will not deactivate until the correct password has been entered. Note that the other screen savers all have the Password option, but may differ in their other options.

FIGURE 8.21:

The Starfield Simulation Setup window

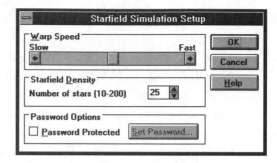

The other features of the Desktop panel are less often changed, and usually should be left alone unless they specifically need to be changed. For an explanation of what Sizing Grid Granularity and other options do, click on the Help button in the Desktop panel, and then click on *Sizing Grid*.

TIP   Help can be a very useful aid in finding out simple facts about the interface. Remember, though, that help files are specific to a particular application. Help on the Desktop control panel, for instance, will provide no assistance on how to change a color scheme, while Help in the Color control panel will.

The 386 Enhanced Panel

Unlike the previous two panels we have looked at, the options in the 386 Enhanced Control Panel are not intended to make the system more aesthetically pleasing or more fun to work with. Rather, the 386 Enhanced panel, shown in Figure 8.22, has a number of options that can distinctly affect the performance of your system. Normal users should stay out of this panel altogether.

FIGURE 8.22:

The 386 Enhanced panel

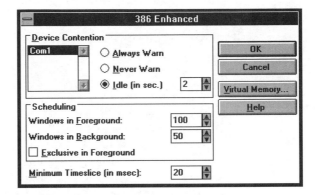

The three options configured in the 386 enhanced panel are:

- Device contention
- Scheduling
- Virtual memory

The device contention configuration allows you to specify how the system should deal with conflicts over resources. If, for instance, two devices are sharing an interrupt, how does the system monitor and arbitrate that relationship? The default here is to use an Idle time of 2 seconds to see if the conflict disappears. Other options are available, but the default is usually fine.

The Scheduling option is an interesting one, and determines how much of the system's resources are dedicated to foreground applications. The foreground application is the application that is currently in front of all the other apps—or, in other words, it is the application whose window is on top of all other open windows. The higher the number, the greater the number of timeslices that will be dedicated to the foreground application (or to the background app if you increase the value in the second spinner box instead). The *Exclusive in Foreground* checkbox takes scheduling to the extreme, and gives

100% of the processor time to the foreground app. If this is checked, the foreground application will run faster, but other applications will not run at all until they are given the focus again (thus bringing them to the foreground).

NOTE

A *spin box* and a *checkbox* are two other types of graphical input tools. The spin box allows the user to select a number from one value range to another simply by clicking the up or down arrow. The value can also be typed in. In the case of the Scheduling spin boxes, the values can range from 1 to 10000. The checkbox is a Boolean field, which has only two values—on (checked) and off (unchecked). Click once to check a box, again to uncheck it.

Probably one of the most important buttons in the Control Panel, and also one that should generally be left alone, is the Virtual Memory button in the 386 Enhanced panel, as shown in Figure 8.23. This button defines the way that your machine will use space on the hard drive to supplement your physical RAM. As the use of this drive space as "virtual memory" is crucial to Windows' performance, you should be careful to set this neither too low *nor* too high.

FIGURE 8.23:

The Virtual Memory window

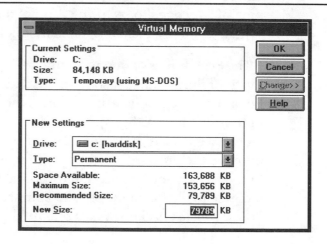

A virtual memory setting which is too low will reduce the size of the "swap file"—the file on the hard drive which acts as virtual RAM—to the point that Windows will not be able to run as many applications concurrently, or may begin to have memory errors. Similarly, a setting that is too high will cause the swap file to be unnecessarily difficult to search for needed information, and will result in a slower system. Because of this the *Recommended Size* value in the Virtual Memory window is almost always the correct value to go with.

A swap file stores information that Windows isn't currently using to a special file on disk. When the particular information is needed by Windows, the information is "swapped" back to main memory for use by Windows. There are two types of swap files: *permanent* and *temporary*. Each swap file has its own unique characteristics.

Permanent swap files are created by Windows the first time it is started. When Windows creates a permanent swap file, it actually creates two files: SPART.PAR and 386SPART.PAR. The first file (SPART.PAR) points to the location of the actual swap file (386SPART.PAR). In order to use a permanent swap file with Windows, you must be running Windows in 386Enhanced mode. Permanent swap files reserve a chunk of the available disk space for their use. That space is not available for use for other files, even when Windows isn't running! Permanent swap files give the best performance, but exact a large "price" in disk space.

TIP   If you ever see one of these files (386SPART.PAR and SPART.PAR) *don't delete them!* Even though they take up a lot of disk space, Windows won't function properly if you delete them. If you need to reclaim some of the space taken up by them, run Windows and use the "Virtual Memory" option in the "386Enhanced" control panel to adjust the size of the permanent swap file.

Temporary swap files, on the other hand, are created every time you start Windows and are deleted when you exit Windows. This kind of swap file is named WIN386.SWP. Temporary swap files are more flexible because their size is dynamic, based on how much disk space is available during Windows startup. Beware, however; they slow Windows down, primarily because they are not as efficient, but also because it takes time during Windows bootup to recreate.

The swap file *can* be deleted, just like any other file, but only if Windows is not running—i.e., it must be deleted through a DOS utility. It will, however, be recreated the next time Windows starts. Do not delete or reduce the size of the swap file to save room on a full drive! When faced with a client who is in a situation where this might seem to be a necessity, recommend instead that the client either delete other seldom-used files or buy an additional or larger hard disk.

If you do want to move or resize the swap file, watch carefully to see how the system performs after the change, and continue making changes to the location or size as necessary until you find that the performance of the system is adequate.

Additional Control Panels

The three Control Panel selections we have examined are by no means the only ones you should take the time to examine. Nonetheless, most of the other options are rather like the 386 Enhanced, in that they should not need to be changed in normal conditions. Nonetheless, the Printers, Drivers, Sound, and other panels do have valuable options, and you should definitely examine them closely.

> **TIP**
>
> Because Windows is a graphical system, the key to learning it inside and out is to click on every option, and examine every window and dialog box. By exploring the system to find out what it can do, you will be better prepared to later decipher what a user has done! Moreover, remember that when you are first learning Windows the solution to a support issue is most often found through your eyes, not your memory. If you have a problem to troubleshoot, begin by looking in all of the windows you can find that may have settings relating to the problem. Often, the answer will actually stare you in the face, in the form of disabled settings that should be enabled, or numbers that are impossibly low (or high) to accomplish what the user is attempting to accomplish!

Windows Setup

The other important configuration area in Windows is Windows Setup, the icon for which is a computer and an open software box, located in the Main group. Windows Setup is not as graphical as the Control panels, and its configuration options are far more advanced. As with the 386 Enhanced control panel, you do not want your users making changes here in most cases. For the technician, though, the Windows Setup window, shown in Figure 8.24, can be a useful area.

FIGURE 8.24:

The Windows Setup window in Windows for Workgroups

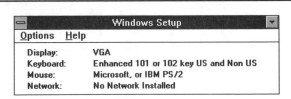

The Windows Setup window shown in Figure 8.24 allows you to quickly see the type of input/output devices installed on a machine. It also has three options in its Options menu that can be used to configure these I/O devices, as well as performing other tasks. The options on the Options menu are:

- Change System Settings
- Set Up Applications
- Add/Remove Windows Components

Changing System Settings

To reconfigure the display, keyboard, or mouse, the Change System Settings option window is used. This window, as shown in Figure 8.25, has either three or four drop-down menus, depending on your version of Windows, and changing any of the selections and clicking OK will change the driver that is used to access that particular device. Note that the graphics shown here includes a fourth menu, used to specify a particular network to attach to. This option is only available on Windows 3.11 (Windows for Workgroups) machines, as they have native network support that is lacking in Windows 3.1.

FIGURE 8.25:

The Change System Settings window in WFW

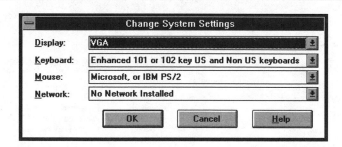

To change a setting, simply select the desired option and click OK. Be sure to have the Windows Setup disks available, because you will usually have to install a new driver, and Windows will ask for one or more of these disks. You have two options here:

- You can search the drop-down list to see if an appropriate driver can be found on the Windows Setup disks.

- Or, if you are setting up a *new* piece of hardware, and it came with a driver disk, select Other (always listed last) and then supply *that* disk when it is requested.

An example of what you will see when you go to change your display settings is shown in Figure 8.26.

FIGURE 8.26:

The Change System Settings window with the Display option menu open

Once you have completed your changes, click OK. At this point the information will be saved, but it won't be active yet. To use the new settings, you must exit Windows. To do this properly, follow these steps:

1. Close all open programs.

2. Click the Control box on the Program Manager and select Close to close Program Manager.

3. Click OK to exit Windows.

4. At a DOS prompt, type **WIN** to start Windows again. This time Windows will run with your changes implemented.

WARNING Changing I/O drivers can be extremely tricky, and a mistake here may render Windows unusable. Luckily, Microsoft realized this, and has included a DOS version of this utility as well. Located by default in C:\windows\setup.exe, this program will allow you to repair ill-advised configuration changes made within Windows Setup. This is especially useful if the Display settings are incorrect, as Windows may be unusable until they are fixed.

Setting Up Applications

The second option in the Setup Windows Option menu is *Setup Applications*. This is a relatively simple utility that allows Windows to go out and look for application programs, and then create an icon for them so they can be accessed through Windows. The initial Setup Applications window has two options, as shown in Figure 8.27, allowing you to either search for applications or set up a particular app. The system will then either allow you to type in a path to the application or will begin a search for .EXE and .COM files, depending on your selection. The programs are then added as new icons to the groups in Program Manager.

FIGURE 8.27:

The Setup Applications window

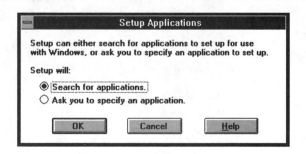

Adding and Removing Windows Components

The last of the Setup options is *Add/Remove Windows Components*. This option brings up a window which allows you to change which optional components are installed on the system. To add or delete an entire group of programs or options, check or uncheck the Component checkbox. The amount of space taken up on the hard drive by a particular component is listed in the Bytes Used column to the right, and the Files button to the far right allows you to add or delete particular pieces of a component without affecting the other pieces. Note that not all components can be modified here. For example, Windows itself cannot be uninstalled from here.

Let's take an example. To uninstall all of the games on the system, for instance, uncheck the Games icon and click OK. To uninstall only some of the game elements, click on the Files button. You'll see the specialized type of dialog box shown in Figure 8.28.

FIGURE 8.28:

The Add/Remove Games window

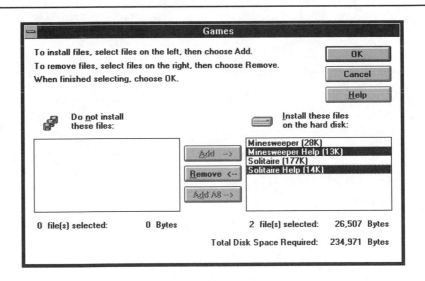

In this box you can select the elements you want to uninstall. Click Remove and the selected elements will move to the *Do not install*

these files: list. Click OK twice to complete the process. Note that by default, *all* the options will have been installed in a standard Windows installation, and so will all appear on the right.

Summary

As you look through the possible options in the dialog boxes we've introduced in this chapter, you will notice that we have not looked at all of the options. We have not, for instance, learned how to use the Paintbrush or the CardFile. These and other productivity utilities are definitely worth taking some time to learn, if only because some of your clients may have questions about them, but you will not be tested on them for A+, as they are not fundamental computing environment issues.

Review Questions for Chapter 8, Windows Interface Overview

Answers to the review questions may be found in Appendix A.

1. Which of the following is not an important function of Windows?

    A. running applications

    B. preparing hard disks for use

    C. managing files and directories

    D. managing printing

2. The Windows Desktop is responsible for what duties?

    A. printing

    B. managing applications

    C. managing files

    D. nothing

3. Which of the following is not included within the Program Manager?

    A. icon

    B. group

    C. Desktop

    D. menu

4. Which of these best describes an icon?

    A. any Windows-based program file

    B. the graphical configuration file needed to run all Windows apps

    C. the graphical shortcut to a file

    D. a graphical application

5. In which of these states does a window have a border?

   A. restored

   B. maximized

   C. minimized

   D. all of the above

6. Which of these is used to close a window?

   A. Restore button

   B. Title bar

   C. Minimize button

   D. Control box

7. Which of the following is not a mouse function?

   A. double-click

   B. skip

   C. drag

   D. click

8. Which of these is not configurable through an icon's Properties window?

   A. its label

   B. its working directory

   C. its group

   D. its icon graphic

9. Where will you *not* find icons?

   A. the Desktop

   B. the Program Manager workspace

    C. in a group

    D. in the Control Panel

10. Which DOS wildcard is used in File Manager to represent any number of characters in a string?

    A. *

    B. %

    C. @

    D. ?

11. In which area do Windows and Windows for Workgroups differ?

    A. file management

    B. network support

    C. local printing

    D. virtual memory settings

12. A printer must be attached to a logical _____.

    A. window

    B. I/O address

    C. device

    D. port

13. The Control Panel is used to configure:

    A. system settings

    B. DOS settings

    C. applications

    D. I/O drivers

14. A set of colors which define the appearance of Windows element is a _____.

    A. scheme

    B. group

    C. palette

    D. rainbow

15. This method of switching between applications can be turned off in the Desktop Control Panel:

    A. Ctrl+Esc

    B. Alt+Tab

    C. Alt+Enter

    D. Ctrl+Tab

16. Which of the following is *not* an option under Windows Setup in Windows 3.1?

    A. Display

    B. Keyboard

    C. Mouse

    D. Network

17. Selecting the Exclusive in Foreground option in the 386 Enhanced control panel affects the foreground application by:

    A. slowing it down

    B. speeding it up

    C. assigning it specific memory

    D. assigning it specific hard disk space

18. Which of the following is used to represent a Boolean (on or off) option?

    A. checkbox

    B. spinner box

    C. drop-down menu

    D. icon

19. Which of the following Control panels is used to password-protect a Windows workstation?

    A. Colors

    B. Keyboard

    C. Enhanced

    D. Desktop

20. Which of the following Windows utilities also comes with a DOS version?

    A. Control Panel

    B. Program Manager

    C. Print Manager

    D. Windows Setup

21. Which Windows component is responsible for displaying program icons?

    A. System Manager

    B. File Manager

    C. Icon Manager

    D. Program Manager

22. To start a program, you must do which of the following?

   A. Select "Run Program" from the File menu.

   B. Drag the icon for the program to the Start button.

   C. Double-click the appropriate icon.

   D. Any of the above.

23. Which of the following is *not* part of the windows interface?

   A. scroll bars

   B. switches

   C. icons

   D. the mouse pointer

24. Which control panel controls the settings for Virtual Memory?

   A. The Memory control panel

   B. The System control panel

   C. The Desktop control panel

   D. The 386 Enhanced control panel

25. What are the two types of swap files used with Windows?

   A. virtual

   B. permanent

   C. temporary

   D. real

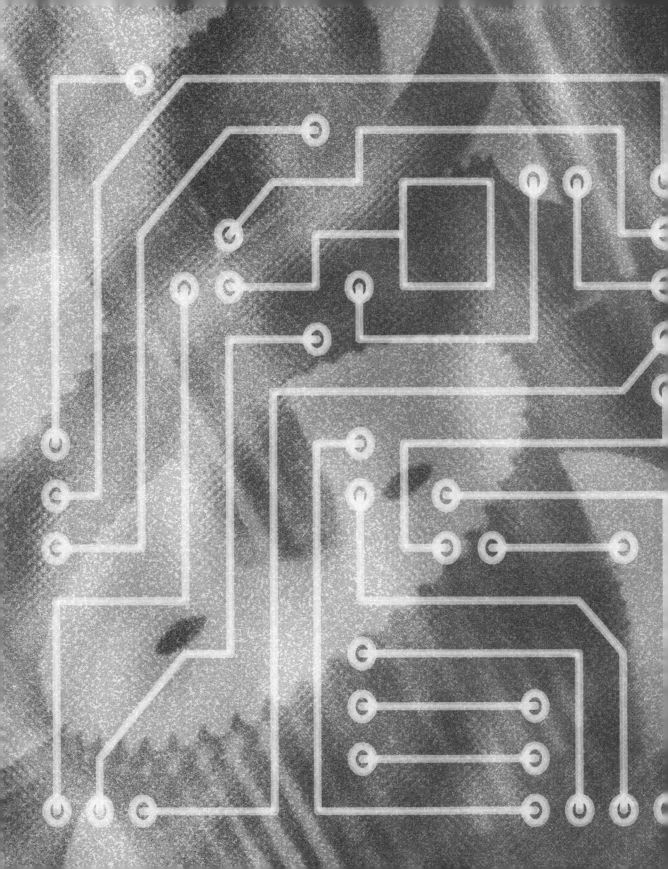

Installing Windows 3.1

- Prerequisites for Windows 3.1 Installation

- Installing Using Express Setup

- Installing Using Custom Setup

- The DOS Portion of Setup

- The Windows Portion of Setup

Now that we have discussed the basics of Windows, we need to discuss how to install it. Installing Windows is a relatively simple act that every technician will have to perform several times throughout their career. The A+ exam covers several Windows installation topics, so we will pay particular attention to the major installation steps:

- Prerequisites for Windows 3.1 Installation
- Installing Using Express Setup
- Installing Using Custom Setup
- The DOS Portion of Setup
- The Windows Portion of Setup

We will actually go into more detail than the exam does. However, you may install Windows so often, you might not think about the exact steps. This chapter may also detail some installation options you may not have used before.

For this chapter we need to make two assumptions

- First, that the version of Windows you are installing is version 3.1 (as the title of this chapter suggests). Installation for Windows 3.11 (Windows for Workgroups) is mostly the same as for Windows 3.1. (Also, the A+ exams cover the Windows 3.1 version only.) From now on, when I say "Windows" in the rest of this book, I will be talking about Windows 3.1 unless otherwise specified.

- Second, we assume that you are installing from 3½" floppy diskettes. This is the default medium, but it is also possible to get Windows on 5¼" disks by writing to Microsoft.

Prerequisites for Windows 3.1 Installation

Just as with the installation of DOS, Windows has its own set of prerequisites. Because Windows is a graphical interface, instead of keyboard-command based, it has a longer list of prerequisites (as well as more stringent ones).

Computer System

Windows 3.1 requires a 286 or better processor. A 286 is required for running Windows in Standard mode, and a 386 or better is required for running Windows in 386-Enhanced mode. (See the sidebar "What Is a Windows Operating Mode?" for an explanation of Standard and 386-Enhanced modes.)

Operating System

Windows is only a shell for an existing operating system and therefore requires that one is installed before you can install Windows. Windows can be installed over MS-DOS or PC-DOS version 3.1 or later. Windows should be installed over DOS versions greater than 5.0.

Disk Space

Windows requires more disk space than DOS alone, so you must take into account your current disk space situation. A new installation of Windows 3.1 requires at least 8 MB (possibly up to 11 MB) available. An upgrade from an earlier version of Windows will require anywhere from 5 MB up to 5.5 MB (in addition to what the current version already uses).

Memory

Windows 3.1 requires at least 640 KB of conventional memory and 1024 KB (1 MB) of Extended memory for 386-Enhanced mode (approximately 2,048 KB). If you are running in Standard mode, those requirements are reduced, somewhat, to 640 KB of conventional and 256 KB of extended. Also, in order to access Extended memory, you must make sure that there is an extended memory manager (like HIMEM.SYS) loaded. If there isn't one currently loaded, the Windows Setup program will make the changes to your CONFIG.SYS to load it.

Mouse

Windows is a graphical interface. As such, it uses a pointer and icons to represent files, programs, and disks. To move this pointer, you need to use a mouse. It is possible to run Windows without a mouse, but it is very difficult. Also, some commands in some Windows programs don't have keyboard shortcuts. In short, you really should have some type of mouse attached to your computer in order to use Windows

Video

DOS uses video circuitry differently than Windows does. DOS uses a video card's character mode (also called text mode). Character mode has a lower resolution than its other mode, graphics mode. Character mode is faster than graphics mode, but graphics mode has a higher resolution and can take advantage of most of any particular video card's features. For this reason, a video card that has a *Windows driver* is also required, as well as a monitor that is compatible with that type of video card.

WARNING Remember that these *prerequisites* are just that. They are *bare minimums*! You can get Windows to run with these settings, but don't expect to get any work done. Windows 3.1 *should* be run on nothing less than a 386 with 4 MB of RAM and 30 MB of disk space free for adequate performance. Increasing any of these resources will improve Windows' performance. We have actually installed Windows on a 286 machine with 1.5 MB of RAM, and it *does* run, but we couldn't do much with it. The NOTEPAD program takes a full minute to launch. And, when typing in windows, it takes a second or two between keypresses and seeing the character appear on the screen!

What Is a Windows Operating Mode?

When Windows 1.0 came out, it was pretty basic. It was designed to run on any PC. At that time, the fastest PC was one based on a 286 processor. When Windows 3.0 was going to come out, Microsoft had a problem. The fastest processor then was the 386 processor which had several new features (multitasking, access to more memory, etc.). They wanted to use the new features of the 386 processor, but still provide compatibility for people running Windows on older hardware. To deal with this, they introduced the *operating mode* feature. When Windows is first started, it detects what kind of hardware it's running on. If the hardware can support it, Windows runs in *386-Enhanced mode* to take advantage of all of the features that the 386 processor had to offer. If the hardware can't support it, Windows drops into what is called *Standard mode*. This mode makes Windows run as if it is running on a 286 processor, even though it may actually be running on a 486.

Installing Windows 3.1

Assuming the machine you are going to install Windows on has met the prerequisites, you now have two choices: Install Windows using Express Setup or install it using Custom Setup. When you run Setup.EXE from the A: drive, you will be presented with a somewhat familiar blue installation screen. This screen will, eventually, ask if you want install via Express or Custom.

Express Setup

Express Setup makes a few assumptions about the way you would like Windows installed. For example, it automatically picks for you which Windows applications and utilities will be installed (i.e. Notepad, Solitaire, and Windows Write). We will detail a little later which specific settings can be chosen.

Because Windows is a unique program, the installation has been divided into two parts: the DOS portion and the Windows portion.

DOS Portion

The first part of Windows installation is the DOS Setup portion. In this portion, the files for Windows Setup portion are copied to the hard disk and decompressed—which brings up a good point: Installing Windows (and most programs these days) doesn't mean simply copying the files from the installation disk to the hard disk. It usually also involves *decompression*. The files were compressed to fit more files on the floppy disks in the first place. Therefore, when you run an installation program (like Setup.EXE), it decompresses the files as it copies them to the hard disk.

Let's run through a typical Windows Express installation.

Starting Setup   The installation program that you use to install Windows to your hard disk (Windows *cannot* be installed to a floppy disk—there isn't nearly enough space) is called Setup.EXE and is located on the first disk of the Windows installation diskettes. This disk is labeled "Disk 1." Normally, to install Windows, you type **Setup** at the A: prompt. However, sometimes there are special situations to consider. For this reason, the Setup program has a few command-line options that can be used to customize how Setup runs. Table 9.1 details these options.

TABLE 9.1:   Windows Setup Command-Line Options

Option	Example	Description
/A	Setup /A	"Administrative Setup." Decompresses the Windows files and places them in a server directory you specify and marks them "read-only." Use this option if you are planning to run Windows from the network. (Used with the "/N" option.)
/N	Setup /N	Sets up a workstation from a network (shared) copy of Windows (set up with the "/A" option above). Run Setup from the network with this option.
/I	Setup /I	Ignores Setup's hardware detection. With this option, Setup ignores any hardware types it detects, and the person installing Windows must manually verify all hardware type information during Setup. Use this option if Setup is locking up before getting to the first screen.
/S:*path*	Setup /S:C:\winSetup	Specifies the path to the Windows compressed files.
/O:*file*	Setup /O:C:\winSetup\Setup.INF	Specifies the path and filename of the Setup.INF file.

TABLE 9.1 CONTINUED: Windows Setup Command-Line Options

Option	Example	Description
/B	Setup /B	Runs Setup with monochrome video options. If you have a black-and-white monitor, run Setup with this option.
/H:*file*	Setup /H:C:\ACME.INF	Runs Setup in batch mode, where *file* specifies the name of the systems settings file (See Microsoft's Windows 3.1 website for information on creating this file.)
/T	Setup /T	Searches the target installation drive for possible conflicting memory-resident (TSR) programs. Check with the manufacturer of a particular TSR to see whether or not it's compatible.
/C	Setup /C	Disables the search for TSR programs. If you need to install Windows and Setup doesn't recognize one of the memory-resident programs, run Setup with this switch.

To start your Windows installation, place the Windows installation disk labeled "Disk 1" into your A: drive and type **A:Setup**, like so:

A:Setup

Setup will present you with a message that says "Please wait…" while it checks the hardware configuration of your computer. After a few seconds, the blue installation welcome screen (Figure 9.1) will appear and welcome you to Windows Setup.

Just like the MS-DOS Setup covered in Chapter 4, the Setup program for Windows has a few keys that perform certain functions during the Setup process. F1 is for help, F3 is for exiting Setup, Enter accepts, and the arrow keys navigate through menu choices. If you wonder what keys you can press, look at the gray bar at the bottom of the screen. It will give you choices for which keys are active.

Windows Setup's wel-
come screen

```
Windows Setup
════════════════

        Welcome to Setup.

        The Setup program for Windows 3.1 prepares Windows
        to run on your computer.

            •   To learn more about Windows Setup before continuing, press F1.

            •   To set up Windows now, press ENTER.

            •   To quit Setup without installing Windows, press F3.
```

If you want to read the HELP information, go ahead and press F1,
otherwise, press Enter to continue.

Choosing Express Setup   At this point, you will see the figure
shown in Figure 9.2. This screen allows you to choose which type
of Setup to use: Express or Custom. The fastest way to do this is to
use the Express Setup. Choosing Express Setup allows Setup to
make the following decisions for the user:

- Setup automatically configures mouse, keyboard, language,
  and network (if there is any). It will also automatically configure AUTOEXEC.BAT and CONFIG.SYS files for optimum Windows performance.

- Setup will suggest that you install Windows to C:\WINDOWS.
  If there is a version of Windows already installed, it will ask the
  user if they want to upgrade.

- Searches for available disk space on other local disk drives if
  there is not enough space available on the C: drive.

- Setup will recommend a partial Setup if there is not enough
  disk space to install the standard install of Windows.

- If you are upgrading from Windows 3.0, Setup will set up any currently installed printers.

- Setup will automatically make icons for any existing Windows (and certain DOS) applications that are on your hard disk. Setup scans your hard disk and looks for Windows applications (and some DOS applications, like EDIT.COM) and makes icons for them.

- When Setup is finished, it will offer some basic instruction on how to use the mouse and some basic Windows concepts.

If you would like to make any of these decisions, you must choose the Custom Setup option by pressing the C key. We will discuss the Custom Setup option later in this chapter.

FIGURE 9.2:

Express or Custom Setup—Your choice

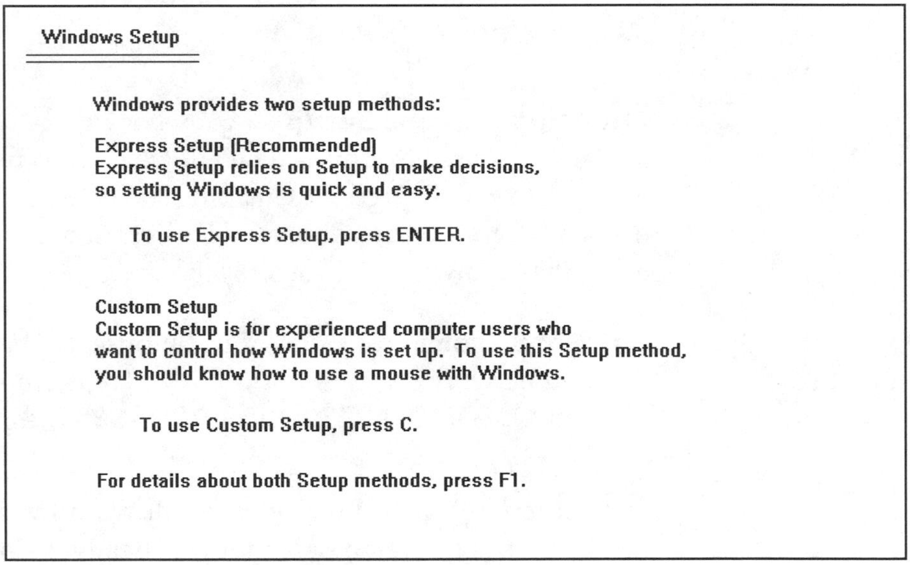

Windows Setup

Windows provides two setup methods:

Express Setup (Recommended)
Express Setup relies on Setup to make decisions,
so setting Windows is quick and easy.

   To use Express Setup, press ENTER.

Custom Setup
Custom Setup is for experienced computer users who
want to control how Windows is set up. To use this Setup method,
you should know how to use a mouse with Windows.

   To use Custom Setup, press C.

For details about both Setup methods, press F1.

To continue setting up Windows, press Enter to choose Express Setup and begin copying files to your hard disk.

NOTE At this point, no files have been copied until you press Enter. Once pressed, Setup will begin copying files to your hard disk. You can press F3 at any point during the installation to cancel it. If you press F3 now, no changes will have been made to your disk.

DOS Setup File Copy At this point, Setup will detect your current hardware configuration and begin copying files to your hard disk and decompressing them (Figure 9.3). You can watch this process in the lower right-hand corner of the screen. This corner will indicate what file is being copied. There is also a status bar at the bottom of the screen that indicates the percentage of files copied.

FIGURE 9.3:

The DOS portion Setup's "file-copy" screen

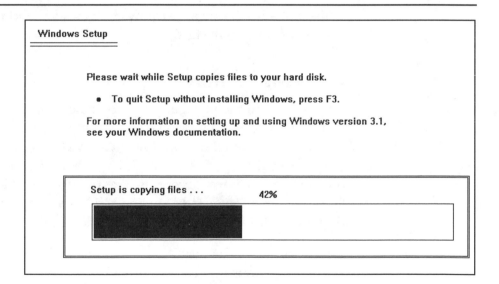

When the status bar reaches about halfway across the screen, Setup will stop and ask you to insert the second disk (Figure 9.4). Remove the first disk from the floppy drive and insert the second one (labeled "Disk 2"). Once this is done, press Enter to continue copying files.

FIGURE 9.4:

The DOS portion Setup asking for Disk #2

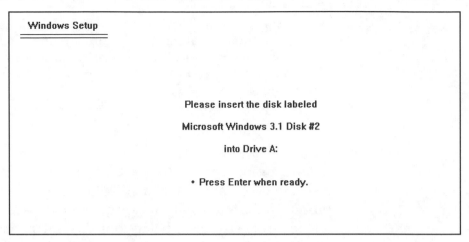

When the file copy has completed, Setup will notify you to wait while it starts Windows. Windows will execute and the Windows portion of Setup will start.

Windows Portion

At this point in the installation, you are now running Windows. It is really a scaled-down version of Windows, since it isn't loading all the drivers and the Program Manager. Once Windows has executed, it will run the Windows Setup utility. This utility performs the same function as its DOS counterpart. The Windows portion of the installation finalizes the installation and modifies both the Windows configuration files and the DOS configuration files.

This portion of the installation is easier with a Mouse attached. There are buttons you can click to answer the various questions that Setup asks you. To click these buttons, Windows needs to be able to communicate with a mouse. If a mouse has been detected by Windows, then when Windows starts you will see a white mouse pointer (See Figure 9.5). If the mouse pointer does not appear, you can still install Windows; just use the Tab key to switch between active buttons, and the Enter key to select them. An "active" button has an extra dark line around it.

FIGURE 9.5:

The Windows mouse
pointer

Entering User Information   The next step in the installation of
Windows is to enter the name and company of the person that is
going to use Windows. This information is stored for future use by
other installation programs (Microsoft products pull their registration information, in part, from these two fields). Figure 9.6 shows an
example of the name and company screen. Enter your name in the
first field, and the company, if applicable, that you are installing
Windows for.

FIGURE 9.6:

Entering user and
company information

> **Windows Setup**
>
> Please type your full name in the box below. You
> may also specify the name of your company if
> Windows will be used for business purposes.
>
> Then choose Continue or press ENTER.
>
> The information you enter will be sued by Setup
> for subsequent installations of Windows
>
> Name: [   ]
>
> Company: [   ]

Once you have entered your name and company information,
click Continue. A window will appear asking you to verify that you
typed your information correctly. If you have entered your information correctly, click Continue again. If not, click Change and you will
be taken back to the screen in Figure 9.6 and you will be asked to
enter that information again.

Windows Portion Setup File Copy   Now that Windows knows who you are, it can proceed to copy files. During the copying of files, you will see a screen similar to the one in Figure 9.7.

FIGURE 9.7:

Windows portion Setup's file-copy screen

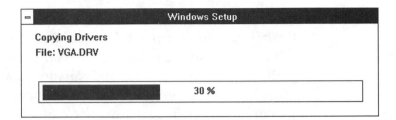

This screen has several similarities to the DOS Copy Files screen (Figure 9.3). First of all, there is a copy status bar, except in the Windows copy screen, it's blue instead of yellow. Also, there is an area that displays which file is being copied, but in the Windows file-copy screen, this area is in the upper left, instead of the lower right. This difference is vitally important, because if you're propping your head on your hands at this point and you're staring generally downward, you may miss the message that can change your life.

When the file copy gets to approximately 30%, Setup will ask for Disk #3 by displaying a screen similar to the one in Figure 9.8. Insert #3 in the floppy drive, and click Continue or hit Enter to allow the file copy to continue.

When the file copy gets to approximately 80%, Setup will ask for Disk #4 and display another "Insert disk..." screen like the one in Figure 9.8. Remove disk #3 and insert #4. Click Continue or hit Enter to allow the file copying to continue.

When the file copy reaches 100%, the file copy is finished and Setup will start setting up any DOS and Windows applications.

FIGURE 9.8:

Windows portion Setup asking for Disk #3

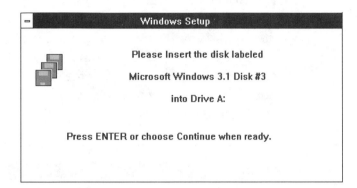

Setting Up Applications   Once the file copy has finished, Setup will create the main program groups (Main, Accessories, Games, Startup and Applications). Then it will search the hard disk for Windows applications and DOS applications (that it knows about through entries in its APPS.INF file). When it finds one, it creates an icon for it in the "Applications" program group. If there are several, it will create a second program group, called Applications 2.

For some reason, Microsoft can never recognize one of its own programs: The MS-DOS Editor (EDIT.COM). Setup always asks what this program is. It does this by presenting you with a dialog box that gives you a choice between "MS-DOS Editor" and "None of the above" (see Figure 9.9). Click on "MS-DOS Editor," then click OK to accept this as the program Setup should make the icon for.

FIGURE 9.9:

Application setup for EDIT.COM

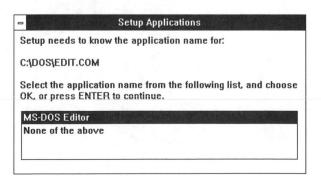

Windows Tutorial   After making the icons for the Windows and DOS applications, Setup is pretty much finished. The last thing it does is ask you if you want to run the tutorial (Figure 9.10). Personally, I've never run the tutorial because I have used Windows several times. If you are in the same situation, click Skip Tutorial. It is not the default, so you will have to hit Tab (or the down arrow key) once before you hit Enter.

FIGURE 9.10:

You can run the Windows tutorial at this point if you wish.

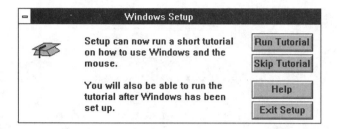

Finishing Up   Windows is now installed. A screen appears telling you just that (Figure 9.11). From this point, you have two choices: Restart Windows or Return to MS-DOS. Restarting Windows loads Windows with the Program Manager and all drivers. Returning to DOS exits Windows and returns you to the DOS command prompt.

FIGURE 9.11:

Setup finished!

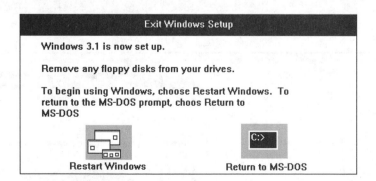

NOTE It is best to choose "Return to MS-DOS" at the Finished screen. Once you've done this, you can reboot the computer so that any changes that may have been made to the CONFIG .SYS or AUTOEXEC.BAT can take effect. If you don't do this, Windows may not function properly.

Custom Setup

The other option for setting up Windows is to use the Custom Setup option. You will choose this option if you would like to be able to choose the Windows settings that the Express Setup chooses for you automatically. (See the list under the "Express Setup" section earlier in this chapter for a list of the possible settings and assumptions that Express Setup makes for you). Just like Express Setup, the installation of Windows under Custom Setup is divided into two portions, the DOS Setup Portion and the Windows Setup Portion. Let's discuss the details of each portion.

NOTE Several items in the Custom Setup are the same as in Express Setup. I will indicate which are the same and which are different as we discuss the Custom Setup.

DOS Portion

The DOS portion of the Custom Setup is responsible for copying files and preparing for the Windows portion, exactly like the DOS portion of the Express Setup. The major difference between the two is that the DOS portion of the Custom Setup allows you to make more choices (as described above).

Let's run through a typical Custom Setup.

Starting Setup   This Setup program is started the same way as Express Setup. Simply insert Disk 1 into the A: drive and type the following at your C: prompt.

`A:Setup`

This will start the Setup program. At this point, Setup will show the "Please Wait…" then the "Welcome to Setup Screen" (as shown previously in Figure 9.1). The same options exist at this screen as in the Express Setup (get help, quit, or set up Windows now). To begin the Setup of Windows, press Enter.

Choosing Custom Setup   At this point, you will see the "Choose Your Setup Method" screen (as shown previously in Figure 9.2) This is the step where the first difference between Express and Custom Setups appears. Instead of pressing Enter to continue with an Express Setup, you need to press the letter C to perform a Custom Setup. This choice will give you more options during the installation.

Specifying Windows Directory   Another difference between the Custom and Express Setup is that Custom Setup lets you specify which directory to install Windows in (Figure 9.12). If C:\WINDOWS

FIGURE 9.12:

Choosing the Windows installation directory

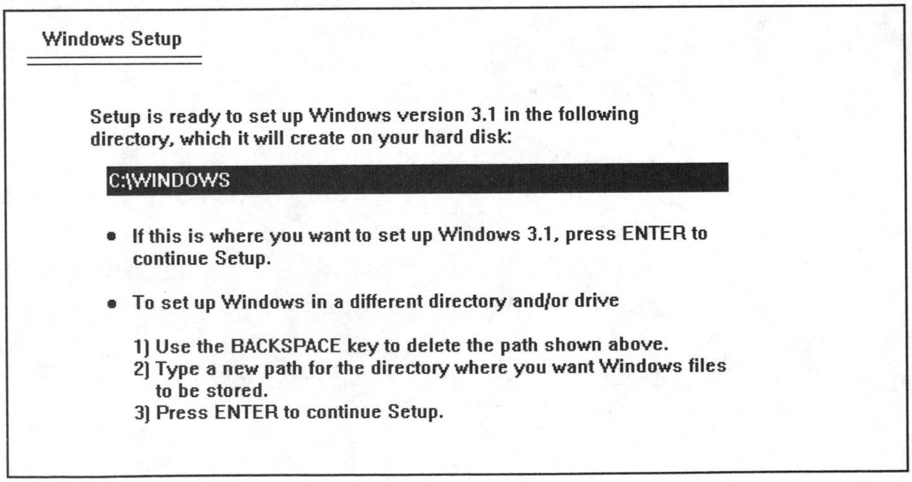

```
Windows Setup
════════════

    Setup is ready to set up Windows version 3.1 in the following
    directory, which it will create on your hard disk:

    ┌────────────────────────────────────────────────────┐
    │ C:\WINDOWS                                          │
    └────────────────────────────────────────────────────┘

    •  If this is where you want to set up Windows 3.1, press ENTER to
       continue Setup.

    •  To set up Windows in a different directory and/or drive

       1) Use the BACKSPACE key to delete the path shown above.
       2) Type a new path for the directory where you want Windows files
          to be stored.
       3) Press ENTER to continue Setup.
```

is the directory you want to install Windows in, go ahead and press Enter to continue. However, if you want to install Windows to another directory, hit Backspace several times to delete C:\WINDOWS from the entry field and type in a new path (for example, C:\WIN31). Once you have accepted the default path or entered a new one, press Enter to continue the installation.

Specifying Windows Settings   The next screen, which appears only in the Custom Setup process, is the Windows settings screen (Figure 9.13). This screen displays the hardware and software Setup detected on your machine when it was first started. Check this list over carefully. If there are any discrepancies between the settings Setup chooses and what hardware and software is installed on your computer, you can change them. To do this, use the up and down arrow keys on your keyboard to move the selection bar to the setting you want to change. Then press Enter. This will bring up another screen with a list of possible choices for the setting. Use the up and down arrows to select the new choice and press Enter. This will accept the change and return you to the screen shown in Figure 9.13. Table 9.2 describes the Windows settings that can be changed from this screen.

FIGURE 9.13:

Changing Windows settings

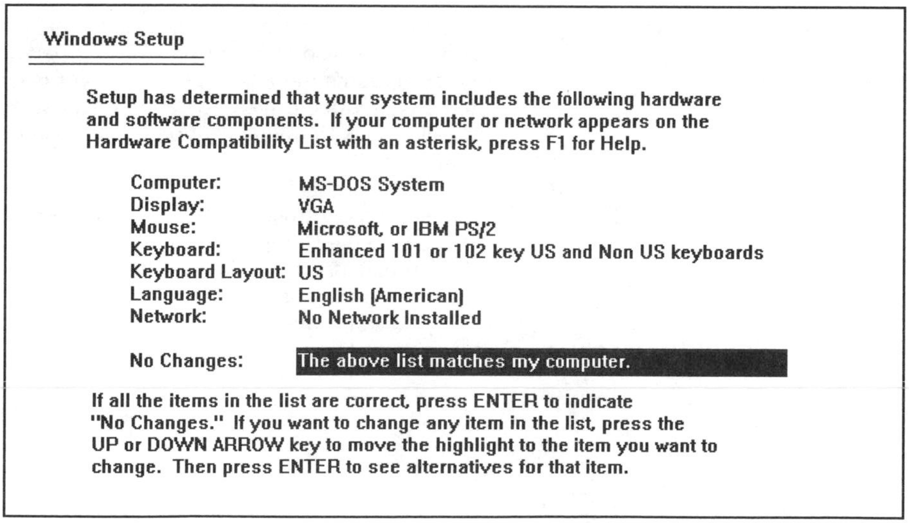

```
Windows Setup
═══════════

      Setup has determined that your system includes the following hardware
      and software components.  If your computer or network appears on the
      Hardware Compatibility List with an asterisk, press F1 for Help.

         Computer:        MS-DOS System
         Display:         VGA
         Mouse:           Microsoft, or IBM PS/2
         Keyboard:        Enhanced 101 or 102 key US and Non US keyboards
         Keyboard Layout: US
         Language:        English (American)
         Network:         No Network Installed

         No Changes:      The above list matches my computer.

      If all the items in the list are correct, press ENTER to indicate
      "No Changes." If you want to change any item in the list, press the
      UP or DOWN ARROW key to move the highlight to the item you want to
      change.  Then press ENTER to see alternatives for that item.
```

WARNING Remember that these settings are detected by Setup and should be considered accurate, unless your documentation says otherwise.

TABLE 9.2: Possible Windows Settings

Setting	Description
Computer	Most often this setting is set to "MS-DOS System" (for generic MS-DOS-based computers). If the computer has special concessions (like a low-power processor that needs to go to sleep every once in awhile) that need to be made, you will need to choose the driver that most closely matches your system. If one isn't listed, check your documentation.
Display	This is a very important setting. This setting is the Windows video driver. If this setting is set to the wrong driver, the Windows portion of Setup won't function correctly (You won't be able to see the Setup screens). Your video card documentation will contain information about which driver to use. It may also include a disk with that driver on it. To use that driver, select the option "Other (Requires disk provided by a hardware manufacturer)" in the drop-down list. Setup will ask you for the location of the driver, which you can type in and press Enter. (This option is available in all of these configuration lists.)
Mouse	This setting allows you to select the mouse driver that Windows uses. This is also an important setting because Windows can't use the computer's mouse unless the driver is correct. It's not as important as the video driver, however, because you can still finish the installation with only a keyboard if you have to (it's mostly pressing Enter).
Keyboard	This setting controls which type of keyboard Windows will be using. Like the Computer setting, most keyboards use one setting ("Enhanced 101 or 102 key US and Non US keyboards"). You would only need to choose a different one if there is a special situation. See your computer's or keyboard's documentation for details if you suspect you're in one of those situations.

TABLE 9.2 CONTINUED: Possible Windows Settings

Setting	Description
Keyboard Layout	This setting controls which keys, when struck, make which extended characters (characters such as @#$!%^;:"'> and < among others). Also, foreign keyboard layouts may contain extra characters (like accented letters) that will need to be mapped to a keyboard.
Language	This setting controls the language of the Windows dialog boxes and help files.
Network	This setting indicates which network Windows will support. With Windows 3.1, it relies on DOS for most network software, but Windows components must be installed to allow Windows to take advantage of the network. If you are not installing Windows on a computer that is hooked to a network, this setting should be "No Network Installed."

When you are finished changing settings, or you agree with the settings Setup has chosen for you, highlight "The above list matches my computer" and hit Enter to begin copying files.

DOS Setup File Copy   The DOS Portion file copy is exactly the same as in the Express Setup. Both file copy operations copy the Windows portion files and expand them (decompress them) to the hard disk. The copy screens both have status bars that indicate the installation's progress. There is only one difference between the DOS file copy for Custom Setup and the DOS file copy for Express Setup, and it's really a trivial one. The screen that asks for disk #2 looks different. Compare Figure 9.4 earlier in the chapter (Express Setup) with Figure 9.14 here (Custom Setup). Notice in Figure 9.14, Setup is actually asking you where the Setup disk is, instead of assuming that it's in Drive A:. To continue, type in the path to the Windows files from Disk #2 (or the drive where Disk #2 is located) and press Enter to continue copying files.

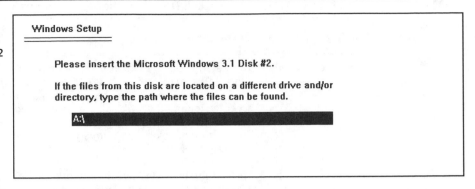

FIGURE 9.14:

The DOS portion file-copy asking for Disk #2

The file copy will continue until the DOS file-copy status bar reaches 100%. At this point, the DOS portion of Setup starts Windows and executes the Windows Setup program.

Windows Portion

The Windows portion of the Custom Setup has the exact same responsibilities as the Windows portion of the Express Setup: copying files and configuring the Windows user interface. When the DOS portion of the Custom Setup is finished, it will start Windows. Since this is the first time Windows has been executed, it will start the Windows Setup program. The installation can then continue.

Entering User Information   Once the Windows portion of the Custom Setup has begun, the first thing it does is ask who you are and what company you work for. (This was shown previously in Figure 9.6.) This step is another one that is just like Express Setup. Enter your name, press Tab to move to the next field, and enter your company name (if applicable), then press Enter or click Continue. Setup will ask you to verify that you have entered the correct information. If it is correct, click Continue, if not, click Change to be taken back to the previous screen.

Windows Setup Choices   This step is unique to the Custom Setup. Figure 9.15 shows the next screen to appear. This screen allows to choose how the Custom Setup proceeds. There are three checkboxes in this screen, one next to each item you want Windows to install. If you want Windows to make a default installation of all programs, you need to click in the checkbox next to the first item in the list ("Set Up Only Windows Components You Select") so that the X is removed from the box. If you leave this checkbox checked, you will be asked which programs and utilities you want Setup to install. All three items in the list are checked by default.

FIGURE 9.15:

You can make your choice of Windows components.

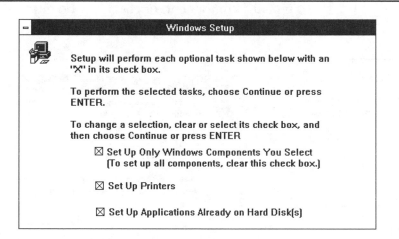

If you want to select a printer driver as part of the installation, make sure the second box is checked (the default). If not, uncheck this box. Finally, if you want Setup to search for Windows applications on the hard disk and make icons for them in the Program Manager, leave the last box checked. If not, uncheck this box.

For the purposes of our installation, leave all three checkboxes checked, and click Continue.

NOTE   If one of these checkboxes is unchecked, you won't see the corresponding screen for the sections we discuss next (i.e. if you uncheck "Set Up Printers" you won't be given the option to add a printer).

Choosing Windows Components   The next screen allows you to choose which Windows applications and utilities to install (Figure 9.16). They are grouped into several categories that Setup calls "components." Just as in the previous step, if you don't want to install a component, uncheck the box in front of the component you don't want to install.

FIGURE 9.16:

Choosing Windows applications and utilities

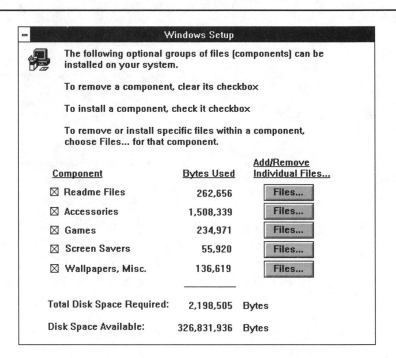

Let's say, for example, you want to install only Solitaire, but not Minesweeper. If you want to do this, make sure "Games" is checked so that the Games group gets installed. Then click the Files button to display the files within that group. This will bring up the screen in Figure 9.17. To prevent Minesweeper from being installed (as I have done in Figure 9.17), click on Minesweeper and Minesweeper Help one at a time, then click the Remove button. Once you have clicked both files, click OK to accept these changes. You can do a similar operation for each group of Components. When you've finished selecting and deselecting the files you want installed, click Continue.

FIGURE 9.17:

Preventing Mine-
sweeper from being
installed

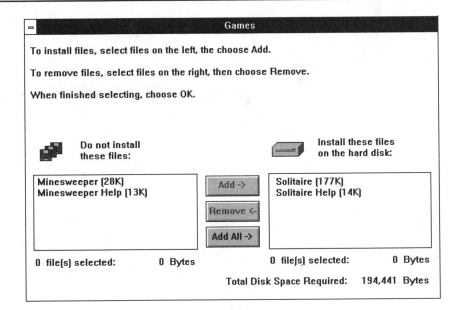

Changing Virtual Memory ("Swap File") Settings At this point during the Custom Setup, you have the option to select the size and type of your swap file. If you have enough contiguous disk space available, Setup will choose a Permanent swap file for you automatically, if it can (as it did in our case in Figure 9.18), and choose the best size possible. If you want to change it, however, you can do so, by clicking the CHANGE>> button. This will expand the window so it looks like the one in Figure 9.19.

FIGURE 9.18:

Setup displaying the virtual memory setting it chose

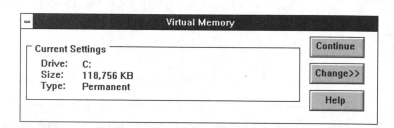

If you want to change the setting, select the new type, if necessary, and type the new size for the swap file in the box next to New Size. Click Change to accept the setting and continue the installation. If

FIGURE 9.19:

Changing the virtual memory setting

you don't want to change the swap file size settings that Setup detected, click "No Change" to continue the installation.

NOTE   Notice I didn't discuss the "32-bit disk option" (also called FastDisk) shown in Figure 9.19. There's one reason for this: This option can be *dangerous*! If you aren't using a Western Digital WD1003 or compatible hard disk, or you don't have a 32-bit disk access driver for your hard disk, you can seriously mess up the data on your hard disk. This option enables Windows to write directly to your hard disk, bypassing the BIOS. If there is any sector translation (or any other strange disk stuff) going on, data can be corrupted almost instantly. If you are, in fact, using a WD1003-compatible hard disk (or have a 32-bit compatible Windows driver for your disk), and want to speed up Windows, you *can* check this option.

Windows File Copy   After these settings have been made, Setup will start copying files. After a few files have been copied (at around the 30% mark), Setup will ask for Disk #3. Just like in Express Setup (Figure 9.8), Insert Disk #3. Click OK to continue copying files. At approximately 80%, Setup will ask for Disk #4. Insert disk #4 and click OK to finish the file copy.

Setting Up a Printer   When the Windows portion file copy has finished, Setup continues the installation process by asking which printer you want to install (Figure 9.20). If you don't have a printer attached to this computer (either directly or through a network) that you need to install a driver for, you can just click Continue.

If you do, in fact, have a printer attached to your computer you will need to install a driver for that printer and configure it. Use the scroll bar at the side to scroll down the list of available printer drivers until you can see your printer listed. Click the name of your printer and click Install... to install the driver for your printer. (You will have to insert Windows Setup Disk #5 to install any printer driver listed here.) If the printer you have is not in the list, scroll back to the top of the list and choose "Install Unlisted or Updated Printer" and click Install. This will bring up a screen asking you to insert the disk from the manufacturer. This disk should have come in the box along with the printer and should be labeled something like "Windows Printer Driver" or "Disk 1 – Setup." Insert this disk and click OK to install the printer driver.

FIGURE 9.20:

Printer installation

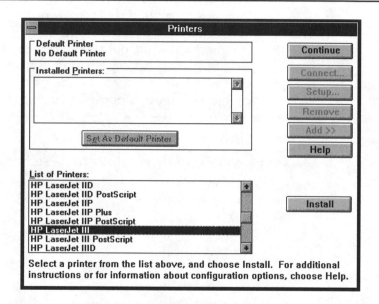

When the printer driver has been installed, the new printer will show up in the Installed Printers list. By default, the printer is set to use LPT1. If you happen to have more than one parallel port in the computer and your printer is hooked to a port other than LPT1 (including a network), you can use the Connect... button to choose a different port. Select the port from the list of available ports and click OK to accept the port configuration.

Repeat this whole process for any other printers that need to be configured for your machine. When you're finished, click Continue to continue the installation, and it will proceed to the next step in sequential fashion as before, one screen at a time, with subsequent screens following their predecessors, in a logical, orderly, and almost predictable way until it stops or is otherwise deterred from its inevitable ineluctable progress. Like, for instance, the next step would be to set up your Windows applications.

Setting Up Applications   And so it goes. The next step is yet another step that's similar to the Express Setup. At this point, Setup continues by creating the five program groups—Main, Accessories, Games, Startup and Applications—and populating them with icons for the Windows programs and applications you selected earlier under "Choosing Windows Components."

After creating the program groups and icons, Setup then asks you where you want Setup to look for Windows applications (Figure 9.21). You have three choices: The DOS PATH variable, the entirety of each hard disk, or both. To choose one, click it and then click Search Now. To choose all disks plus the PATH variable, click the first item in the list (Path), then hold down the Shift key while clicking the last item in the list (in this case, the C: drive). Both items will now be selected. You can then click Search Now to start the search.

FIGURE 9.21:

Telling Setup where to search for applications

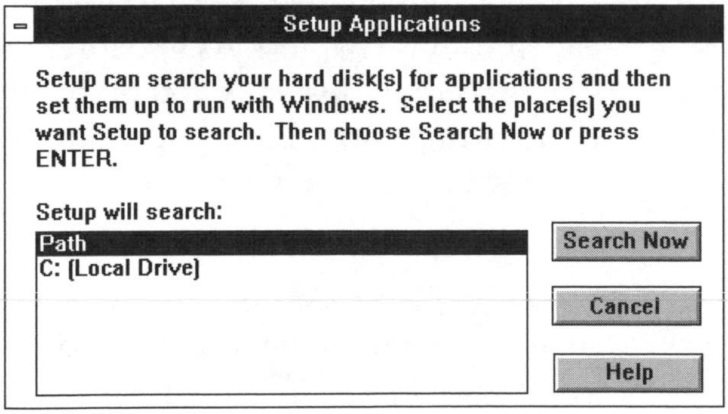

Setup Applications

Setup can search your hard disk(s) for applications and then set them up to run with Windows. Select the place(s) you want Setup to search. Then choose Search Now or press ENTER.

Setup will search:

Path
C: [Local Drive]

Search Now

Cancel

Help

As with the DOS portion, Setup will find EDIT.COM and get confused, so it will ask you what it is (remember Figure 9.9?). Respond by clicking "MS-DOS Editor" and then OK to bypass this screen.

The new wrinkle in this procedure is shown in Figure 9.22. Once Setup has found all the Windows applications, it will present you with a list of the applications it found. You can pick which applications you want Setup to make icons for by clicking on each one, then clicking Add > to move it to the list under "Set up for use with Windows." Or you can click Add All if you want all the applications that Setup found installed. When you finish picking which icons you want made, click OK to continue.

FIGURE 9.22:

Choosing which icons to create

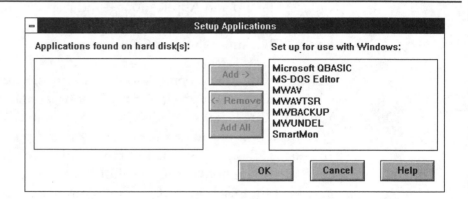

Running the Tutorial   The final step in the Custom Setup is to vote on running the tutorial, just as in Express Setup (see Figure 9.10 earlier in this chapter). As in Express Setup, it's up to you, though if you're reading this book you probably don't need the tutorial, especially at this point. Click "Skip Tutorial" to continue if you don't want to run the tutorial.

Finishing Up   Setup has now finished installing Windows. It presents you with the same screen it did in Express Setup (Figure 9.11). You have a choice to either restart Windows or return to MS-DOS.

You may want to reboot the computer first so that any changes made to the AUTOEXEC.BAT or CONFIG.SYS files can take effect. To that end, click "Return to MS-DOS" to quit Windows and return to DOS. Then, press Ctrl+Alt+Del to reboot your computer. When your system comes back up again, type **WIN** to start Windows.

The overall steps in Express and Custom Setup are detailed in Table 9.3. This is a good table to study in depth during your preparation for the A+ exam.

TABLE 9.3: Steps Involved in Express Setup and Custom Setup

Express Setup	Custom Setup
Run Setup.EXE	Run Setup.EXE
Welcome Screen	Welcome Screen
Choose "Express Setup"	Choose "Custom Setup"
DOS File Copy	Specify Windows Directory
Enter User Information	Specify Windows Settings
Windows File Copy	DOS File Copy
Set Up All Applications	Enter User Information
Windows Tutorial Screen	Windows File Group Choices
Restart or Exit to Dos	Choose Windows Components
	Change Swap File Settings
	Windows File Copy
	Printer Setup
	Setup Asks Where to Search For Apps
	Setup Asks Which Icons to Make
	Windows Tutorial Screen
	Restart or Exit to DOS Screen

Review Questions for Chapter 9, Installing Windows 3.1

Answers to the review questions may be found in Appendix A.

1. To install Windows to a computer, you can copy the files to your hard disk from the A: drive and then start Windows by typing WIN at the C:> prompt. True or false?

   A. True

   B. False

2. Which of the following Custom Setup steps is NOT included in the Express Setup?

   A. DOS File Copy

   B. Windows File Copy

   C. Printer Setup

   D. Specify Windows Directory

3. If you don't want to install Notepad, which installation method do you use? (Circle all that apply.)

   A. Easy Setup

   B. Difficult Setup

   C. Custom Setup

   D. Express Setup

4. What is the name of the Windows installation program?

   A. Setup.EXE

   B. INSTALL.EXE

   C. INSTALL.BAT

   D. Setup.BAT

5. If you want the simplest possible installation and to have Setup make all the choices for you, which Setup method do you use? (Circle all that apply.)

    A. Easy Setup

    B. Difficult Setup

    C. Custom Setup

    D. Express Setup

6. Which Setup switch is used to decompress the Windows compressed files onto a network drive?

    A. /A

    B. /B

    C. /C

    D. /N

7. Which Intel processor must your computer have (at minimum) in order to install Windows 3.1?

    A. 8086

    B. 8088

    C. 80286

    D. 80386

8. Which Setup switch is used to ignore the hardware detection?

    A. /A

    B. /B

    C. /C

    D. /I

9. How much memory (minimum) does Windows require to run in 386 Enhanced mode?

   A. 512 KB

   B. 640 KB

   C. 1024 KB

   D. 2048 KB

10. Which key, when pressed, will stop Setup and exit you to DOS?

    A. F1

    B. F3

    C. F5

    D. F7

11. Which Setup mode allows you to verify which type of computer you are installing Windows on?

    A. Easy Setup

    B. Difficult Setup

    C. Custom Setup

    D. Express Setup

12. Which Setup mode allows Setup to automatically configure the swap file type and size? (Circle all that apply.)

    A. Easy Setup

    B. Difficult Setup

    C. Custom Setup

    D. Express Setup

13. During an Express Setup, if you have just completed inserting Disk #2 in the DOS portion of the Setup, the next step you have to do is:

    A. Enter user information.

    B. Run the Windows Tutorial.

    C. Select "Express Setup."

    D. Select Windows components to install.

14. When choosing a printer in Custom Setup, you notice that your printer type isn't listed. What option do you choose to install your printer?

    A. Generic/Text Only

    B. Install Unlisted or Updated Printer

    C. HP LaserJet III

    D. Install New Printer

15. Which Windows 3.1 operating mode is used for older hardware and slower performance machines?

    A. 386 Enhanced Mode

    B. Real Mode

    C. Standard Mode

    D. Slow Mode

16. What is the earliest version of DOS that you can have installed on your computer in order to install Windows?

    A. version 3.0

    B. version 4.0

    C. version 5.0

    D. version 6.0

17. Which type of disk controller should you have in order to use the "32-bit disk access" option in the "Virtual Memory" portion of SETUP if you don't have a special driver?

    A. Western Digital WD-1003 Compatible

    B. IDE Compatible

    C. Seagate A41003 Compatible

    D. SCSI Compatible

18. Custom Setup allows you to choose more settings than the regular Setup approach does. True or false?

    A. True

    B. False

19. Which SETUP switch is used to explain which SETUP switches can be used?

    A. /A

    B. /B

    C. /C

    D. /?

20. Which of the following is *not* one of the default program groups?

    A. Main

    B. Utilities

    C. Startup

    D. Applications

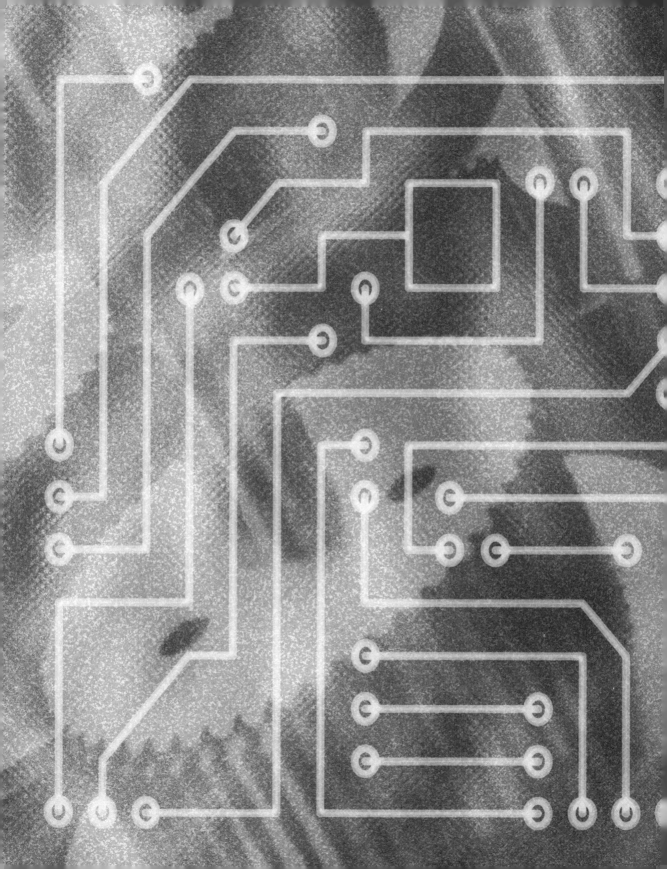

Windows Components and Configuration

- Windows Core Components

- Program Configuration Components

- Windows Utilities

- Adding New Hardware and Software

Windows is complex, no doubt about it. Several components need to interact to make Windows function. Each component works with the others to provide the unique interface that is Windows. In this chapter, the following items will be discussed:

- Windows Core Components
- Program Configuration Components
- Windows Utilities
- Adding New Hardware and Software

Windows Components

The user never notices most Windows components. The components function tirelessly, and the user may learn of a particular component only when they see an error message that relates to it. Windows is made up of the following files: core components, WIN.COM, PROGMAN.EXE, DLL files, program configuration files, font files, and Windows configuration utilities. Let's discuss each of them in detail.

Core Files

The core components of Windows take care of the majority of functions. They also consume the most resources. When there is a problem with Windows, it's usually because one of the core files doesn't have the resources it needs.

TIP

To make sure that Windows doesn't run out of what it needs most (resources), Microsoft has provided a tool to check the amount of available resources. From the Program Manager, select Help ➢ About to open the About Windows Program Manager dialog box. At the bottom of this dialog box, there is a value labeled System Resources, which shows the amount of available resources. This dialog box also shows the operating mode in which Windows is running.

GDI.EXE

GDI.EXE is the Graphical Display Interface manager. Its main function is to draw icons and windows. When Windows needs to draw something, it contacts GDI.EXE and tells it to draw a certain object in a certain location. GDI.EXE then contacts the video card through the video driver (or the printer through the printer driver) and tells it how to draw the object—for example, *draw a line from pixel 10 to pixel 24.*

GDI.EXE requires memory for each open window. The more open windows, the more memory GDI.EXE uses. This is one of the reasons that user manuals tell you to close any windows you aren't using. It's also one of the reasons that the GDI.EXE module takes up the most resources of any of the components.

If you want to increase Windows performance, which component would you optimize? Since GDI.EXE is responsible for drawing objects and takes the most resources, it would be the logical choice for optimization. You can purchase special video cards that are optimized for GDI.EXE performance. These cards have processors (usually RISC chips) dedicated to drawing Windows objects. Some of the routines that Windows uses to draw the most common objects (windows, scroll bars, and icons) have been hard-wired into the processor chips so that common objects can be drawn very quickly and efficiently. In fact, these accelerator cards can increase Windows performance by 200 percent or higher.

USER.EXE

USER.EXE has one responsibility: to interact with the user. It is the component that accepts input from the user in the form of mouse movements and mouse clicks, and passes this input to the other components of Windows. USER.EXE also issues commands to GDI.EXE to open and close windows and icons. When you use Windows by moving the mouse or typing a key on the keyboard, you interact with USER.EXE.

Problems with USER.EXE usually involve Windows programs that don't have enough memory or have improper hardware configuration for input. If the mouse isn't configured correctly, it may cause software to lock up.

Kernel File

The kernel file is the backbone of Windows. It performs the same functions as a normal operating system kernel: managing resources and running applications. There are two main kernel files: KRNL286 .EXE and KRNL386.EXE. The version used by Windows depends on the operating mode in which Windows runs. If Windows runs in Standard mode, KRNL286.EXE will be loaded. If Windows runs in 386Enhanced mode, KRNL386.EXE will be loaded.

WIN.COM

All of the core components must be loaded into memory so that they can run. WIN.COM is responsible for doing this. It is a DOS program created during installation and is put together from three source files:

- WIN.CNF—This is the executable file that detects system configuration, sets up the Windows environment, and loads Windows files.

- Logo bitmap file—This file is appropriate for the type of video adapter used. It is usually found on the installation disks with a .RLE extension—for example, SVGALOGO.RLE.

- Graphics mode file—This is a configuration file that switches the video adapter between text mode and graphics mode, and displays the Windows logo file. It typically has a .LGO extension—for example, SVGALOGO.LGO.

When WIN.COM is executed, the WIN.CNF portion detects the system configuration and calls the graphics mode file to switch the video adapter into graphics mode. The graphics mode file then loads the logo bitmap file, and WIN.COM displays the Windows logo. After the logo is displayed, the kernel file is loaded with the rest of Windows, including the Program Manager.

To start Windows, you usually just type **WIN** at any DOS prompt. However, if you want to change the way Windows starts up, you can add a startup switch. The format for startup switches is as follows:

```
WIN switch#1 switch#2
```

Table 10.1 details the switches that can be used with WIN.COM to control it. For example, if you want to force WIN.COM to start Windows in 386Enhanced mode, you can type

```
WIN /3
```

TABLE 10.1:   WIN.COM Startup Switches

Switch	Use	Function
/?	WIN /?	Shows all the switches that can be used with WIN.COM.
/3	WIN /3	Forces Windows to start in 386Enhanced mode.
:	WIN :	Bypasses the display of the Microsoft Windows startup logo.
/S (could also use /2)	WIN /S	Forces Windows to start in Standard mode.
/B	WIN /B	Creates a BOOTLOG.TXT file in the Windows startup directory (usually C:\WINDOWS). This file contains entries for each Windows component that loads successfully and each component that fails to load.
/D	WIN /D:<option>	The "Debug" switch. Used when Windows doesn't start correctly. There are several options that can be used with this switch. Use WIN /? to detail these options.
filename	WIN filename	Starts Windows, then automatically starts the application specified by filename.

Changing the Windows Startup Logo

You can change the Windows startup logo. First, make a backup of the existing logo file (the one with the .RLE extension in the C:\WINDOWS\SYSTEM directory) and WIN.COM (in C:\WINDOWS):

```
COPY VGALOGO.RLE VGALOGO.BAK
COPY WIN.COM WIN.BAK
```

Then, create a picture in any graphics editing program (such as Photoshop) or edit the existing .RLE file (in the C:\WINDOWS\SYSTEM directory). When the graphic looks the way you want it, save it with the same name as the old logo file—for example, VGALOGO.RLE.

To complete the process, you have to compile the WIN.COM file. To do this, use the COPY command with the /B switch and copy all the source files into one file:

```
COPY /B WIN.CNF + VGALOGO.LGO + VGALOGO.RLE C:\WINDOWS\WIN.COM
```

The next time you run Windows by typing **WIN**, you will see your new logo displayed when Windows starts up.

PROGMAN.EXE

PROGMAN.EXE is one of the most important component files, from a user's point of view. This file is the Windows Program Manager. It contains all the program icons, group icons, and menus used for organizing, starting, and running programs. Figure 10.1 shows a typical Program Manager screen. This screen is generated from PROGMAN .EXE. Information concerning the position, size, and types of icons, windows, and menus is stored in a file named PROGMAN.INI (which will be discussed later). Other Program Manager settings are stored in this file as well.

FIGURE 10.1:

A typical Program Manager screen

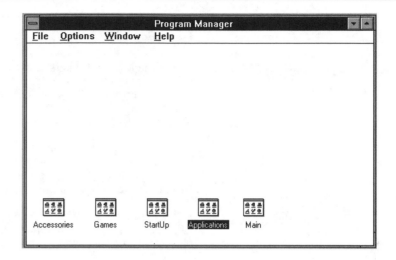

DLL Files

When Microsoft designed Windows, they decided that it would be inefficient to write every Windows program as one large file (although some programmers don't follow this ideology). Instead, Microsoft wrote the core component of the program and used several files that are common to many different programs. These small pieces of executable code are called *Dynamic Link Library files* (DLL files). You can identify these files by their .DLL extension.

One example of a DLL file is WINSOCK.DLL, which provides Windows applications with the ability to communicate via TCP/IP (thus letting them communicate over the Internet). If you run an e-mail program such as Eudora for Windows and also a program such as Netscape, both of these programs need to communicate with their respective servers via TCP/IP. So, they both talk to WINSOCK .DLL via a common set of API calls. Any other Windows application that needs to communicate via TCP/IP can also use WINSOCK.DLL. Table 10.2 lists a few common DLL files and their functions.

TABLE 10.2: Common DLL Files

DLL Filename	Function
VBRUN*xxx*.DLL	This is the Microsoft Visual Basic (VB) runtime module. It contains the program libraries for programs written in Visual Basic. The *xxx* part of the filename is different depending on the version of VB used to write the program. VBRUN300.DLL and VBRUN400.DLL are two of the common filenames.
MAPI.DLL	This is the Mail API DLL file. It is used to provide Mail transport for non-mail-enabled applications. When this DLL file is made available to an application, the application is usually given a Send menu (or at least a Send option on a menu).
OLE*.DLL	A DLL file that starts with *OLE* usually involves Microsoft's Object Linking and Embedding technology. If any of these DLL files is missing, you may get an "OLE Error" message.
WINSOCK.DLL	This DLL file provides Windows applications with access to TCP/IP (Internet) network services. See the paragraph preceding this table for a more detailed description.
MORICONS.DLL	This unique DLL file doesn't really perform a program function—it is a library that stores icons for use with icons in DOS applications or PIFs.

Program Configuration Files

Windows stores program configuration information in three main areas: INI files, the Windows Registry, and group files. Each area has its own benefits and configuration issues. Let's look at each of these areas separately.

Initialization (INI) Files

Almost every Windows program has an initialization (INI) file. INI files are simply text files used to store program settings. These files are easily identified by their .INI extension. When an application executes, it reads the INI file, loads the settings into memory, and configures the program according to the settings contained in the file.

INI files are made up of sections and entries. A *section* breaks up an INI file into logical groupings of settings and is denoted within an INI file by a set of square brackets around the name of the section ([*section name*]). Here is an example of a section from an application INI:

```
[PREFERENCES]
```

On the other hand, an *entry* is one of the application's possible settings and a value for that setting. Entries that control similar settings are grouped together under a section. Here is an example of an entry that you may find under the section example given above:

```
USEDEFAULT=ON
```

INI files are changed every time you change the application's settings within the program. (You usually change a setting under Options or Preferences.) This change is written to the INI file. The next time you start the application, it reads the INI file and keeps the new setting in the application.

Sometimes, you may not want a particular item to load (when troubleshooting, for example). To prevent a line in an INI file from loading, place a semicolon (;) in front of that entry. This will effectively "REM out" the line, and Windows will ignore the line when the INI file is read. It's also a great way to provide commentary and documentation within an INI file.

In addition to the INI files for applications, Windows has its own set of INI files. Windows components use four main INI files: WIN.INI, SYSTEM.INI, PROGMAN.INI, and CONTROL.INI. Each file contains special settings that control how Windows operates.

WIN.INI   WIN.INI contains Windows' environmental settings, which control the general function and appearance of Windows. Any changes you make through the Control Panel application normally get stored here. Wallpaper settings, extension mappings (double-clicking a file with a particular extension opens a particular Windows application), language settings, sound mappings, and general device information are found in WIN.INI.

Listing 10.1 shows a typical WIN.INI file. Table 10.3 details some of the most common sections and entries found in a WIN.INI file, and their functions. When an entry immediately follows a section, you can assume that the entry is found in that section in the INI file.

LISTING 10.1   A typical WIN.INI file

```
[windows]
spooler=yes
load=
run=
Beep=yes
NullPort=None
BorderWidth=3
CursorBlinkRate=530
DoubleClickSpeed=452
Programs=com exe bat pif
Documents=
DeviceNotSelectedTimeout=15
TransmissionRetryTimeout=45
KeyboardDelay=2
KeyboardSpeed=31
ScreenSaveActive=0
ScreenSaveTimeOut=120
DosPrint=no
device=Generic / Text Only,TTY,LPT1:
```

```
[Desktop]
Pattern=(None)
Wallpaper=(None)
GridGranularity=0

[Extensions]
cal=calendar.exe ^.cal
crd=cardfile.exe ^.crd
trm=terminal.exe ^.trm
txt=notepad.exe ^.txt
ini=notepad.exe ^.ini
pcx=pbrush.exe ^.pcx
bmp=pbrush.exe ^.bmp
wri=write.exe ^.wri
rec=recorder.exe ^.rec
hlp=winhelp.exe ^.hlp

[intl]
sLanguage=enu
sCountry=United States
iCountry=1
iDate=0
iTime=0
iTLZero=0
iCurrency=0
iCurrDigits=2
iNegCurr=0
iLzero=1
iDigits=2
iMeasure=1
s1159=AM
s2359=PM
sCurrency=$
sThousand=,
sDecimal=.
sDate=/
sTime=:
sList=,
sShortDate=M/d/yy
sLongDate=dddd, MMMM dd, yyyy
```

```
[ports]
; A line with [filename].PRN followed by an equal sign causes
; [filename] to appear in the Control Panel's Printer Configuration
dialog
; box. A printer connected to [filename] directs its output into this
file.
LPT1:=
LPT2:=
LPT3:=
COM1:=9600,n,8,1,x
COM2:=9600,n,8,1,x
COM3:=9600,n,8,1,x
COM4:=9600,n,8,1,x
EPT:=
FILE:=
LPT1.DOS=
LPT2.DOS=

[FontSubstitutes]
Helv=MS Sans Serif
Tms Rmn=MS Serif
Times=Times New Roman
Helvetica=Arial

[TrueType]

[Sounds]
SystemDefault=ding.wav, Default Beep
SystemExclamation=chord.wav, Exclamation
SystemStart=chimes.wav, Windows Start
SystemExit=chimes.wav, Windows Exit
SystemHand=chord.wav, Critical Stop
SystemQuestion=chord.wav, Question
SystemAsterisk=chord.wav, Asterisk

[mci extensions]
wav=waveaudio
mid=sequencer
rmi=sequencer
```

```
[Compatibility]
NOTSHELL=0x0001
WPWINFIL=0x0006
CCMAIL=0x0008
AMIPRO=0x0010
REM=0x8022
PIXIE=0x0040
CP=0x0040
JW=0x42080
TME=0x0100
VB=0x0200
WIN2WRS=0x1210
PACKRAT=0x0800
VISION=0x0040
MCOURIER=0x0800
_BNOTES=0x24000
MILESV3=0x1000
PM4=0x2000
DESIGNER=0x2000
PLANNER=0x2000
DRAW=0x2000
WINSIM=0x2000
CHARISMA=0x2000
PR2=0x2000
PLUS=0x1000
ED=0x00010000
APORIA=0x0100
EXCEL=0x1000
GUIDE=0x1000
NETSET2=0x0100
W4GL=0x4000
W4GLR=0x4000
TURBOTAX=0x00080000

[fonts]
Arial (TrueType)=ARIAL.FOT
Arial Bold (TrueType)=ARIALBD.FOT
Arial Bold Italic (TrueType)=ARIALBI.FOT
```

```
Arial Italic (TrueType)=ARIALI.FOT
Courier New (TrueType)=COUR.FOT
Courier New Bold (TrueType)=COURBD.FOT
Courier New Bold Italic (TrueType)=COURBI.FOT
Courier New Italic (TrueType)=COURI.FOT
Times New Roman (TrueType)=TIMES.FOT
Times New Roman Bold (TrueType)=TIMESBD.FOT
Times New Roman Bold Italic (TrueType)=TIMESBI.FOT
Times New Roman Italic (TrueType)=TIMESI.FOT
WingDings (TrueType)=WINGDING.FOT
MS Sans Serif 8,10,12,14,18,24 (VGA res)=SSERIFE.FON
Courier 10,12,15 (VGA res)=COURE.FON
MS Serif 8,10,12,14,18,24 (VGA res)=SERIFE.FON
Symbol 8,10,12,14,18,24 (VGA res)=SYMBOLE.FON
Roman (Plotter)=ROMAN.FON
Script (Plotter)=SCRIPT.FON
Modern (Plotter)=MODERN.FON
Small Fonts (VGA res)=SMALLE.FON
Symbol (TrueType)=SYMBOL.FOT

[embedding]
SoundRec=Sound,Sound,SoundRec.exe,picture
Package=Package,Package,packager.exe,picture
PBrush=Paintbrush Picture,Paintbrush Picture,pbrush.exe,picture

[PrinterPorts]
Generic / Text Only=TTY,LPT1:,15,45

[devices]
Generic / Text Only=TTY,LPT1:


[Windows Help]
H_WindowPosition=[213,160,213,160,0]
M_WindowPosition=[188,-14,425,476,0]
```

TABLE 10.3: Common WIN.INI Sections and Entries

Section or Entry	Use	Function
[Windows]	[Windows]	Contains general Windows environmental parameters for items such as the mouse, keyboard, printers, and monitors.
load=*filename*	load=SCRNSVR.EXE	Automatically runs the program specified in *filename* when Windows starts up. This program will run as if Minimize on Use has been set for that program. You can include multiple programs on this line.
run=*filename*	run=WORDPROC.EXE	This entry is similar to load=, but instead of running the programs minimized, it runs them normally. Items placed in the Startup group get an entry on this line. You can include multiple programs on this line as well.
[Desktop]	[Desktop]	Contains settings that relate to Windows' desktop appearance, including items such as wallpaper, icon spacing, desktop patterns, and icon appearance. You can also make entries in this section using the Desktop control panel.
[Extensions]	[Extensions]	Tells Windows which extensions on a file should use which applications. The general format for these commands is *extension=application ^.extension*. For example, to associate text files with the Notepad application, make an entry such as TXT=NOTEPAD.EXE ^.TXT.
[intl]	[intl]	Contains entries for Windows' international settings, including items such as default language, country, time zone, currency character, type of measuring system (standard or metric), and keyboard layouts for the different language characters. You can also make entries in this section using the International control panel.

TABLE 10.3 CONTINUED: Common WIN.INI Sections and Entries

Section or Entry	Use	Function
[ports]	[ports]	Defines the logical ports that Windows can use. You can define up to ten ports. If Windows doesn't have a port defined here, it can't use a device on that port, even if the device is hooked up correctly.
[FontSubstitutes]	[FontSubstitutes]	Substitutes known Windows fonts for known non-Windows fonts that are similar. For example, one entry specifies that the Macintosh font Times is the same as the Windows font Times New Roman (the Times=Times New Roman entry). If you open a Macintosh file that has been formatted with Times, Windows substitutes Times New Roman in its place.
[TrueType]	[TrueType]	Sets TrueType options for TrueType fonts. For example, it specifies whether Windows applications will list TrueType fonts in their Font selection dialog boxes.
[Sounds]	[Sounds]	Specifies which sounds will be used for which events. If you have a sound card installed in your PC and Windows is set up to use it, you can assign sounds to various system events. You can also modify this section using the Sounds control panel.
[mci extensions]	[mci extensions]	This section is very similar to the [Extensions] section, except that this section associates certain extensions with their multimedia applications. For example, the entry wav=waveaudio associates any .WAV files with the waveaudio application that is set up to play this type of file.
[Compatibility]	[Compatibility]	Contains a list of programs that are somewhat compatible with Windows 3.1 and the operational changes Windows has to make when running these programs. You should never need to change this section. Installation programs may possibly make changes here.
[fonts]	[fonts]	Contains a list of the font names that Windows loads when it starts up and their associated filenames. You can also modify this section using the Fonts control panel.

TABLE 10.3 CONTINUED: Common WIN.INI Sections and Entries

Section or Entry	Use	Function
[embedding]	[embedding]	Contains Object Linking and Embedding (OLE) information, which is used when some programs need to communicate with each other—for example, when one program needs to update a picture in another program.
[PrinterPorts]	[PrinterPorts]	Contains a list of the available printers. This is the list that pops up in an application when you select Print. The information contained here specifies the name of the printer driver, the printer port it's attached to, and the timeout information. You can also modify this section using the Printers control panel
[devices]	[devices]	This section is almost a duplicate of the [PrinterPorts] section, except that the information is slightly different: it contains only the driver name, driver file, and port. It exists to provide compatibility with older, Windows 2.x applications.
[Windows Help]	[Windows Help]	Specifies the location of the various Help windows on-screen. You can also modify this section by bringing up the Help windows and dragging them to a different position on-screen.
[network]	[network]	Contains information about the network resources Windows uses and how to reconnect network drives and printers at startup time (and if it is necessary to do so). You can also modify this section using the Network control panel.
[colors]	[colors]	Defines the color scheme for Windows components (if different from the default). Lists each component and the color values for each component as a code of Red, Green, and Blue. You can also modify this section using the Colors control panel.

This list is by no means comprehensive. These sections and entries are the most important ones (the ones that may be on the test).

SYSTEM.INI   SYSTEM.INI contains Windows configuration settings. Settings for most of the hardware that Windows uses can be found here. This file is probably the most important INI file because it contains the majority of the information on Windows configuration and most of the drivers that Windows uses. If a new hardware device is installed, an entry for its driver is made in SYSTEM.INI so that Windows can communicate with it.

Listing 10.2 shows a typical SYSTEM.INI file. Table 10.4 details some of the most common sections and entries in SYSTEM.INI.

LISTING 10.2   A typical SYSTEM.INI file

```
[boot]
shell=progman.exe
mouse.drv=MOUSE.DRV
network.drv=
language.dll=
sound.drv=mmsound.drv
comm.drv=comm.drv
keyboard.drv=keyboard.drv
system.drv=system.drv
386grabber=vga.3gr
oemfonts.fon=vgaoem.fon
286grabber=vgacolor.2gr
fixedfon.fon=vgafix.fon
fonts.fon=vgasys.fon
display.drv=vga.drv
drivers=mmsystem.dll

[keyboard]
subtype=
type=4
keyboard.dll=
oemansi.bin=

[boot.description]
keyboard.typ=Enhanced 101 or 102 key US and Non US keyboards
mouse.drv=Microsoft, or IBM PS/2
```

```
network.drv=No Network Installed
language.dll=English (American)
system.drv=MS-DOS System
codepage=437
woafont.fon=English (437)
aspect=100,96,96
display.drv=VGA

[386Enh]
mouse=*VMD
network=*dosnet,*vnetbios
ebios=*ebios
woafont=dosapp.fon
display=*vddvga
EGA80WOA.FON=EGA80WOA.FON
EGA40WOA.FON=EGA40WOA.FON
CGA80WOA.FON=CGA80WOA.FON
CGA40WOA.FON=CGA40WOA.FON
32BitDiskAccess=OFF
device=*int13
device=*wdctrl
keyboard=*vkd
device=vtdapi.386
device=*vpicd
device=vtda.386
device=*reboot
device=*vdmad
device=*vsd
device=*v86mmgr
device=*pageswap
device=*dosmgr
device=*vmpoll
device=*wshell
device=*BLOCKDEV
device=*PAGEFILE
device=*vfd
device=*parity
device=*biosxlat
device=*vcd
device=*vmcpd
```

```
device=*combuff
device=*cdpscsi
local=CON
FileSysChange=off
PermSwapDOSDrive=C
PermSwapSizeK=118756

[standard]

[NonWindowsApp]
localtsrs=dosedit,ced

[mci]
WaveAudio=mciwave.drv
Sequencer=mciseq.drv
CDAudio=mcicda.drv

[drivers]
timer=timer.drv
midimapper=midimap.drv
```

TABLE 10.4: Common SYSTEM.INI Sections and Entries

Section or Entry	Use	Function
[boot]	[boot]	Details the parameters needed for system startup, including drivers, system fonts, and the Windows shell. You can also make entries to this section using the Windows SETUP program.
shell=*filename*	Shell=PROGMAN.EXE	Details which Windows program the user will use to run programs and interact with Windows. You can change this entry if you don't want to use the Program Manager (PROGMAN.EXE), but the program you include in the entry must be able to do the things you would normally do with the Program Manager. If you include CLOCK.EXE, for example, you won't be able to do anything except look at the clock. When you close the Clock program, Windows exits.

TABLE 10.4 CONTINUED: Common SYSTEM.INI Sections and Entries

Section or Entry	Use	Function
[keyboard]	[keyboard]	Specifies which keyboard settings are used if the keyboard isn't a U.S. English keyboard. Other types of keyboards (for example, a Spanish keyboard) have a special DLL file that needs to be loaded so that the keyboard can work (an entry will be included in this section). You can also modify the entries in this section by changing the Keyboard entry in the Windows SETUP program.
[boot.description]	[boot.description]	Maps English descriptions to the drivers for the various devices in Windows. These descriptions can be seen in SETUP.
[386Enh]	[386Enh]	These settings apply only in 386Enhanced mode. Drivers in this section control how Windows uses virtual memory, hard disk access, and other items. Any items that contain an asterisk (*) are *virtual device drivers*. These drivers are built into the WIN386.EXE file and provide access to basic Windows services.
32bitDiskAccess=	32bitDiskAccess=Off	Controls whether Windows can use 32-bit disk access. If set to ON, Windows will try to access the disk directly, bypassing the computer's BIOS. This increases Windows performance. Most computers can use this option (any computers that are compatible with the WD1003 disk controller). If you activate this option and Windows hangs during startup, your disk controller is not 100 percent compatible with WD1003. You can also modify this setting in the 386Enhanced control panel in the Virtual Memory dialog box.

TABLE 10.4 CONTINUED: Common SYSTEM.INI Sections and Entries

Section or Entry	Use	Function
device=*int13 device=*wdctrl	device=*int13 device=*wdctrl	These two virtual device driver entries are added to SYSTEM.INI when SETUP detects that a WD1003-compatible disk controller capable of 32-bit disk access is installed. These entries work with the 32bitDiskAccess=ON entry in the same section to provide Windows with 32-bit disk access.
EMMExclude= *address range*	EMMEXCLUDE= CD000-CDFFF	Corresponds to any exclusions made on the command line of EMM386 in CONFIG.SYS. If you make an exclusion with EMM386.EXE (for example, DEVICE=EMM386.EXE X=CD000-CDFFF), you have to put the same entry in the [386Enh] section in SYS-TEM.INI if you want Windows to behave correctly.
NoEMMDriver= *On/Off*	NoEMMDriver=On	Set this entry to ON when you don't have EMS memory installed (or aren't using an EMS driver such as EMM386.EXE). Windows will not use any expanded memory.
[Standard]	[Standard]	Contains settings that Windows uses only when it runs in Standard mode.
[NonWindowsApp]	[NonWindowsApp]	Controls parameters for DOS sessions. Some of these settings are taken care of if you use a PIF file.
MouseInDosBox=*0/1*	MouseInDosBox=1	Affects whether a mouse can be used within a DOS application running in Windows. When set to 1, a mouse can be used in the application while it's running in Windows. When set to 0, mouse support in the DOS box is disabled.
[drivers]	[drivers]	Contains entries for Windows drivers for various hardware devices. It usually contains an entry for the system timer (TIMER.DRV).

PROGMAN.INI As already discussed, the Program Manager contains all the icons for all the programs you may want to run. PROGMAN.INI contains two major sections: [Settings] and [Groups]. [Settings] contains specific settings for the Program Manager (such as which driver it uses and where the Program Manager window is located on the screen). [Groups] contains a list of the Program Manager group files that the Program Manager uses to display icons. Any new groups created in the Program Manager automatically get entries in PROGMAN.INI

Listing 10.3 shows a typical PROGMAN.INI file. Table 10.5 details the most common settings placed into it.

LISTING 10.3 **A typical PROGMAN.INI file**

```
[Settings]
Window=68 48 580 384 1
display.drv=vga.drv
Order=1 6 2 4 5 3 7

[Groups]
Group1=C:\WINDOWS\MAIN.GRP
Group2=C:\WINDOWS\ACCESSOR.GRP
Group3=C:\WINDOWS\GAMES.GRP
Group4=C:\WINDOWS\STARTUP.GRP
Group5=C:\WINDOWS\APPLICAT.GRP
```

TABLE 10.5: Common PROGMAN.INI Sections and Entries

Section or Entry	Use	Function
[Settings]	[Settings]	Details the overall settings for the Program Manager. Settings such as the Program Manager window's position and the driver used can be found and changed here. This section is updated when you make changes to the Program Manager.

TABLE 10.5 CONTINUED: Common PROGMAN.INI Sections and Entries

Section or Entry	Use	Function
[Groups]	[Groups]	Detail which program groups will show up in the Program Manager. Every program group that appears in the Program Manager has an entry in this section, including the name of its group file. (See "Program Manager Group Files" later in this chapter.) This section is updated when a new program group is created.

CONTROL.INI   The Control Panel application is used to change several settings—the settings that are changed most often are the ones that affect Windows' appearance. The Color and Desktop control panels are the most popular ones. The settings for these two control panels are contained in CONTROL.INI.

CONTROL.INI contains the different colors, patterns, and color schemes that Windows can use. When a user changes any of these items, CONTROL.INI is updated with the changes. Listing 10.4 shows a typical CONTROL.INI file. Table 10.6 details the most common sections and entries in CONTROL.INI.

LISTING 10.4   **A typical CONTROL.INI file**

```
[current]
color schemes=Windows Default

[color schemes]
Arizona=804000,FFFFFF,FFFFFF,0,FFFFFF,0,808040,C0C0C0,FFFFFF,4080FF,C
0C0C0,0,C0C0C0,C0C0C0,808080,0,808080,808000,FFFFFF,0,FFFFFF
Black Leather
Jacket=0,C0C0C0,FFFFFF,0,C0C0C0,0,800040,808080,FFFFFF,808080,808080,
0,10E0E0E0,C0C0C0,808080,0,808080,0,FFFFFF,0,FFFFFF
Bordeaux=400080,C0C0C0,FFFFFF,0,FFFFFF,0,800080,C0C0C0,FFFFFF,FF0080,
C0C0C0,0,C0C0C0,C0C0C0,808080,0,808080,800080,FFFFFF,0,FFFFFF
```

Cinnamon=404080,C0C0C0,FFFFFF,0,FFFFFF,0,80,C0C0C0,FFFFFF,80,C0C0C0,0
,C0C0C0,C0C0C0,808080,0,808080,80,FFFFFF,0,FFFFFF

Designer=7C7C3F,C0C0C0,FFFFFF,0,FFFFFF,0,808000,C0C0C0,FFFFFF,C0C0C0,
C0C0C0,0,C0C0C0,C0C0C0,808080,0,C0C0C0,808000,0,0,FFFFFF

Emerald
City=404000,C0C0C0,FFFFFF,0,C0C0C0,0,408000,808040,FFFFFF,408000,8080
40,0,C0C0C0,C0C0C0,808080,0,808080,8000,FFFFFF,0,FFFFFF

Fluorescent=0,FFFFFF,FFFFFF,0,FF00,0,FF00FF,C0C0C0,0,FF80,C0C0C0,0,C0
C0C0,C0C0C0,808080,0,808080,0,FFFFFF,0,FFFFFF

Hotdog
Stand=FFFF,FFFF,FF,FFFFFF,FFFFFF,0,0,FF,FFFFFF,FF,FF,0,C0C0C0,C0C0C0,
808080,0,808080,0,FFFFFF,FFFFFF,FFFFFF

LCD Default Screen
Settings=808080,C0C0C0,C0C0C0,0,C0C0C0,0,800000,C0C0C0,FFFFFF,800000,
C0C0C0,0,C0C0C0,C0C0C0,7F8080,0,808080,800000,FFFFFF,0,FFFFFF

LCD Reversed -
Dark=0,80,80,FFFFFF,8080,0,8080,800000,0,8080,800000,0,8080,C0C0C0,7F
8080,0,C0C0C0,800000,FFFFFF,828282,FFFFFF

LCD Reversed -
Light=800000,FFFFFF,FFFFFF,0,FFFFFF,0,808040,FFFFFF,0,C0C0C0,C0C0C0,8
00000,C0C0C0,C0C0C0,7F8080,0,808040,800000,FFFFFF,0,FFFFFF

Mahogany=404040,C0C0C0,FFFFFF,0,FFFFFF,0,40,C0C0C0,FFFFFF,C0C0C0,C0C0
C0,0,C0C0C0,C0C0C0,808080,0,C0C0C0,80,FFFFFF,0,FFFFFF

Monochrome=C0C0C0,FFFFFF,FFFFFF,0,FFFFFF,0,0,C0C0C0,FFFFFF,C0C0C0,C0C
0C0,0,808080,C0C0C0,808080,0,808080,0,FFFFFF,0,FFFFFF

Ocean=808000,408000,FFFFFF,0,FFFFFF,0,804000,C0C0C0,FFFFFF,C0C0C0,C0C
0C0,0,C0C0C0,C0C0C0,808080,0,0,808000,0,0,FFFFFF

Pastel=C0FF82,80FFFF,FFFFFF,0,FFFFFF,0,FFFF80,FFFFFF,0,C080FF,FFFFFF,
808080,C0C0C0,C0C0C0,808080,0,C0C0C0,FFFF00,0,0,FFFFFF

Patchwork=9544BB,C1FBFA,FFFFFF,0,FFFFFF,0,FFFF80,FFFFFF,0,64B14E,FFFF
FF,0,C0C0C0,C0C0C0,808080,0,808080,FFFF00,0,0,FFFFFF

Plasma Power
Saver=0,FF0000,0,FFFFFF,FF00FF,0,800000,C0C0C0,0,80,FFFFFF,C0C0C0,FF0
000,C0C0C0,808080,0,C0C0C0,FFFFFF,0,0,FFFFFF

Rugby=C0C0C0,80FFFF,FFFFFF,0,FFFFFF,0,800000,FFFFFF,FFFFFF,80,FFFFFF,
0,C0C0C0,C0C0C0,808080,0,808080,800000,FFFFFF,0,FFFFFF

The
Blues=804000,C0C0C0,FFFFFF,0,FFFFFF,0,800000,C0C0C0,FFFFFF,C0C0C0,C0C
0C0,0,C0C0C0,C0C0C0,808080,0,C0C0C0,800000,FFFFFF,0,FFFFFF

```
Tweed=6A619E,C0C0C0,FFFFFF,0,FFFFFF,0,408080,C0C0C0,FFFFFF,404080,C0C
0C0,0,10E0E0E0,C0C0C0,808080,0,C0C0C0,8080,0,0,FFFFFF
Valentine=C080FF,FFFFFF,FFFFFF,0,FFFFFF,0,8000FF,400080,FFFFFF,C080FF
,C080FF,0,C0C0C0,C0C0C0,808080,0,808080,FF00FF,0,FFFFFF,FFFFFF
Wingtips=408080,C0C0C0,FFFFFF,0,FFFFFF,0,808080,FFFFFF,FFFFFF,4080,FF
FFFF,0,808080,C0C0C0,808080,0,C0C0C0,808080,FFFFFF,0,FFFFFF

[Custom Colors]
ColorA=FFFFFF
ColorB=FFFFFF
ColorC=FFFFFF
ColorD=FFFFFF
ColorE=FFFFFF
ColorF=FFFFFF
ColorG=FFFFFF
ColorH=FFFFFF
ColorI=FFFFFF
ColorJ=FFFFFF
ColorK=FFFFFF
ColorL=FFFFFF
ColorM=FFFFFF
ColorN=FFFFFF
ColorO=FFFFFF
ColorP=FFFFFF

[Patterns]
(None)=(None)
Boxes=127 65 65 65 65 65 127 0
Paisley=2 7 7 2 32 80 80 32
Weave=136 84 34 69 136 21 34 81
Waffle=0 0 0 0 128 128 128 240
Tulip=0 0 84 124 124 56 146 124
Spinner=20 12 200 121 158 19 48 40
Scottie=64 192 200 120 120 72 0 0
Critters=0 80 114 32 0 5 39 2
50% Gray=170 85 170 85 170 85 170 85
Quilt=130 68 40 17 40 68 130 1
Diamonds=32 80 136 80 32 0 0 0
Thatches=248 116 34 71 143 23 34 113
Pattern=224 128 142 136 234 10 14 0
```

```
[installed]
3.1=yes
TTY.DRV=yes
TTY.HLP=yes

[MMCPL]
NumApps=12
X=44
Y=44
W=430
H=240
```

TABLE 10.6: Common CONTROL.INI Section and Entries

Section or Entry	Use	Function
[current]	[current]	Specifies which color scheme is currently used.
[color schemes]	[color schemes]	Specifies the color schemes that Windows can use and the colors for the various items in Windows. The hexadecimal numbers after the style names are separated by commas. Each hexadecimal number represents a particular color for a particular item in Windows. You can make additional entries to this section using the Color control panel.
[patterns]	[patterns]	Defines the various patterns that can be used for the desktop. You can also modify this section using the Desktop control panel.
[installed]	[installed]	Contains the Windows version number and lists installed printer drivers and DLL files.
3.1=?	3.1=Yes	If set to Yes, indicates that Windows 3.1 is installed.
[MMPCL]	[MMPCL]	Defines settings for multimedia devices.

TIP

INI files can be edited with any ASCII text editor (including the DOS EDIT command and NOTEPAD.EXE in Windows). Some INI files can be edited with the SYSEDIT utility, which will be discussed in "Windows Configuration Utilities" later in this chapter.

The Registry

Configuration information is also stored in a special configuration database known as *the Registry*. This centralized database contains environmental settings for various Windows programs. It also contains what is known as *registration* information, which details which types of file extensions are associated with which applications. So, when you double-click a file in File Manager, the associated application runs and opens the file you double-clicked.

The Registry is unique in a couple of ways. First, it is a database. Most of the configuration files that have been discussed so far have been ASCII text files, which can be edited with almost any text editor. However, the Registry database is contained in a special binary file named REG.DAT, which can be edited only with the special Registry Editor provided with Windows. The Registry Editor program is called REGEDIT.EXE, and its icon is not typically created during Windows installation—you must create the icon manually. You can also run the program manually by choosing File ➤ Run from the Program Manager, typing **REGEDIT**, and clicking OK.

Once you have successfully run REGEDIT.EXE, you will see a screen similar to the one shown in Figure 10.2. This screen lists the types of files that have been registered with Windows. This registration is another difference between INI files and the Registry. When a program is installed, the installation program registers the file types with the Registry database so that Windows is familiar with the file types that the application uses. INI files just store the configuration information. If you want the information to be centralized, you have to edit the WIN.INI or SYSTEM.INI file.

FIGURE 10.2:

REGEDIT.EXE window

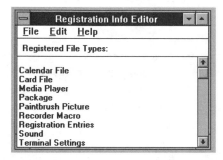

> **NOTE**   Windows 95 extensively uses the Registry to store all kinds of information. It is a major task to modify the Registry in Windows 95—you should try it only under the direction of a Technical Support Engineer.

Program Manager Group Files

Program Manager group files are the files in the Windows directory (for example, C:\WINDOWS) that store information about which application icons are contained in which Program Manager groups. Group filenames always have a .GRP extension and names similar to their actual program group names. The names may be truncated to fit within the DOS naming convention of eight letters, a period, and a three-letter extension. For example, the Accessories group has a group file named ACCESSOR.GRP, and the Main group has a group file named MAIN.GRP.

You cannot edit group files with a text editor. You must make an icon in the associated program group in Program Manager. When you add an icon to a program group, the group file is updated with information such as the path to the application, the name of the icon, the icon's picture, and the icon's position within the group.

When you delete a program group in Program Manager, the group file gets deleted as well.

> **TIP**
>
> If a program group gets deleted from the Program Manager accidentally and you have a backup of the group file, you can restore the program group without needing to create new icons. First, copy the group file back into the Windows directory. Then, select File ➤ New in Program Manager. When asked whether you want to create a group or an icon, select Group. Finally, instead of typing a new name for the group, type the name of the group file (for example, TEST.GRP) and click OK. The group will be created with its old name, and all the icons will be exactly where they were (as of the last backup).

Font Files

Font files are one of the Windows components that receive very little attention (and people know very little about them). Fonts (also called *typefaces*) are different ways of presenting the same letters. A font usually has a name and a size. The size is measured in points (a point is 1/72 of an inch). Several fonts come with Windows, and you can add several more using the Fonts control panel. Figure 10.3 shows some examples of the fonts that came with Windows 3.1. Font files are stored in C:\WINDOWS\SYSTEM (unless Windows was installed in a different directory).

FIGURE 10.3:

Font examples

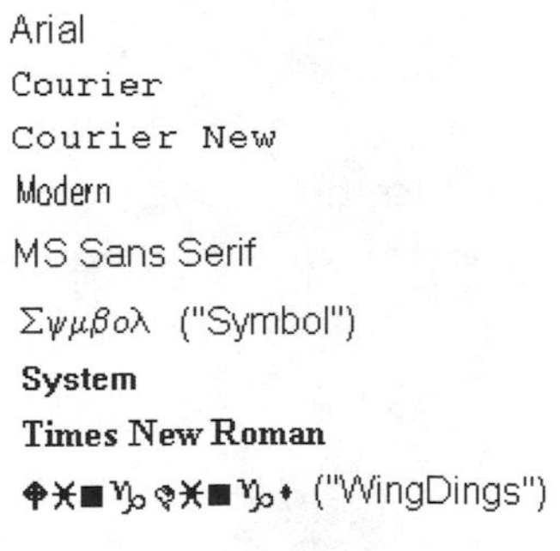

Arial
Courier
Courier New
Modern
MS Sans Serif
Σψμβολ ("Symbol")
System
Times New Roman
✦✖■ℓ♭ ✦✖■ℓ♭✦ ("WingDings")

Windows uses three main types of font files: raster fonts, vector fonts, and printer fonts. Each type has a specific use.

Raster Fonts

Raster fonts (also called *bitmap* or *screen* fonts) are designed pixel by pixel, and each size family is stored as a separate file (for example, 12-point fonts are stored in one file, 10-point fonts in another). These fonts display quickly and are great for viewing text on-screen. You cannot scale a raster font without losing image quality (the letters will look as if they were drawn with blocks instead of smooth, continuous lines), and you cannot rotate them. Typically, these files have a .FON extension.

The main disadvantage of raster fonts is that you must have the font file installed for the type and size you need to display (for example, if you need to display 12-point Arial, you must have the .FON file for that type and size installed on your system). This problem was addressed with the introduction of vector fonts.

Vector Fonts

Vector fonts (also called *scalable* or *TrueType* fonts) are stored as mathematical formulas. When a vector font is displayed, Windows reads the instructions in the formula—for example, *draw a line from* X *to* Y, *then from* Y *to* Z, *then from* A *to* B. (See Figure 10.4 for an illustration of this process.) To enlarge the font size, Windows just moves A, B, X, Y, and Z farther apart (also shown in Figure 10.4). These fonts scale and rotate well. However, they are more complex and take more time for Windows to process so that they can be displayed. TrueType fonts have the extensions .TTF and .FOT. One file of each type must be installed on the system for Windows to be able use the font.

FIGURE 10.4:

Drawing a vector font

Printer Fonts

Printer font files contain the instructions that the printer needs to print a particular font. There are three types of printer fonts: device fonts, printable screen fonts, and soft fonts.

Device Fonts   *Device* fonts (also called *hardware* fonts) print the quickest because the routines needed to draw these fonts are stored inside the printer. These fonts are either hardwired in the printer's control circuitry or added through a removable cartridge.

Printable Screen Fonts   It is difficult to find a device font for some of the TrueType and bitmap fonts. In these cases, the screen font is translated into a printer font by Windows and downloaded to the printer. This type of printer font is called a *printable screen* font. These fonts are the regular fonts used to display text on-screen (either raster or vector fonts), but are translated and downloaded to the printer so that they can be printed. Printable screen fonts are probably the most popular type of font for the average user. Their main advantage is that they allow any screen font to be printed. Their main disadvantage is that this process takes resources away from Windows. If you print a several-page document with only printable screen fonts, it may take longer than it would with screen and printer fonts.

Soft Fonts   *Soft* fonts come on a disk and are downloaded via a special utility to the printer's memory or hard disk. (Some printers have hard disks on which they store fonts and print jobs.) Soft fonts usually include a screen font.

Most publishers use a combination of screen fonts and either device or soft printer fonts. To use a font in a design program, you must make sure that both the screen and printer fonts for that type-face are available. If they aren't, the screen font will be translated and downloaded to the printer, and the printing process will take several minutes longer.

Windows Configuration Utilities

Windows configuration utilities are a class of Windows components that don't get much attention. These utilities are provided by Micro-soft to make managing Windows parameters easier. There are two main utilities used for this purpose: SYSEDIT.EXE and the Windows PIF Editor.

SYSEDIT.EXE

Often, you have to modify DOS and Windows configuration files simultaneously. For this reason, Microsoft included the SYSEDIT.EXE program (see Figure 10.5). This utility typically doesn't have an icon created for it during installation. However, you *can* create an icon for it. It's located in the C:\WINDOWS\SYSTEM directory. You can also run the utility by choosing File ➤ Run in the Program Manager.

In Figure 10.5, notice that the only files SYSEDIT.EXE can edit are SYSTEM.INI, WIN.INI, and DOS's CONFIG.SYS and AUTOEXEC .BAT. All other configuration files must be edited by some other means (using either DOS's EDIT.COM or the Windows Notepad).

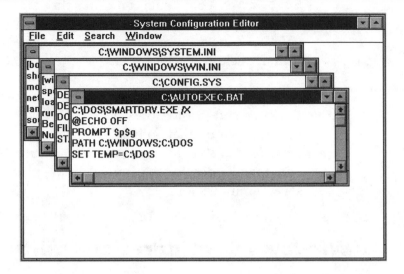

FIGURE 10.5:

SYSEDIT.EXE's main screen

To edit any of the files listed above, just click the window that represents the file you wish to edit. Then, make the change (delete an entry, add an entry, or modify an entry). To make the change permanent, choose File ➢ Save or exit the program—SYSEDIT.EXE will ask you whether you want to save the changes you made.

TIP The SYSEDIT.EXE program can also give you information about available system resources. Choose File ➢ About. At the bottom of the dialog box that appears, you will see the amount of system resources available (as a percentage).

PIF Editor

A common practice these days is to run DOS applications in Windows, as shown in Figure 10.6. There are no special requirements to run a DOS application in Windows. (Although, if you want a

DOS application to show within a window instead of full-screen, you must run Windows in 386Enhanced mode.) However, some older DOS applications try to access hardware directly instead of going through the operating system and BIOS. If this type of application tries to run in Windows, Windows may not know how to handle it.

FIGURE 10.6:

Running a DOS application (EDIT.COM) in Windows

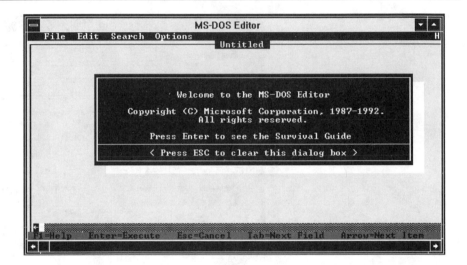

For this reason, Windows includes a utility for making *program information files (PIFs),* which tell Windows how to handle DOS applications that try to run in the Windows environment. PIF files are associated with a DOS application and have .PIF extensions. The PIF Editor (found in the Main program group) is the utility used to create these files.

NOTE If a DOS application doesn't have its own PIF file, Windows will use the settings from a PIF file called _DEFAULT.PIF (located in the C:\WINDOWS directory).

When you first open the PIF Editor, you will see a screen similar to the one shown in Figure 10.7. Notice that there are several options for making a DOS application run in Windows. Some settings (such as any settings that relate to memory) are crucial, while others don't affect the way the application runs—they are simply cosmetic (such as the Windows Title setting).

FIGURE 10.7:

The PIF Editor's main screen

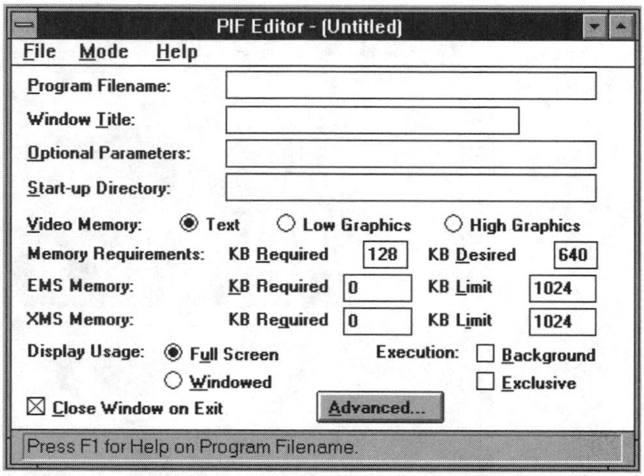

NOTE   You will see the screen shown in Figure 10.11 only if you run Windows in 386Enhanced mode and are making a PIF file to run in 386Enhanced mode. You can change the PIF file type by selecting an operating mode from the Mode menu.

Let's discuss each setting and what it does. If you need more details, press F1 while in the PIF Editor—the Windows PIF Editor Help program will give you a description of the parameter and how to use it.

Program Filename   This field should include the name and path of the DOS executable. When you double-click the icon for this executable in Windows, Windows looks for the application specified in this field.

Window Title   This field specifies the text that appears at the top of the window when running the application in Windows. In Figure 10.6 (shown earlier in the chapter), this field has been filled in (in the PIF Editor for EDIT.COM) with "MS-DOS Editor".

Optional Parameters   Some DOS applications require parameters (or switches) after their name to run properly. Instead of putting the parameters in Program Filename, put them here.

Start-up Directory   Some DOS applications require a working directory. This directory is specified so that the DOS application can find the files it needs. The application usually uses the same directory in which the application resides.

Video Memory   This setting specifies the video mode the DOS application uses in Windows. It also specifies how much memory the video portion takes. Text mode uses the least amount of memory; High Graphics mode uses the most. If you are unsure of which mode to use, check the documentation for the application. This setting is important—if you don't give the application enough memory, it may hang or scramble the video display when switching between the DOS application and Windows. Or, it may not run at all.

Memory Requirements   This setting specifies how much conventional memory the application requires. There are two values here: KB Required and KB Desired. The amount *required* is how much available conventional memory the manufacturer recommends. The amount *desired* is usually set to 640 so that the application uses as much conventional memory as is available.

EMS Memory   This setting is similar to Memory Requirements, except that these fields specify the minimum amount of expanded memory the application needs and the maximum amount it can use.

XMS Memory   This setting is also similar to Memory Requirements, except that it is used for extended memory.

Display Usage   This radio button specifies how the application runs, either using the whole display (Full Screen) or running in a window (Windowed). This setting is important—the Windowed mode requires more resources from Windows and isn't as efficient (but it's easier to switch between Windows and DOS applications). No matter which setting you've specified, you can usually switch between Windowed and Full Screen mode by holding down the Alt key and pressing Enter.

Execution   This setting specifies how Windows treats this application with regard to the multitasking abilities of Windows. When the Background option is checked, this application continues to run in the background, even if it is not the active application. For example, this option allows you to switch to another program in Windows while this application calculates a long list of numbers. When the Exclusive option is checked, no other application can run in the background while this application is active (even DOS applications with PIF files that have the Background option checked). You can check one or both of these options.

Close Window on Exit   This option controls what happens to the window when you exit the DOS application from its own menus (for example, by pressing Esc or Ctrl + Q). If this option is checked, Windows closes the window automatically. If this option is unchecked, Windows leaves the window open and puts the word "Inactive" in front of the application name at the top of the window. To close the window, you must double-click the box in the upper-left corner or click it once and choose Close.

Advanced   The Advanced button opens the window shown in Figure 10.8, which details the 386Enhanced options for the PIF Editor. If you are in Standard mode, this button won't be available. Click it to bring up the next set of PIF options

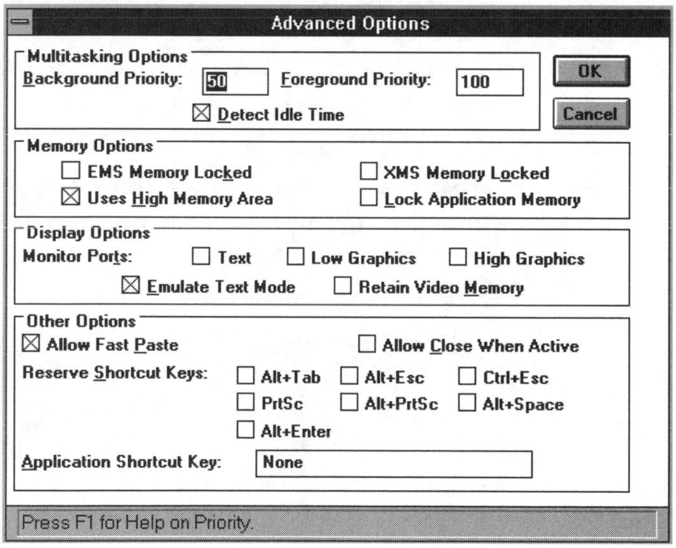

FIGURE 10.8:

The PIF Editor's Advanced Options screen

Multitasking Options   These options control how the application receives processor time. The numbers in Background Priority and Foreground Priority specify the priority of receiving processor time (the range of these numbers is 0 to 10,000). If you want the application to receive most of the processor time in one of these situations, set the corresponding value to 10,000.

- Background Priority—This number specifies the priority of the application when it runs in the background. The larger the number, the more processor time the application receives when running in the background.

- Foreground Priority—This number specifies the priority of the application when it runs in the foreground. The larger the number, the more processor time the application receives when running in the foreground as the active application.

- Detect Idle Time—If this option is checked, another application can steal CPU cycles from this application while waiting for keyboard input. You should keep this option checked most of the time so that other applications can benefit from a user's indecision. If an application hangs while waiting for keyboard input, uncheck this option.

Memory Options   These options specify the memory settings unique to running this application in 386Enhanced mode:

- EMS Memory Locked—When an application is pushed to the background, the information it had in memory is sometimes swapped to the disk. When this option is checked, the information the application had in expanded memory will not be swapped to the disk—it will remain in memory. Most applications don't have a problem with swapping memory. However, if you have an application that does, check this box so that the information stays put.

- XMS Memory Locked—This option is similar to EMS Memory Locked, except that it prevents the application's extended memory from being swapped to the disk. If this box is unchecked, the application can use Windows' virtual memory. However, some DOS applications don't like memory swapping and may crash if this option is unchecked, especially if the application tries to directly access memory instead of going through DOS.

- Lock Application Memory—When this option is checked, it performs the same functions as EMS Memory Locked and XMS Memory Locked, except that it functions for conventional memory. It prevents the application's conventional memory from being swapped to the disk when the application goes to the background.

- Uses High Memory Area—This option allows the application to use the High Memory Area (HMA). Most recent DOS applications have access to the DOS HMA, but only if there is nothing loaded there. If the HMA is available when Windows starts, the DOS application can allocate its own HMA. If the HMA is unavailable when Windows starts, uncheck this box so that the application won't try to use HMA.

Display Options   These options specify how an application uses video in Windows in 386Enhanced mode:

- Monitor Ports—This setting specifies whether Windows can verify the settings that the application uses for video while it runs in a particular mode. For example, if Text is checked, Windows will monitor all video transactions that the application makes while in Text mode. If there is a problem, Windows tries to correct the display. If you have problems switching between graphics modes, check the option that corresponds to the mode that has the problem. If none of these options are checked, the application can access the full-screen display quicker.

- Emulate Text Mode—Some DOS applications run in Text mode and display information using standard ROM BIOS services for output. If your application does this, check this box to increase the speed of the video display. When you check this box, if you get garbage on your screen when you display information in the application, uncheck this option.

- Retain Video Memory—When this option is unchecked, it allows Windows to allocate the memory given to the DOS application for displaying information to other applications when the DOS application is in the background. If this option is checked, the memory is allocated to the DOS application for video memory and is not given back to the system until the application is closed.

Other Options This is the miscellaneous section of the PIF Editor. It contains the options that don't fit into any of the other areas:

- Allow Fast Paste—This option allows Windows to use a faster method of pasting information from the Windows Clipboard to the DOS application. Some applications can handle this faster method, others cannot. Test it by trying to paste information from the Clipboard to the application. If it works, you can use this option.

- Allow Close When Active—This option allows you to make Windows automatically force the application to shut down when you close Windows. This is dangerous because an application that is forcibly shut down can corrupt data. Never use this option for applications that consistently use the hard disk (such as word processors or graphics-intensive applications).

- Reserve Shortcut Keys—These checkboxes deactivate the selected key combinations in Windows so that when the key combinations are pressed, they perform a function in the DOS application rather than in Windows. If you use a DOS word processor, you may have to reserve several of these key combinations. Check the box next to the key combination that you want the DOS application to be able to use.

- Application Shortcut Key—This option allows you to start a DOS application from within Windows by typing a key combination. To set the key combination, click within this field and press the keys that you want to use to start the application (the key combination that you press can't already be used by another application). As you press the keys, their names are displayed in this field.

When you are finished entering settings for the application, save the PIF file with a name similar to the name of the application (for example, if the DOS application is called FURBLE.EXE, you should name the PIF file something like FURBLE.PIF). To finish, make an icon for the PIF file in the Program Manager. When you double-click the PIF file, Windows runs the DOS application with the settings contained in the PIF file.

NOTE　Before you create your own PIF file for a DOS application, check the installation directory for an existing PIF file. If there isn't one, check the technical support Web site of the company that made the application for an updated PIF file. You will find a list of technical support Web sites in Appendix D.

Adding New Hardware and Software

When you add new hardware or software to Windows, remember one thing: it will change your configuration. Before you change a machine running Windows, back up your INI files, GRP files, AUTOEXEC.BAT, and CONFIG.SYS, either to a floppy disk or to another directory. If the installation is unsuccessful, you can return the machine to its former state by copying those files back to the correct directories in place of the current, nonworking ones.

Adding New Hardware

When adding new hardware to Windows, there are very few new elements in addition to the ones you encountered when adding new hardware to DOS. The key items that Windows requires so that it can use the new hardware are drivers. If you install a new sound card in the computer and install drivers for DOS, it doesn't necessarily mean that Windows can take advantage of the new hardware. Windows needs its own drivers.

Typically, when you install a new piece of hardware, you will install software immediately after installing the device in the computer. Most installation programs install two portions of software for the new device: the DOS portion and the Windows portion. The DOS portion usually consists of drivers for CONFIG.SYS or AUTOEXEC.BAT and, possibly, one or two DOS utilities. The Windows portion consists of Windows applications needed to use the new device. Usually, there are *no* Windows drivers. Access to the device is provided to the application through its DLL files via their communication to DOS and the device drivers.

Adding New Software

When adding new software to Windows, the process is usually the same as adding new software to DOS. Insert the installation disk into the disk drive. Then, choose File ➤ Run in the Program Manager. When the Run dialog box appears (see Figure 10.9), type **A:\SETUP.EXE** or **A:\INSTALL.EXE**, depending on the application—check your documentation to find out the name of the installation program—to run the installation program. Follow the prompts that appear.

FIGURE 10.9:

The Run dialog box

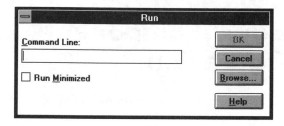

Remember that a new application adds additional INI files and takes up disk space. Some of the Office Suites take up more than 150 MB (and that's the Typical installation).

Review Questions for Chapter 10, Windows Components and Configuration

Answers to the review questions may be found in Appendix A.

1. Which Windows core component handles user input?

    A. INPUT.EXE

    B. USER.EXE

    C. WIN.COM

    D. WIN386.EXE

2. Which INI file contains settings for color schemes?

    A. WIN.INI

    B. SYSTEM.INI

    C. PROGMAN.INI

    D. CONTROL.INI

3. Generally speaking, the SYSTEM.INI file gets updated when you run which Windows program and make changes?

    A. CONTROL.EXE

    B. PIFEDIT.EXE

    C. SETUP.EXE

    D. PAINT.EXE

4. Which Windows core-component file is responsible for displaying Windows and drawing icons?

    A. GDI.EXE

    B. WINDOWS.EXE

    C. ICONIFY.EXE

    D. KRNL386.EXE

5. What does *PIF* stand for?

   A. Programmable Initialization File

   B. Program Information File

   C. Program Instant File

   D. Program Instruction File

6. Which Windows component is a small piece of executable code shared between many applications to reduce the size of each application that shares it?

   A. USER.EXE

   B. INI files

   C. The Registry

   D. DLL files

7. Which file(s) cannot be edited with SYSEDIT? (Circle all that apply.)

   A. AUTOEXEC.BAT

   B. CONFIG.SYS

   C. WIN.INI

   D. SYSTEM.INI

   E. PROGMAN.INI

   F. CONTROL.INI

   G. COMMAND.COM

8. Which type of font file prints fastest?

   A. Bitmap

   B. TrueType

   C. Hardware printer

   D. Screen

9. Which part of WIN.COM contains the Windows startup logo?

    A. WIN.CNF

    B. VGALOGO.RLE

    C. VGALOGO.LGO

    D. WIN.COM

10. Which section of the SYSTEM.INI file contains the drivers and programs that are loaded at system startup?

    A. [boot]

    B. [drivers]

    C. [boot.description]

    D. [386Enh]

11. Which WIN.COM startup switch forces Windows to start in 386Enhanced mode?

    A. /B

    B. /S

    C. /E

    D. /3

12. Which core component file acts as the backbone of Windows?

    A. WIN.INI

    B. KRNL386.EXE

    C. USER.EXE

    D. WINSOCK.DLL

13. Which entry do you place in WIN.INI to make a program start automatically as a minimized application?

    A. Minimize=*filename*

    B. Run=*filename*

    C. Load=*filename*

    D. Start=*filename*

14. Which entry do you place in WIN.INI to make a program start automatically as a regular, full-screen application?

    A. Minimize=*filename*

    B. Run=*filename*

    C. Load=*filename*

    D. Start=*filename*

15. What is the extension of TrueType font files?

    A. .TTF

    B. .TT

    C. .FOT

    D. .FNT

16. Which WIN.COM startup switch forces Windows to start in Standard mode?

    A. /B

    B. /S

    C. /E

    D. /3

17. Which executable(s) are typically used to install new Windows programs? (Circle all that apply.)

    A. START.EXE

    B. INSTALL.EXE

    C. WINSTRT.EXE

    D. SETUP.EXE

    E. INSTALL.COM

    F. PROGMAN.EXE

18. Which WIN.COM startup switch prevents the display of the Windows logo?

    A. /B

    B. /D

    C. /E

    D. :

19. You can only use one startup switch with WIN.COM to customize the startup of Windows. True or false?

    A. True

    B. False

20. You are troubleshooting a Windows program that keeps quitting with a "General Protection Fault in module VBRUN300.DLL." What is VBRUN300.DLL?

    A. Visual Basic RUNtime DLL

    B. Very Big RUNning DLL

    C. Vital Bit RUNtime DLL

    D. Virtual Bit RUNtime DLL

21. What is the correct syntax for a section marker in an INI file?

    A. :SECTION

    B. {SECTION}

    C. [SECTION]

    D. (SECTION)

22. What is the main reason it may be necessary to create a PIF?

    A. It's used to get a DOS program to run properly under Windows 3.x.

    B. It's used to specify Windows program settings.

    C. It's needed after you install new hardware.

    D. It's used to capture program output in a graphic file, like a TIF.

23. If a DOS program does not have a PIF, and you did not create one, where does Windows get the settings needed in order to run the DOS program?

    A. WIN.INI

    B. SYSTEM.INI

    C. _DEFAULT.PIF

    D. PROGMAN.INI

24. Where does Windows 3.x store the settings relating to the color and/or picture used as the Desktop background?

    A. WIN.INI

    B. SYSTEM.INI

    C. _DEFAULT.PIF

    D. PROGMAN.INI

25. Which of the following of Windows core components provides Windows applications with access to TCP/IP (and, subsequently, the Internet)?

    A. WIN.INI

    B. KRNL386.EXE

    C. USER.EXE

    D. WINSOCK.DLL

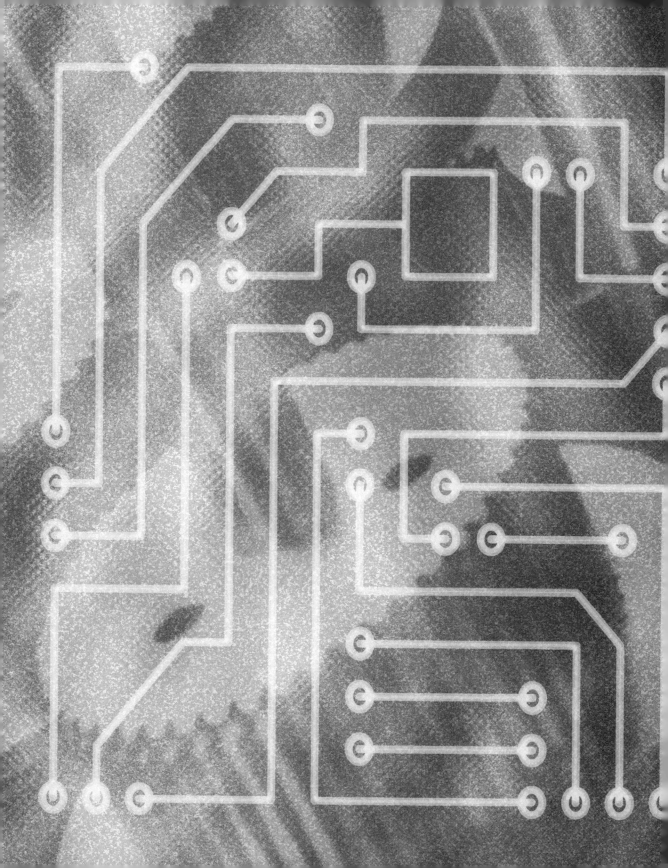

CHAPTER

ELEVEN

DOS and Windows System Optimization

- DOS Memory Optimization

- Windows Memory Optimization

- Disk System Optimization

The goal of optimization is to make the most system resources available (for example, memory, disk space, and processor time) while preserving system stability. Several items can increase system performance:

- DOS Memory Optimization
- Windows Memory Optimization
- Disk System Optimization

DOS Memory Optimization

Because of the increasing number of drivers that need to be loaded and the increasing size of programs, it is very common to lack sufficient conventional memory. When people discuss memory optimization, they usually refer to making as much conventional memory available as possible.

Memory optimization is one of the most important skills of a technician. Because of the large number of DOS applications, a technician who knows how to optimize memory will continue to be valuable. In general, DOS-based PCs run best when they have the most conventional memory available as possible—ideally, 600 KB or more.

Determining Memory Utilization with MEM.EXE

You already understand what conventional memory is, but to optimize it, you must first determine whether memory optimization is needed. For DOS systems, you use the MEM.EXE program to do this. This program allows you to determine how memory is utilized within DOS. The syntax for the MEM command is as follows:

MEM *option*

If you execute the MEM command without an option, it lists how much of each type of memory is installed, as shown in Figure 11.1. The available options are described in Table 11.1.

FIGURE 11.1:

A report from the MS-DOS MEM command when executed without options

```
C:\WINDOWS>mem

Memory Type         Total       Used       Free
----------------   --------   --------   --------
Conventional          640K        44K       596K
Upper                   0K         0K         0K
Reserved              384K       384K         0K
Extended (XMS)     15,360K     2,240K    13,120K
----------------   --------   --------   --------
Total memory       16,384K     2,668K    13,716K

Total under 1 MB      640K        44K       596K

Total Expanded (EMS)            20M (20,463,616 bytes)
Free Expanded (EMS)             13M (13,434,880 bytes)

Largest executable program size   596K (609,968 bytes)
Largest free upper memory block     0K       (0 bytes)
MS-DOS is resident in the high memory area.
```

TABLE 11.1: MEM.EXE Command-Line Options

Option	Description
/?	Help switch—Shows basic information on the syntax of the MEM command and how it is used, and shows all the switches listed in this table and how they are used.
/C	Classify switch—Gives output similar to that shown in Listing 11.1 following this table.
/D	Debug switch—Details how the first 640 KB of conventional memory is used. This switch is helpful when you want to determine the memory addresses of the various programs that are loaded. (Remember that MEM itself is a program and should be listed.) A sample report of MEM /D is shown in Listing 11.2 following this table.

TABLE 11.1 CONTINUED: MEM.EXE Command-Line Options

Option	Description
/F	Free memory switch—Shows all the free memory blocks in the first 640 KB of conventional memory and their starting addresses. It is also useful in memory optimization.
/M *module*	Module switch—Shows the starting addresses of the data, program, and free memory allocated to the module you specify.
/P	Pause switch—When used in conjunction with the other switches, halts the display of the command's output until a key is pressed for each page that is displayed.

NOTE

In IBM's PC-DOS, the CONFIG.EXE program shows some of the same information as the MS-DOS MEM.EXE program, as well as information regarding fixed disks.

Listing 11.1   **A report from the MEM /C command**

```
Modules using memory below 1 MB:
```

Name	Total		Conventional		Upper Memory	
SYSTEM	48,880	(48K)	10,592	(10K)	38,288	(37K)
HIMEM	1,168	(1K)	1,168	(1K)	0	(0K)
EMM386	4,320	(4K)	4,320	(4K)	0	(0K)
WIN	3,696	(4K)	3,696	(4K)	0	(0K)
————	288	(0K)	288	(0K)	0	(0K)
vmm32	102,064	(100K)	448	(0K)	101,616	(99K)
COMMAND	7,456	(7K)	7,456	(7K)	0	(0K)
IBMIDECD	10,848	(11K)	0	(0K)	10,848	(11K)
IFSHLP	2,864	(3K)	0	(0K)	2,864	(3K)
DOSKEY	4,688	(5K)	0	(0K)	4,688	(5K)
Free	627,120	(612K)	627,120	(612K)	0	(0K)

Memory Summary:

Type of Memory	Total	Used	Free
Conventional	655,360	28,240	627,120
Upper	158,304	158,304	0
Reserved	393,216	393,216	0
Extended (XMS)	32,347,552	95,648	32,251,904
Total memory	33,554,432	675,408	32,879,024
Total under 1 MB	813,664	186,544	627,120

Largest executable program size   627,104   (612K)
Largest free upper memory block   0   (0K)
MS-DOS is resident in the high memory area.

Listing 11.2 **A report from the MEM /D command**

Conventional Memory Detail:

Segment	Total	Name	Type
00000	1,024 (1K)		Interrupt Vector
00040	256 (0K)		ROM Communication Area
00050	512 (1K)		DOS Communication Area
00070	1,424 (1K)	IO	System Data
		CON	System Device Driver
		AUX	System Device Driver
		PRN	System Device Driver
		CLOCK$	System Device Driver
		A: - C:	System Device Driver
		COM1	System Device Driver
		LPT1	System Device Driver
		LPT2	System Device Driver
		LPT3	System Device Driver
		CONFIG$	System Device Driver
		COM2	System Device Driver
		COM3	System Device Driver

			COM4	System Device Driver
000C9	5,120	(5K)	MSDOS	System Data
00209	7,632	(7K)	IO	System Data
	1,024	(1K)		Relocated EBIOS data
	1,152	(1K)	XMSXXXX0	Installed Device=HIMEM
	4,304	(4K)	$MMXXXX0	Installed Device=EMM386
	544	(1K)		Sector buffer
	512	(1K)		BUFFERS=50
003E6	80	(0K)	MSDOS	System Program
003EB	32	(0K)	WIN	Data
003ED	288	(0K)	----	Data
003FF	256	(0K)	WIN	Environment
0040F	3,408	(3K)	WIN	Program
004E4	48	(0K)	vmm32	Data
004E7	400	(0K)	vmm32	Program
00500	288	(0K)	COMMAND	Data
00512	5,728	(6K)	COMMAND	Program
00678	1,440	(1K)	COMMAND	Environment
006D2	288	(0K)	MEM	Environment
006E4	90,464	(88K)	MEM	Program
01CFA	536,656	(524K)	MSDOS	– Free –

Upper Memory Detail:

Segment	Region	Total		Name	Type
0C95C	1	51,968	(51K)	IO	System Data
		10,832	(11K)	IBMCD001	Installed Device=IBMIDECD
		2,848	(3K)	IFSHLP	Installed Device=IFSHLP
		464	(0K)		Block device tables
		4,736	(5K)		FILES=85
		256	(0K)		FCBS=4
		26,800	(26K)		BUFFERS=50
		2,816	(3K)		LASTDRIVE=`
		3,072	(3K)		STACKS=9,256
0D60C	1	272	(0K)	vmm32	Data
0D61D	1	4,688	(5K)	DOSKEY	Program
0D742	1	101,344	(99K)	vmm32	Data

```
Memory Summary:

Type of Memory        Total          Used           Free
_____  _____    _____        _____         _____

Conventional         655,360         28,240        627,120
Upper                158,304        158,304              0
Reserved             393,216        393,216              0
Extended (XMS)    32,347,552         95,648     32,251,904
_____  _____    _____        _____         _____

Total memory      33,554,432        675,408     32,879,024

Total under 1 MB     813,664        186,544        627,120

Memory accessible using Int 15h              0      (OK)
Largest executable program size        627,104      (612K)
Largest free upper memory block              0      (OK)
MS-DOS is resident in the high memory area.

XMS version  3.00; driver version  3.95
```

Approaches to Memory Optimization

Once you have determined how much conventional memory you have available (and, in all likelihood, that you need to optimize your conventional memory), you must then determine how to best optimize it. If you installed DOS with the default installation, you will have the CONFIG.SYS file shown below.

DEVICE=C:\DOS\HIMEM.SYS

Files=40

Buffers=9,256

SHELL=C:\DOS\COMMAND.COM /E:1024

The most important procedure that you can perform to increase available conventional memory is to add the line **DOS=HIGH** to

CONFIG.SYS. This moves DOS to the HMA, which frees up the first 64KB block (minus a small amount to keep HIMEM.SYS and a few smaller files in conventional memory).

The next procedure is to load some or all of your device drivers and TSRs into upper memory. This procedure is also called *loading them high,* which is a misnomer because you don't load them into the HMA—you load them into upper memory (the other name for reserved memory, which is *higher* than conventional memory, but not typically referred to as the high memory area). This is accomplished by doing three things:

1. Add **DEVICE=C:\DOS\EMM386.EXE** to your CONFIG.SYS file so that DOS can manage the UMBs (upper memory blocks).

2. Make sure that you have some free UMBs. You can do this with the MEM /C command, which shows the available upper memory in the Memory Summary portion of its output.

3. Add something to each command that loads a driver or TSR so that the driver or TSR loads into upper memory.

The command used to load a driver into upper memory is DEVICEHIGH=*driver name*. Use this command like you use the DEVICE= command in CONFIG.SYS. When you replace each of the DEVICE= commands in CONFIG.SYS with DEVICEHIGH=, the driver attempts to load itself into upper memory. You can determine whether this was successful by using the MEM /C command to show how much of the driver is loaded in upper memory. The driver will be displayed, with a number in the Upper Memory column, if it successfully loaded into upper memory. In addition, if you have drivers loaded from AUTOEXEC.BAT, use LOADHIGH *driver name* (or LH, for short) to load that driver or TSR into an upper memory block.

Also, you should check whether you have a program that uses expanded memory. If you don't, you can place the NOEMS line after C:\DOS\EMM386.EXE in CONFIG.SYS. This frees up the 64KB area used by the page frame so that it can be used for UMBs.

Automating Memory Management with MEMMAKER and RAMBOOST

The memory-optimization tricks discussed above are simple enough, but most users don't want or need to know memory-optimization theory. So, Microsoft and IBM included intelligent memory-optimization utilities with their DOS operating systems—MEMMAKER (by Microsoft) and RAMBOOST (by IBM). These utilities already know the theory behind memory optimization, and can examine the system and determine how to optimize it most efficiently. Each utility accomplishes the same tasks by different means. MEMMAKER scans CONFIG.SYS and AUTOEXEC.BAT, and adds DEVICEHIGH and LOADHIGH statements to optimize memory. RAMBOOST, on the other hand, is a TSR that runs constantly. Anytime you change CONFIG.SYS or AUTOEXEC.BAT, RAMBOOST detects the change, reboots the computer, and rearranges the drivers in upper memory to secure the best possible memory configuration. RAMBOOST saves all its information in a file called RAMBOOST.INI.

NOTE   For more information on RAMBOOST, refer to its user manual.

One thing to be careful about regarding MEMMAKER is that it isn't as smart as it could be. For example, if you have the following CONFIG.SYS:

```
DEVICE=C:\DOS\HIMEM.SYS
DEVICE=C:\DOS\EMM386.EXE
FILES=50
BUFFERS=9,256
DEVICE=C:\SB16\CTMMCD.SYS
```

MEMMAKER may optimize it to read as follows:

```
DEVICE=C:\DOS\HIMEM.SYS
DEVICE=C:\DOS\EMM386.EXE NOEMS
FILES=50
BUFFERS=9,256
DOS=UMB
DEVICEHIGH=C:\SB16\CTMMCD.SYS
```

Memory utilization would be more efficient after MEMMAKER has run, but there is one glaring problem: where is DOS=HIGH? If MEMMAKER included this statement, it would free up a 64KB block of conventional memory. However, MEMMAKER didn't include this statement. So, while it's good at general optimization, MEMMAKER can't beat an intuitive technician with a good grasp of memory theory.

Another factor of memory optimization is the *order* in which drivers are loaded into memory. When optimizing memory, you sometimes run into a situation in which you need only 1 or 2 KB more conventional memory and you've done all you can to secure the most available conventional memory. The final trick in your bag is to change the order in which the drivers load. To do this, load the driver that needs the most memory first. Then, load the next largest driver, etc. When you build a wall, do you put down the smallest stones first, then the largest? Or, do you put down the largest stone first, then the smallest? It is obvious that you use the latter method so that your wall is stable.

TIP

Before running MEMMAKER, make sure you have a bootable DOS diskette handy in case MEMMAKER makes changes to your configuration that cause your system to crash. (Or, you can press F5 or Shift at bootup to bypass config.sys and autoexec.bat.)

Starting MEMMAKER

Start MEMMAKER by typing its name at the command line:

MEMMAKER

You will see the opening screen for the MEMMAKER program. Hit Enter—you will see another MEMMAKER screen, which offers a choice between Express or Custom setup. If you choose the Express setup, MEMMAKER makes all the decisions, and only asks you to press Enter a couple of times and reboot the system—once to analyze the memory requirements of your drivers and programs, and a second time to initiate the changes.

MEMMAKER Setup Options

The Custom setup offers you several options. Here are some suggestions for selecting from the advanced options:

- Don't let MEMMAKER set aside upper memory for EMS page frames unless your system uses expanded memory.

- Let MEMMAKER create upper memory in the monochrome region unless your monitor uses hex memory addresses B000–B7FF.

- Keep current EMM386.EXE exclusions and inclusions only if someone has manually performed memory mapping of the system to improve performance. The exclusions and inclusions are found in the EMM386.EXE command as I= and X= statements in CONFIG.SYS, and are hexadecimal memory addresses.

Using MEMMAKER

An example of this process will help clarify what MEMMAKER does and how memory management works in a DOS environment.

Suppose that the CONFIG.SYS file looks as follows before MEM-MAKER enters the picture:

```
DEVICE=C:\WINDOWS\HIMEM.SYS
DOS=HIGH
DEVICE=C:\WINDOWS\SETVER.EXE
DEVICE=C:\WINDOWS\COMMAND\ANSI.SYS
DEVICE=C:\CRIDE\SBIDE.SYS /D:MSCD001 /P:170,15
```

When the memory configuration is checked by typing the MEM /C command at the command line, the screen shown in Figure 11.2 appears.

FIGURE 11.2:

DOS 6.22 memory configuration before running MEMMAKER

```
Modules using memory below 1 MB:

    Name         Total           Conventional      Upper Memory
    --------   ----------------   ----------------  ----------------
    MSDOS       17,680   (17K)    17,680   (17K)        0    (OK)
    SBIDE       14,864   (15K)    14,864   (15K)        0    (OK)
    SETVER         832   (1K)        832   (1K)         0    (OK)
    ANSI         4,320   (4K)      4,320   (4K)         0    (OK)
    HIMEM        1,120   (1K)      1,120   (1K)         0    (OK)
    DBLBUFF      2,448   (2K)      2,448   (2K)         0    (OK)
    IFSHLP       2,864   (3K)      2,864   (3K)         0    (OK)
    COMMAND      7,328   (7K)      7,328   (7K)         0    (OK)
    MOUSE       17,152   (17K)    17,152   (17K)        0    (OK)
    SMARTDRV    29,024   (28K)    29,024   (28K)        0    (OK)
    Free       557,584  (545K)   557,584  (545K)        0    (OK)

Memory Summary:

    Type of Memory      Total          Used          Free
    ----------------  ------------  ------------  -----------
    Conventional         655,360        97,776       557,584
    Upper                      0             0             0
    Reserved             393,216       393,216             0
    Extended (XMS)    15,728,640     2,166,784    13,561,856
                      ------------  ------------  -----------
    Total memory      16,777,216     2,657,776    14,119,440

    Total under 1 MB     655,360        97,776       557,584
```

The HIMEM.SYS extended memory driver let DOS load much of itself into high memory with the DOS=HIGH command. High memory, you will recall, is the first 64 KB of extended memory. The third column in the upper half of Figure 11.2 shows that all the programs and drivers have been loaded into conventional memory, for a total of 97 KB.

The last column in the upper half of Figure 11.2 shows clearly that there is no upper memory in use at all. You will find a very interesting statistic in the lower half of the screen in the Upper memory category—there is zero KB of free memory. If there is no upper memory available, it is certain that none can be used. If you manually place EMM386.EXE into CONFIG.SYS and reboot, it would revise this figure drastically. MEMMAKER, however, performs that feat admirably well. After you run MEMMAKER and use another MEM /C command, the screen shown in Figure 11.3 appears.

FIGURE 11.3:

DOS 6.22 memory configuration after running MEMMAKER

```
Modules using memory below 1 MB:

    Name          Total           Conventional      Upper Memory
    --------    -------------    --------------    ---------------
    SYSTEM       17,696  (17K)     9,520   (9K)      8,176   (8K)
    HIMEM         1,120   (1K)     1,120   (1K)          0   (0K)
    EMM386        4,320   (4K)     4,320   (4K)          0   (0K)
    DBLBUFF       2,448   (2K)     2,448   (2K)          0   (0K)
    SBIDE        14,896  (15K)         0   (0K)     14,896  (15K)
    ANSI          4,320   (4K)         0   (0K)      4,320   (4K)
    IFSHLP        2,864   (3K)         0   (0K)      2,864   (3K)
    SETVER          864   (1K)         0   (0K)        864   (1K)
    COMMAND       7,168   (7K)         0   (0K)      7,168   (7K)
    MOUSE        17,152  (17K)         0   (0K)     17,152  (17K)
    SMARTDRV     29,024  (28K)         0   (0K)     29,024  (28K)
    Free        744,352 (727K)   637,744 (623K)    106,608 (104K)

Memory Summary:

    Type of Memory      Total          Used           Free
    ----------------  -----------   -----------    -----------
    Conventional         655,360        17,616        637,744
    Upper                191,072        84,464        106,608
    Reserved             393,216       393,216              0
    Extended (XMS)    15,537,568     2,340,256     13,197,312
    ----------------  -----------   -----------    -----------
    Total memory      16,777,216     2,835,552     13,941,664

    Total under 1 MB     846,432       102,080        744,352
```

If you examine this output, you will notice that the SBIDE device driver has been loaded into upper memory, along with SETVER and ANSI. The MOUSE driver is loaded from the AUTOEXEC.BAT file. When you examine the post-MEMMAKER CONFIG.SYS file, you will notice some important additions and changes:

```
DEVICE=C:\WINDOWS\EMM386.EXE NOEMS
DOS=UMB
```

MEMMAKER loaded the upper memory manager and issued a DOS command that instructs a portion of the operating system to load into upper memory.

MEMMAKER also altered existing lines in CONFIG.SYS, as follows:

```
DEVICEHIGH /L:1,24992 =C:\WINDOWS\SETVER.EXE
DEVICEHIGH /L:1,16976 =C:\WINDOWS\COMMAND\ANSI.SYS
DEVICEHIGH /L:1,9728 =C:\CRIDE\SBIDE.SYS /D:MSCD001 /P:170,15
```

The /L switches describe the portion of upper memory to load the drivers into (region *1* is the lowest block of available memory addresses). The second number indicates the minimum size of the UMB for the driver to load into that location.

If you examine the AUTOEXEC.BAT file, you will notice that MEMMAKER added a LOADHIGH command to the MOUSE program to push it into upper memory.

SYSTEM is representative of the operating system—much of DOS loaded into upper memory. Notice that SYSTEM replaced the MSDOS program shown previously in Figure 11.2.

TIP

If you use MEMMAKER for memory optimization and Windows is installed on your system, you may need to manually add the DOS=HIGH statement to your CONFIG.SYS file. If you don't, Windows may not load DOS into high memory, which it typically does by default. If MEM /C reports that an inordinate amount of conventional memory is used by SYSTEM, add the DOS=HIGH statement to CONFIG.SYS.

For ideal memory optimization, set the BUFFERS and FILES commands low enough that their reserved memory addresses fit into the high memory area from 1024 KB to 1088 KB. (HIMEM.SYS and DOS=HIGH must be loaded in CONFIG.SYS for high memory to be utilized.) BUFFERS and FILES are best utilized in high memory because few programs can take advantage of that space (in fact, most programs must be specially written to do so). MEM /C will reveal whether DOS loaded BUFFERS and FILES into the high memory area. If DOS loaded BUFFERS and FILES high, the MSDOS or SYSTEM program in MEM /C will use a relatively small amount of space (perhaps 17 KB). If BUFFERS and FILES use upper memory instead, SYSTEM may use over 50 KB. Experiment with the BUFFERS and FILES commands by changing their numbers and rebooting (perhaps several times) to determine how high their numbers can be set.

Windows Memory Optimization

Windows memory works slightly differently than DOS memory. Therefore, you can use different techniques and utilities to optimize it. Windows primarily uses extended memory. However, most of the programs (including Windows) use a portion of conventional memory to get started. For that reason, it is still advisable to first optimize DOS conventional memory when optimizing Windows memory. After all, Windows is a DOS program, and what DOS program runs well without enough conventional memory?

Choosing a Swap File Type

Do you remember when swap files were discussed in Chapter 8? A swap file is a file on the hard disk that is used to emulate physical memory. Information is swapped between this file and main memory. There are two main types of swap files: permanent and temporary. Table 11.2 offers a quick review of the difference between these two types.

TABLE 11.2: Permanent vs. Temporary Swap Files

Permanent Swap File	Temporary Swap File
Requires contiguous disk space	Doesn't require contiguous disk space
Can be created only on a local drive (for example, C: or D:)	Can be created on a local drive or a redirected network drive (for example, C:, D:, F:, or G:)
Has excellent performance	Has average performance
Has a fixed size	Has a dynamic size—disk space is allocated at Windows startup
Filenames are 386SPART.PAR and SPART.PAR	Filename is WIN386.SWP

Optimizing the Swap File

You optimize Windows memory by optimizing the swap file. You can do several things to optimize the swap file. First, if possible, change the swap file type to Permanent in the Virtual Memory page of the 386Enhanced control panel (see Figure 11.4). Windows automatically detects the best size for your swap file and enters that number in the New Size field. If this number is the same as the Size value in Current Settings, click the Cancel button and don't change your swap file—it's already optimized for your current disk configuration (as far as type and size are concerned).

Another thing you can do to optimize the swap file is to make sure you have enough contiguous disk space on the disk drive that contains the swap file. You can check the amount of fragmented files by running the DOS utility DEFRAG.EXE. This program not only tells you how fragmented your disk is, but helps you defragment it. DEFRAG.EXE will be covered in the next section of this chapter.

FIGURE 11.4:

Changing the swap file
type to Permanent

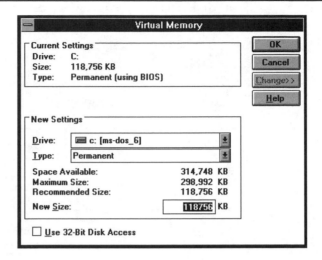

The last thing you can do to optimize the swap file is to check
the Use 32-Bit Disk Access option in the Virtual Memory page of the
386Enhanced control panel (see Figure 11.4). This was briefly discussed in Chapter 10. When this option is checked, Windows directly
accesses the disk system, bypassing the BIOS. When this is done, all
disk accesses (including swap file accesses) are faster. In addition,
the amount of system resources Windows has available increases. If
you enable 32-bit disk access, it is probably the single best thing you
can do to increase Windows performance.

TIP

To enable 32-bit disk access, you must have a disk controller
that is compatible with the Western Digital-1003. If you don't
have one, check with the manufacturer of your hard disk to
determine whether there is a 32-bit disk driver available for
Windows. If not, you can't enable 32-bit disk access.

Click OK. Windows will ask you whether you want to make the
changes. Click OK to accept the changes you have made. Windows
will then issue a warning (see Figure 11.5) that informs you that

32-bit disk access may not work on portable computers—BIOS may shut down the disk to conserve power without telling Windows about it. If this happens and Windows tries to access the disk, it may cause data loss. At the very least, it will return a strange error message and may cause Windows to hang. Click Yes to accept this change if your machine doesn't have a problem with this option.

FIGURE 11.5:

32-bit disk access warning

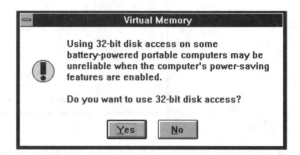

Disk System Optimization

Disk system optimization involves squeezing every possible iota of speed out of a disk subsystem. It also involves making sure that there is enough disk space for all the applications and files (including swap files) that reside on your hard disk.

Optimizing Disk Space

You can use four major utilities to optimize disk space. The first utility is the DEL (and, to a certain extent, DELTREE) command. Disk space is like closet space—you can never have enough. If you currently have 500 MB of data on your disk and you have a 1000MB disk, you will fill it eventually. When you fill it, you won't have any space left in which to put data. In addition, the less disk space that remains, the less disk space that is available for a swap file. Windows performance will be degraded as you run out of disk space.

You may see more program crashes and Not Enough Memory error messages.

In this case, to optimize disk space, you must back up then delete some unused programs or data from the disk. It is pretty easy to decide which data are unneeded: which programs or data have not been used in a while? If you don't use a program or data often, you can get rid of it. Programs can simply be deleted because you have the installation diskettes or CDs. Data should be backed up to floppy disks or tape before deletion so that you can access them later. Finally, use the DEL command to remove unused programs or data.

Enhancing Performance with Disk Caching

You can use a disk-caching utility to optimize disk performance. A *disk cache* improves performance by requiring that all disk reads and writes are temporarily stored in a section of memory, because it is fairly time-consuming to go from disk to memory, but it is quick to go from memory to processor. The disk cache can store several MB of disk data. Every time the processor issues a read request to the disk controller, the data are sent from the disk to the cache. Then, the processor can read the information from the cache as it needs it. The same process happens in reverse for disk writes. The processor writes the data to the cache. Then, in the background, the data are written to the disk little by little. Between disk-read caching and disk-write caching, you can gain an increase in disk performance of 10 to 20 percent.

Disk Caching with SMARTDrive

There are several disk-caching programs—the one that comes with DOS and Windows is called SMARTDrive (SMARTDRV.EXE). There are two versions of it—one comes with DOS, the other comes with Windows. The different versions are optimized for their respective software. SMARTDrive uses a portion of extended memory for read and write caching—you must have an extended memory manager (such as HIMEM.SYS) loaded in your CONFIG.SYS file.

To start disk caching, type the following line in your AUTOEXEC.BAT file:

C:\DOS\SMARTDRV.EXE

Or, if you are running Windows, type

C:\WINDOWS\SMARTDRV.EXE

This will produce the output shown in Figure 11.6, which lists the drives that are cache-enabled, the type(s) of caches that are enabled (read, write, or both), and the size of the cache. You can customize these settings with command-line switches, which you will find by executing SMARTDRV at the command line with the special /? switch. This switch gives you a list of switches and their use, and the syntax of the SMARTDRV command in general.

FIGURE 11.6:

Disk-caching status in SMARTDrive

```
C:\WINDOWS>smartdrv
Microsoft SMARTDrive Disk Cache version 4.0
Copyright 1991,1992 Microsoft Corp.

Cache size: 2,097,152 bytes
Cache size while running Windows: 2,097,152 bytes

                  Disk Caching Status
  drive    read cache     write cache     buffering
  ----------------------------------------------------
    A:         yes            no              no
    B:         yes            no              no
    C:         yes            yes             no

For help, type "Smartdrv /?".
```

Defragmenting a Disk

When files are stored, they are typically stored in sequential clusters so that as the disk rotates, the entire file can be read without moving the position of the read/write heads. However, as the disk fills up, sequential clusters get harder and harder to find on the disk. So, pieces of some files are strewn about in different places on the disk, and the read/write heads have to move to several different places to read one file. As the disk fills up, this will cause slower file access than on a new disk. This situation is known as disk *fragmentation*. However, you can cure this ailment.

NOTE Permanent swap files require a large chunk of contiguous disk space. If the disk is severely fragmented, you won't be able to create a permanent swap file.

When a large, sequential file is deleted, its clusters become available for storing files again. However, the fragmented files don't automatically jump to these large, available clusters. You must run the DEFRAG.EXE utility to consolidate these file fragments and place them in the sequential clusters. When you run DEFRAG.EXE, it asks you which disk you want to optimize. You can run DEFRAG.EXE on either floppy or hard disks. After you select the disk you want to defragment, DEFRAG.EXE analyzes the disk and reports the percentage that is *not* fragmented (for example, *80 percent of drive C: is not fragmented*). If this percentage is greater than 90 percent, you won't gain very much by defragmenting the disk. However, if the percentage is less than 90 percent, you can initiate a defragmentation— DEFRAG.EXE will rearrange the files and put them in contiguous clusters (where possible). While DEFRAG.EXE does this, it displays a graphic that shows DEFRAG.EXE's progress.

To get more information about how DEFRAG.EXE works, run DEFRAG.EXE and press F1 to bring up the Help screen.

Using RAM Disks

If you have lots of RAM installed in your computer and you want to increase disk performance, you can make a RAM disk to hold the data that you most frequently access. A *RAM disk* (also called a *virtual disk)* is an area of memory that has been set aside and assigned a drive letter. You can use this area as if it is a regular disk. Because it is memory, not disk space, access to programs and the data stored there is much faster.

To create a RAM disk on a DOS machine, place the RAMDRIVE.SYS driver in the CONFIG.SYS file as follows:

```
DEVICE=C:\DOS\RAMDRIVE.SYS 1024 /E
```

The *1024* directs RAMDRIVE.SYS to allocate 1024 KB (or 1 MB) of RAM for the RAM disk. The /E parameter directs RAMDRIVE.SYS to use extended memory for the RAM disk. To use expanded memory for the RAM disk, use the /A switch instead.

TIP　If you have several drive letters already, you may have to increase the value of LASTDRIVE= in the CONFIG.SYS file to a higher drive letter so that DOS can allocate a drive letter for it.

WARNING　Because a RAM disk's information is stored in RAM, all information placed in it is erased when you shut down the machine. Remember to copy information that you want to keep back to a disk before shutting down the machine.

Review Questions for Chapter 11, DOS and Windows System Optimization

1. Which type of swap file requires contiguous disk space?

   A. Temporary

   B. Permanent

   C. Memory

   D. Contiguous

2. Which DOS utility can you use to optimize DOS conventional memory?

   A. MEMMOPT

   B. MEMMAKER

   C. OPTIMIZE

   D. SMARTDRV

3. Which item increases Windows performance the most?

   A. Temporary swap file

   B. Permanent swap file

   C. 32-bit disk access

   D. None of the above

   E. All of the above

4. You can use the DEFRAG utility to defragment floppy disks. True or false?

   A. True

   B. False

5. Which driver (loaded in CONFIG.SYS) enables you to use a chunk of RAM as a virtual disk?

   A. RAMDISK.SYS

   B. VDISK.EXE

   C. VDISK.SYS

   D. RAMDRIVE.SYS

6. Which of the following items is *not* a requirement for running Windows with a permanent swap file?

   A. swap file on a local drive (not a network drive)

   B. swap file stored in contiguous disk space

   C. swap file named WIN386.SWP

   D. swap file of a fixed size

7. Which utility provides DOS with disk-caching functionality?

   A. CACHE.EXE

   B. SMARTDRV.EXE

   C. SMRTDRIV.COM

   D. DISKCACH.COM

8. Which utility can you use with IBM PC-DOS to optimize conventional memory?

   A. MEMMAKER

   B. PCMEM

   C. RAMBOOST

   D. RAMMAKER

9. Which CONFIG.SYS command allows DOS to load itself into the HMA?

    A. DOS=HIGH

    B. DOS=HMA

    C. DOS=UMB

    D. DOS=LOADHIGH

10. MEMMAKER is the best way to optimize MS-DOS conventional memory. True or false?

    A. True

    B. False

11. When you reboot a computer that uses a RAM disk, the information that was in the disk before the reboot will be there after the reboot. True or false?

    A. True

    B. False

12. A user complains that their computer has gotten slower in the last few months. They haven't added any new hardware, but they are starting to get Out of Memory error messages in Windows. What is a possible reason for this?

    A. A corrupt Windows application is causing the crash.

    B. There is not enough conventional memory.

    C. The disk is full (or almost full).

    D. The disk cache is full.

13. To prevent EMM386.EXE from using a particular memory address range (for example, C0000–CFFFF) for UMBs, how would you state the DEVICE line in CONFIG.SYS?

    A. DEVICE=EMM386.EXE OFF=C0000-CFFFF

    B. DEVICE=EMM386.EXE NO=C0000-CFFFF

    C. DEVICE=EMM386.EXE I=C0000-CFFFF

    D. DEVICE=EMM386.EXE X=C0000-CFFFF

14. A good guideline for defragmenting your hard disk is to do it when more than what percent of your hard disk is fragmented?

    A. 10

    B. 20

    C. 80

    D. 90

15. To change a swap file, which control panel should you go to first?

    A. Swap File

    B. 386Enhanced

    C. Virtual Memory

    D. Memory

16. You have just added a new sound card to a machine running MS-DOS 6.22 and Windows 3.1. After installing the software for it and rebooting, you can no longer run some DOS programs. They quit with an "Out of Memory" error message. Which of the following is the most likely cause of the problem?

    A. hardware I/O port conflict with the new hardware

    B. not enough expanded memory available after the install

    C. software conflict with the new software

    D. not enough conventional memory available after the install

17. Running MEMMAKER.EXE is *not* the best way to increase the amount of available conventional memory. True or false?

    A. True

    B. False

18. Deleting files to save disk space has no effect on the performance of a machine that is running MS-DOS without Windows installed. True or false?

    A. True

    B. False

19. Which of the following files is created when Windows is using a permanent swap file? (Circle all that apply.)

    A. SPART.PAR

    B. 386SPART.PAR

    C. WIN386.SWP

    D. WIN386.PART

20. Which of the following files is created when Windows is using a temporary swap file? (Circle all that apply.)

    A. SPART.PAR

    B. 386SPART.PAR

    C. WIN386.SWP

    D. WIN386.PART

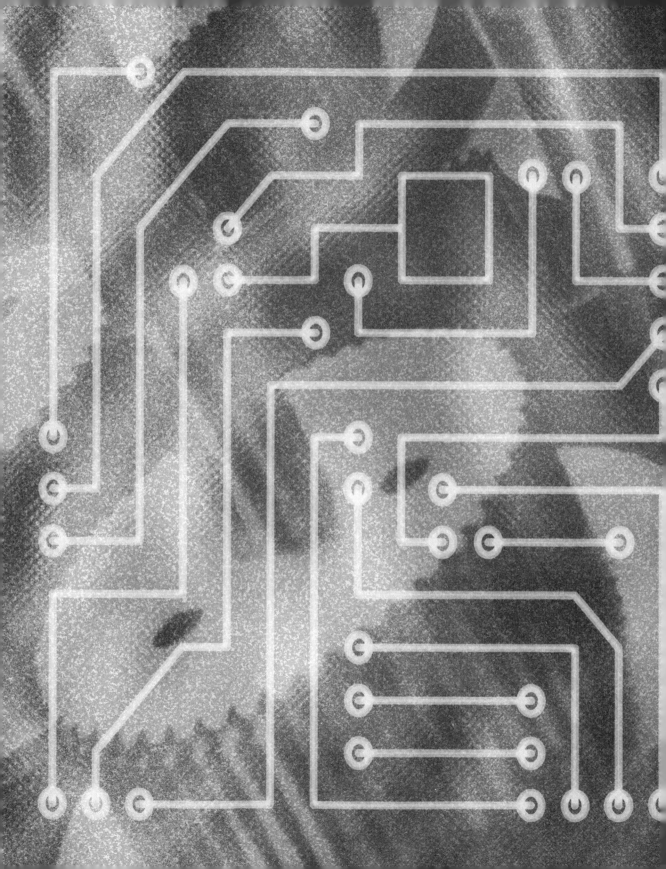

DOS and Windows Troubleshooting

- Troubleshooting Resources

- Software Troubleshooting

- DOS Troubleshooting

- Windows Troubleshooting

*T*roubleshooting is the process of identifying a computer problem so that you can fix it. This book can give you the basic knowledge you need to be a good troubleshooter, but not the instinct you need to be a great one. Very few people have mastered the art of troubleshooting because it is, indeed, an art, not a science. Anyone can paint, but very few people are truly good at it. The same is true for computer repair.

As with any art, excellence comes from experience, and the best way to gain experience is to practice. However, until you've had the opportunity to troubleshoot several computers with several different types of customers, the best way to gain the skills you will rely on as a certified technician is to learn from other people's experiences. The A+ exam tests your skills as a troubleshooter and your ability to regurgitate information. This chapter covers the following A+ troubleshooting topics in detail:

- Troubleshooting Resources
- Software Troubleshooting
- DOS Troubleshooting
- Windows Troubleshooting

Troubleshooting Resources

Like an artist uses brushes, a great troubleshooter uses several resources to make their job easier; and just like the artist's brushes and palette, different resources work together to accomplish a common goal: identifying a problem.

The first major resource you can use to identify and troubleshoot a problem is your brain. Your brain holds lots of information. You remember almost everything to which you're exposed. For this reason, the best troubleshooters are usually the people who have been exposed to the most problems; they have seen several different types of problems and their solutions. Therefore, when they run into a particular problem, they may have seen it before and can quickly fix the problem.

Most technicians love computer problems, because they know that a problem is a chance to find a solution. This feeling is almost like being the first astronomer to discover a star or comet, although you rarely get to name a problem or its solution (for example, *The Roger Smith General Protection Fault Solution* or *The Dan Jones AUTOEXEC .BAT Conundrum*). Each time a technician solves a new problem, they mature mentally. They know that if they ever run into that problem again, they will be able to fix it easily (or, at least, have a starting point for troubleshooting).

Another intellectual resource that is not used as often as it should be is service documentation. When a new product is released, several items are released at the same time (or very shortly after), including the owner's manual, the buyer's guide, and (most importantly) service documentation. These items can be a valuable source of troubleshooting information and can also contain replacement-parts information, such as which part(s) should be replaced when a particular component is found to be faulty. Also, these items usually contain exploded diagrams of a model being repaired.

In recent times, the Internet has become a valuable resource for troubleshooting. Almost every technology company has a Web site. One feature of most technology companies' Web sites is the knowledge base (it may have a different name, but the concept is the same). This area of a company's Web site contains several pieces of information that are valuable to technicians. First, the knowledge base contains several Frequently Asked Questions (FAQs) files. These files are summaries of the questions (and answers) that technical-support technicians get. You may have to go to the Support section or perform a search to find them. In addition, knowledge bases are usually searchable, so you can see whether any other technician has experienced this problem and, possibly, found the solution. The final intellectual resource that is seldom used, except in the most difficult cases, is a coworker. If you don't have the knowledge to troubleshoot or repair the component, a coworker may. This resource is seldom used because people hate to admit that they don't know something. However, as the saying goes, *the beginning of wisdom is "I don't know."*

Software Troubleshooting

This section deals with a canvas that the troubleshooting artist may have to paint often: software problems. More than half of all computer problems are software-related. These problems usually don't stem from the software itself, but the interaction of that software with other software that may be running on that machine. However, before you can start troubleshooting, you must determine whether the problem is hardware-related or software-related. To determine the source of a problem (hardware or software), you can take the following steps to narrow it down:

1. **In DOS or Windows computers, boot the computer "clean."** Booting it clean means starting the computer with no software drivers loading. The only things that should be in AUTOEXEC .BAT or CONFIG.SYS (the two DOS configuration files) are the necessary memory managers and settings to get the computer up and running. Leave out sound card, CD-ROM, network, and other device drivers. You can also boot clean by using a bootable floppy disk (see the sidebar "Making a Bootable Diskette"). If the computer functions normally, the problem is usually software-related. Although, it could be a hardware problem and the device driver just enabled the device, causing the conflict to show itself. (You can also do this with the F8 key and step through the settings, saying N to the ones you don't want.)

2. **Identify operating system error messages.** Every operating system has built-in error-detection routines. These routines are designed to intercept problems and notify the user. If there is a major problem, these routines display an error message for the software or hardware component that caused the problem. For example, when you try to print to a printer connected to your primary parallel port (LPT1) and the system returns an error message such as Error Writing to Device LPT1, it is likely a hardware-related problem because a hardware device was mentioned (or alluded to) in the error message.

Making a Bootable Diskette

A DOS bootable diskette is a valuable tool for troubleshooting. The creation process is very simple: insert a blank 1.44MB or 720KB diskette into your floppy-disk drive and type the following line at a DOS prompt:

```
FORMAT A: /S
```

You can replace A: with the drive letter that represents your floppy-disk drive. If the diskette is already formatted, you can add the system files to the diskette and make it bootable by typing the following line at a DOS prompt:

```
SYS A:
```

When the computer is done, the System Transferred message appears, telling you that the computer has finished making the diskette bootable. This diskette, when you insert it before turning on the computer, allows the computer to be booted because it contains the smallest portion of DOS necessary to start the computer.

3. **Uninstall and then reinstall the application in question**. This ensures that you have the correct versions of all the application's components and that there are no missing files.

4. **Look for ways to repeat the problem**. If it is a phantom problem, ask the user to help you out by finding a way to repeat the problem or looking for some type of pattern to the problem.

5. **Ensure that you use the latest patches**. This is especially important with machines that are on a network—always make sure they have the latest version of the network client. If you have a buggy network client, it can cause a lot of strange application problems. Also, ensure that there are no bug fixes for the application itself by looking on the publisher's Web site.

6. **Check the Internet**. Often, software publishers post FAQs and have a searchable knowledge base on the Internet with useful resources for troubleshooting.

7. **Compare and isolate**. Often, it can be difficult to determine whether an application problem is caused by the software or hardware. The best troubleshooting tools in this case are comparison and isolation. Try comparing how the application behaves on known working machines, or remove and replace hardware components to eliminate possible causes and isolate the solution.

These steps, with your experience, should help you narrow the problem to either a hardware or a software problem.

DOS Troubleshooting

DOS troubleshooting is a fundamental skill that most technicians get several chances to practice. If you understand and can modify the two main configuration files of DOS—CONFIG.SYS and AUTOEXEC.BAT—you can solve most DOS problems.

These topics apply to both MS-DOS and PC-DOS.

DOS Configuration Files: CONFIG.SYS and AUTOEXEC.BAT

DOS is a simple operating system. It requires very few system resources to operate. It is also simple to operate. Unless you've damaged or misplaced part of DOS itself, you just type the command you want the computer to execute—and it does it. Despite the fact that it can take a lot of study to familiarize yourself with *all* the commands that DOS has to offer, you don't need to know very many of them to take advantage of DOS's most useful capabilities. For these reasons, DOS stands as the most popular operating system of all time.

DOS requires two main configuration files: CONFIG.SYS and AUTOEXEC.BAT. Each file is a simple ASCII text file that contains commands and variables that set up the user environment in DOS.

- The CONFIG.SYS file is the main configuration file that DOS uses and, as such, it can be the source of several problems with DOS. The problems that you normally experience are things such as insufficient conventional memory, incorrect drivers loading, and not enough file handles. CONFIG.SYS also has a detailed role in the logical mapping of the PC's memory. It loads memory drivers (such as EMM386.EXE and HIMEM .SYS) and specifies the location of the DOS files (with statements such as DOS=HIGH, UMB). It can also load device drivers by using lines that start with a DEVICE= statement.

- The AUTOEXEC.BAT file, on the other hand, is a special batch file that executes automatically at system startup. This configuration file establishes the user environment and loads system drivers. Because it's a batch file, you can add statements to it that automatically start other programs.

If either file becomes damaged or corrupted (with incorrect entries), the best two tools that you have are REM statements and backup files.

REM Statements

Suppose that the PC you're working on inconsistently locks up. Further, suppose that you have already determined that the problem is software-related, because when you boot clean with a bootable diskette, the computer functions normally. This means that one of the statements in CONFIG.SYS or AUTOEXEC.BAT is causing the problem.

To solve the problem, you must remove (or change) the line that is causing the problem. However, you must first find the offending line. This is accomplished with REM statements. The REM command is short for *remark* and is placed before the suspect command in either configuration file. When this is done, the suspect command is skipped. (The initial purpose for the REM command was to insert comments—remarks—into batch files so that the programmer or curious user could annotate what was going on in different sections of the files without requiring the computer to run the comment.) By editing both CONFIG.SYS and AUTOEXEC.BAT and "REMing out" one command at a time (rebooting between each change), you can progressively eliminate statements that may be the cause of the problem.

Let's take a look at a sample computer problem: the computer randomly locks up. CONFIG.SYS and AUTOEXEC.BAT are as follows (the lines are numbered to facilitate our discussion here—the real files would not have the numbers):

CONFIG.SYS

```
1. DEVICE=C:\DOS\HIMEM.SYS
2. DEVICE=C:\WINDOWS\EMM386.EXE
3. DOS=HIGH
```

4. FILES=40
5. BUFFERS=9,256
6. DEVICE=C:\SB16\DRV\CTSB16.SYS /UNIT=0 /BLASTER=A:220 I:5 D:1 H:5
7. DEVICE=C:\SB16\DRV\DRV\SBCD.SYS /D:MSCD001 /P:220

AUTOEXEC.BAT

1. @ECHO OFF
2. SET BLASTER=A220 I5 D1 T4
3. C:\DOS\MSCDEX.EXE /D:MSCD001
4. SET PATH=C:\DOS;C:\;C:\WINDOWS;C:\MOUSE
5. SET TEMP=C:\TEMP
6. C:\WINDOWS\SMARTDRV.EXE
7. PROMPT=PG

When troubleshooting software problems, the first thing to always check is the non-DOS items in either configuration file. Lines 6 and 7 of CONFIG.SYS and line 2 of AUTOEXEC.BAT are from a recent sound card installation. To check whether one of these drivers is the problem, always start by "REMing out" the non-DOS items. So, if you edit both of the configuration files and "REM out" the non-DOS items, CONFIG.SYS and AUTOEXEC.BAT look as follows:

CONFIG.SYS

1. DEVICE=C:\DOS\HIMEM.SYS
2. DEVICE=C:\WINDOWS\EMM386.EXE
3. DOS=HIGH
4. FILES=40
5. BUFFERS=9,256
6. rem DEVICE=C:\SB16\DRV\CTSB16.SYS /UNIT=0 /BLASTER=A:220 I:5 D:1 H:5
7. rem DEVICE=C:\SB16\DRV\DRV\SBCD.SYS /D:MSCD001 /P:220

AUTOEXEC.BAT

1. @ECHO OFF
2. rem SET BLASTER=A220 I5 D1 T4

```
3. C:\DOS\MSCDEX.EXE /D:MSCD001
4. SET PATH=C:\DOS;C:\;C:\WINDOWS;C:\MOUSE
5. SET TEMP=C:\TEMP
6. C:\WINDOWS\SMARTDRV.EXE
7. PROMPT=$P$G
```

If the computer boots and operates normally with this configuration, you can assume that the problem was related to one of the non-DOS entries—that is, a driver for a peripheral. It should be noted that "REMing out" the statements (like we did above) causes the devices that the statements configured to not function at all. This is not a failure, but simply the way computers work. In our example, because the only device drivers were for the sound card, the sound card may be configured improperly. You will have to test each possibility to find out.

Sherlock Holmes said it best, "When you have eliminated the impossible, whatever remains, no matter how improbable, must be the truth." Troubleshooting with REM statements is a process of elimination. One by one, you must eliminate the impossible so that you can find the improbable.

Backup Files

Whenever you install drivers for a hardware device, the installation program asks you whether you want it to modify CONFIG.SYS and AUTOEXEC.BAT for you, or whether you want to modify the files yourself. When the installation program modifies these files, it makes duplicates (or *backups*) of them in case the drivers it installs cause problems. That way, if there *is* a problem, you can reboot using the backup files instead of the ones modified during the installation process.

To reboot using the backup files, you first need to rename the new CONFIG.SYS and AUTOEXEC.BAT files (to anything other than those names). A good way to keep track of them is to replace the .SYS and .BAT extensions with your initials. Then, you need to rename (to CONFIG.SYS and AUTOEXEC.BAT, of course) the backups that the installation process created.

Of course, before you can rename your backups to CONFIG.SYS and AUTOEXEC.BAT, you have to find them. Installation programs usually name the backup file for CONFIG.SYS with a name like CONFIG.BAK or CONFIG.OLD, or, if you already have files with those names, by providing a numbered filename extension, such as CONFIG.001 or CONFIG.002. Similarly, installation programs rename the backup file for AUTOEXEC.BAT with a .BAK, .OLD, or numbered filename extension.

TIP Since a system can contain numerous backups from different installations over time, it can be very helpful to view the list of files according to date (or Last Modified) so that you can easily find the most recently modified files—the ones created and modified by the problem installation.

Windows Troubleshooting

Windows problems are the most troublesome of all software-related problems, mainly because several components work together in Windows. If any of these components develop a problem or corruption, they can bring Windows to a screeching halt. You can check three primary areas to find troubleshooting information in Windows: system resources, general protection faults, and Windows configuration files.

NOTE These topics apply to most versions of Windows, including Windows 3.1, Windows 3.11, and Windows 95.

System Resources

When Windows runs out of memory, hard disk space, or both, it is said to have run out of *system resources*. Windows 3.1 has an About Program Manager window (select Help ➤ About in the Windows Program Manager) that you can use to check the amount of available system resources (see Figure 12.1 for an example of the About Program Manager window). For optimal Windows performance, the available system resources should be above 80 percent. If they are below 80 percent, you need to add RAM, disk space, or both.

FIGURE 12.1:

Windows 3.1 system resources

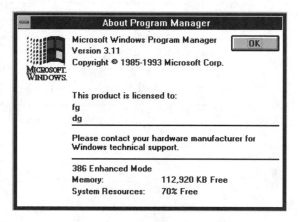

By way of comparison, if you are using Windows 95, you can check the system resources by using the Resource Meter (available by choosing Start ➤ Programs ➤ Accessories ➤ System Tools). The Resource Meter shows up as a small bar graph on your taskbar at the bottom of the screen. If you double-click the bar graph, it brings up a screen that shows the available system resources (similar to the Windows 3.1 statistics). Figure 12.2 shows this window.

FIGURE 12.2:

Windows 95 system resources

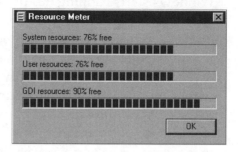

> **NOTE** There are a couple of other ways to increase the amount of system resources. One is to increase the amount of virtual memory available to Windows. You can do this in the Enhanced control panel in the Windows Control Panel. The other is to reduce the number of fonts you are using in Windows. This can be done through the Fonts control panel.

General Protection Faults

A misbehaving Windows program may overstep its bounds and try to take memory from another application. When a program does this, Windows halts the misbehaving program and displays an error called a *general protection fault* (or *GPF*). This type of error is one of the most common Windows errors—and the most frustrating. Such errors are generally the result of bad programming. The programmer took shortcuts in their programming and left out the safety nets that prevent a program from taking memory away from another running program.

There is no way to make a system 100-percent GPF-free. You can, however, reduce the number of GPFs that occur by taking a couple of precautions. First, monitor your system resources carefully. When

Windows starts running out of available memory, the programs that are running are tightly packed in memory. In a system with only a little space available, the likelihood is relatively great that a program will use another program's memory when it looks for more memory—and, thus, cause a GPF. (By comparison, when a program tries to take more memory in a system that has *plenty* of available memory, the chances are good that the program will find memory that is *not* being used by another program.) This underscores the guideline that *you can never have enough closet space or RAM.*

Second, exercise some discipline, and use only the *released* versions of software—the retail versions, the ones available commercially. Software goes through three major steps of development: *Alpha, Beta,* and *Release.* In the Alpha release, the program is intended only for testing within the software company itself, and it may not include all the features that are intended to be included in the eventual actual release. Also, the software, at this stage, still has many errors (called *bugs*) that need to be worked out. The Beta release is ready for consumer testing—it includes all the features that will be included in the Release version, and the installation program. Some of the loose ends may need to be tightened up, but the software is basically ready. When the software is released, the developers consider it to be more-or-less bug-free. There may be a few minor bugs that crop up after the initial release, but the software is stable for use.

WARNING *Never* use Alpha or Beta software on your computer. These software programs *are* buggy and *will* cause problems and GPFs.

There are two ways to fix the bugs that appear after the initial release of the software: you can either use a patch (a type of software "Band-Aid" that fixes the problem until the next release) on the software or wait until the next release of the software. This brings us to the next tip: try to avoid version 1 of any piece of software. Because this version is the first release, it usually contains the most bugs. Wait until the software has been out for a few months (and has gone through a few revisions) before you buy it and install it on your computer. By version 1.2, most of the bugs have been worked out, and the software can be considered stable.

How to Read the Version Numbers of Software

When you read the version numbers of most software titles, you can deduce a few things: the leftmost number indicates the *major release version*. Each major release introduces several new features and may completely change the way the software operates.

The first number to the right of the decimal point is the *revision number*. When a single feature (or small set of features) needs to be introduced, with several bug fixes, a new revision of the software is released. Revision numbers increment until the software developers decide to release another major release.

Any numbers to the right of the revision number can be considered *patch levels*. When software is released with a second number to the right of the decimal point, it usually means that it is a bug fix only. No new features are released in this version.

For example, let's examine the following version number:

```
FURBLE 1.24
```

This version number indicates that it contains all the features of the first major release of the FURBLE program. In addition, it is the second revision of that release and the fourth patch at that level. This software should be quite stable by this stage.

It should also be noted that some vendors (mainly Microsoft) have abandoned this convention in favor of naming the software with the year it was released (for example, Windows 95, Office 97, etc.). However, production schedules fall behind, and software is sometimes released the following year.

Windows Configuration Files

When Windows programs are installed, their files are copied to the hard disk and entries are made in the Windows configuration files: INI files and the Registry (also known as the REG.DAT file). The entries made in these files control various settings and tell the program (or Windows itself) how to operate. Let's discuss each of them.

INI Files

Primarily used for Windows 3.x programs, INI files (short for initialization files) are made for each program and for Windows. When a new application is installed, the installation program creates an INI file that contains the new application's settings. INI files are text files that can be edited with any text editor, if necessary.

The three primary INI files that Windows uses are as follows: SYSTEM.INI, WIN.INI, and PROGMAN.INI. You should back up each of them before you make changes. SYSTEM.INI contains settings for the drivers that Windows uses. It is probably the most critical of the three files. Changes made to this file affect Windows' resource usage and resource availability.

WIN.INI controls the Windows operating environment. It contains entries for the programs that Windows starts automatically, screensaver settings, desktop color schemes, wallpaper, and system-compatibility information. Changes made to this file aren't critical (for example, your screen may come up in a different color), but you should take care when modifying the [Compatibility] section, because it could cause problems with older programs.

Finally, PROGMAN.INI contains settings for the Program Manager. These settings control the number and filenames of the program groups in the Program Manager. When you change these settings, it modifies which program groups appear in the Program Manager. You can also control Program Manager security (such as which menu options appear or are grayed out in the Program Manager) by modifying the [Security] section.

NOTE   If you delete the INI file of some programs, they will create a new one with the default settings.

You can track a problem to an INI file if a setting was made in a Windows 3.1 program and now the program doesn't function properly or "GPFs" frequently. To solve this type of problem, it is best to rename an old INI file to replace the corrupt one (for example, WINWORD.OLD to WINWORD.INI). As with DOS installation programs, Windows setup programs make backups of the configuration files they change and name them with .BAK or .OLD extensions, or with number extensions (.001, .002, etc.). If you have a problem with a new INI file, you can rename one of the backups (preferably the most recent one) to the .INI extension to make *it* the active INI file.

The Registry

With the introduction of Windows 95, Microsoft did away with the practice of using several INI files to contain program-configuration information. Microsoft introduced a special database called the Registry to provide a single common location for all configuration and program-setting information. It is a little known fact that Windows 3.x has a registry as well, but it is not used to the extent that it is in Windows 95. Every Windows program, upon installation, registers itself so that Windows knows about it. When other programs need information about which printers and devices are available in Windows, they query the Registry to get this information. Windows 3.x used its registry in a similar fashion, but primarily used INI files for the storage of its program configuration information.

You can view and edit the Registry with REGEDIT.EXE. When you run this program, it presents the screen shown in Figure 12.3. Each folder represents a section (or *key*) that contains specific information. The settings for the Windows programs are kept within these keys.

FIGURE 12.3:

Viewing the Registry with REGEDIT.EXE

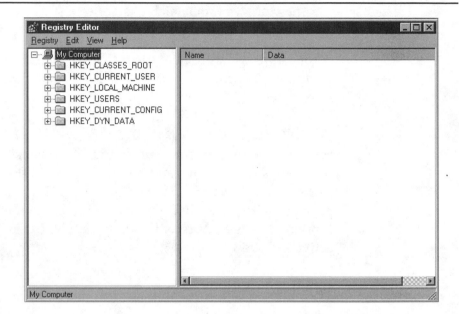

In general, you should not make changes to the Registry. Registry changes can be exceedingly complex and are not covered on the A+ exams, so no more space will be devoted to the Registry here.

Review Questions for Chapter 12, DOS and Windows Troubleshooting

Answers to the review questions may be found in Appendix A.

1. Suppose that a user calls you and reports that their computer is giving them a general protection fault in the program XXXX.EXE. What are some possible causes? (Circle all that apply.)

   A. The XXXX.EXE program is bad and should be replaced or patched (a bug fix applied).

   B. There is not enough memory in the computer.

   C. There is not enough hard disk space in the computer.

   D. all of the above

   E. none of the above

2. Which Windows error is caused by an application being greedy and taking memory away from other programs?

   A. general system error

   B. general protection fault

   C. system fault

   D. memory protection fault

3. Which two files are used by DOS to configure a computer?

   A. INI files

   B. AUTOEXEC.BAT

   C. CONFIG.BAT

   D. CONFIG.SYS

4. Suppose that a Windows program constantly "GPFs" (at least a couple of times a day). It has always been this way, although it gets worse when there are several programs loaded. What is the first thing you should check?

   A. whether the computer is out of disk space

   B. the Internet knowledge base, to see whether there is a patch or upgrade for this problem

   C. your Windows resources

   D. whether the computer is fast enough

5. Which menu in the Windows 3.1 Program Manager contains the option to view the Windows resources?

   A. Options

   B. File

   C. Resources

   D. Help

6. Which statement can be placed in the AUTOEXEC.BAT or CONFIG.SYS file to "comment out" suspect lines?

   A. REM

   B. ""

   C. STOP

   D. NO

7. Suppose that one day you start Windows and none of the program groups show up in the Program Manager. Which Windows file may have been edited (or deleted)?

   A. .GRP files

   B. WIN.INI

   C. SYSTEM.INI

   D. PROGMAN.INI

8. Which INI file is not critical and doesn't need to be backed up?

    A. WIN.INI

    B. SYSTEM.INI

    C. PROGMAN.INI

    D. CONTROL.INI

    E. none of the above

9. To solve problems related to AUTOEXEC.BAT, you should "REM out" all entries and "un-REM" each entry one at a time to find the problem entry. True or false?

    A. True

    B. False

10. Suppose that you just installed a new sound card in a client's computer. Upon rebooting, the computer locks up after the message HIMEM.SYS Is Testing Extended Memory ... Done. On which configuration file should you focus your troubleshooting efforts?

    A. CONFIG.SYS

    B. AUTOEXEC.BAT

    C. WIN.INI

    D. SYSTEM.INI

11. Which DOS command(s) can create a bootable diskette?

    A. FORMAT A: /S

    B. FORMAT A: /B

    C. SYS A:

    D. BOOT A:

12. What condition(s) are likely to occur when Windows runs out of resources?

    A. Windows gets more resources.

    B. All programs restart.

    C. Windows closes, returning to DOS.

    D. General protection faults (GPFs).

    E. all of the above

13. Suppose that you want to find out whether a Windows program you are having trouble with is supposed to be compatible with the network you have. Where could you check to find this information?

    A. other technicians

    B. the program manufacturer's Web site

    C. the program's manual

    D. all of the above

    E. none of the above

14. Which Windows 95 configuration file replaces the INI files that were used by previous versions of Windows?

    A. the database

    B. CONFIG.SYS

    C. MS-DOS.SYS

    D. the Registry

APPENDIXES

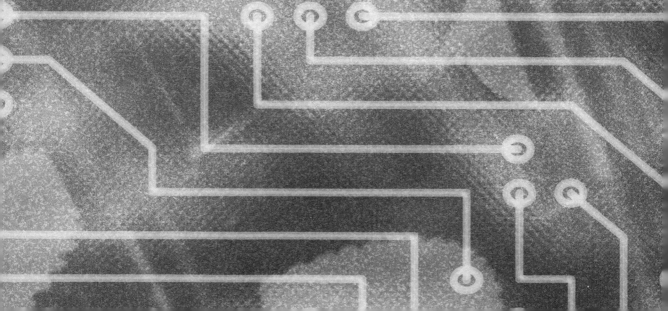

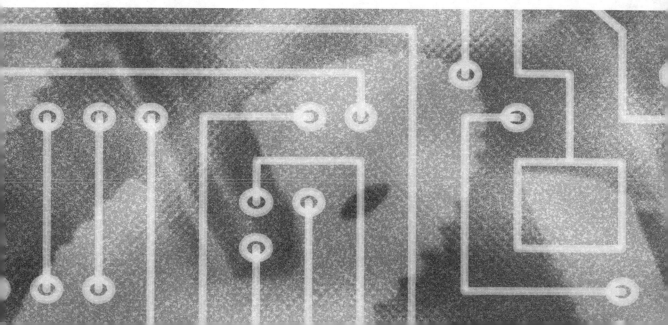

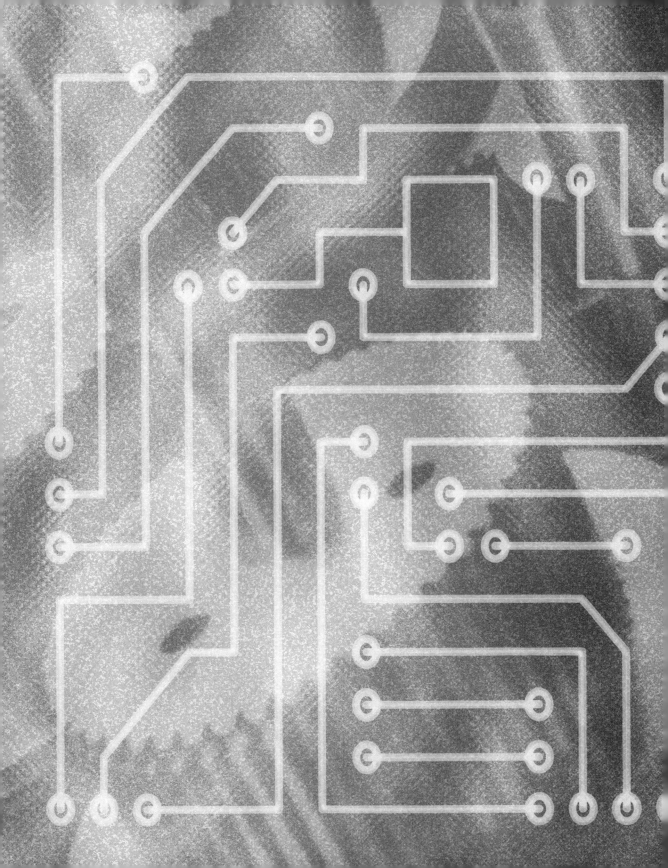

Answers to Review Questions

Answers to Review Questions for Chapter 2, An Overview of the DOS Operating System

1. Which of the following is *not* true of an upgrade?

    A. usually cheaper than a new purchase

    B. requires the buyer to own an earlier version of the software

    C. available only for applications, not operating systems

    D. created to add new features to an existing piece of software

    Answer: C

2. Which of the following is *not* a standard feature of DOS?

    A. network support

    B. running programs

    C. managing files

    D. managing disks

    Answer: A

3. Which of these is used to add and configure new software?

    A. SETUP.EXE

    B. ADDPROG.EXE

    C. INSTALL.EXE

    D. both A and C

    Answer: D

4. Which of the following is a program?

   A. Windows 3.1

   B. WordPerfect 5.1

   C. FORMAT.EXE

   D. all of the above

   Answer: D

5. Which of the following are typical requirements of newer applications? (Circle all that apply.)

   A. need greater amounts of free drive space to install the software

   B. need newer versions of DOS to run properly

   C. more likely to run off of a floppy drive instead of the hard disk

   D. need more memory (RAM) and a faster system (updated CPU, etc.)

   Answer: A, B, D

6. Which of the following filenames are invalid in DOS?

   A. myfile.txt

   B. my file.txt

   C. myfile

   D. myfile.

   E. MYFILE.TXT

   Answer: B

7. Which is a disk-related service provided by DOS?

   A. creating and deleting partitions on hard drives

   B. compressing files to increase the number of files stored on a drive

   C. copying and backing up disks

   D. all of the above

   Answer: D

8. Which utility allows you to view memory usage?

   A. MEM

   B. MEMORY

   C. TIME

   D. FORMAT

   Answer: A

9. Which utility allows you to view the system's processor type?

   A. MEM

   B. MSD

   C. FDISK

   D. PROC

   Answer: B

10. Which of the following actually talks to a computer's hardware?

    A. the ROM BIOS

    B. the DOS System Files

    C. COMMAND.COM

    D. the processor

    Answer: A

11. What is the Basic Input/Output System also known as?

    A. RAM

    B. ROM

    C. COMMAND.COM

    D. BIOS

    Answer: B, D

12. Which is *not* a function of COMMAND.COM?

    A. provide a consistent user interface to all DOS system files

    B. present the results of a command to the user

    C. receive input from the user

    D. format requests so they can be sent directly to the processor

    Answer: D

13. Which DOS attribute is used by backup programs?

    A. Read-only

    B. Archive

    C. Hidden

    D. System

    Answer: B

14. Which command allows you to see the syntax of the DATE command?

    A. DATE /?

    B. DATE ?

    C. HELP /DATE

    D. HELP /DATE /SYNTAX

    Answer: A

15. What do you have to do to run a Windows-based program in DOS without the Windows interface?

    A. Use the DOS Shell to run the program.

    B. Configure DOS to support a mouse.

    C. Run the Windows program as the only program on the machine.

    D. Dream on. Windows programs do not run under DOS alone.

    Answer: D

16. Which DOS command displays your current directory structure, including any subdirectories?

    A. SUBDIR

    B. DIRSTRUCT

    C. TREE

    D. DIR

    Answer: C

17. It is possible to have two files, one having the name file.txt and another having the name FILE.TXT in the same directory. True or false?

    A. True

    B. False

    Answer: B

18. The exact location of a file in the DOS directory structure is known as the file's _____.

    A. absolute reference

    B. path

    C. reference

D. location

Answer: B

19. If the COMMAND.COM file was missing from the boot disk of a computer, which of the following would you *not* be able to do?

    A. interact with DOS

    B. boot the computer

    C. run Programs

    D. none of the above

    Answer: D

20. Which function of DOS deals with file compression?

    A. managing hardware

    B. managing disks

    C. managing files

    D. executing programs

    Answer: B

Answers to Review Questions for Chapter 3, Prerequisites for Installation

1. Format is what type of DOS command?

    A. core

    B. internal

    C. external

    D. extended

    Answer: C

2. FDISK allows all of the following except:

    A. creating a partition

    B. deleting a partition

    C. moving a partition

    D. marking a partition as active

    Answer: C

3. Logical drives exist for which of the following?

    A. primary partition

    B. extended partition

    C. floppy drives

    D. all of the above

    Answer: B

4. Formatting a partition will delete the files on that partition in which of the following circumstances?

    A. only if the partition is a primary partition

    B. only if the partition is an extended partition

    C. Never. (Formatting never deletes existing data.)

    D. Always. (Formatting always deletes existing data.)

    Answer: D

5. Which switch tells FORMAT to transfer the system to a newly formatted partition?

    A. /s

    B. \s

    C. -s

    D. -t

    Answer: A

6. Which file system type is used by DOS?

   A. NTFS

   B. HPFS

   C. FAT

   D. CP/M

   Answer: C

7. Which partition type can have more than one logical drive?

   A. extended partition

   B. primary partition

   C. both A and B

   D. neither A nor B

   Answer: A

8. Which utility can *sometimes* recover a partition that has been reformatted with DOS 6?

   A. FORMAT with the /u switch

   B. UNDELETE

   C. UNFORMAT

   D. No utility can do this. The information is gone.

   Answer: C

9. What is the maximum partition size with DOS 3.3?

   A. 12 MB

   B. 23 MB

   C. 32 MB

   D. 42 MB

   Answer: C

10. On a new drive, in which order must the following commands be executed in order to install DOS? (Assume that at least two logical drives are needed on the drive.)

    A. FORMAT

    B. SYS

    C. FDISK

    D. DOS SETUP

    Answer: C, A, B, D

11. Which utility allows you to view the current disk configuration of a system?

    A. FDISK.EXE

    B. SYS.COM

    C. FORMAT.COM

    D. COMMAND.COM

    Answer: A

12. When can the /q switch be used with FORMAT?

    A. on a new partition only

    B. on any partition

    C. only on partitions with an existing FAT file system

    D. only on an extended partition

    Answer: C

13. Which of the following utilities allows you to recover a partition deleted through FDISK?

    A. UNDELETE

    B. UNFORMAT

  C. none, because partitions cannot be deleted through FDISK

  D. none, because partitions deleted through FDISK cannot be recovered

Answer: D

14. Which of the following commands work on floppy disks?

  A. FDISK

  B. FORMAT

  C. SYS

  D. both B and C

  E. A, B, and C

Answer: D

15. SYS can be performed on which of the following partition types?

  A. primary

  B. extended

  C. both A and B

  D. neither A nor B

Answer: A

16. In a normal DOS install, where are FORMAT and FDISK located on the hard drive?

  A. Nowhere. They are only available if you have a boot disk.

  B. the root of the C: drive

  C. C:\DOS

  D. C:\DOSUTILS

Answer: C

17. A boot disk can have which of the following?

    A. DOS system files

    B. DOS external commands

    C. specific device drivers

    D. all of the above

    Answer: D

18. Which of these cannot be part of a DOS volume label?

    A. a blank space

    B. \

    C. !

    D. %

    E. all of the above

    Answer: B

19. What is the maximum length of a volume label?

    A. 8 characters

    B. 11 characters

    C. 16 characters

    D. 24 characters

    Answer: B

20. If you need only one partition on a new 500 MB drive, and want to use all the space on the drive for that partition, *and* you want to format the partition and install DOS, what is the most efficient way to do this?

    A. Use a boot disk to configure the partition and format it, then run DOS Setup.

    B. Run DOS Setup.

C. Run SYS, then DOS SETUP.

D. You cannot create just one partition on a drive.

Answer: B

21. How many primary partitions can be created on a DOS disk using FDISK?

    A. 1

    B. 2

    C. 3

    D. several

    Answer: A

22. How many Extended partitions can be created on a DOS disk using FDISK?

    A. 1

    B. 2

    C. 3

    D. several

    Answer: A

23. You cannot adjust the size of partition, once it has been created, using the FDISK program. True or false?

    A. True

    B. False

    Answer: A

24. Which drive letter is assigned to the first, active, primary partition in DOS?

    A. A:

    B. B:

    C. C:

    D. D:

    Answer: C

25. Which DOS command(s) can be used to make a disk bootable?

    A. SYS

    B. FDISK

    C. FORMAT

    D. BOOT

    Answer: A, C

26. Which FORMAT switch(es) can be used to format a 360K low-density floppy disk in a high-density drive?

    A. /1

    B. /f

    C. /4

    D. /8

    Answer: B, C

27. Which utilities can be used to format a hard disk?

    A. FORMAT.COM

    B. FORMAT.EXE

    C. the DOS SETUP.EXE program

    D. INSTALL.EXE

    Answer: A, C

28. Suppose your hard disk contains two partitions, a primary and an extended partition. There are three logical drive letters in the extended partition (D:, E:, & F:). You want to delete the primary partition and recreate it. What do you do?

    A. Using FDISK, delete the primary partition and recreate it.

    B. Using FDISK, delete the extended DOS partition, then the primary partition.

    C. Using FDISK, delete the drive letters in the order D:, E:, F:, then the extended partition, then the primary partition.

    D. Using FDISK, delete the drive letters in the order F:, E:,D:, then the extended partition, then the primary partition.

    Answer: D

29. What must be created before you can create the logical drive letter D: on the first disk?

    A. the primary partition

    B. the secondary partition

    C. the extended partition

    D. the logical drive pointer C:

    D. none of the above

    E. all of the above

    Answer: A, C, D

30. Before you can boot to a hard disk, what three things must you do to it?

    Answer: FDISK it with a primary, active partition; format the partition; and transfer the system files to the boot partition using the SYS command (or FORMAT /S).

Answers to Review Questions for Chapter 4, Installing DOS

1. Which program is used to install DOS?

   A. INSTALL.EXE

   B. INSTALL.BAT

   C. SETUP.EXE

   D. STEPUP.EXE

   Answer: C

2. Which utility (or utilities) can be used to determine the amount of disk space on a machine that already has a version of DOS installed? (Circle all that apply.)

   A. DIR

   B. CHKDSK

   C. SPACE /DISK

   D. DISK /SPACE

   Answer: A, B

3. When upgrading DOS, SETUP renames the AUTOEXEC.BAT to what?

   A. AUTOEXEC.BAK

   B. AUTOEXEC.001

   C. AUTOEXEC.OLD

   D. AUTOEXED.DAT

   Answer: D

4. DOS can be installed on IBM-compatible computers. True or false?

   A. True

   B. False

   Answer: A

5. How many disks are required to do a regular DOS installation?

   A. 1

   B. 2

   C. 3

   D. 4

   Answer: C

6. If you are upgrading from MS-DOS 6.20 to 6.22, how many disks (not counting uninstall diskettes) will you use to do the upgrade?

   A. 1

   B. 2

   C. 3

   D. 4

   Answer: A

7. It is necessary to back up the entire hard disk before doing a DOS upgrade. True or false?

   A. True

   B. False

   Answer: B

8. Which of the following prerequisites is *not* required to upgrade DOS?

    A. Back up the configuration files.

    B. Verify that the computer is IBM-compatible.

    C. Ensure that the computer has more than 10 MB of available disk space.

    D. Format the hard disk.

    Answer: D

9. When installing DOS for the first time, you must do which of the following?

    A. FDISK and FORMAT the disk.

    B. Delete any unnecessary files.

    C. Back up the entire disk.

    D. Turn off the computer, then turn it back on.

    Answer: A

10. If you are installing DOS onto the A: floppy drive, you must:

    A. Boot to the C: drive. Insert the DOS setup disk 1 in the A: drive and run SETUP from the A: drive manually.

    B. Boot to the C: drive. Insert the DOS setup disk 1 in the B: drive and run SETUP from the B: drive manually.

    C. Boot to Drive B:. Insert DOS setup disk 1 in the A: drive and run SETUP from the A: drive manually.

    D. Boot to Drive A:. Insert DOS setup disk 1 in the B: drive and run SETUP from the B: drive manually.

    Answer: D

11. Which function key, when pressed, will halt SETUP and leave you at a DOS command prompt?

   A. F1

   B. F3

   C. F5

   D. F7

   Answer: B

12. Which program is used to upgrade DOS from version 6.20 to 6.22?

   A. SETUP.COM

   B. SETUP.EXE

   C. STEPUP.EXE

   D. STEPUP.COM

   Answer: C

13. Which function key will display help in the SETUP program?

   A. F1

   B. F3

   C. F5

   D. F7

   Answer: A

14. Which of the following is a DOS installation step unique to a DOS upgrade?

    A. booting to the A: drive

    B. adding Windows components of DOS utilities

    C. running SETUP.EXE

    D. pressing F3 to exit

    Answer: B

15. A computer with an AMD K5 processor (an Intel-compatible CPU) can run MS-DOS. True or false?

    A. True

    B. False

    Answer: A

16. You can install DOS 6.22 on Macintosh computers without any special hardware or software. True or false?

    A. True

    B. False

    Answer: B

17. Which key could you press to give you information about the SETUP process while running it?

    A. F1

    B. F3

    C. F5

    D. F7

    Answer: A

18. Suppose you have just performed an upgrade from MS-DOS 6.0 to MS-DOS 6.22. You are wondering what the new features of this new version of DOS are. What command can you type at the C:\> prompt to detail these commands and features?

    A. HELP

    B. INFO

    C. HELP WHATSNEW

    D. WHATSNEW INFO

    Answer: C

19. What executable is used to upgrade DOS to a new version?

    A. INSTALL.EXE

    B. SETUP.EXE

    C. UPGRADE.EXE

    D. INSTALL.BAT

    Answer: A

20. How many disks are used to install DOS?

    A. 1

    B. 3

    C. 5

    D. 4

    Answer: B

21. How many disks are used during a DOS upgrade? (Assume the current version of DOS is 6.0 and you are upgrading to 6.22.)

    A. 1

    B. 2

    C. 3

    D. as many as 4

    Answer: D

22. Assume that you don't have an operating system installed on the hard disk of your computer. You insert the disk labeled "Disk 1 – SETUP" into the A: drive and turn the computer on. What do you have to do next?

    A. Use a different disk. "Disk 1" isn't boot**b.**   le

    B. Type **SETUP** from the C:\> prompt, when it appears

    C. Type **INSTALL** at the C:\> prompt, when it appears

    D. Nothing, the installation program will start automatically

    Answer: D

23. During a DOS upgrade, you happen to drop something on your keyboard and it hits the F5 key. What happens?

    A. Nothing.

    B. Your screen changes color.

    C. The installation quits.

    D. Your computer reboots, forcing you to delete the DOS directory and start over.

    Answer: B

24. Which system settings can you change during a fresh DOS install? (Circle all that apply.)

    A. time zone

B. date

C. hardware configuration

D. time

E. keyboard layout

F. DOS components to install

Answer: B, D, E

25. The DOS installation installs some Windows programs. True or false?

A. True

B. False

Answer: A

Answers to Review Questions for Chapter 5, DOS Startup and Configuration

1. Place the following MS-DOS files in order by placing a number next to them to indicate their loading order (i.e., 1=first, 2=second, and so on)

_____ MSDOS.SYS

_____ CONFIG.SYS

_____ IO.SYS

_____ AUTOEXEC.BAT

_____ COMMAND.COM

Answer: 2, 3, 1, 5, 4

2. If SMARTDRV.EXE is used, which CONFIG.SYS parameter's value should be reduced?

   A. FILES=20

   B. CACHE=10

   C. BUFFERS=50

   D. SMARTDRV=10

   Answer: C

3. The PATH environment variable specifies what kind of directories?

   A. directories that DOS uses

   B. directories that COMMAND.COM searches to find programs to run

   C. directories that COMMAND.COM searches to find files

   D. directories that DOS searches to find files

   Answer: B

4. Which memory driver controls access to the High Memory Area (HMA)?

   A. HIMEM.SYS

   B. EMM386.EXE

   C. SMARTDRV.EXE

   D. MEM.EXE

   Answer: A

5. Which DOS components can be used for caching?

   A. BUFFERS=

   B. CACHE=

C. SMARTDRIVE

D. SMARTDRV

Answer: A, D

6. Name the three files that MS-DOS requires in order to boot.

   Answer: MSDOS.SYS, IO.SYS, and COMMAND.COM

7. Name the three files that PC-DOS requires in order to boot.

   Answer: IBMBIO.COM, IBMDOS.COM, and COMMAND.COM

8. Which command replaces the "DEVICE=" command in the CONFIG.SYS, but performs the same function and adds the ability to load drivers into free UMBs?

   A. LOADUMB=

   B. DEVICEUMB=

   C. LOADHIGH=

   D. DEVICEHIGH=

   Answer: D

9. Which MS-DOS file must be loaded in order for the AUTOEXEC.BAT to execute?

   A. MSDOS.SYS

   B. COMMAND.COM

   C. IO.SYS

   D. IBMBIO.COM

   Answer: B

10. Which MS-DOS command controls the appearance of the MS-DOS command prompt?

    A. CSET

    B. DOSPROMPT

    C. PROMPT

    D. CONFIG.SYS

    Answer: C

11. Which CONFIG.SYS area (in a multiconfig setup) contains commands that execute regardless of the menu option chosen?

    A. :ALL

    B. [ALL]

    C. :COMMON

    D. [COMMON]

    Answer: D

12. Which CONFIG.SYS loads device drivers into memory?

    A. DEVICE=

    B. LOAD=

    C. START=

    D. DOS=

    Answer: A

13. Which type of DOS command is contained within COMMAND .COM?

    A. .EXE

    B. Internal

C. External

D. .COM

Answer: B

14. What DOS utility is used for disk compression?

A. DRVSPACE

B. DISKSPACE

C. DUBDRIVE

D. DoubleSpace

Answer: D

15. Which of the following is *not* an internal DOS command?

A. CLS

B. COPY

C. MORE

D. PAUSE

Answer: C

16. Which DOS system file(s) must be loaded in order for the CONFIG.SYS to be executed?

A. IO.SYS

B. MSDOS.SYS

C. COMMAND. COM

D. MSDOS.COM

Answer: A, B

17. You are troubleshooting a computer that is having CD-ROM read problems. You look on the CD-ROM manufacturers web site and discover that the driver has an incompatibility with SMARTDRV. The customer requires SMARTDRV for use with their proprietary program. What do you do?

    A. Inform the customer they will need to buy a new CD-ROM, one that is compatible with SMARTDRV.

    B. Disable CD-ROM caching at the SMARTDRV command line with the /U switch.

    C. Disable CD-ROM caching at the SMARTDRV command line with the /CD switch.

    D. Disable CD-ROM caching at the SMARTDRV command line with the /Q switch.

    Answer: B

18. You want to change the DOS prompt to look like

    C:\=

    What prompt command do you place in the AUTOEXEC.BAT?

    A. PROMPT=PE

    B. PROMPT=PV

    C. PROMPT=PQ

    D. PROMPT=PS

    Answer: C

19. Which key(s) can be pressed at the appearance of the message "Starting MS-DOS…," and will bypass the CONFIG.SYS and AUTOEXEC.BAT, preventing them from being executed?

    A. F5

    B. Ctrl

    C. Esc

    D. Shift

Answer: A, D

20. Suppose you have a Token Ring network adapter card installed in a computer. The computer keeps locking up on boot-up. It usually does this right after the phrase "HIMEM.SYS is testing Extended Memory." Since your computer uses Expanded memory, you conclude that the problem is that there were no memory range exclusions on the EMM386.EXE command line for the Token Ring card's ROMs. How would you modify the DEVICE=EMM386.EXE line in the CONFIG.SYS?

    A. Add the line I=*<Memory Range>* after EMM386.EXE on the same line.

    B. Add the line X=*<Memory Range>* after EMM386.EXE on the same line.

    C. Add the line NOEMS after EMM386.EXE on the same line.

    D. Add the line ROM=*<Memory Range>* after EMM386.EXE on the same line.

Answer: B

21. Which MS-DOS Startup Menu command determines which menu option will be chosen automatically after a timeout period?

    A. Menutimeout

    B. Menuoption

    C. Menudefault

    D. Menuchoice

Answer: C

22. Which key(s) can be pressed at the appearance of the message "Starting MS-DOS...," and will allow you to "step through" the CONFIG.SYS and AUTOEXEC.BAT, allowing commands or preventing them at each step at your discretion?

    A. F2

    B. F3

    C. F5

    D. F8

    Answer: D

23. Which is the proper way to indicate CONFIG.SYS sections for use with the MS-DOS Startup Menu?

    A. :*<Section Name>*:

    B. [*<Section Name>*]

    C. :*<Section Name>*

    D. [*<Section Name>*

    Answer: B

24. Which DOS system file is responsible for processing the CONFIG.SYS?

    A. IO.SYS

    B. MSDOS.SYS

    C. COMMAND.COM

    D. AUTOEXEC.BAT

    Answer: A

25. Which kind of DOS command is TIME in MS-DOS?

    A. Internal

    B. External

    Answer: A

Answers to Review Questions for Chapter 6, Basic DOS Commands

1. Which DOS command(s) allow you to delete files?

   A. ERASE

   B. BEGONE

   C. DEL

   D. PURGE

   Answer: A, C

2. Which DOS command(s) allow you to create directories?

   A. CREATE

   B. MD

   C. DIR

   D. CD

   Answer: B

3. Which external DOS command is a text editor for PC-DOS?

   A. E

   B. EDIT

   C. TEXT

   D. ASCII

   Answer: A

4. Which switch for the DIR command displays the output one page at a time?

   A. /W

   B. /O

   C. /S

   D. /P

   Answer: D

5. The command **COPY CON FILE.TXT** will create a file called FILE.TXT on the hard drive from keyboard input, once the input has finished and the author has pressed Ctrl+Z. True or false?

   A. True

   B. False

   Answer: A

6. If you have used the ATTRIB command to set the Hidden attribute on a file, can you delete the file?

   A. Yes

   B. No

   C. Maybe, if the file isn't a text file

   D. Maybe, if the file isn't an application (.COM or .EXE) file

   Answer: B

7. Which files will be listed via the command **DIR *.TXT** if the command is issued at the root of the C: drive?

   A. all files

   B. all text files

   C. all files with the .TXT extension

   D. all word processing files

   Answer: C

8. Which switch for the DIR command displays the output in "Wide" format, with no other information except for the filenames?

    A. /W

    B. /O

    C. /S

    D. /P

    Answer: A

9. Which of these COPY commands will work?

    A. COPY A*?.DOC

    B. COPY $A.DOC

    C. COPY *A*.DOC

    D. COPY A*.DOC

    Answer: D

10. Which program is used to backup PC-DOS disks?

    A. MSBACKUP

    B. BACKUP

    C. CPBACKUP

    D. PCBACKUP

    Answer: C

11. Which DOS command can copy directories, subdirectories, and files all at once to a new location, preserving their structure?

    A. COPY

    B. XCOPY

    C. COPYTREE

    D. COPYFILE

    Answer: B

12. Which syntax for the ATTRIB command is correct for setting the Read Only attribute on the file TEXT.DOC?

    A. ATTRIB +R TEXT.DOC

    B. ATTRIB –R TEXT.DOC

    C. ATTRIB +O TEXT.DOC

    D. ATTRIB –O TEXT.DOC

    Answer: A

13. MSBACKUP will work with floppy disk and tape drive backup media. True or false?

    A. True

    B. False

    Answer: B

14. What information will the command **XCOPY *.* /s A:** copy to the A: drive?

    A. everything in the current directory

    B. everything on the current disk

    C. everything in the current directory, including all subdirectories and files

    D. everything on the current disk, including all subdirectories and files

    Answer: C

15. If you wanted to rename a file from JOHNS.TXT to JSMITH.TXT, how could you do it? (Choose all that apply.)

    A. REN JOHNS.TXT JSMITH.TXT

    B. REN JSMITH.TXT JOHNS.TXT

    C. COPY JOHNS.TXT JSMITH.TXT and then DELete the original

    D. COPY JSMITH.TXT JOHNS.TXT and then DELete the original

    Answer: A, C

16. Which command should you use to display a directory listing in wide format, one page at a time, sorted alph**b.** etically (backwards Z to A)?

    A. DIR /S /P /Z

    B. DIR /W /P /S:-A

    C. DIR /W /P /S:-O

    D. DIR /W /P /:-N

    Answer: D

17. What is the name of the disk compression utility for PC-DOS?

    A. DiskComp

    B. SuperStore

    C. Disk Doubler

    D. DoubleSpace

    Answer: B

18. Which of the following are external DOS commands?

    A. CLS

    B. FORMAT

    C. XCOPY

    D. COPY

    Answer: B, C

19. Which of the following DOS utilities can be used to edit an ASCII text file?

    A. any word processor

    B. EDITOR.COM

    C. E.EXE

    D. EDIT.COM

    Answer: A, C, D

20. Which type of backup backs up the entire hard disk at one time?

    A. Full

    B. Differential

    C. Incremental

    D. Total

    Answer: A

Answers to Review Questions for Chapter 7, Batch Files

1. Batch files can be made with word processors. True or false?

    A. True

    B. False

    Answer: A

2. If you name a batch file with the same name as a DOS utility or program and execute it by name only (no extension), it will run instead of the DOS utility or program. True or false?

    A. True

    B. False

    Answer: B

3. Which batch command executes another batch file and then returns to the original?

   A. ECHO

   B. IF... THEN...

   C. CHOICE

   D. CALL

   Answer: D

4. Which batch command displays text to the screen?

   A. ECHO

   B. IF... THEN...

   C. CHOICE

   D. CALL

   Answer: A

5. Which of the following sample outputs would be generated by this batch file?

```
@ECHO OFF
ECHO       Menu
ECHO.
ECHO Hello, User
ECHO This is the current time
TIME
```

   OUTPUT A:

```
Menu

.

Hello, User
This is the current time
11:02:56.10p
```

OUTPUT B:

```
Menu

Hello, User
This is the current time
Current time is 11:02:56.10p
Enter new time:
```

OUTPUT C:

```
Hello, User
11:02:56.10p
```

OUTPUT D:

```
Hello, User
Current time is 11:02:56.10p
Enter new time:
```

Answer: B

6. Batch files can contain what commands?

   A. any DOS command

   B. ECHO, CHOICE, IF …THEN… statements

   C. variables

   D. none of the above

   E. all of the above

   Answer: E

7. Which key needs to be pressed to resume execution when the PAUSE command is used to halt batch file execution?

    A. Ctrl+Break

    B. Ctrl+C

    C. Any key will work.

    D. the spacebar

    Answer: C

8. Which of the following commands would successfully interpret a variable that the user would type after the name of the batch file (when issuing the batch file at the command line) in order to specify how a batch file should executes command "X"?

    A. IF EXIST CMDLINE THEN X

    B. IF %1="Y" THEN X

    C. IF Z<=Y THEN X

    D. IF %TEMP%="C:\TEMP" THEN X

    Answer: B

9. If the CHOICE command that follows is implemented, which ERRORLEVEL would be considered TRUE if the answer given is "Y"?

    ```
    CHOICE Do you want to continue?
    ```

    A. IF ERRORLEVEL=1 THEN X

    B. IF ERRORLEVEL=Y THEN X

    C. IF ERRORLEVEL=N THEN X

    D. IF ERRORLEVEL=0 THEN X

    Answer: A

10. To use the TEMP environment variable in a batch file, which syntax must you follow?

    A. TEMP

    B. #TEMP

    C. %TEMP

    D. %TEMP%

    E. %%TEMP

    Answer: D

11. Which programs can be used to make batch files? (Circle all that apply.)

    A. COPY

    B. EDIT.COM

    C. a word processor

    D. E.EXE

    E. none of the above

    Answer: A, B, C, D

12. Batch files have to be in the DOS directory to execute. True or false?

    A. True

    B. False

    Answer: B

13. Which of the following Boolean operators has the most conditions?

    A. AND

    B. NOT

C. OR

D. ELSE

Answer: C

14. Which command-line switch for the CHOICE command prevents the displaying of the questionmark and answer choices?

    A. /S

    B. /T

    C. /Q

    D. /N

    Answer: D

15. Which of the following illustrates the proper syntax for the GOTO command to branch the batch file to the :END label?

    A. GOTO END

    B. GOTO :END

    C. GOTO %END

    D. GOTO %:END%

    Answer: A

16. Which key combination(s) will halt a batch file during its execution? (Choose all that apply.)

    A. Ctrl+Break

    B. Ctrl+Del

    C. Ctrl+Alt+Del

    D. Ctrl+C

    Answer: A, D

17. Which is better (that is, which is more efficient, design-wise): a large batch file, or several smaller batch files?

    A. One large batch file

    B. Several smaller batch files

Answer: B

18. If you create a batch file and you want it to operate differently depending on what name was placed after the name of the batch file, like so:

MYBATCH Name

then which parameter would you place in the batch file?

    A. %1

    B. %2

    C. %A

    D. %B

Answer: A

19. Which command(s) turn off the displaying of each batch file command?

    A. ECHO OFF

    B. ECHO

    C. DISPLAY

    D. DISPLAY OFF

Answer: A

20. If, within a batch file, you want to execute another batch file, then continue on in the original batch file, which command do you use?

    A. GOTO

    B. CALL

    C. RUN

    D. GOSUB

    Answer: B

Answers to Review Questions for Chapter 8, Windows Interface Overview

1. Which of the following is not an important function of Windows?

    A. running applications

    B. preparing hard disks for use

    C. managing files and directories

    D. managing printing

    Answer: B

2. The Windows Desktop is responsible for what duties?

    A. printing

    B. managing applications

    C. managing files

    D. nothing

    Answer: D

3. Which of the following is not included within the Program Manager?

   A. icon

   B. group

   C. Desktop

   D. menu

   Answer: C

4. Which of these best describes an icon?

   A. any Windows-based program file

   B. the graphical configuration file needed to run all Windows apps

   C. the graphical shortcut to a file

   D. a graphical application

   Answer: C

5. In which of these states does a window have a border?

   A. restored

   B. maximized

   C. minimized

   D. all of the above

   Answer: A

6. Which of these is used to close a window?

   A. Restore button

   B. Title bar

   C. Minimize button

   D. Control box

   Answer: D

7. Which of the following is not a mouse function?

    A. double-click

    B. skip

    C. drag

    D. click

    Answer: B

8. Which of these is not configurable through an icon's Properties window?

    A. its label

    B. its working directory

    C. its group

    D. its icon graphic

    Answer: C

9. Where will you *not* find icons?

    A. the Desktop

    B. the Program Manager workspace

    C. in a group

    D. in the Control Panel

    Answer: B

10. Which DOS wildcard is used in File Manager to represent any number of characters in a string?

    A. *

    B. %

    C. @

    D. ?

    Answer: A

11. In which area do Windows and Windows for Workgroups differ?

    A. file management

    B. network support

    C. local printing

    D. virtual memory settings

    Answer: B

12. A printer must be attached to a logical _____.

    A. window

    B. I/O address

    C. device

    D. port

    Answer: D

13. The Control Panel is used to configure:

    A. system settings

    B. DOS settings

    C. applications

    D. I/O drivers

    Answer: A

14. A set of colors which define the appearance of Windows element is a _____.

    A. scheme

    B. group

    C. palette

    D. rainbow

    Answer: A

15. This method of switching between applications can be turned off in the Desktop Control Panel:

    A. Ctrl+Esc

    B. Alt+Tab

    C. Alt+Enter

    D. Ctrl+Tab

    Answer: B

16. Which of the following is *not* an option under Windows Setup in Windows 3.1?

    A. Display

    B. Keyboard

    C. Mouse

    D. Network

    Answer: D

17. Selecting the Exclusive in Foreground option in the 386 Enhanced control panel affects the foreground application by:

    A. slowing it down

    B. speeding it up

    C. assigning it specific memory

    D. assigning it specific hard disk space

    Answer: B

18. Which of the following is used to represent a Boolean (on or off) option?

    A. checkbox

    B. spinner box

    C. drop-down menu

    D. icon

    Answer: A

19. Which of the following Control panels is used to password-protect a Windows workstation?

    A. Colors

    B. Keyboard

    C. Enhanced

    D. Desktop

    Answer: D

20. Which of the following Windows utility also comes with a DOS version?

    A. Control Panel

    B. Program Manager

    C. Print Manager

    D. Windows Setup

    Answer: D

21. Which Windows component is responsible for displaying program icons?

    A. System Manager

    B. File Manager

    C. Icon Manager

    D. Program Manager

    Answer: D

22. To start a program, you must do which of the following?

    A. Select "Run Program" from the File menu.

    B. Drag the icon for the program to the Start button.

C. Double-click the appropriate icon.

D. Any of the above.

Answer: C

23. Which of the following is *not* part of the windows interface?

   A. scroll bars

   B. switches

   C. icons

   D. the mouse pointer

   Answer: B

24. Which control panel controls the settings for Virtual Memory?

   A. The Memory control panel

   B. The System control panel

   C. The Desktop control panel

   D. The 386 Enhanced control panel

   Answer: D

25. What are the two types of swap files used with Windows?

   A. virtual

   B. permanent

   C. temporary

   D. real

   Answer: B, C

Answers to Review Questions for Chapter 9, Installing Windows 3.1

1. To install Windows to a computer, you can copy the files to your hard disk from the A: drive and then start Windows by typing WIN at the C:> prompt. True or false?

    A. True

    B. False

    Answer: B

2. Which of the following Custom Setup steps is NOT included in the Express Setup?

    A. DOS File Copy

    B. Windows File Copy

    C. Printer Setup

    D. Specify Windows Directory

    Answer: D

3. If you don't want to install Notepad, which installation method do you use? (Circle all that apply.)

    A. Easy Setup

    B. Difficult Setup

    C. Custom Setup

    D. Express Setup

    Answer: C

4. What is the name of the Windows installation program?

    A. Setup.EXE

    B. INSTALL.EXE

C. INSTALL.BAT

D. Setup.BAT

Answer: A

5. If you want the simplest possible installation and to have Setup make all the choices for you, which Setup method do you use? (Circle all that apply.)

   A. Easy Setup

   B. Difficult Setup

   C. Custom Setup

   D. Express Setup

   Answer: D

6. Which Setup switch is used to decompress the Windows compressed files onto a network drive?

   A. /A

   B. /B

   C. /C

   D. /N

   Answer: A

7. Which Intel processor must your computer have (at minimum) in order to install Windows 3.1?

   A. 8086

   B. 8088

   C. 80286

   D. 80386

   Answer: C

8. Which Setup switch is used to ignore the hardware detection?

    A. /A

    B. /B

    C. /C

    D. /I

    Answer: D

9. How much memory (minimum) does Windows require to run in 386 Enhanced mode?

    A. 512 KB

    B. 640 KB

    C. 1024 KB

    D. 2048 KB

    Answer: D

10. Which key, when pressed, will stop Setup and exit you to DOS?

    A. F1

    B. F3

    C. F5

    D. F7

    Answer: B

11. Which Setup mode allows you to verify which type of computer you are installing Windows on?

    A. Easy Setup

    B. Difficult Setup

    C. Custom Setup

    D. Express Setup

    Answer: C

12. Which Setup mode allows Setup to automatically configure the swap file type and size? (Circle all that apply.)

    A. Easy Setup

    B. Difficult Setup

    C. Custom Setup

    D. Express Setup

    Answer: D

13. During an Express Setup, if you have just completed inserting Disk #2 in the DOS portion of the Setup, the next step you have to do is:

    A. Enter user information.

    B. Run the Windows Tutorial.

    C. Select "Express Setup."

    D. Select Windows components to install.

    Answer: A

14. When choosing a printer in Custom Setup, you notice that your printer type isn't listed. What option do you choose to install your printer?

    A. Generic/Text Only

    B. Install Unlisted or Updated Printer

    C. HP LaserJet III

    D. Install New Printer

    Answer: B

15. Which Windows 3.1 operating mode is used for older hardware and slower performance machines?

    A. 386 Enhanced Mode

    B. Real Mode

    C. Standard Mode

    D. Slow Mode

    Answer: C

16. What is the earliest version of DOS that you can have installed on your computer in order to install Windows?

    A. version 3.0

    B. version 4.0

    C. version 5.0

    D. version 6.0

    Answer: C

17. Which type of disk controller should you have in order to use the "32-bit disk access" option in the "Virtual Memory" portion of SETUP if you don't have a special driver?

    A. Western Digital WD-1003 Compatible

    B. IDE Compatible

    C. Seagate A41003 Compatible

    D. SCSI Compatible

    Answer: A

18. Custom Setup allows you to choose more settings than the regular Setup approach does. True or false?

    A. True

    B. False

    Answer: A

19. Which SETUP switch is used to explain which SETUP switches can be used?

    A. /A

    B. /B

    C. /C

    D. /?

    Answer: D

20. Which of the following is *not* one of the default program groups?

    A. Main

    B. Utilities

    C. Startup

    D. Applications

    Answer: D

Answers to Review Questions for Chapter 10, Windows Components and Configuration

Answers to the review questions may be found in Appendix A.

1. Which Windows core component handles user input?

    A. INPUT.EXE

    B. USER.EXE

    C. WIN.COM

    D. WIN386.EXE

    Answer: B

2. Which INI file contains settings for color schemes?

   A. WIN.INI

   B. SYSTEM.INI

   C. PROGMAN.INI

   D. CONTROL.INI

   Answer: D

3. Generally speaking, the SYSTEM.INI file gets updated when you run which Windows program and make changes?

   A. CONTROL.EXE

   B. PIFEDIT.EXE

   C. SETUP.EXE

   D. PAINT.EXE

   Answer: C

4. Which Windows core-component file is responsible for displaying Windows and drawing icons?

   A. GDI.EXE

   B. WINDOWS.EXE

   C. ICONIFY.EXE

   D. KRNL386.EXE

   Answer: A

5. What does *PIF* stand for?

   A. Programmable Initialization File

   B. Program Information File

   C. Program Instant File

D. Program Instruction File

Answer: B

6. Which Windows component is a small piece of executable code shared between many applications to reduce the size of each application that shares it?

   A. USER.EXE

   B. INI files

   C. The Registry

   D. DLL files

   Answer: D

7. Which file(s) cannot be edited with SYSEDIT? (Circle all that apply.)

   A. AUTOEXEC.BAT

   B. CONFIG.SYS

   C. WIN.INI

   D. SYSTEM.INI

   E. PROGMAN.INI

   F. CONTROL.INI

   G. COMMAND.COM

   Answer: E, F, G

8. Which type of font file prints fastest?

   A. Bitmap

   B. TrueType

   C. Hardware printer

   D. Screen

   Answer: C

9. Which part of WIN.COM contains the Windows startup logo?

   A. WIN.CNF

   B. VGALOGO.RLE

   C. VGALOGO.LGO

   D. WIN.COM

   Answer: B

10. Which section of the SYSTEM.INI file contains the drivers and programs that are loaded at system startup?

    A. [boot]

    B. [drivers]

    C. [boot.description]

    D. [386Enh]

    Answer: A

11. Which WIN.COM startup switch forces Windows to start in 386Enhanced mode?

    A. /B

    B. /S

    C. /E

    D. /3

    Answer: D

12. Which core component file acts as the backbone of Windows?

    A. WIN.INI

    B. KRNL386.EXE

    C. USER.EXE

    D. WINSOCK.DLL

    Answer: B

13. Which entry do you place in WIN.INI to make a program start automatically as a minimized application?

    A. Minimize=*filename*

    B. Run=*filename*

    C. Load=*filename*

    D. Start=*filename*

    Answer: C

14. Which entry do you place in WIN.INI to make a program start automatically as a regular, full-screen application?

    A. Minimize=*filename*

    B. Run=*filename*

    C. Load=*filename*

    D. Start=*filename*

    Answer: B

15. What is the extension of TrueType font files?

    A. .TTF

    B. .TT

    C. .FOT

    D. .FNT

    Answer: A

16. Which WIN.COM startup switch forces Windows to start in Standard mode?

    A. /B

    B. /S

    C. /E

    D. /3

    Answer: B

17. Which executable(s) are typically used to install new Windows programs? (Circle all that apply.)

    A. START.EXE

    B. INSTALL.EXE

    C. WINSTRT.EXE

    D. SETUP.EXE

    E. INSTALL.COM

    F. PROGMAN.EXE

    Answer: B, C

18. Which WIN.COM startup switch prevents the display of the Windows logo?

    A. /B

    B. /D

    C. /E

    D. :

    Answer: D

19. You can only use one startup switch with WIN.COM to customize the startup of Windows. True or false?

    A. True

    B. False

    Answer: B

20. You are troubleshooting a Windows program that keeps quitting with a "General Protection Fault in module VBRUN300.DLL." What is VBRUN300.DLL?

    A. Visual Basic RUNtime DLL

    B. Very Big RUNning DLL

C. Vital Bit RUNtime DLL

D. Virtual Bit RUNtime DLL

Answer: A

21. What is the correct syntax for a section marker in an INI file?

    A. :SECTION

    B. {SECTION}

    C. [SECTION]

    D. (SECTION)

    Answer: C

22. What is the main reason it may be necessary to create a PIF?

    A. It's used to get a DOS program to run properly under Windows 3.x.

    B. It's used to specify Windows program settings.

    C. It's needed after you install new hardware.

    D. It's used to capture program output in a graphic file, like a TIF.

    Answer: A

23. If a DOS program does not have a PIF, and you did not create one, where does Windows get the settings needed in order to run the DOS program?

    A. WIN.INI

    B. SYSTEM.INI

    C. _DEFAULT.PIF

    D. PROGMAN.INI

    Answer: C

24. Where does Windows 3.x store the settings relating to the color and/or picture used as the Desktop background?

    A. WIN.INI

    B. SYSTEM.INI

    C. _DEFAULT.PIF

    D. PROGMAN.INI

    Answer: A

25. Which of the following Windows core components provides Windows applications with access to TCP/IP (and, subsequently, the Internet).

    A. WIN.INI

    B. KRNL386.EXE

    C. USER.EXE

    D. WINSOCK.DLL

    Answer: D

Answers to Review Questions for Chapter 11, DOS and Windows System Optimization

1. Which type of swap file requires contiguous disk space?

    A. Temporary

    B. Permanent

    C. Memory

    D. Contiguous

    Answer: B

2. Which DOS utility can you use to optimize DOS conventional memory?

   A. MEMMOPT

   B. MEMMAKER

   C. OPTIMIZE

   D. SMARTDRV

   Answer: B

3. Which item increases Windows performance the most?

   A. Temporary swap file

   B. Permanent swap file

   C. 32-bit disk access

   D. None of the above

   E. All of the above

   Answer: C

4. You can use the DEFRAG utility to defragment floppy disks. True or false?

   A. True

   B. False

   Answer: A

5. Which driver (loaded in CONFIG.SYS) enables you to use a chunk of RAM as a virtual disk?

   A. RAMDISK.SYS

   B. VDISK.EXE

   C. VDISK.SYS

   D. RAMDRIVE.SYS

   Answer: D

6. Which of the following items is *not* a requirement for running Windows with a permanent swap file?

    A. swap file on a local drive (not a network drive)

    B. swap file stored in contiguous disk space

    C. swap file named WIN386.SWP

    D. swap file of a fixed size

    Answer: C

7. Which utility provides DOS with disk-caching functionality?

    A. CACHE.EXE

    B. SMARTDRV.EXE

    C. SMRTDRIV.COM

    D. DISKCACH.COM

    Answer: B

8. Which utility can you use with IBM PC-DOS to optimize conventional memory?

    A. MEMMAKER

    B. PCMEM

    C. RAMBOOST

    D. RAMMAKER

    Answer: C

9. Which CONFIG.SYS command allows DOS to load itself into the HMA?

    A. DOS=HIGH

    B. DOS=HMA

    C. DOS=UMB

    D. DOS=LOADHIGH

    Answer: A

10. MEMMAKER is the best way to optimize MS-DOS conventional memory. True or false?

    A. True

    B. False

    Answer: B

11. When you reboot a computer that uses a RAM disk, the information that was in the disk before the reboot will be there after the reboot. True or false?

    A. True

    B. False

    Answer: B

12. A user complains that their computer has gotten slower in the last few months. They haven't added any new hardware, but they are starting to get Out of Memory error messages in Windows. What is a possible reason for this?

    A. A corrupt Windows application is causing the crash.

    B. There is not enough conventional memory.

    C. The disk is full (or almost full).

    D. The disk cache is full.

    Answer: C

13. To prevent EMM386.EXE from using a particular memory address range (for example, C0000–CFFFF) for UMBs, how would you state the DEVICE line in CONFIG.SYS?

    A. DEVICE=EMM386.EXE OFF=C0000-CFFFF

    B. DEVICE=EMM386.EXE NO=C0000-CFFFF

    C. DEVICE=EMM386.EXE I=C0000-CFFFF

    D. DEVICE=EMM386.EXE X=C0000-CFFFF

    Answer: D

14. A good guideline for defragmenting your hard disk is to do it when more than what percent of your hard disk is fragmented?

   A. 10

   B. 20

   C. 80

   D. 90

   Answer: A

15. To change a swap file, which control panel should you go to first?

   A. Swap File

   B. 386Enhanced

   C. Virtual Memory

   D. Memory

   Answer: B

16. You have just added a new sound card to a machine running MS-DOS 6.22 and Windows 3.1. After installing the software for it and rebooting, you can no longer run some DOS programs. They quit with an "Out of Memory" error message. Which of the following is the most likely cause of the problem?

   A. hardware I/O port conflict with the new hardware

   B. not enough expanded memory available after the install

   C. software conflict with the new software

   D. not enough conventional memory available after the install

   Answer: D

17. Running MEMMAKER.EXE is *not* the best way to increase the amount of available conventional memory. True or false?

    A. True

    B. False

    Answer: A

18. Deleting files to save disk space has no effect on the performance of a machine that is running MS-DOS without Windows installed. True or false?

    A. True

    B. False

    Answer: A

19. Which of the following files is created when Windows is using a permanent swap file? (Circle all that apply.)

    A. SPART.PAR

    B. 386SPART.PAR

    C. WIN386.SWP

    D. WIN386.PART

    Answer: A, B

20. Which of the following files is created when Windows is using a temporary swap file? (Circle all that apply.)

    A. SPART.PAR

    B. 386SPART.PAR

    C. WIN386.SWP

    D. WIN386.PART

    Answer: C

Answers to Review Questions for Chapter 12, DOS and Windows Troubleshooting

1. Suppose that a user calls you and reports that their computer is giving them a general protection fault in the program XXXX.EXE. What are some possible causes? (Circle all that apply.)

   A. The XXXX.EXE program is bad and should be replaced or patched (a bug fix applied).

   B. There is not enough memory in the computer.

   C. There is not enough hard disk space in the computer.

   D. all of the above

   E. none of the above

   Answer: D

2. Which Windows error is caused by an application being greedy and taking memory away from other programs?

   A. general system error

   B. general protection fault

   C. dystem fault

   D. memory protection fault

   Answer: B

3. Which two files are used by DOS to configure a computer?

   A. INI files

   B. AUTOEXEC.BAT

   C. CONFIG.BAT

   D. CONFIG.SYS

   Answer: B, D

4. Suppose that a Windows program constantly "GPFs" (at least a couple of times a day). It has always been this way, although it gets worse when there are several programs loaded. What is the first thing you should check?

   A. whether the computer is out of disk space

   B. the Internet knowledge base, to see whether there is a patch or upgrade for this problem

   C. your Windows resources

   D. whether the computer is fast enough

   Answer: C

5. Which menu in the Windows 3.1 Program Manager contains the option to view the Windows resources?

   A. Options

   B. File

   C. Resources

   D. Help

   Answer: D

6. Which statement can be placed in the AUTOEXEC.BAT or CONFIG.SYS file to "comment out" suspect lines?

   A. REM

   B. ""

   C. STOP

   D. NO

   Answer: A

7. Suppose that one day you start Windows and none of the program groups show up in the Program Manager. Which Windows file may have been edited (or deleted)?

   A. .GRP files

   B. WIN.INI

   C. SYSTEM.INI

   D. PROGMAN.INI

   Answer: D

8. Which INI file is not critical and doesn't need to be backed up?

   A. WIN.INI

   B. SYSTEM.INI

   C. PROGMAN.INI

   D. CONTROL.INI

   E. none of the above

   Answer: E

9. To solve problems related to AUTOEXEC.BAT, you should "REM out" all entries and "un-REM" each entry one at a time to find the problem entry. True or false?

   A. True

   B. False

   Answer: B

10. Suppose that you just installed a new sound card in a client's computer. Upon rebooting, the computer locks up after the message HIMEM.SYS Is Testing Extended Memory ... Done. On which configuration file should you focus your troubleshooting efforts?

    A. CONFIG.SYS

    B. AUTOEXEC.BAT

C. WIN.INI

D. SYSTEM.INI

Answer: A

11. Which DOS command(s) can create a bootable diskette?

    A. FORMAT A: /S

    B. FORMAT A: /B

    C. SYS A:

    D. BOOT A:

    Answer: A, C

12. What condition(s) are likely to occur when Windows runs out of resources?

    A. Windows gets more resources.

    B. All programs restart.

    C. Windows closes, returning to DOS.

    D. General protection faults (GPFs).

    E. all of the above

    Answer: D

13. Suppose that you want to find out whether a Windows program you are having trouble with is supposed to be compatible with the network you have. Where could you check to find this information?

    A. other technicians

    B. the program manufacturer's Web site

    C. the program's manual

    D. all of the above

    E. none of the above

    Answer: B, C

14. Which Windows 95 configuration file replaces the INI files that were used by previous versions of Windows?

    A. the database

    B. CONFIG.SYS

    C. MS-DOS.SYS

    D. the Registry

    Answer: D

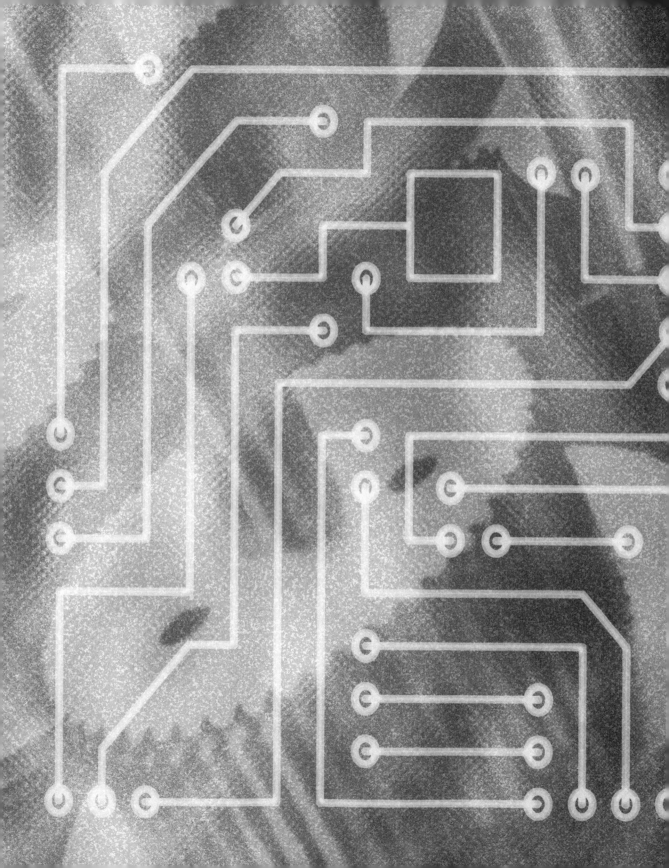

APPENDIX

B

Familiarizing Yourself with Windows 95

- Windows 95 System Requirements

- The Windows 95 Interface

- Upgrading from Windows 3.x and DOS

- Configuring New Hardware under Windows 95

- Troubleshooting Windows 95 Hardware Problems

At the time this book is being written, the most current version of Windows is Windows 95. Of course, although Windows 95 was introduced in early 1996, there are still millions of Windows 3.1 users, and, as the A+ test administrators recognize, these users will likely be a large part of the client base you will be serving in your job providing general computer support. However, it would be ignorant to pretend that you won't run into questions from your clients regarding Windows 95 (and, soon enough, Windows 98 as well). To that end, we provide this overview of Windows 95 for your benefit, in an effort to provide some needed instruction beyond the strictly DOS and Windows 3.x certification of the current A+ exam.

There are quite a few similarities (and more than a few differences) between Windows 3.x and Windows 95. In this chapter we'll take a look some of the most significant ones.

The major topics we'll cover in this chapter are as follows:

- Windows 95 System Requirements

- The Windows 95 Interface

- Upgrading from Windows 3.x and DOS

- Configuring New Hardware under Windows 95

- Troubleshooting Windows 95 Hardware Problems

NOTE For more detailed information on Windows 95, check out other books from Sybex (available at most large bookstores), or browse Microsoft's website at *http://www.microsoft.com/*.

Windows 95 System Requirements

As with any software requirements, as the version number increases, usually the hardware requirements increase as well.

Because Windows 95 is a newer generation of software than Windows 3.x, a more powerful computer is required to run it. Table B.1 lists the minimum requirements needed to run Windows 95.

TABLE B.1: Minimum System Requirements for Installing Windows 95

Resource	Requirement
Processor	386DX or higher
Memory	4 MB (8 MB or higher recommended)
Disk Space	35 to 40 MB free. (This is for a typical installation. If all components are installed, the installation may take up to 60 MB.)
Video Card	VGA or compatible
Other Hardware	Mouse, Keyboard

Remember that the requirements listed in Table B.1 are *minimums*. If you equip your machine with only the minimum requirements, you *will* be able to run Windows 95—but not much else. If you want to run other programs, you'll want to increase the number of resources that you give to Windows 95 accordingly.

And Now for the Real World...

In order to run applications in Windows 95, you really should have a computer that is at least a 486DX/33 with 16 MB of RAM and at least a 300MB disk drive (with at least 125 MB free to allow for a decent swap file). As with Windows 3.x, the more resources you can give Windows, the better it will function.

The Windows 95 Interface

The most obvious difference between Windows 95 and Windows 3.x is the new interface. You will notice some drastic changes between this interface and the older, Windows 3.x interface. Figure B.1 shows an example of the Windows 95 interface. Each major component is labeled in the figure.

FIGURE B.1:

The new Windows 95 interface

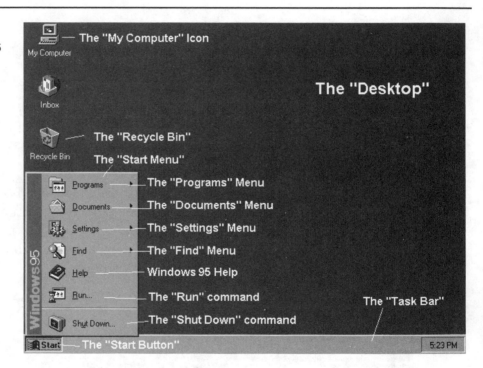

Let's take a look at some of the more common elements of the Windows 95 interface.

The Desktop

You can change the Desktop's background patterns, screen saver, color scheme, and Desktop size easily by "right clicking" on any area of the Desktop that doesn't contain an icon. When you right click, you'll get a menu that pops up in front of the Desktop (Figure B.2). This menu allows you to do several things, like creating new icons (now called *shortcuts*), new directories (now called *folders*), a command for arranging icons, and a special command called *Properties*. This command is available through several other right-click options throughout Windows 95.

FIGURE B.2:

A popup menu

When you right click on the Desktop and choose Properties, you will see the screen shown in Figure B.3. This is the Display Properties screen. From this screen you can click the various tabs at the top to move to the different screens of information about the way Windows 95 looks. For example, if you want to change the screen saver, click the Screen Saver tab, then choose a different screen saver from the drop down list. Make any other changes you want (like changing the Desktop pattern wallpaper or screen resolution) and click OK to save them.

TIP   The Display Properties screen performs the same function as the Desktop control panel does under Windows 3.x.

TIP   You can also access the Display Properties settings by using the Display control panel under Start ➢ Settings ➢ Control Panel.

FIGURE B.3:

The Display Properties
screen

FIGURE B.3:

The Display Properties
screen

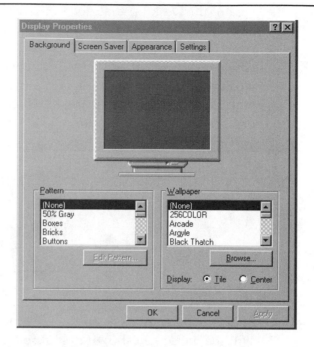

The Taskbar

The Taskbar (Figure B.4) is yet another new feature of the Windows 95 interface. It contains two major items: the Start Menu and the System Tray. The Start menu is discussed in the next subsection. The System Tray is located on the right side of the Taskbar and contains a clock (by default). Other Windows 95 utilities (for example, screen savers, virus-protection utilities) may put their icons here when running to indicate that they are running and also to provide the user with a quick way to get access to their features.

FIGURE B.4:

The Taskbar

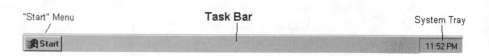

Whenever you open a new window or program, it gets a button on the Taskbar with an icon that represents the window or program. To bring that window or program to the front (or maximize it if it was minimized), you can click on the representative button on the Taskbar. As the Taskbar fills up with buttons, the buttons make themselves smaller to fit all the programs on the Taskbar.

You can increase the size of the Taskbar by moving the mouse pointer to the top of the Taskbar and pausing until the pointer turns into a double-headed arrow. Once this happens, you can click the mouse and move it up to make the Taskbar bigger. Or, you can move it down to make the Taskbar smaller. You can also move the Taskbar to the top or sides of the screen by simply clicking on the Taskbar and dragging it to the new location.

TIP

You can make the Taskbar automatically "hide" itself when not being used (thus freeing up that space for use by the Desktop or other Windows). To do this, right click on the Taskbar and choose Properties. (You can also do this by selecting Start ➤ Settings ➤ Taskbar). This will bring up the Taskbar Properties screen. From this screen you can customize the appearance of the Taskbar (like removing the clock from the System Tray, making the Start menu's icons smaller so they take up less room, and choosing which programs appear on the Start menu). If you check the Auto Hide option and then click OK, the Taskbar will minimize itself when the pointer is not over it. When you move the mouse pointer back to the area of the screen where the Taskbar is hidden, the Taskbar will pop up and can be used as normal.

The Start Menu

When Microsoft officially introduced Windows 95 to the world, it bought the rights to use the Rolling Stones song "Start Me Up" in its advertisements and at the introduction party. The reason they chose that particular song is because it's the Start menu that is the central point of focus in the new Windows 95 interface. It functions a lot like the File menu does in the Windows 3.x Program Manager, except there are a lot more functions. Figure B.5 shows the Start menu and all of its components.

FIGURE B.5:

The Windows 95
Start menu

To display the Start menu, click on the word "Start" in the Taskbar. You will then see the menu as shown previously in Figure B.5. From this menu, you can select any of the various options the menu presents. An arrow pointing to the right means that there is a submenu. To select a submenu, move the mouse pointer over the submenu title and pause. The submenu will then appear; you don't even have to click. (You have to click to choose an option *on* the submenu, though.) Let's discuss each of the default Start menu's submenu options and how to use them.

Programs Submenu

The Programs submenu holds the program groups and program icons that you can use (a lot like the Program Manager does under Windows 3.x). When you select this submenu, you will be shown yet another submenu, with a submenu for each program group (Figure B.6). You can navigate through this menu and its submenus and click on the program you wish to start.

FIGURE B.6:

The Programs
submenu

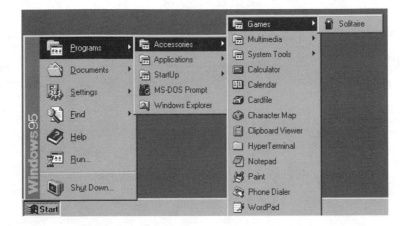

You can add programs to this submenu in any one of three ways: via the application's installation program, via the Taskbar Properties screen, or via the Windows 95 Explorer program. The first (and simplest) way is to use the application's installation program. The installation program will not only copy the files for the program, but will automatically make a program group and shortcuts for the programs under the Programs submenu.

TIP

You can add shortcuts to the top of the Start menu (above the Programs submenu) by clicking on a program or shortcut and dragging it to the Start menu. A shortcut for that item will appear in the Start menu, above a divider between Programs and the new shortcut.

Another way to make shortcuts under the Programs submenu is to use the Taskbar Properties screen to add them. To get to this screen, right click on the Taskbar and choose Properties. When the Taskbar Properties screen appears, click the Start Menu Programs tab to bring it to the front. You will then see the screen shown in Figure B.7. From here you can click Add to add a new program or

Remove to remove one. A Wizard (a special sequence of screens designed to "walk you through" the necessary steps to accomplish certain tasks) will help you create or delete the shortcut(s).

FIGURE B.7:

Using the Taskbar Properties screen to add/remove programs from the Programs submenu

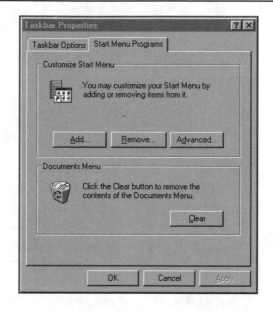

Finally, you can add program shortcuts to the Programs submenu by using another new component introduced in Windows 95: the Windows 95 Explorer (EXPLORER.EXE). Explorer performs a lot of the same functions of the File Manager under Windows 3.x, but adds quite a few more features. Start the Explorer by navigating to Start ➢ Programs ➢ Windows Explorer. You will see a window similar to the one in Figure B.8. From here you can see all of the crucial elements in Windows 95. Navigate on the C: drive to C:\Windows*Start Menu* by either double-clicking on parent folders or clicking the + signs next to the parent folders. This will display any subfolders. Once you click the plus sign next to Start Menu you should see the Programs subfolder. You can either navigate further to a particular program group, or create the shortcut at the root of the Programs submenu. To create a shortcut in Explorer, right click *in the right pane*, and follow the steps in the Wizard to create the new shortcut.

FIGURE B.8:

The Windows 95
Explorer

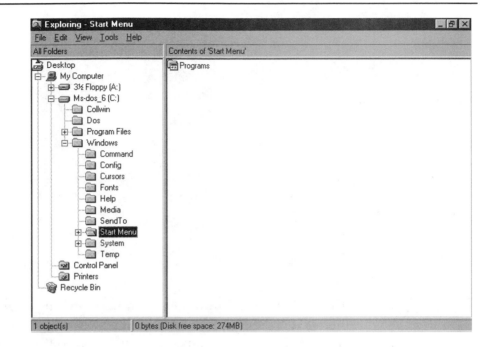

Documents Submenu

The Documents submenu has one and only one function: to keep track of all of the data files you open. Whenever you open a file, a shortcut is automatically made in this menu. This menu makes it easier to open the same document again if you need to. Just click on the document in the Documents menu to open the document in its associated application. Figure B.9 shows an example of a Documents submenu.

TIP

If you want to "clear" the list of documents shown in the Documents submenu, go to the Taskbar Properties screen (shown earlier in Figure B.7). Then, click the Clear button within the Documents Menu section.

FIGURE B.9:

The Windows 95
Documents submenu

Settings Submenu

The Settings submenu (Figure B.10) is provided so you have easy access to the configuration of Windows 95. There are three submenus to the Settings submenu: Control Panel, Printers, and Taskbar. These submenus give you access to the Control Panel, printer driver, and Taskbar configuration areas, respectively. You can also access the first two areas from the My Computer icon, but they are placed here together to provide a common area to access Windows 95 settings.

FIGURE B.10:

The Settings submenu

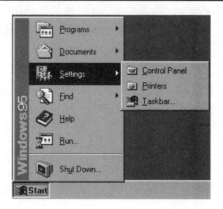

Find Submenu

The Find submenu (Figure B.11) is used for an obvious purpose: to find things. The Find command can be used to find either files (stored on a local computer or a network drive) or to find a computer that is hooked to the same network.

FIGURE B.11:

The Find submenu

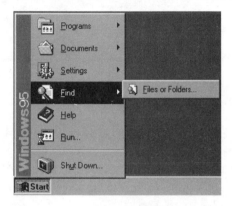

TIP

If your computer is connected to a network, then the Find submenu shows an extra option—Computer—to allow you to search for other computers on the network

When you select the Find submenu, then select Files or Folders, you will be presented with a figure similar to the one in Figure B.12. Next to the *Named:* field in this dialog box, simply type in the name of the file or directory you are looking for, and click Find Now. Windows 95 will search whatever is specified in the *Look in:* parameter for the file or directory. Matches will be listed in a window underneath the Find window. You can use wildcards (* and ?) to look for multiple files and directories. You can also click the Advanced tab to further refine your search.

FIGURE B.12:

The Find Files screen

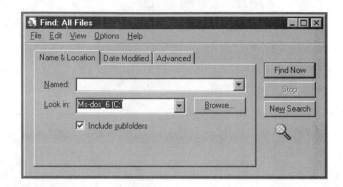

Help Command

Windows 95 includes a *very* good help system. Not only is it arranged by topic, but it is fully indexed and searchable. Because of its usefulness and power, it was placed into the Start menu for easy access. When you select this command, it will bring up the Windows 95 Help screen (Figure B.13). From this screen you can double click on a manual to show a list of subtopics, then click on a subtopic to view the text of that topic.

FIGURE B.13:

Windows 95 Help Contents tab

Or, you can click the Index tab to show an alphabetic listing of topics (Figure B.14). To select a topic, type the first few letters of the topic (for example, type **prin** to move to the section that talks about printing), then click Display to display the text on the topic.

FIGURE B.14:

Windows 95 Help
Index tab

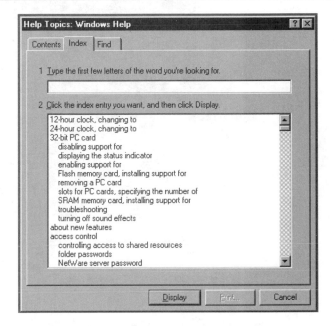

Or, you can click the Find tab to find any text you want in the help files (Figure B.15). Simply type the text. As you type, Help will display a list of topics that contain the characters you are typing. You will see the list of topics get shorter as you type, because the more you type, the more you are narrowing down your search. When the topic you want appears in the list, click on the one(s) you want to read about, then click Display.

Run Command

The Run command can be used to start programs if they don't have a shortcut on the Desktop or in the Programs submenu. When you choose Run from the Start menu, the screen in Figure B.16 appears. To execute a particular program, just type its name and path into the *Open:* field. If you don't know the exact path, you can browse to find the file by clicking the Browse button. Once you have typed in the executable name and path, click OK to run the program.

TIP

If the program you want to run has been run recently, you can find it listed on the drop-down list next to the Run box's Open: field. Click the down arrow to display the list, then select the program you want by clicking on its name and then on OK.

FIGURE B.16:

FIGURE B.16:

The Start menu's Run command

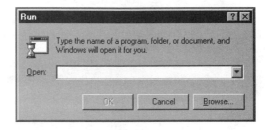

Shut Down Command

Windows 95 is a very complex operating system. At any one time, there are several files open in memory. Because of this, if you accidentally hit the power switch and turn the computer off while these files are open, there is a good chance these files will be corrupted. For this reason, Microsoft has added the Shut Down command under the Start menu. When you select this option, Windows 95 presents you with three choices, as shown in Figure B.17.

FIGURE B.17:

Shut Down command options

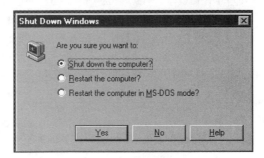

The three Shut Down choices are:

- **Shut down the computer.** This option will write any unsaved data to disk, close any open applications, and get the computer ready to be powered off. When you see a black screen with the message "It's now safe to turn off your computer" in orange text, it is, in fact, safe to power off the computer.. You can also hit Ctrl+Alt+Del to reboot the computer at this point.

- **Restart the computer.** This option works the same as the first option, but instead will automatically reboot the computer with a warm reboot.

- **Restart the computer in MS-DOS Mode.** This option is special. It does the same as the previous option, except upon reboot, Windows 95 will execute the command prompt only and will not start the graphic portion of Windows 95. You can then run DOS programs as though the machine were a DOS machine. When you are finished running these programs, type **exit** to reboot the machine back into the "full" Windows 95 with the GUI.

The My Computer Icon

Another new addition to the Windows 95 Desktop is the My Computer icon (Figure B.18). This icon represents just that, your computer. If you double-click on it, it will display all the disk drives installed in your computer as well as the Control Panel and Printers folders (Figure B.19) which can be used to configure the system. If you double click on a disk drive, you will see the contents of that disk drive.

FIGURE B.18:

The My Computer icon

You can delve deeper into each disk drive and open a window for each subdirectory by double clicking on them. You can copy and move files between drives and between directories using these windows.

FIGURE B.19:

The My Computer window

If you were to right click on the My Computer icon and choose Properties, you would see a screen similar to the one in Figure B.20. This screen is called the System Properties screen and can give you information about the current configuration of your computer—for example, what type of processor your computer uses and how much RAM is installed. It also will tell you what version of Windows 95 is being used.

FIGURE B.20:

System Properties screen

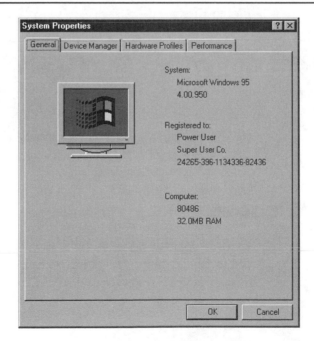

The Recycle Bin

Under Windows 3.x, when you delete a file from Windows, it warns you, then allows you to permanently delete the file. In Windows 95, when you delete a file, it still asks you, but instead of deleting it permanently from the disk, it places it in the "Recycle Bin" (Figure B.21).

FIGURE B.21:

The Recycle Bin

You can retrieve a file that you have deleted by simply opening the Recycle Bin icon, then dragging the file from the Recycle Bin back to the disk it came from. To permanently erase the file, you need to "empty" the Recycle Bin. This is accomplished by right clicking on the Recycle Bin and choosing *Empty Recycle Bin*. Figure B.22 shows the difference between a full Recycle Bin (one that contains deleted files) and an empty Recycle Bin (one without any deleted files).

FIGURE B.22:

The full (left) and empty (right) Recycle Bins

Windows

The final interface component that has changed is the set of buttons in the upper right-hand corner of any window. Figure B.23 shows these buttons. Under Windows 3.x, there were only two buttons, but in Windows 95, there are three, each with a different function. The leftmost button is the *Minimize* button. When clicked, it causes the window to be minimized into an icon on the Taskbar. The middle button is the *Minimize/Maximize* button. Depending on the size of the screen when you click this button, the window is either maximized so that it takes up the whole screen or reduced if the window is already at its largest size. The rightmost button is the *Window Close* button. This button, when clicked, will close the window.

FIGURE B.23:

Window control buttons

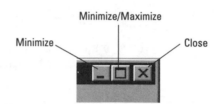

Other Differences between Win 95 and Win 3.x

Another difference between Windows 95 and Windows 3.x is that Windows 95 is an operating system that manages its own resources, whereas Windows 3.x is a Graphical User Interface (GUI) for DOS. As such, any hardware that Windows 95 needs to talk to must have its own drivers installed for Windows 95 to be able to talk to it.

Additionally, Windows 95 can run 32-bit (Windows 95) applications simultaneously with older, 16-bit (Windows 3.x) applications. This provides for backwards compatibility with 16-bit applications. However, if a 16-bit application misbehaves it can take down the whole system. This drawback is one of the reasons you should upgrade all of your older, 16-bit applications to their newer, 32-bit counterparts.

Upgrading from Windows 3.x and DOS

If you are currently running Windows 3.x and want to upgrade to Windows 95, you're not alone. By the time of the millennium, most Intel-based computers will be running Windows 95. That's due, in part, to the benefits and ease of use that Windows 95 offers. It can also be attributed to the fact that the upgrade process is very easy (almost painless, in fact). Let's run through a typical upgrade.

Starting the Upgrade

There are three major steps that you need to follow when upgrading from an earlier version of Windows. The steps are, in order:

1. Gather information about your computer.

2. Copy files to your computer.

3. Finish Setup.

These steps are performed by the Windows 95 installation program, SETUP.EXE. In order to start the upgrade, you need to start the SETUP.EXE program. If you are upgrading to Windows 95 using the floppy disk installation method, insert the first disk (the one labeled "Disk 1-SETUP") into your A: drive. Then, from Windows, select the Run command under the File menu in Program Manager and type the following in the box that appears:

```
A:\SETUP.EXE
```

To run the program, click OK. The screen in Figure B.24 will appear, after a short examination of your hard disk to make sure it doesn't have any serious flaws. This screen asks you to read the license agreement and either accept it or decline it. If you decline, SETUP will exit and the installation cannot continue. So, to continue the installation, click Accept.

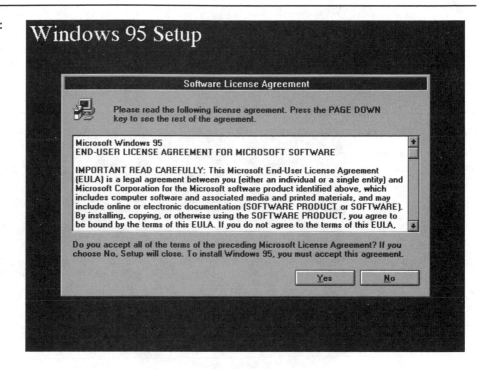

FIGURE B.24:

Microsoft License Agreement screen

Step 1: Gathering Information

The next screen that SETUP shows you is the one that details what the generic steps in the installation are (Figure B.25). As we have already discussed, there are three general steps to the upgrade: Gathering Information, Copying Files, and Finishing Setup. To continue, click the Next button.

Specifying Windows Directory

There are several pieces of information that SETUP needs to gather before it can complete the setup. The first of these is the directory you want to install Windows in. By default, SETUP wants to install

Windows in the C:\Windows directory (Figure B.26), which is the same directory it was installed in for Windows 3.1. You can change it if you want by clicking the box next to *Other directory:* and typing in a new path for the Windows installation. If C:\Windows is acceptable, click Next to continue the installation.

FIGURE B.25:

Gathering Information screen

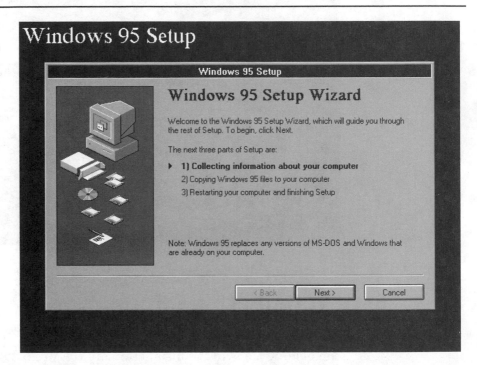

TIP

If you want to be able to use your DOS / Windows 3.x combination after the upgrade, you still can. You may need to revert to DOS or Windows 3.x for an application that is incompatible with Windows 95. Any DOS program that accesses hardware directly would fall into this category. To make sure the Windows files don't get overwritten and are available, you must install Windows 95 in a directory other than C:\Windows (for example, *C:\WIN95*). Then, after the installation is complete, you can press F8 during boot-up and select *Previous version of MS-DOS*. Your computer will boot up as it was immediately before the upgrade.

FIGURE B.26:

Selecting Windows
Directory

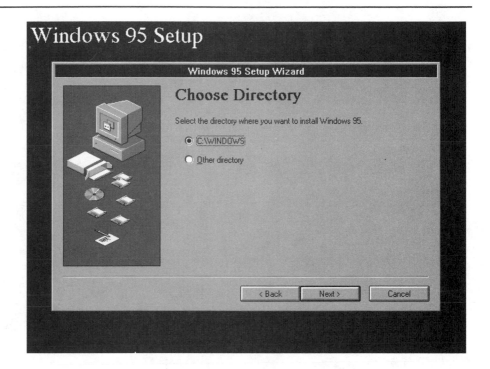

FIGURE B.26:

Selecting Windows
Directory

Once you have specified the installation directory, SETUP will scan the hard disk and make sure the C:\Windows directory exists. If it doesn't, SETUP will make it. It will also scan the disk and check to see that there is enough disk space to upgrade Windows (Figure B.27). You can click Cancel at any time to cancel the scan.

Saving Existing System Files

At this point, SETUP asks you if you want to save your old system files (Figure B.28). This should be done, in case the installation doesn't work properly and you want to uninstall Windows 95. If you answer Yes to this question, SETUP will make a duplicate of the existing DOS and Windows files (this will take about 6 MB of extra disk space) that can be used to uninstall Windows 95.

FIGURE B.27:

Windows checking the disk

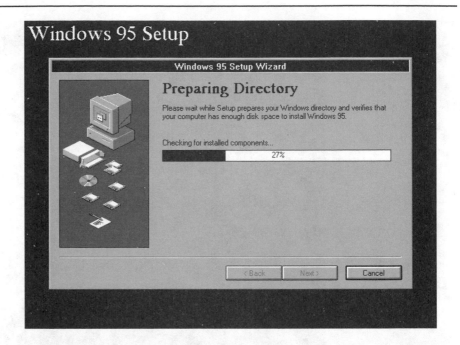

FIGURE B.28:

"Do You Want to Save Your System Files?"

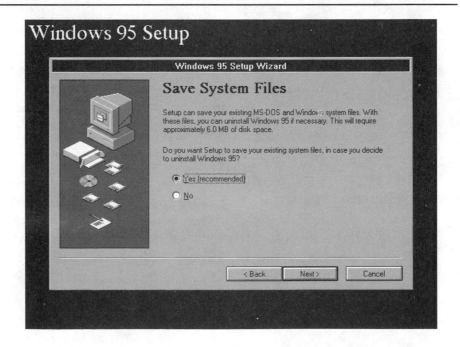

Click Next to continue the installation. The screen in Figure B.29 will appear. While this screen is being displayed, the system files are being compressed and "tucked away" until they are needed. If not needed, they can be deleted using the Add/Remove Programs control panel. When you open this control panel, there will be a listing of all the programs that were installed since the time Windows 95 was installed. In this list will be the categories *Old Windows 3.x and MS-DOS system files* and *Windows 95*. If you want to uninstall Windows 95, click on the *Windows 95* entry and click the Add/Remove button. It will then start the uninstall and ask you to reboot. After rebooting, your system will be as it was before the upgrade.

FIGURE B.29:

Saving your existing system files

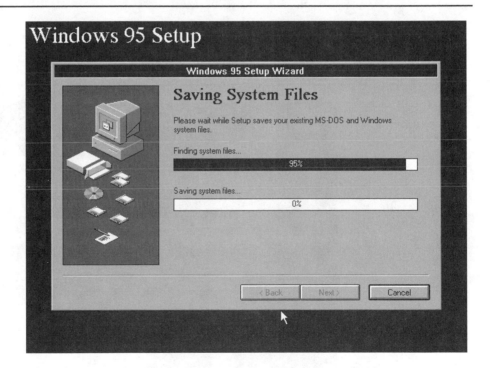

Choosing a "Typical Installation"

When SETUP is done saving the system files, it will present you with the screen in Figure B.30. This screen allows you to choose from the following options to customize the way SETUP runs.

- **Typical.** This option allows SETUP to choose the most popular options

- **Portable.** This option sets up the most common applications and utilities for portable computers. This option will install PCMCIA support and Advanced Power Management (APM).

- **Compact.** This option, when selected, will install the bare minimum components of Windows 95.

- **Custom.** This option will allow you to choose which components to install. If you select this option, SETUP will present you with a list of utilities and programs to install. This option allows you to make the most choices about how Windows 95 gets installed.

For this discussion, choose Typical and click Next.

FIGURE B.30:

Choosing a typical installation

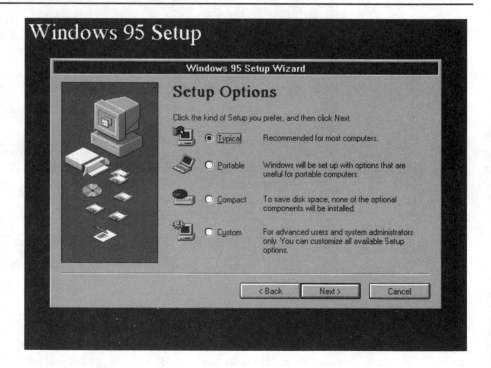

Verifying Name and Company Information

The next step in the upgrade is to verify the registration information you typed in when you installed Windows 3.x. This is a very simple process. The user and company are automatically entered (Figure B.31). All you need to do is click Next.

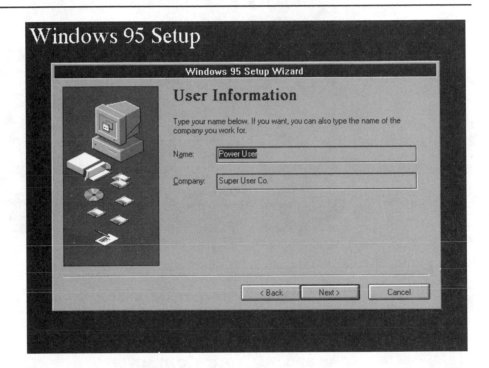

Product Identification Number

Another screen that requires your acknowledgement is the Product Identification Number. This number is used by Microsoft to register the product in your name, for things like Technical Support. This screen displays the Product Registration ID number for your installation of Windows 95 (Figure B.32). Before you send in your warranty card for Windows 95, you should write this number on it in the space provided.

FIGURE B.32:

Production identifica-
tion number

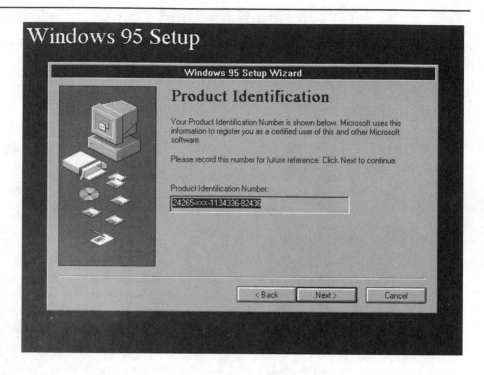

When you have written the number down and are ready to continue, click Next to continue the installation.

Analyzing Your Computer

The next thing that SETUP does is check to see what hardware is
installed in your computer. It does that so you don't have to manually choose every driver that Windows needs. To start this process, it
presents you with a list of the multimedia and network components
you might have installed in your computer (Figure B.33). If you have
any of those devices installed in your computer, click the checkbox
next to the device(s) you have installed and click the Next button to
continue the hardware device detection.

FIGURE B.33:

Selecting multimedia
and network compo-
nents to install

FIGURE B.33:

Selecting multimedia
and network compo-
nents to install

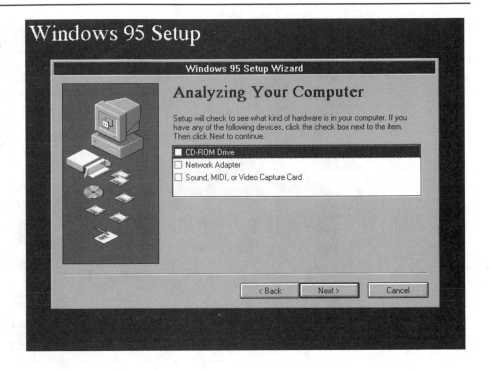

SETUP will now scan the system and look for hardware devices (Figure B.34). For each device it finds, SETUP will install the drivers and utilities for each type of device you have installed in your computer. This screen will disappear automatically when the progress bar reaches 100%.

NOTE   If the progress bar stops moving for more than ten minutes, and there is no hard disk activity, more than likely the machine is locked up. Reboot the computer and rerun setup. SETUP will detect that a partial installation wasn't completed and it will try to resume where it left off. Neat, huh?

FIGURE B.34:

Hardware detection process

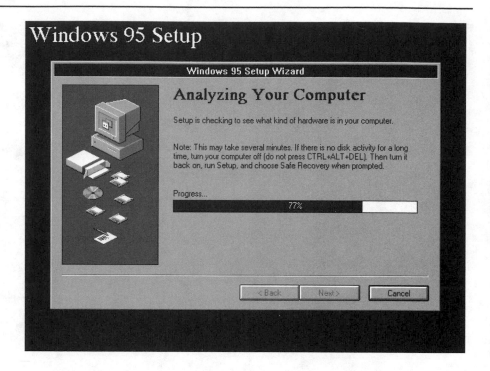

Selecting Windows 95 E-Mail Options

When the hardware detection is complete, SETUP presents you with the screen in Figure B.35. This screen allows you to select which E-mail services you want to install and configure for use with Windows 95. The Microsoft Network (MSN) is Microsoft's own, private online service (similar to America Online). If you choose not to install it, don't worry. You can install it later, after Windows 95 is installed. Microsoft leaves it right there on the Desktop and all you have to do is double-click on it to install it.

> **NOTE** The "Set Up The Microsoft Network" icon on the Desktop can't be dragged to the trash, but you can delete it by right clicking on it, then selecting Delete from the popup menu.

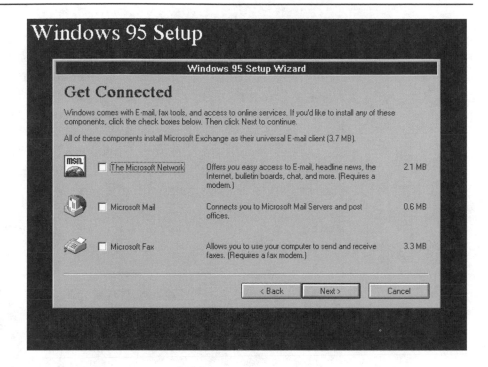

The second mail option is Microsoft Mail. This option will install the MS Exchange Universal Inbox client which can connect to Internet (POP3) mail servers, and MS Mail or Exchange post offices. If you want to use this mail client, check the checkbox next to it, otherwise leave it blank. The final mail option isn't really an e-mail option; it's a fax option. Microsoft Fax allows you to send faxes from within almost any Windows 95 application (assuming you have a fax-capable modem installed in your computer). When installed, a Microsoft Fax printer will be created. When you select this printer from within an application, instead of printing the document, a window will pop up and allow you to fax the page to someone using your fax/modem.

Select which option(s) you want to install, then click Next to continue the installation.

Selecting Windows 95 Components

After choosing which E-mail options you want, you can customize the Windows 95 installation and decide which components you want to install. At this point in the installation, SETUP will present you with the screen shown in Figure B.36. If you want to let the SETUP program install the most common components, choose the *Install the most common components (recommended)* option by checking the button next to that item. This is the most common option to choose during installation if you want the installation to be as simple as possible. If you choose the other option, *Show me a list of components so I can choose*, and click Next, SETUP will present you a list of the possible components and you can select the ones you want to install.

FIGURE B.36:

Telling SETUP to auto-
matically choose which
components are
installed

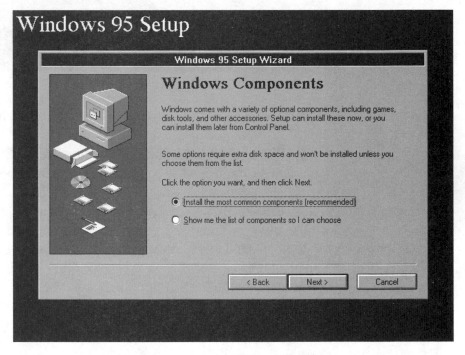

For your upgrade, allow SETUP to choose your components and click Next to continue.

Creating a Startup Disk

It should already be apparent that Windows 95 and DOS are different. We have discussed several differences between Windows 95 and the DOS/Windows combination. There is another difference that we haven't discussed. There is a different way to create a startup disk. During the upgrade, SETUP will ask you if you want to create a startup disk (Figure B.37). If you select Yes, you will need to insert a blank floppy disk (either a 1.2MB 5¼" floppy disk or 1.44MB diskette) so that SETUP can copy the startup files to the diskette.

FIGURE B.37:

Creating a Windows 95 startup disk

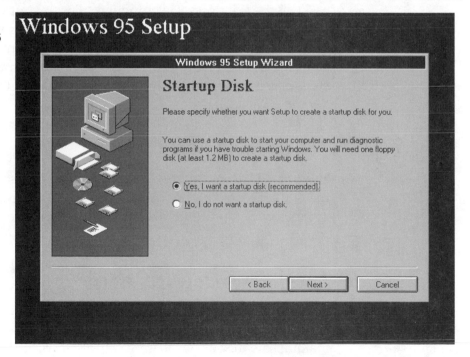

TIP	You can create a startup disk after installation (if you select No to the "Create Startup Disk" question during the upgrade installation process, for example). Go to the Start ➤ Settings ➤ Control Panel and double click on the Add/Remove Programs control panel. Within this control panel is a tab called Startup Disk. Click this tab to bring it to the front. On this page will be a button that says Create Startup Disk. When you click it, it will start the startup disk creation process.

Step 2: Copying Files to Your Computer

Once the entering of information is complete, the next step is to copy all the Windows 95 component files to your computer. During this step, SETUP will copy the files from their compressed archive files on the disk or CD (called *CAB files* because they have the extension *.CAB) to the hard disk. This step is the simplest of the three steps because there are only two parts: initiating the file copy and the file copy itself.

Start Copying Files

To initiate the file copy, SETUP returns you to a screen similar to the one presented earlier back in Figure B.25. Figure B.38 shows the screen that Setup presents to allow you to initiate the file copy. To start the file copy, click the Next button.

Copying Windows 95 Files

During the file copy, a status bar will appear and indicate how far along the file copy is (Figure B.39). You will also see various screens that indicate the various features of Windows 95. During this process, you can cancel the file copy by pressing the F3 key at any time (or by clicking the Exit button).

FIGURE B.38:

Starting the file copy

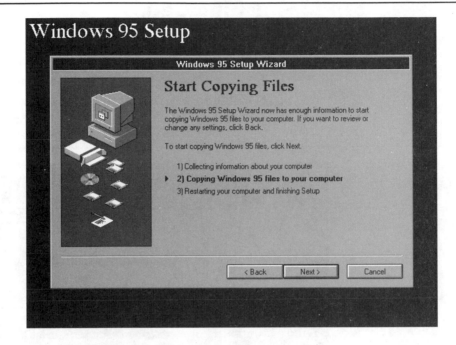

FIGURE B.39:

Windows 95 installation
file copy

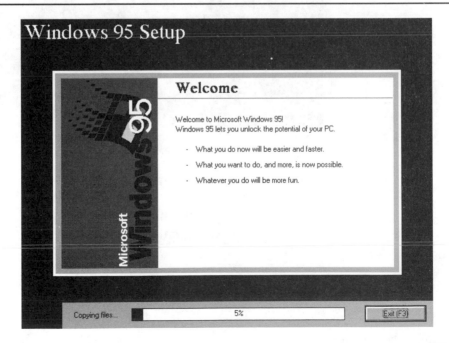

Step 3: Finishing Setup

After the file copy, the installation is basically complete. To complete the installation, only two things must be done: reboot the computer and enter final Windows settings. As soon as the file copy is complete, SETUP will present you with the screen shown in Figure B.40. To finish the installation, click Finish and the computer will reboot.

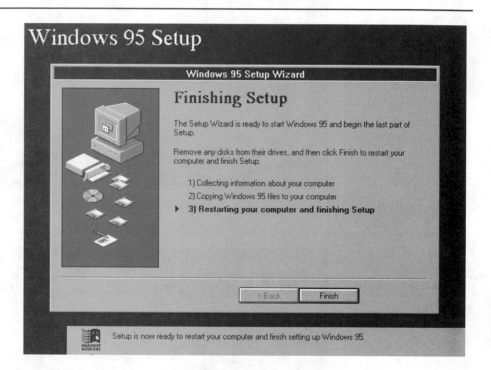

After the machine has rebooted, Windows 95 will start up and indicate that setup is "preparing to run Windows 95 for the first time." After this, it will indicate that it is "Finalizing settings for Windows 95" and present a small list of the settings it is making permanent. SETUP will make icons for the control panel and upgrade your Windows 3.x Program Manager program groups and program icons into groups and icons for the Start menu. After that, SETUP will index the Windows Help file so it can be searched. Then, SETUP will modify the generic MS-DOS program properties so that DOS programs can be run under Windows 95.

The final step is to set up the time zone that this computer resides in (Figure B.41). This gives Windows 95 information it can use to automatically adjust the time when sending e-mail across time zones, for example. Windows 95 can also automatically adjust the built-in BIOS clock during daylight savings time.

FIGURE B.41:

Setting Windows 95 time information

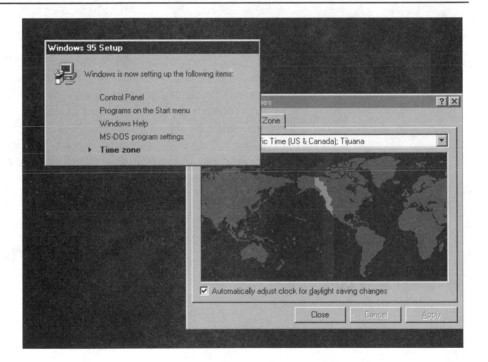

To select the proper time zone, choose the time zone from the drop-down list. I live in Fargo, ND, which is in the Central Time Zone, six hours behind GMT (Greenwich Mean Time). To finish the installation, click Apply to make the settings permanent, then click Close.

After setting the time zone, SETUP will restart the computer for a final time. After this restart, the computer will be a fully functional Windows 95 computer.

TIP If it's not functioning properly, try rebooting the computer in *Safe Mode*. This mode of operation loads Windows 95 with a minimal set of drivers and can help you determine if the problem is hardware or software related. To boot the computer in safe mode, turn the computer on and press the F8 key when you see "Starting Windows 95." This will present you with a list of boot-up choices, the third of which is "Boot computer in Safe Mode." Select this option (number 3) and press Enter. When Windows 95 comes up, it will be running in safe mode. This is indicated by the words "Safe Mode" in all four corners of the screen. To exit safe mode, restart the computer. Upon reboot, the computer will be operating normally.

Configuring New Hardware under Windows 95

Adding new hardware devices is very simple under Windows 95. When you start Windows 95 after installing a new hardware device, normally Windows 95 will detect the new device and automatically install the software for it. If not, you need to run the Add New Hardware Wizard.

Starting the New Hardware Installation Wizard

To start adding the new device, open the My Computer icon by double clicking on it. Then, double click on the Control Panels folder. To start the Wizard, double click Add New Hardware in the Control Panel window (Figure B.42).

FIGURE B.42:

Control Panel window

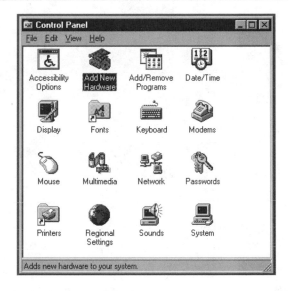

TIP   You can also bring up this window by clicking the Start menu, then the Settings submenu, then the Control Panels folder.

Once you have started the Add New Hardware Wizard, you will see a figure similar to the one in Figure B.43. This is the introduction to the Wizard. To start the configuration of the new hardware, click Next.

FIGURE B.43:

Add New Hardware
Wizard

Telling Windows 95 to Search for the Hardware

The next screen that is presented (Figure B.44) allows you to select whether or not the Wizard will search for the hardware or if you need to specify the type and settings of the hardware. If you choose

FIGURE B.44:

Telling Windows to
search for the new
hardware

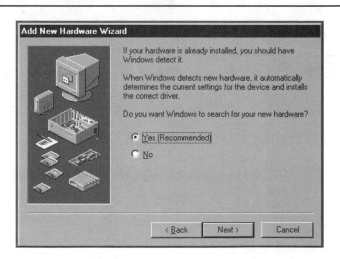

Yes, then in the next step Windows will search for the hardware and install the drivers for it automatically. It is the easiest method (especially if the hardware is Plug-and-Play compliant) and is the least complex. If you choose No, you will have to select the type, brand, and settings for the new hardware. For our example, choose Yes (recommended) and click Next.

Automatic Hardware Detection

The next screen will tell you that Windows 95 is ready to search for the new hardware. To begin the detection, click Next again. Windows 95 will make an intensive scan of the hardware (you should notice the hard disk light will be on almost constantly and you will hear the hard disk thrashing away during the detection). During this scan, you will see a progress bar at the bottom of the screen (Figure B.45) that indicates Windows 95's progress with the detection.

FIGURE B.45:

Detecting new hardware

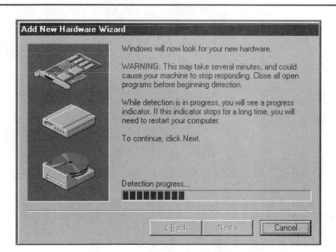

You can stop the detection at any time by clicking the Cancel button.

Finishing Hardware Setup

When the progress indicator gets all the way to the right, Windows 95 will tell you that it found some hardware that it can install (Figure B.46). You can see which hardware it found by clicking the Details button. To finish the setup of the new hardware, click the Finish button. When you do this, Windows 95 will copy the drivers from the installation disks or CD for the device. Once it has done that, it may ask you for configuration information, if necessary. To finish the hardware setup, it will ask you to reboot Windows 95 so that the changes take effect and Windows can recognize (and use) the new hardware.

FIGURE B.46:

Finishing new hardware installation

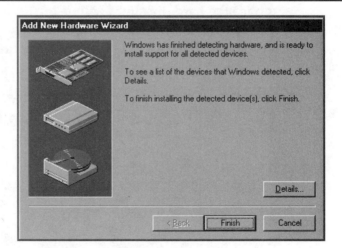

Troubleshooting Windows 95 Hardware Problems

Hardware problems under Windows 95 can be located fairly easily. First of all, when you're having hardware problems, the hardware won't work. This should be fairly obvious. If you are having problems, the first place you should go is the Device Manager in the System Properties control panel. This can be located in the Control Panels folder or by right clicking on the My Computer icon and choosing Properties. Once you are in the System Properties control panel, choose the Device Manager tab (Figure B.47). If there is any malfunctioning hardware, you will notice a yellow circle with an exclamation point inside it next to the malfunctioning device.

FIGURE B.47:

Device Manager tab of the System Properties control panel

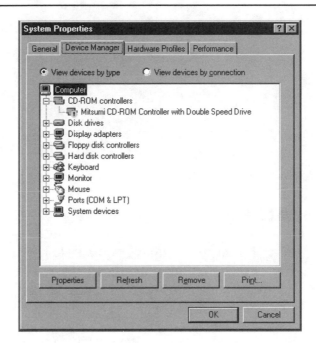

If you click on the offending device and click Properties, you will see a screen similar to the one in Figure B.48. This screen can tell you (through its various tabs) what the problem is. In the case of the error shown in the previous figure (Figure B.47), the device is misconfigured. To solve this problem, you just need to change the settings on the device to ones that don't conflict.

FIGURE B.48:

Device Properties
screen

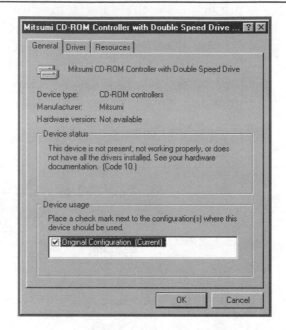

Summary

This Appendix gave you a taste for the new look and feel of Windows 95. Within the next revision of the A+ exams (and the next revision of this book), you can expect a great deal more Windows 95 information. If you haven't already started, you should start working with Windows 95 on one of your own computers to familiarize yourself with its operation, and begin studying the various aspects of configuring, troubleshooting, and using Windows 95 at your workplace.

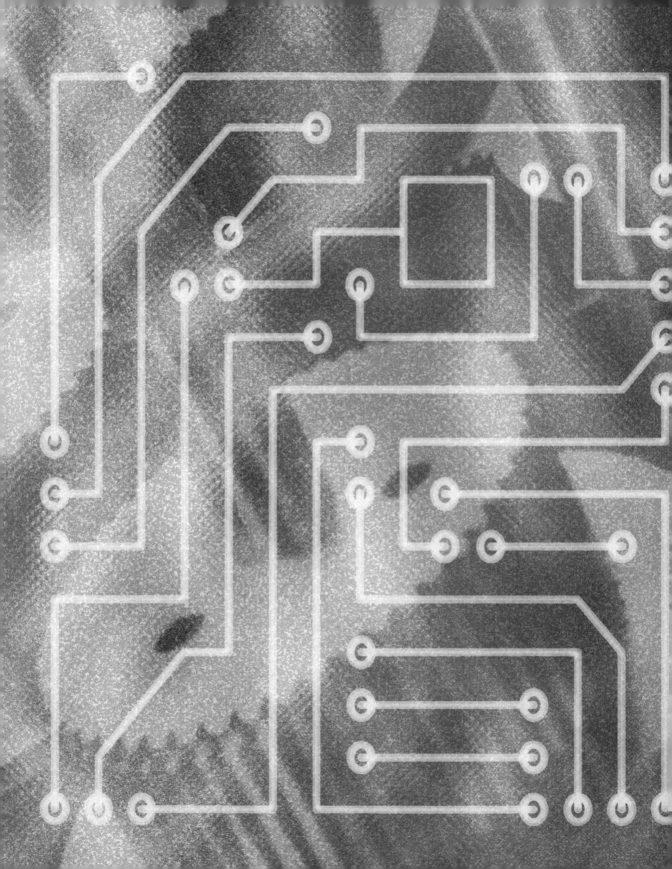

C

A+ Certification Training Centers

- United States
- Australia
- Canada
- United Kingdom

This book provides you with all the information covered by the questions of the A+ Certification Windows/DOS exam. There is no substitute, however, to hands-on training to make a concept "stick." The companies listed in this appendix are those that provide A+ Certification training. Many of these programs will not only increase your chances of passing the test, but will give you some experience in the practical matters of PC repair, as a number of them offer hands-on programs. This list is current as of the time of writing of this book. For an updated list, visit the CompTIA website at http://www.comptia.org/.

The training centers are listed by country, then by state or province. Each listing gives the type of training the center offers. The appendix includes listings for the following countries:

- United States
- Australia
- Canada
- United Kingdom

United States

Arizona

MindWorks Professional Education
1525 N. Hayden Road Suite F-7
Scottsdale, AZ 85257
(800) 874-1516
www.mindwork.com
Training Locations: AZ, MI, NC, OK
• Self-study materials
• Classroom-based courses

California

Aerotek Data Services Group
2299 Perimeter Park Drive, Suite 140
Atlanta, GA 30341
(800) 733-9783
www.aerotek.com/dataservices
Training Locations: CA, FL, GA, IL, MD, NY, TX

DataTrain Institute
301 Madison Ave., 5th Flr.
New York, NY 10017
(800) U-DATATRAIN or
(800) 832-8287
Fax (212) 286-9596
Training Locations: CA, GA,Washington DC, MD, NJ, NY, PA, UK
• Customized training programs, classroom-based
• Self-study, computer-based

Executive 2000
3800 Parkview Lane
Suite 16D
Irvine, CA 92612
(714) 552-3387
Fax (714) 552-4931
• Comprehensive, hands-on training

Graymark Int'l
P.O. Box 2015
Tustin, CA 92681
(714) 544-1414
www.labvolt.com
• Classroom-based courses
• Self-study kits

Ingram Micro Tech Education
1600 E. St. Andrews Place
P.O. Box 25125
Santa Ana, CA 92799-5125
(800) 234-9220
Training Locations: CA, IL
• Classroom-based courses
• Self-study materials

Learning Tree Int'l
6053 W. Century Blvd.
Suite 200
Los Angeles, CA 90045
(800) 843-8733
• Classroom-based courses

Irvine Valley College
Joyce Amston
5500 Irvine Ctr. Dr.
Irvine, CA 92720
Fax (714) 559-4328

Simi Valley Adult School
Kerry O. Selway
3192 Los Angeles Ave.
Simi Valley, CA 93065
(805) 579-6200
Fax (805) 522-8902

Training Directions College
David Koenig
6920 Mirmar Rd., Suite 309
San Diego, CA 92121
(619) 695-2755
Fax (619) 695-2756

Total Seminars, LLC
10733 Gulf Freeway
Houston, TX 77034
(800) 446-6004 or
(713) 943-3888
Fax (713) 943-8550
www.totalsem.com
Training Locations: NY, PA, NJ, DC,
MD, VA, NC, IL, WI, MI, IN, OH,
CA, TX, MO, FL, GA
• Classroom-based courses

Wave Technologies
10845 Olive Blvd., Suite 250
St. Louis, MO 63141-7777
(800) 828-2050 or (314) 995-5767
www.wavetech.com
Training Locations: GA, MA, IL, TX,
CA (San Jose, West LA), MN, NY,
PA, VA, UK, Australia
• Classroom-based courses
• Self-study and computer-based
materials

West Valley College
Pat Senton
14000 Fruit Vail Ave.
Saratoga, CA 95070
(408) 741-2433
Fax (408) 741-2127

Colorado

Micro House International
2477 55th St., Suite 101
Boulder, CO 80301
(800) 473-4595 ext. 3028
Fax (303) 443-3323

Streamlined Systems
1516 1/2 Mesa Ave
Colorado Springs, CO 80906
(719) 471-3836
Fax (719) 471-3837

Florida

CHS/Merisel Latin America, Inc.
1629 N.W. 84th Ave.
Miami, FL 33126
(305) 718-2590
Fax (305) 718-2599
• Classroom-based courses
• Disk-based practice tests

Forefront Direct
25400 US Highway 19N
Suite 285
Clearwater, FL 34623
(800) 653-4933
Fax (813) 726-6922
www.ffg.com/banners/ctia1/
• Computer-based self-study kit

Total Seminars, LLC
10733 Gulf Freeway
Houston, TX 77034
(800) 446-6004 or
(713) 943-3888
Fax (713) 943-8550
www.totalsem.com
Training Locations: NY, PA, NJ, DC,
MD, VA, NC, IL, WI, MI, IN, OH,
CA, TX, MO, FL, GA
• Classroom-based courses

Georgia

Aerotek Data Services Group
2299 Perimeter Park Drive, Suite 140
Atlanta, GA 30341
(800) 733-9783
www.aerotek.com/dataservices
Training Locations: CA, FL, GA, IL,
MD, NY, TX

Chattahoochee Technical Institute
980 S. Cobb Drive
Marietta, GA 30060
(770) 528-4524
www.chat-tec.com/coned/home.html
• Classroom-based courses

DataTrain Institute
301 Madison Ave., 5th Flr.
New York, NY 10017
(800) U-DATATRAIN or
(800) 832-8287
Fax (212) 286-9596
Training Locations: CA, GA, Washington DC, MD, NJ, NY, PA, UK
• Customized training programs, classroom-based
• Self-study, computer-based

IBM Education Company
3100 Windy Hill Road
Marietta, GA 30067
(800) IBM-TEACH, Ext. 999
Scranton, PA 18515
• Self-study kit, self-study text, disk-based practice test

Self Test Software
4651 Woodstock
Suite 203, M/S 281
Roswell, GA 30075-1686
(800) 200-6446
US/Canada (800) 200-6446
Europe 31-348-484646
Pac Rim 61-2-320-5497
• Disk-based practice test

Total Seminars, LLC
10733 Gulf Freeway
Houston, TX 77034
(800) 446-6004 or
(713) 943-3888
Fax (713) 943-8550
www.totalsem.com
Training Locations: NY, PA, NJ, DC, MD, VA, NC, IL, WI, MI, IN, OH, CA, TX, MO, FL, GA
• Classroom-based courses

Wave Technologies
10845 Olive Blvd., Suite 250
St. Louis, MO 63141-7777
(800) 828-2050 or (314) 995-5767
www.wavetech.com
Training Locations: GA, MA, IL, TX, CA (San Jose, West LA), MN, NY, PA, VA, UK, Australia
• Classroom-based courses
• Self-study and computer-based materials

Idaho

Boise State University Outreach Programs
Dian Batt
2407 Caldwell Blvd.
Nampa, ID 83651
(208) 467-5707
Fax (208) 466-2933

Illinois

Aerotek Data Services Group
2299 Perimeter Park Drive, Suite 140
Atlanta, GA 30341
(800) 733-9783
www.aerotek.com/dataservices
Training Locations: CA, FL, GA, IL,
MD, NY, TX

Ingram Micro Tech Education
1600 E. St. Andrews Place
P.O. Box 25125
Santa Ana, CA 92799-5125
(800) 234-9220
Training Locations: CA, IL
• Classroom-based courses
• Self-study materials

PCDC
401 Tomahawk Drive
Maumee, OH 43537
Phone: (419) 891-9700
(800) 322-7232
Fax (419) 891-9702
Training Locations: IL, IN, MI,
OH, PA
• Classroom-based; hands-on

Total Seminars, LLC
10733 Gulf Freeway
Houston, TX 77034
(800) 446-6004 or
(713) 943-3888
Fax (713) 943-8550
www.totalsem.com
Training Locations: NY, PA, NJ, DC,
MD, VA, NC, IL, WI, MI, IN, OH,
CA, TX, MO, FL, GA
• Classroom-based courses

Triton College
Richard J. Zoladz
Electronics/PC Maintenance Inst.
2000 5th Ave.
River Grove, IL 60171-1995
(708) 456-0300
Fax (708) 583-3105

Wave Technologies
10845 Olive Blvd., Suite 250
St. Louis, MO 63141-7777
(800) 828-2050 or (314) 995-5767
www.wavetech.com
Training Locations: GA, MA, IL, TX,
CA (San Jose, West LA), MN, NY,
PA, VA, UK, Australia
• Classroom-based courses
• Self-study and computer-based
materials

Indiana

PCDC
401 Tomahawk Drive
Maumee, OH 43537
Phone: (419) 891-9700
(800) 322-7232
Fax (419) 891-9702
Training Locations: IL, IN, MI,
OH, PA
• Classroom-based, hands-on

Total Seminars, LLC
10733 Gulf Freeway
Houston, TX 77034
(800) 446-6004 or
(713) 943-3888
Fax (713) 943-8550
www.totalsem.com
Training Locations: NY, PA, NJ, DC,
MD, VA, NC, IL, WI, MI, IN, OH,
CA, TX, MO, FL, GA
• Classroom-based courses

Louisiana

Nunez Community College
3700 LaFontaine St.
Chalmette, LA 70043
(504) 278-7440
Fax (504) 278-7463

Maryland

Aerotek Data Services Group
2299 Perimeter Park Drive, Suite 140
Atlanta, GA 30341
(800) 733-9783
www.aerotek.com/dataservices
Training Locations: CA, FL, GA, IL,
MD, NY, TX

DataTrain Institute
301 Madison Ave., 5th Flr.
New York, NY 10017
(800) U-DATATRAIN or
(800) 832-8287
Fax (212) 286-9596
Training Locations: CA, GA,Wash-
ington DC, MD, NJ, NY, PA, UK
• Customized training programs,
classroom-based
• Self-study, computer-based

Howard Community College
Vinitha Nithianandam
109001 Little Patuxent Parkway
Columbia, MD 21044
(410) 992-4800
Fax (410) 992-4822

SHL Key Systems
1 Mall North
10025 Govenor Warfield Pkwy. #400
Columbia, MD 21044
(401) 715-8652
• Classroom-based courses

Total Seminars, LLC
10733 Gulf Freeway
Houston, TX 77034
(800) 446-6004 or
(713) 943-3888
Fax (713) 943-8550
www.totalsem.com
Training Locations: NY, PA, NJ, DC,
MD, VA, NC, IL, WI, MI, IN, OH,
CA, TX, MO, FL, GA
• Classroom-based courses

Massachusetts

Boston University
Sales Department
72 Tying Road
Tyngsboro, MA 01879
(508) 649-9731
Fax (508) 649-6926

Newbury College
129 Fisher Avenue
Brookline, MA 02146
(617) 738-2467
Fax (617) 730-7208

Wave Technologies
10845 Olive Blvd., Suite 250
St. Louis, MO 63141-7777
(800) 828-2050 or (314) 995-5767
www.wavetech.com
Training Locations: GA, MA, IL, TX,
CA (San Jose, West LA), MN, NY,
PA, VA, UK, Australia
• Classroom-based courses
• Self-study and computer-based
materials

Michigan

Heathkit Educational Systems
455 Riverview Dr.
P.O. Box 1288
Benton Harbor, MI 49022
(800) 253-0570
www.heathkit.com
• Self-study kit

MindWorks Professional Education
1525 N. Hayden Road Suite F-7
Scottsdale, AZ 85257
(800) 874-1516
www.mindwork.com
Training Locations: AZ, MI, NC, OK
• Self-study materials
• Classroom-based courses

PCDC
401 Tomahawk Drive
Maumee, OH 43537
Phone: (419) 891-9700
(800) 322-7232
Fax (419) 891-9702
Training Locations: IL, IN, MI,
OH, PA
• Classroom-based, hands-on

Total Seminars, LLC
10733 Gulf Freeway
Houston, TX 77034
(800) 446-6004 or
(713) 943-3888
Fax (713) 943-8550
www.totalsem.com
Training Locations: NY, PA, NJ, DC,
MD, VA, NC, IL, WI, MI, IN, OH,
CA, TX, MO, FL, GA
• Classroom-based courses

Minnesota

Wave Technologies
10845 Olive Blvd., Suite 250
St. Louis, MO 63141-7777
(800) 828-2050 or (314) 995-5767
www.wavetech.com
Training Locations: GA, MA, IL, TX,
CA (San Jose, West LA), MN, NY,
PA, VA, UK, Australia
• Classroom-based courses
• Self-study and computer-based
materials

Missouri

Total Seminars, LLC
10733 Gulf Freeway
Houston, TX 77034
(800) 446-6004 or
(713) 943-3888
Fax (713) 943-8550
www.totalsem.com
Training Locations: NY, PA, NJ, DC,
MD, VA, NC, IL, WI, MI, IN, OH,
CA, TX, MO, FL, GA
• Classroom-based courses

New Jersey

DataTrain Institute
301 Madison Ave., 5th Flr.
New York, NY 10017
(800) U-DATATRAIN or
(800) 832-8287
Fax (212) 286-9596
Training Locations: CA, GA,Wash-
ington DC, MD, NJ, NY, PA, UK
• Customized training programs,
classroom-based
• Self-study, computer-based

**MicroAge Meadowlands Learning
Center, Inc.**
187 East Union Ave.
East Rutherford, NJ 07073
Phone: (201) 935-4100
Fax (201) 935-8785
• Classroom-based

Total Seminars, LLC
10733 Gulf Freeway
Houston, TX 77034
(800) 446-6004 or
(713) 943-3888
Fax (713) 943-8550
www.totalsem.com
Training Locations: NY, PA, NJ, DC,
MD, VA, NC, IL, WI, MI, IN, OH,
CA, TX, MO, FL, GA
• Classroom-based courses

New York

A+ Learning Center
27 West 34th Street
New York, NY 10001
(212) 563-6241
Fax (212) 279-6215
• Classroom-based courses

Aerotek Data Services Group
2299 Perimeter Park Drive, Suite 140
Atlanta, GA 30341
(800) 733-9783
www.aerotek.com/dataservices
Training Locations: CA, FL, GA, IL,
MD, NY, TX

American Institute
708 Third Ave.
New York, NY 10017
(212) 661-3500
• Classroom-based courses
• Self-study kits

Corning Community College
George Gifford
1 Academic Dr.
Corning, NY 14830
(607) 962-9011
Fax (607) 962-9537

DataTrain Institute
301 Madison Ave., 5th Flr.
New York, NY 10017
(800) U-DATATRAIN or
(800) 832-8287
Fax (212) 286-9596
Training Locations: CA, GA, Washington DC, MD, NJ, NY, PA, UK
• Customized training programs,
classroom-based
• Self-study, computer-based

Long Island University
Ian Fisher
Brooklyn Campus
Brooklyn, NY 11201-5372
(718) 488-1359
Fax (718) 780-4052

Total Seminars, LLC
10733 Gulf Freeway
Houston, TX 77034
(800) 446-6004 or
(713) 943-3888
Fax (713) 943-8550
www.totalsem.com
Training Locations: NY, PA, NJ, DC,
MD, VA, NC, IL, WI, MI, IN, OH,
CA, TX, MO, FL, GA
• Classroom-based courses

Wave Technologies
10845 Olive Blvd., Suite 250
St. Louis, MO 63141-7777
(800) 828-2050 or (314) 995-5767
www.wavetech.com
Training Locations: GA, MA, IL, TX,
CA (San Jose, West LA), MN, NY,
PA, VA, UK, Australia
• Classroom-based courses
• Self-study and computer-based
materials

Xincon Technologiess
875 6th Ave., #401
New York, NY 10001
Phone: (212) 465-8633
Fax (212) 947-0285
• Classroom-based courses
• Self-study courses

North Carolina

MindWorks Professional Education
1525 N. Hayden Road Suite F-7
Scottsdale, AZ 85257
(800) 874-1516
www.mindwork.com
Training Locations: AZ, MI, NC, OK

The Computer Lab
2700 Gateway Center, Suite 300
Morrisville, NC 27560
(919) 319-9999
Fax (919) 319-9134

Total Seminars, LLC
10733 Gulf Freeway
Houston, TX 77034
(800) 446-6004 or
(713) 943-3888
Fax (713) 943-8550
www.totalsem.com
Training Locations: NY, PA, NJ, DC,
MD, VA, NC, IL, WI, MI, IN, OH,
CA, TX, MO, FL, GA
• Classroom-based courses

**Wake Technical Community
College**
Witold Sieradzan
9101 Fayetteville Rd.
Raleigh, NC 27603
(919) 662-3400

North Dakota

Corporate Technologies
1700 42nd Street S.
Fargo, ND 58103
(701) 277-0011
Fax (701) 277-0012
www.corptechnologies.com
• Comprehensive, classroom-based courses

Ohio

PCDC
401 Tomahawk Drive
Maumee, OH 43537
Phone: (419) 891-9700
(800) 322-7232
Fax (419) 891-9702
Training Locations: IL, IN, MI, OH, PA
• Classroom-based, hands-on

Total Seminars, LLC
10733 Gulf Freeway
Houston, TX 77034
(800) 446-6004 or
(713) 943-3888
Fax (713) 943-8550
www.totalsem.com
Training Locations: NY, PA, NJ, DC, MD, VA, NC, IL, WI, MI, IN, OH, CA, TX, MO, FL, GA
• Classroom-based courses

Oklahoma

Central Oklahoma Area Vo-Tech
Janice Hermanski
1720 S. Main
Sapula, OK 74066
(918) 227-0331
Fax (918) 224-0744

MindWorks Professional Education
1525 N. Hayden Road Suite F-7
Scottsdale, AZ 85257
(800) 874-1516
www.mindwork.com
Training Locations: AZ, MI, NC, OK
• Self-study materials, classroom-based courses

Pioneer Technology Center
Frank J. Vascellaro
2101 N. Ash St.
Ponca City, OK 74601

Wes Watkins Area Vo-Tech Center
Frank Alexander
Rt. 2 Box 159-1
Wetumka, OK 74883
(405) 452-5500
Fax (405) 452-3561

Pennsylvania

DataTrain Institute
301 Madison Ave., 5th Flr.
New York, NY 10017
(800) U-DATATRAIN or
(800) 832-8287
Fax (212) 286-9596
Training Locations: CA, GA,Washington DC, MD, NJ, NY, PA, UK
• Customized training programs, classroom-based
• Self-study, computer-based

IBM Education Company
3100 Windy Hill Road
Marietta, GA 30067
(800) IBM-TEACH, Ext. 999
Scranton, PA 18515
• Self-study kit, self-study text, disk-based practice test

PCDC
401 Tomahawk Drive
Maumee, OH 43537
Phone: (419) 891-9700
(800) 322-7232
Fax (419) 891-9702
Training Locations: IL, IN, MI, OH, PA
• Classroom-based, hands-on

Total Seminars, LLC
10733 Gulf Freeway
Houston, TX 77034
(800) 446-6004 or
(713) 943-3888
Fax (713) 943-8550
www.totalsem.com
Training Locations: NY, PA, NJ, DC, MD, VA, NC, IL, WI, MI, IN, OH, CA, TX, MO, FL, GA
• Classroom-based courses

Wave Technologies
10845 Olive Blvd., Suite 250
St. Louis, MO 63141-7777
(800) 828-2050 or (314) 995-5767
www.wavetech.com
Training Locations: GA, MA, IL, TX, CA (San Jose, West LA), MN, NY, PA, VA, UK, Australia
• Classroom-based courses
• Self-study and computer-based materials

Texas

Aerotek Data Services Group
2299 Perimeter Park Drive, Suite 140
Atlanta, GA 30341
(800) 733-9783
www.aerotek.com/dataservices
Training Locations: CA, FL, GA, IL, MD, NY, TX

Total Seminars, LLC
10733 Gulf Freeway
Houston, TX 77034
(800) 446-6004 or
(713) 943-3888
Fax (713) 943-8550
www.totalsem.com
Training Locations: NY, PA, NJ, DC, MD, VA, NC, IL, WI, MI, IN, OH, CA, TX, MO, FL, GA
• Classroom-based courses

Wave Technologies
10845 Olive Blvd., Suite 250
St. Louis, MO 63141-7777
(800) 828-2050 or (314) 995-5767
www.wavetech.com
Training Locations: GA, MA, IL, TX, CA (San Jose, West LA), MN, NY, PA, VA, UK, Australia
• Classroom-based courses
• Self-study and computer-based materials

Virginia

Computer Dynamics Institute
5361 Virginia Beach Blvd.
Virginia Beach, VA 23462
(804) 499-4900
• Classroom-based courses

Systems Coordinators, Inc.
11260 Roger Bacon Dr.
Suite 100
Reston, VA 22090
(703) 437-6714
www.syscoord.com
• Classroom-based courses
• Disk-based practice test

Total Seminars, LLC
10733 Gulf Freeway
Houston, TX 77034
(800) 446-6004 or
(713) 943-3888
Fax (713) 943-8550
www.totalsem.com
Training Locations: NY, PA, NJ, DC, MD, VA, NC, IL, WI, MI, IN, OH, CA, TX, MO, FL, GA
• Classroom-based courses

Wave Technologies
10845 Olive Blvd., Suite 250
St. Louis, MO 63141-7777
(800) 828-2050 or (314) 995-5767
www.wavetech.com
Training Locations: GA, MA, IL, TX, CA (San Jose, West LA), MN, NY, PA, VA, UK, Australia
• Classroom-based courses
• Self-study and computer-based materials

Washington

Marcraft International Corp.
P.O. Box 2694
1620 E. Hillsboro St.
Pasco, WA 99302
(509) 547-0030
• Classroom-based courses
• Self-study and computer-based
materials

Washington D.C.

DataTrain Institute
301 Madison Ave., 5th Flr.
New York, NY 10017
(800) U-DATATRAIN or
(800) 832-8287
Fax (212) 286-9596
Training Locations: CA, GA,Wash-
ington DC, MD, NJ, NY, PA, UK
• Customized training programs,
classroom-based
• Self-study, computer-based

Total Seminars, LLC
10733 Gulf Freeway
Houston, TX 77034
(800) 446-6004 or
(713) 943-3888
Fax (713) 943-8550
www.totalsem.com
Training Locations: NY, PA, NJ, DC,
MD, VA, NC, IL, WI, MI, IN, OH,
CA, TX, MO, FL, GA
• Classroom-based courses

Wisconsin

Total Seminars, LLC
10733 Gulf Freeway
Houston, TX 77034
(800) 446-6004 or
(713) 943-3888
Fax (713) 943-8550
www.totalsem.com
Training Locations: NY, PA, NJ, DC,
MD, VA, NC, IL, WI, MI, IN, OH,
CA, TX, MO, FL, GA
• Classroom-based courses

**Waukesha County Technical
College**
Tom Biddick
800 Main St.
Pewaukee, WI 53072
(414) 691-5354
Fax (414) 691-5499

Australia

Wave Technologies
10845 Olive Blvd., Suite 250
St. Louis, MO 63141-7777
(800) 828-2050 or (314) 995-5767
www.wavetech.com
Training Locations: GA, MA, IL, TX,
CA (San Jose, West LA), MN, NY,
PA, VA, UK, Australia
• Classroom-based courses
• Self-study and computer-based
materials

Canada

Ontario

**Applied Information Management
Services Inc.**
5353 Dundas Street West, Suite 500
Etobicote, Ontario M9B 6H8
(416) 234-2227
Fax (416) 234-2231

Indus Systems
2240 Midland Ave.
Suite 203
Scarbourgh, Ontario MIP 4R8
(416) 754-0499
Fax (416) 754-0754
• Classroom-based courses

The Permond Solutions Group
90 Matheson Blvd., West
Mississauga, Ontario L5R 3R3,
Canada
(905) 712-3434
• Classroom-based courses
(405) 762-8336
Fax (405) 762-3107

United Kingdom

DataTrain Institute
301 Madison Ave., 5th Flr.
New York, NY 10017
(800) U-DATATRAIN or
(800) 832-8287
Fax (212) 286-9596
Training Locations: CA, GA, Washington DC, MD, NJ, NY, PA, UK
• Customized training programs,
classroom-based
• Self-study, computer-based

Wave Technologies
www.wavetech.com
Training Location: Surrey, England
• Classroom-based courses
• Self-study and computer-based
materials

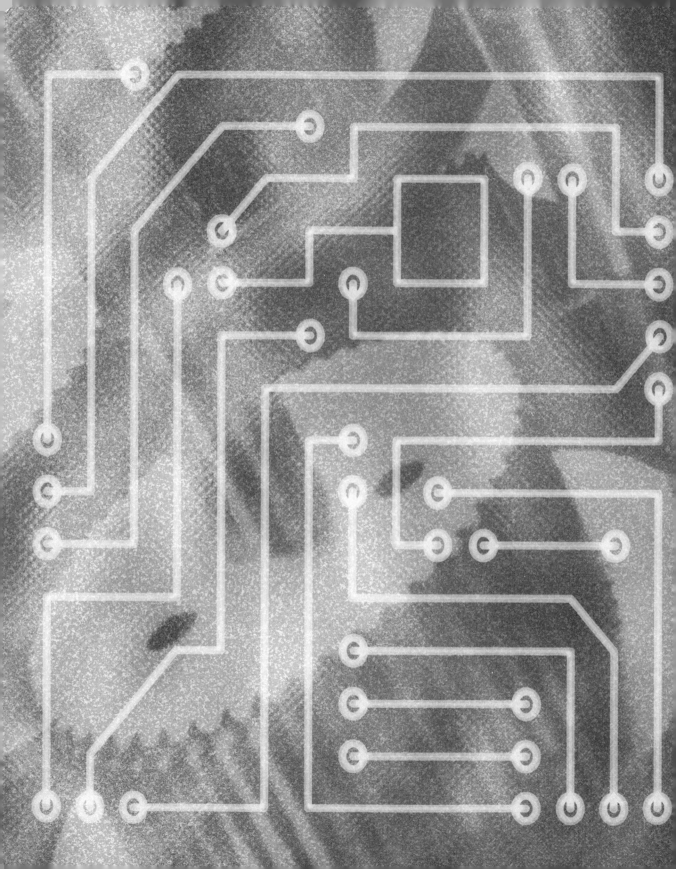

Computer Service Information Website Directory

- Computer Hardware Vendors

- Computer Software Vendors

- Third-Party Technical Support

Within this appendix are several tables of URLs for service information that can be found on the Internet (specifically, on the World Wide Web). Most of the URLs listed point to the companies' support websites. Where a support page was unavailable, we give the URL of the company's home page, where you can at least get an idea of how to contact the company for questions about their products or services.

In this appendix, we offer URLs for the following selected websites:

- Computer Hardware Vendors
- Computer Software Vendors
- Third-Party Technical Support

Computer Hardware

Table D.1 is a listing of the service and support websites of some of the most popular computer hardware vendors. While this is not a comprehensive list, it includes most of the important manufacturers that have useful websites as of this writing.

TABLE D.1: Major Hardware Vendor Support Sites

Company	Address
3Dfx	http://www.3dfx.com/download/
Acer	http://www.aceramerica.com/aac/support/index.htm
Advanced Logic Research (ALR)	http://www.alr.com/service/service.htm
Apple	http://support.info.apple.com/tso/tsohome/tso-home.html
AST	http://www.ast.com/support/support.htm
ATI	http://support.atitech.ca/

TABLE D.1 (CONTINUED): Major Hardware Vendor Support Sites

Company	Address
Boca Research	http://www.bocaresearch.com/support/
Creative Labs (*Soundblaster multi-media equipment*)	http://www-nt-ok.creaf.com/wwwnew/tech/support/support.html
CTX	http://www.ctxintl.com/techsup.htm
Diamond Multimedia	http://207.1.65.7/vweb/
Digital Equipment Corp.	http://www.dec.com/info/services/mcs/mcs_hardware.htm
DTK	http://www.dtkcomputer.com/tech.html
Epson	http://www.epson.com/connects/
ESS Technology	http://www.esstech.com/
Fujitsu	http://www.8fujitsu.com/
Gateway 2000	http://www.gw2k.com/corp/support/cs_techdocs/
Hayes	http://www.hayes.com/support/index.htm
Hewlett-Packard (HP)	http://hpcc923.external.hp.com/wcso-support/Services/services.html
IBM	http://www.ibm.com/Support/
Leading Edge	http://www.primenet.com/~fwagner/le/
Logitech	http://support.logitech.com/support.nsf/support?OpenView
Matrox	http://www.matrox.com/mgaweb/techsupp/ftp.htm
Media Vision	http://www.svtus.com/new/new.html
Megahertz	http://www.mhz.com/intransit/support/index.html
Micron	http://www.micronpc.com/support/support.html
Midwest Micro	http://www.mwmicro.com/support/
Multi-Tech	http://www.multitech.com/servsupp.htp

TABLE D.1 (CONTINUED): Major Hardware Vendor Support Sites

Company	Address
NCR	http://www.ncr.com/support/
NEC	http://www.nec.com/support.html
Okidata	http://www.okidata.com/services/
Packard Bell	http://support.packardbell.com/
Panasonic	http://www.panasonic.com/host/support/index.html
PNY Technologies	http://www.pny.com/Tech/index.stm
Power Computing	http://support.powercc.com/service.html
Practical Peripherals	http://www.practinet.com/support.htm
Quantum	http://support.quantum.com/
S3	http://www.s3.com/bbs/0main/topindex.htm
Samsung	http://www.sec.samsung.co.kr/Support/support.html
Seagate	http://www.seagate.com/support/supporttop.shtml
Sony	http://www.ita.sel.sony.com/support/
SUN Microsystems	http://www.sun.com/service/
Supermac	http://www.supermac.com/service/index.html
Toshiba	http://www.toshiba.com/tais/csd/support/
US Robotics	http://infodeli.3com.com/
Viking Components	http://www.vikingmem.com/support/index.html
VisionTek	http://www.visiontek.com/htdocs/services/support.html
Western Digital	http://www.wdc.com/support/
Zenith Data Systems	http://support.zds.com/default.asp

Computer Software

In addition to hardware vendors, we have compiled a list of some of the major software vendors (Table D.2). Again, it's not a comprehensive list, but should be useful for getting you the information you need.

TABLE D.2: Major Software Vendor Support Sites

Company	Address
Adobe	http://www.adobe.com/supportservice/main.html
Caldera	http://www.caldera.com/tech-ref/
Claris	http://www.claris.com/support/support.html
Corel	http://www.corel.com/support/index.htm
Lotus	http://www.support.lotus.com/
Microsoft	http://www.microsoft.com/support/
Netscape	http://home.netscape.com/comprod/products/support_programs/index.html
Novell	http://support.novell.com/

Other Technical Support Information

Of course, there are all sorts of sources for technical support information besides the websites of the vendors. In this table (Table D.3), we provide the URLs for some useful websites that are run, not by vendors, but by informed third parties.

TABLE D.3: Other Technical Support Sites

Description	Address
HealthyPC.com *Offers computing advice columns and software patch downloads*	http://www.zdnet.com/hpc/
HelpMeNow.com *A free technical support forum and chat area*	http://www.HelpMeNow.com/
CMP Techweb *An e-zine for all aspects of the technical support industry. Check out the encyclopedia for a definition of almost any technical term.*	http://www.techweb.com/
PC Week *The magazine's website. Great for information on PC developments. Also, you can download the Ziff-Davis benchmarking utilities.*	http://www.pcweek.com/
Help Desk Institute *Great source of help desk resources*	http://www.HelpDeskInst.com/
The Computer Technology Industry Association *Information on computer resources as well as information on the A+ certification*	http://www.comptia.org/
Ask a Geek *('nuf said?)*	http://www.flash.net/~cge/java/ask.htm
Software.net *A vendor directory that lists vendors offering technical support information*	http://www.software.net/directory.htm
Software Support Professionals Association *Provides support professionals a place to chat and exchange support information*	http://www.sspa-online.com/
The Technical Support Nightmare *A humorous look at technical support*	http://www.geocities.com/SiliconValley/Vista/9426/
Scott's page o' Computer Literacy *Another technical support humor page*	http://www.center-net.com/8888/
Association of Support Professionals *Another professional support organization*	http://www.asponline.com/
SupportHelp.com *A database of technical support websites, addresses, phone numbers, and other support resources*	http://www.supporthelp.com/

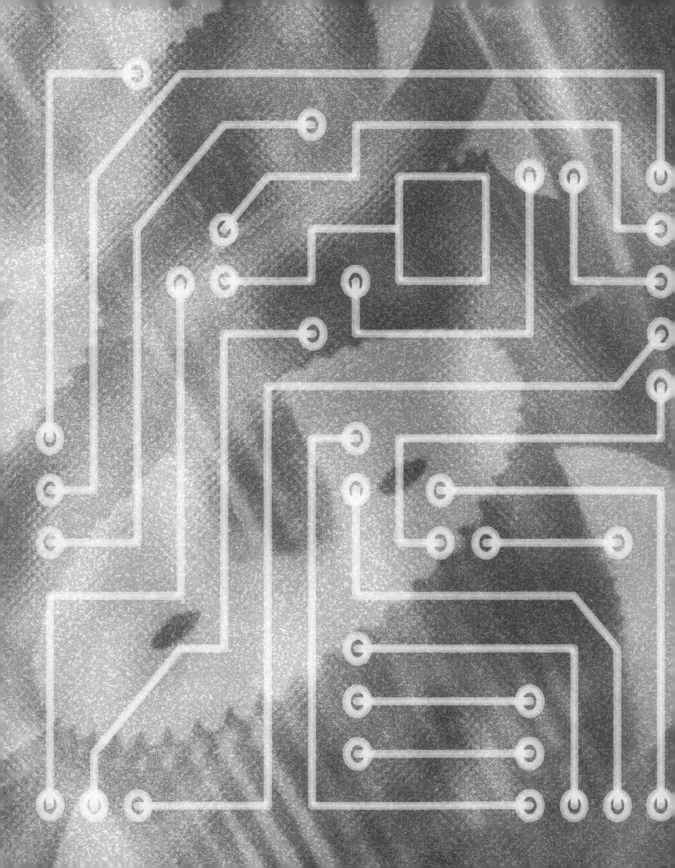

APPENDIX

E

Windows/DOS Glossary

A

active partition

The DOS partition which will be read at startup and will be expected to have the necessary system files on it to boot the computer.

Add/remove windows components

Windows 95 option that brings up a window which allows you to change which optional components are installed on the system.

Alpha release

The release of software that is intended only for testing within the software company itself and may not include all the features that are intended to be included in the eventual release.

archive

Attribute used to mark files that have been modified since they were last backed up. It is set with the DOS ATTRIB command.

ATTRIB

Command used to alter a file's attributes.

attribute

Unique properties of a DOS file that are altered using an external DOS command called ATTRIB.

B

BACKUP

Program that is used to back up a small amount of data on a floppy disk.

batch file

File with a .BAT extension that contains other DOS commands. Simply by typing the name of the batch file and pressing ENTER, DOS will process all of the batch file commands, one at a time, without need for any additional user input.

beta release

The release of a piece of software that is given to a select group of testers. The software has 95% of its functionality and usually only needs a few bug fixes to be a full, released version of software

BIOS (Basic Input /Output System)

The ROM-based software on a motherboard that acts as a kind of "interpreter" between an operating system and a computer's hardware.

Boolean Logic

A type of math where the operators are represented by English words (i.e., AND, NOT, BUT, OR). The result of any Boolean equation is usually TRUE or FALSE. This type of logic is often used in DOS batch files to allow for some branching.

boot disk

A diskette which allows the technician to load a limited version of DOS and then do troubleshooting and configuration tasks on the PC.

booting

Term used for starting up a computer and loading the operating system into memory.

BUFFERS

CONFIG.SYS command that determines the number of buffers DOS creates so that it can store cache information in RAM before it stores it on disk.

C

cache "hit"

Indicates that the requested information was found in the cache.

cache miss

Indicates that the system did not find required data in the cache, which necessitated a disk read.

CALL

Batch file command that executes the commands in another batch file and returns control back to the batch file that "CALLed" it.

Central Point Backup

The disk backup program that is included with PC-DOS.

CHDIR (CD)

Internal command that is used to change the current or default directory.

CHKDSK.EXE

Program that provides information about the size of the disk as well as how many bytes are left on the disk.

"Cold boot"

The process of rebooting the computer by turning off and on the power switch.

COMMAND.COM

Takes commands issued by the user through text strings or click actions and translates them back into calls that can be understood by the lower layers of DOS. It is the vital command interpreter for DOS. See also *Command interpreter.*

Command Interpreter

The primary vehicle used by DOS that allows the user to communicate with the computer and vice-versa.

CONTROL.INI

File that contains all the colors, patterns, and color schemes that Windows can use.

control panel

The Windows component that allows a user to customize the look and operation of Windows.

command-line execution parameters

Parameters that are passed to the batch file or program from its command line.

conditional statement

A statement (usually in a program or batch file) that performs an operation based on some condition (usually a Boolean logic statement like IF *<some condition>* IS TRUE THEN *<do operation>*).

CONFIG.SYS

The DOS system file that controls hardware configuration and general system environment parameters.

contiguous memory

Memory occurring in a single, continuous block.

COPY

Internal DOS command which is used to copy files from location to location.

current path

Refers to the order in which COMMAND.COM searches specified subdirectories for programs typed in and entered at the command prompt.

D

DBR (DOS Boot Record)

The area on a hard disk that contains the MS-DOS system files. This area contains MS-DOS startup files and configuration files.

disk-caching program

A program that reads the most commonly accessed data from disk and keeps it in memory for faster access.

DEL

Internal command contained within COMMAND.COM that is used to delete files from a disk.

Desktop

Contains the visible elements of Windows, and defines the limits of graphic environment.

Desktop Control Panel

Windows panel that is used to configure the system so that is it more easily usable. This control panel contains the settings for the background color and pattern as well as screen saver settings.

DEVICE=

Command found in the DOS CONFIG.SYS that tells DOS which driver to find and load into memory at boot time.

device fonts

Windows fonts that print the fastest because the printer has the routines to "draw" those fonts inside the printer.

DEVICEHIGH=

Command that is used to load the device drivers into Upper Memory Blocks, therefore freeing up space in conventional memory.

differential backup

Backs up files that have changed since the last full backup.

DIR (directory)

An internal command contained within COMMAND.COM. DIR is the principal means by which you examine the contents of your computer's storage media.

DOS Environment Variables

Variables that specify global things like the PATH that DOS searches to find executables.

DoubleSpace

DOS Program that allows for doubling of disk space through disk compression.

Dynamic Link Library (DLL) files

Windows component files that contain small pieces of executable code that are shared between multiple Windows programs. They are used to eliminate redundant programming in certain Windows applications.

E

EDIT

Command in MS-DOS that invokes the MS-DOS Editor which is used to create new text files or modify existing text files.

EMM386.EXE

Reserved memory manager that emulates Expanded Memory in the Extended Memory area (XMS) and provides DOS with the ability to utilize upper memory blocks to load programs and device drivers.

ERASE

See DEL

Extended Memory (XMS)

Memory above 1,024 KB that is used by Windows and Windows-based programs. This type of memory cannot be accessed unless the HIMEM.SYS memory manager is loaded in the DOS CONFIG.SYS with a line like DEVICE=HIMEM.SYS.

extended partition

The type of DOS partition that can be created after the primary partition. It is the only other partition allowed on a disk once the primary partition has been made using FDISK.

extensions

Defines the file's type and function. Extensions are the 1, 2, or 3 characters which appear after the dot in a DOS filename.

external commands

Commands that are not contained within COMMAND.COM. They are represented by a .COM or .EXE extension.

F

FORMAT.COM

External DOS command that prepares the partition to store information using the FAT system as required by DOS.

FAT (File Allocation Table)

A special file located on a DOS-formatted disk that specifies where each DOS file is located on the disk.

FDISK.EXE

The DOS utility that is used to partition hard disks for use with DOS.

File manager

Windows utility that allows the user to accomplish a number of important file-related tasks from a single interface (e.g., copying files, making directories, moving files, and deleting files and directories).

FILES=

CONFIG.SYS command that describes how many file handles DOS can keep track of at one time.

font files

Windows files that specify the different typefaces that can be used to display letters.

formatting

The act of preparing a disk for DOS and creating the DOS File Allocation Table (FAT) so the DOS can place and retrieve files on the disk.

fragmentation

A disk storage problem that exists after several smaller files have been deleted from a hard disk. The deletion of files leaves the disk with areas of free disk space scattered throughout the disk. The fact that these areas of disk space are located so far apart on the disk causes slower performance because the disk read/write heads have to move all around the disk's surface to find the pieces of one file.

full backup

A method of backup that backs up all the files on a disk.

G

GDI.EXE

Windows core component that is responsible for drawing icons and windows in Windows 3.*x*.

General Protection Fault

A Windows error that typically occurs when a Windows program tries to access memory currently in use by another program.

GOTO

Batch file command that allows a batch file execution to "branch." The execution of a batch file starts at the top of the file and executes one line at a time until it reaches the end. But if you need a batch file to be written in one order, then execute in another, you can use GOTO to specify the order of the commands.

group icons

A type of Windows icon that groups Windows program icons together in the Program Manager.

H

HIMEM.SYS

The DOS memory manager which enables Extended Memory above 1,024 KB on your system.

hidden attribute

Attribute of DOS used to keep files from being seen in a normal directory search.

I

IBM-compatible

A computer that has a processor that is compatible with the original IBM PC 8088.

icons

On-screen graphics that act as doors through which programs are started and therefore used to spawn windows. They are shortcuts that allow a user to open a program or a utility without knowing where that program is, or how it needs to be configured.

incremental backup

Backs up every file that has changed since the last full or incremental backup.

INI files

Text files that are used to store program settings.

internal command

Commands contained within COMMAND.COM.

internal DOS commands

Commands like DEL and DIR that are part of COMMAND.COM.

IO.SYS

Hidden, read-only system file that manages the input/output routines of your computer. IO.SYS deals with the basic issues of data communication between various hardware devices such as the hard disk, printers, floppy disk drives etc.

K

kernel file

Windows core component that is responsible for managing Windows resources and running applications.

M

MBR (Master Boot Record)

File that contains information on how the hard disk is divided into partitions.

MKDIR (MD)

Internal command for "Make Directory," DOS command used to create new directories.

MSBACKUP

A DOS program that allows the user to make backup copies of all the programs and data that is stored on the hard disk. This program is menu-driven and allows the user to set up options that can be used each time you back up the hard drive.

MEM.EXE

DOS command that allows you to examine the total and used memory on the system.

multitasking

A feature of an operating system that allows more than one program to run simultaneously.

MSD (Microsoft Diagnostics)

Program that allows the user to examine many different aspects of a system's hardware and software setup.

MSDOS.SYS

The hidden, read-only system file for MS-DOS that handles program and file management.

P

partitioning

The carving out of disk space that DOS can use.

path

The location of the file on the disk. It is composed of the logical drive letter the file is on and any directories the file is contained with in.

Personal NetWare

Peer-to-peer network operating system developed by Novell, Inc. It allows computers to function as both servers and workstations on small networks.

PIF editor

A Windows program used to create PIF files.

primary partition

The first partition created on a disk.

printable screen font

The regular fonts used to display text on the screen that are translated and downloaded to the printer when printed.

printer font

Files that contain the instructions that the printer needs to print a particular typeface.

Print Manager

Windows program used to install printers for use with Windows.

Program Groups

See group icons.

Program Information File (PIF)

File that tells Windows how to handle DOS programs that are trying to run in the Windows environment.

PROGMAN.INI

The INI file that contains the configuration settings for the Windows Program Manager.

Program Manager

The primary interface to Windows that allows you to organize and execute numerous programs by double-clicking on an icon in a single graphical window.

Program Manager Group (GRP) Files

Files in the Windows directories that store information about which application icons are contained in which group icons.

PROMPT

DOS Command that is used to modify the appearance of the command line prompt .

R

RAM disk

An area of memory that has been set aside and assigned a drive letter.

raster fonts

Fonts that are designed pixel-by-pixel and each size family is stored as a separate file.

ROM (Read Only Memory)

A type of computer memory that is retains its data permanently, even when power is removed. Once the data is written to this type of memory, it cannot be changed.

Read-Only

Attribute of DOS that prevents a file from being modified, deleted or overwritten.

Registry

Centralized database that contains environmental settings for some Windows 3.x and Windows 95 programs.

RENAME (REN)

Internal DOS command used to change the name of a file.

REMARK (REM)

Batch file command that is placed into a batch file before a command or set of commands to detail their use. Can also be used to prevent a comment from executing since any line beginning with this command will be ignored by COMMAND.COM while the batch file is executing.

Reserved Memory Area

The area in the DOS memory map that resides between 640 KB and 1,024 KB. Typically contains the EMS Page Frame as well as any ROMs for expansion devices and video display circuitry.

S

SETUP.EXE

Program that is configured to run a setup automatically when the computer is booted to this disk.

screen saver

Program originally designed to prevent damage to a computer monitor from being left on too long. These programs usually include moving graphics so that no one pixel is left on all the time. These programs detect computer inactivity and activate after a certain period of inactivity.

scheduling option

Windows option that determines how much of the system's resources are dedicated to foreground applications.

Sections

Breaks up the INI file into logical groupings of settings.

SMARTDRV.EXE (SmartDrive)

A disk-caching program used to improve Windows and DOS performance on a DOS-based system.

soft font

Font that comes on a disk and is downloaded via a special utility to the printers memory or hard disk.

SYSEDIT

A Windows utility that can be used to edit the CONFIG.SYS, AUTOEXEC.BAT, WIN.INI, and SYSTEM.INI simultaneously.

SYSTEM.INI

File that contains Windows hardware configuration settings.

Swapfile

The file on the hard drive which acts as virtual RAM for Windows.

switches

Command line options for some DOS commands that determine how simply a DOS command will be executed or what special features will be invoked. Switches are sometimes bracketed and therefore optional.

System attribute

Attribute of DOS that is used to tell the OS that this file is needed by the OS and should not be deleted. Marks a file as part of the operating system and will also prevent the file from deletion.

T

timeout

Specifies in seconds how long Multiconfig will wait for you to select one of the configurations.

TREE

Command that allows you to examine your file structure and see the directories and subdirectories that have been created.

troubleshooting

The process of identifying a computer problem so that it can be fixed.

U

UMBs (upper memory blocks)

The blocks of free memory in the upper memory area between 640 KB and 1,024 KB.

unattended backup

Backs up files to the destination you specify at the time you specify.

upgrade

Inexpensive way to purchase a new version of any software product.

upper memory area

See reserved memory area.

USER.EXE

Windows core component that allows a user to interact with Windows. It is the component responsible for interpreting keystrokes and mouse movements and sending the appropriate commands to the other core components

W

warm boot

Refers to pressing Ctl+Alt+Del to reboot the computer. This type of booting doesn't require the computer to perform all of the harware and memory checks that a cold boot does.

wildcard characters

Characters such as * or ? used in place of letters or words. They are used when you want to do a particular operation with several files at once.

windows

Rectangular display areas that provide the space in which a particular program or utility can function.

Windows Desktop

See Desktop.

Windows Program Manager

File that contains all of the program icons, group icons, and menus used for organizing, starting, and running programs.

WIN.INI

Files that contains Windows environmental settings that control the general function and appearance.

WINSOCK

A DLL that is responsible for providing Windows applications with the ability to communicate via TCP/IP (communication over the Internet).

X

XCOPY

Command used to copy entire subdirectories or the entire contents of disk.

INDEX

Note to the Reader: Throughout this index **boldfaced** page numbers indicate primary discussions of a topic. *Italicized* page numbers indicate illustrations.

C

D

E

F

G

H

I

J

K

L

M

N

Q

T

U

V

W

X

Y

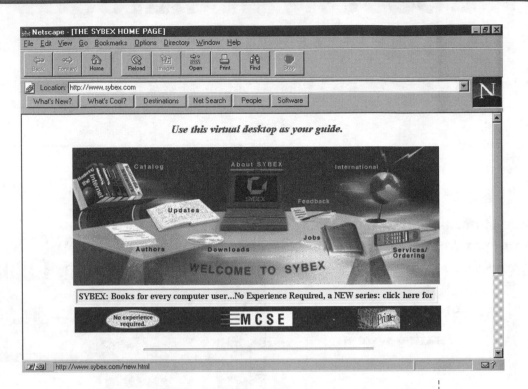